The Power of the Female

Devāṅganā Sculptures on Indian Temple Architecture

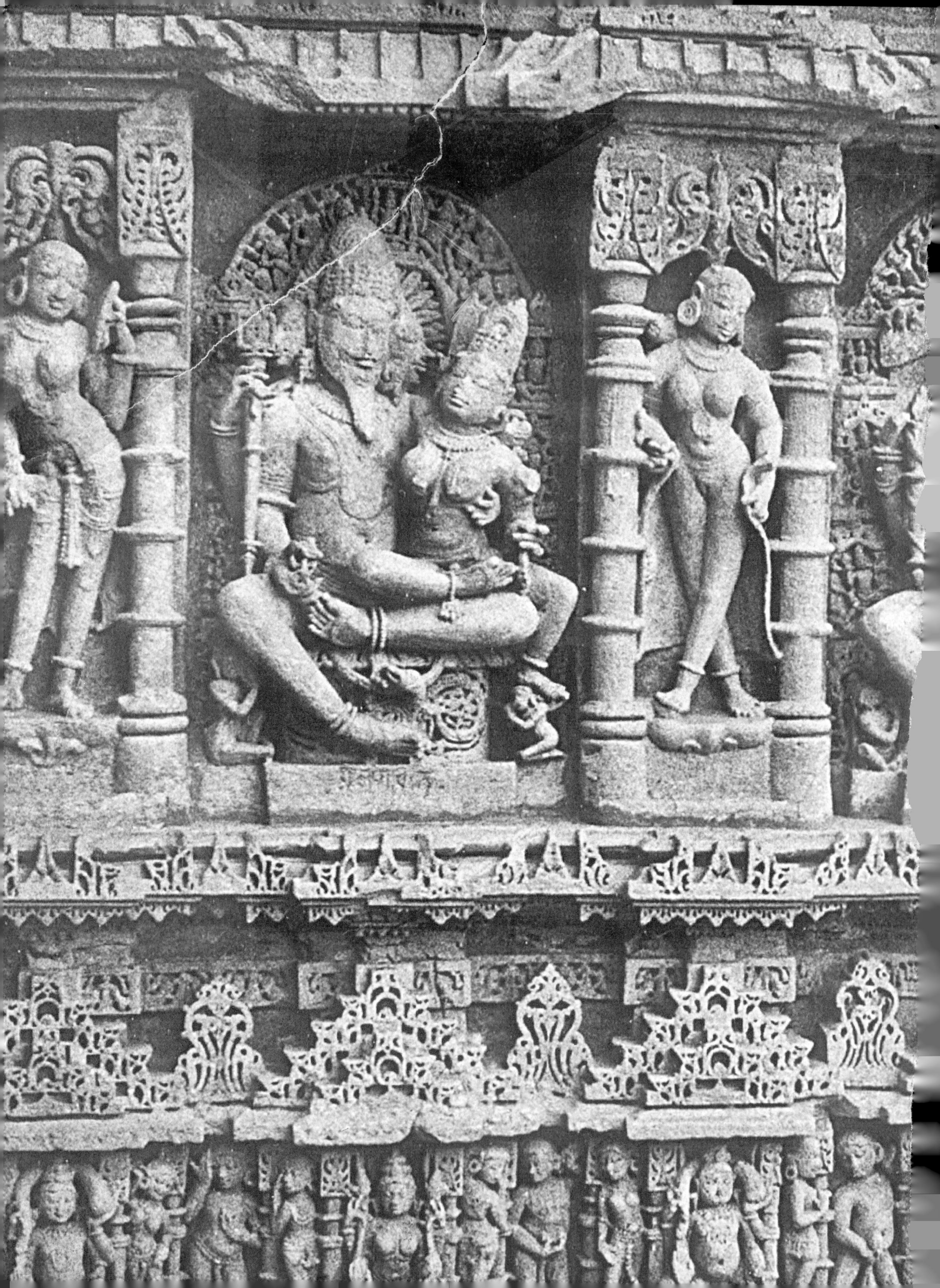

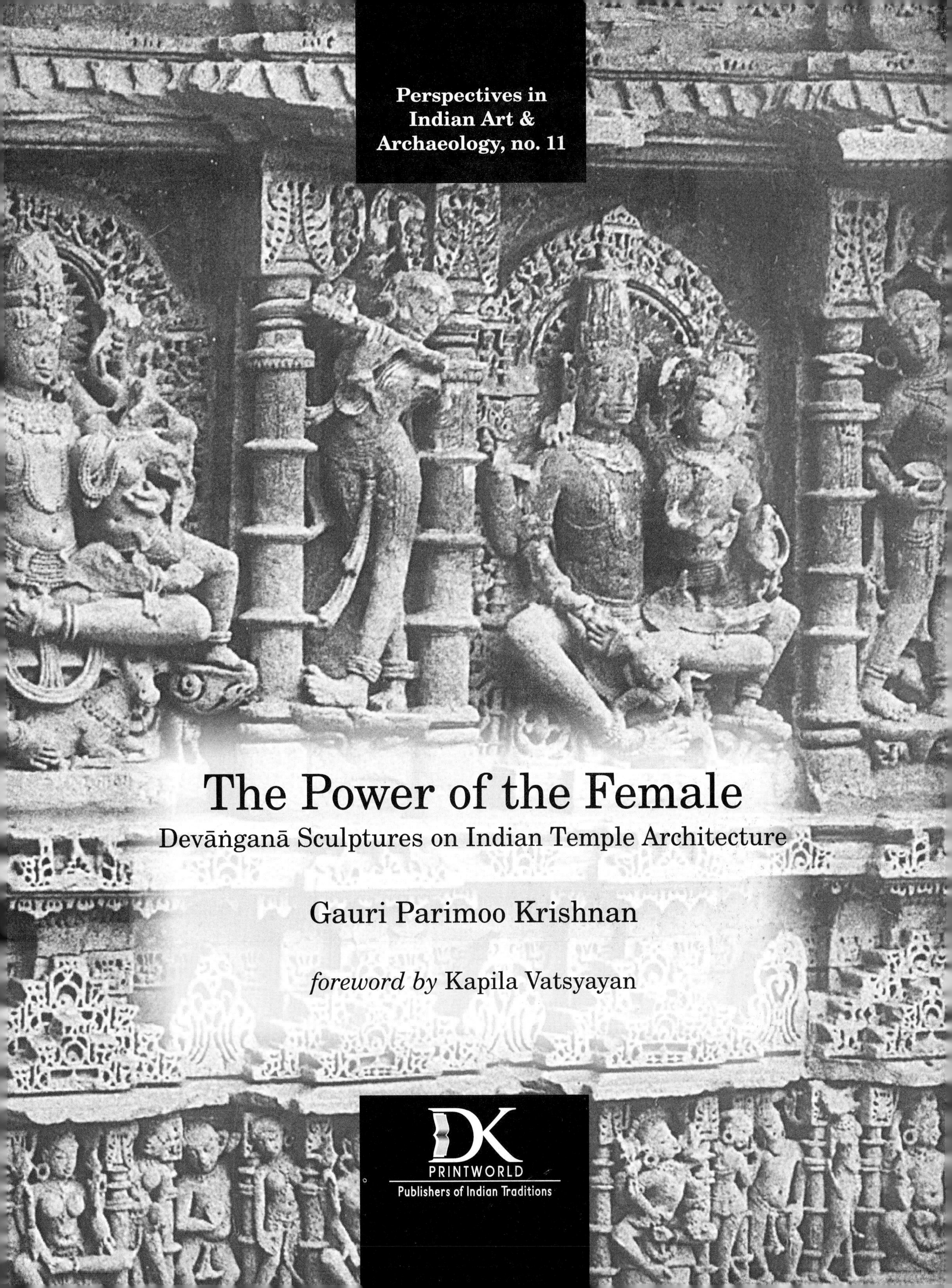

Perspectives in Indian Art & Archaeology, no. 11

The Power of the Female

Devāṅganā Sculptures on Indian Temple Architecture

Gauri Parimoo Krishnan

foreword by Kapila Vatsyayan

DK PRINTWORLD
Publishers of Indian Traditions

Cataloging in Publication Data — DK
[Courtesy: D.K. Agencies (P) Ltd. <docinfo@dkagencies.com>]

Krishnan, Gauri, 1963–
The power of the female : devāṅganā sculptures on Indian temple architecture / Gauri Krishnan.
p. 29 cm.
Includes bibliographical references (p.) and index.
ISBN 13 : 9788124606872

1. Apsarases in art. 2. Women in art. 3. Sculpture, Hindu — India — History. 4. Temples, Hindu — India — History. 5. Architecture, Hindu — India — History. I. Title. II. Series : Perspectives in Indian art & archaeology, no. 11.

DDC 704.942 409 54 22

ISBN 13: 978-81-246-0687-2
First Published in India in 2014

Printed and published by:
D.K. Printworld (P) Ltd.
Regd. Office: *Vedaśrī*, F-395, Sudarshan Park
(Metro Station: Ramesh Nagar), New Delhi - 110 015
Phones: (011) 2545 3975, 2546 6019; *Fax*: (011) 2546 5926
e-mail: indology@dkprintworld.com
Web: www.dkprintworld.com

This book is dedicated to

My loving parents,
my first and lifelong teachers.
Their passion for creativity and
academic excellence still inspires me;

My late parents-in-law,
who whole-heartedly encouraged
my pursuit of academic career;

My *guru*s and teachers
at school and university.
Their *gurudakṣiṇā* is long overdue
in the form of this book;

and

to my
Satguru Param Pujya Swamiji of Savali.
May his unconditional love and guidance
enrich our lives!

Naṭa Maṇḍapa, Sūrya Temple, Moḍhera, Gujarat

Foreword

Gauri Parimoo Krishnan represents a younger generation of art historians who have imbibed the knowledge and approach to Indian art of their peers but who have also critiqued their work with sharp incisive insights. Her book concentrates on investigating a "motif" in Indian art which pervades all schools and styles of Indian art, from about the second century BCE to the fourteenth or fifteenth century CE. The "woman and tree" motif has been the subject of investigation by historians of Indian art ranging from Ferguson (*Tree and Nature Worship*) to Vincent Smith and, more importantly, Vasudeva Saran Agrawala, A.K. Coomaraswamy, Stella Kramrisch as also the present writer (Kapila Vatsyayan).

The *śālabhañjikā,* known by her various names — *surasundarī, apsaras*, *madanikā, alasā kanyā* and many others — are integral to the architectural schema. They can be as bracket figures as in Sāñcī, they can be railing figures as in Mathurā, they can hang loosely from pediments, and they can even surround the outer and inner walls of temples, Hindu and Jaina alike. A.K. Coomaraswamy delves into the subject, focusing his attention on water cosmology. Vasudeva Saran Agrawala classifies them into sub-categories, especially in the context of Kuṣāṇa (Mathurā). Stella Kramrisch elucidates upon them in the context of the Hindu temples, particularly Khajurāho. Devangana Desai investigates them within the framework of her principal argument of religious imagery. Kapila Vatsyayan examines the motif from the point of view of movement. And now Gauri Parimoo Krishnan looks at this subject anew, while maintaining continuity but not repetition. She has assiduously perused the critical analyses of her predecessors and has gone further by concentrating attention on the morphology of architecture and the place of *devāṅganā* sculptures within the architectural schema.

Gauri Parimoo Krishnan meticulously looks at the critical

literature of the twentieth-century scholarship and re-examines some of the earlier classifications. She extends her investigation very pointedly to medieval western Indian sculptures, modelling, form and style. Here she takes into account the valuable and path-breaking work of U.P. Shah as also M.A. Dhaky. However, here, there are both fresh insights, and new material.

Gauri Parimoo Krishnan commences her study with an introduction clearly outlining the scope of her study, as also the methodologies and strategies she proposed to adopt. The introduction takes into account studies on the subject as mentioned above, but it states clearly that at the level of methodology, she proposes to apply both Erwin Panofsky's formulation in studies in iconology (1950) as also Ānandavardhana's theory of *dhvani* (i.e. theory of meaning). She elaborates on the latter. This juxtaposition is a welcome fresh approach which will stimulate critical reflection.

Gauri Parimoo Krishnan carries her narration through seven chapters from these multiple perspectives and methodologies of interpretation. All this is brought together in the final eighth chapter. Here she presents her own formulation on the iconological and semiotic interpretation of the *devāṅganā* motif. She adopts the "semiotic method" and subscribes to the Morris' view of semiotics. She returns to juxtaposing this with theories of Ānandavardhana. She elucidates on semiosis, the semantical paradigramatic dimensions and returns to state that it is truly significant that the principle of *dhvani* in Indian literary criticism is so closely analogous to the semiotic analysis. She carries forward her argument convincingly to enunciate a "diagrammatic analysis of the *devaṅganā* motif" (p. 381). This diagrammatical analysis is a new and welcome theoretical formulation. I have no doubt that the arguments given and the conclusion drawn will engage scholars in the future.

It has been a great pleasure and education for me to read this seminal impressingly comprehensive study.

The discipline of art history is multi-dimensional, always inviting the scholar to undertake new journeys on age-old material. Painstaking, sincere endeavours such as this are significant milestones.

Kapila Vatsyayan

Contents

	Foreword by Kapila Vatsyayan	vii
	Acknowledgement	xi
	List of Photographs	xiii
1.	Introduction	1
2.	A Medieval Historical Backdrop	31
3.	Apsaras Imagery from Sanskrit and Prākr̥t Sources	53
4.	Weaving the Architectural Fabric: Morphology of Architectural Style and Placement of Devāṅganā Sculptures	105
5.	Devāṅganā Sculptural Image Study I: Emergence and Evolution of Individual Motif Types	185
6.	Devāṅganā Sculptural Image Study II: Post-Gupta and Medieval Devāṅganās	271
7.	Medieval Western Indian Sculpture: Modelling the Medieval Form and Style	357
8.	Iconological and Semiotic Interpretation of the Devāṅganā Motif	377
	Appendix	421
	Glossary	429
	Bibliography	433
	Index	445

Rānī Vāv, step-well,
Pāṭan, Gujarat

Acknowledgement

I wish to acknowledge the guidance, help, support and well wishes of several people for the past twenty-five years — from the beginning of field and library research to the completion of the PhD and its extensive revision in the form of this publication. This book is shaped by many technological devices ranging from typewriters to large format MS-DOS computer systems and floppy discs to CD-Roms and Microsoft Word formats. Despite technological changes, the material examined in this book and its interpretation are still fresh and relevant.

My foremost gratitude is due to my guide and teacher, Prof. Ratan Parimoo, who generously shared his knowledge on Indian and Western art history with generations of students, for more than forty years, at the Department of Art History and Aesthetics, Faculty of Fine Arts, Maharaja Sayajirao University of Baroda, Vadodara, Gujarat, India. I consider myself fortunate to be his student. I owe my entire grounding in art history to his teaching, writing and documenting, and lecturing at archaeological sites and museum collections all over India. My teachers and colleagues — Prof. Shivaji Panikkar, Prof. Deepak Kannal and Prof. Vaijayanti Navangule — were very encouraging in shaping the content, research methodology and Sanskrit references, especially Vaijayanti for coining new terms for *devaṅganā*s, which did not have references in Sanskrit literature. Initial consultations with Mr M.A. Dhaky and Prof. R.N. Mishra to shape the structure of the thesis and its details were very constructive and their on-going support and encouragement over the years were reassuring. Consultations with Dr Kapila Vatsyayan, Dr Anandakrishna, Dr K.D. Tripathi and Mr K.S. Srinivasan were very fruitful, and their timely direction for further research to incorporate newer material to my core research area is well lauded.

I could not have travelled to 100-plus temple sites cited in this book without funding, and the help of a professional photographer. The research fellowships during the course of my data collection during 1987-90 were therefore very useful. The American Institute of Indian Studies, Ramnagar and Gurgaon, allowed me to access their enormous photo archive and exhaustive library by giving me Junior Research Fellowship for two seasons. I thank Mr M.A. Dhaky, and the staff of the library and the archives for their friendly support. This was followed by the Special Assistance Grant given to the Art History Department during which period I was able to join the group of teachers and researchers to temple sites that enabled me to study the *apsaras* and *devaṅganā* on temple architecture *in situ*. The Nehru Trust for Indian Collections at Victoria and Albert Museum, London, granted me a small Study Research Grant which was sufficient to produce the presentation copies of the PhD thesis in 1993. I thank Mr Piplani of the Teen Murti Bhavan for his support and encouragement. Following libraries and their staff are acknowledged herewith: the Oriental Institute Library, Museum and Picture Gallery Library at Vadodara; National Centre for Performing Arts and Prince of Wales Museum Library, Mumbai; Lalit Kala Akademi Library, Sahitya Akademi Library, Indira Gandhi National Centre for the Arts Library, Nehru Memorial Library at Teen Murti House, New Delhi; and Bharat Kala Bhavan Library at Varanasi. The hospitality and unconditional love from the family of Mr O.P. Tandon and Mrs Usha Tandon provided me a "home away from home" during two summers spent at Varanasi. The motherly love of late Mrs Gitanjali Dhaky nurtured my soul.

At M.S. University of Baroda, where I taught art history during 1987-93, my colleagues and students were like my family members. I fondly remember the help of colleagues Dr Shailendra Khushwaha, Neelanjana Bhattacharya, Rita Sodha, Himanshu Pahad, H.S. Kadam and Ravi Kadam. Students Pallavi Sharma, Rajesh Singh, Mrinal Kulkarni, Sonali Soni, Renuka Kadapatti, Vaibhav Vishal, Monal Iyer and Shaili Sharma helped me in preparing the photo albums for the PhD thesis volumes and the indices.

During the sabbatical leave generously granted to me by the senior management of the National Heritage Board, Singapore, in 2003-04 to revise the thesis for publication, I was kindly offered honorary visiting research fellowship by the Monash Asia Institute which gave me access to various Monash University libraries and I thank Marica Vicziany for her support. During this period, Prof. Ian Mabbett was kind enough to go through the chapters of the manuscript and gave valuable suggestions for revision.

My late in-laws — Mrs Sarojini and Mr R. Jagannathan — had ungrudgingly supported my pursuit of academic research and professional work. Their continued support saw the completion of my PhD thesis. My mother Naina Parimoo and my sister Gayatri were like my backbone, and their role was lovingly taken over by my husband Krishnan after our marriage. He is always there for me — supporting, encouraging and critiquing my work. Without his encouragement in my pursuit of excellence, I could not have gone very far in balancing professional work with family life, and raising our two lovely children, Sarang and Katya. They have seen me busy at work throughout their growing-up stages. Their understanding and care have always been a source of inspiration for me.

The publisher D.K. Printworld has done a commendable job of production, and I thank Mr Susheel Mittal and Mr Rajendra Agarwal along with their entire team, for their interest and support in executing this project with commitment.

List of Photographs

fig. 1. Harihara I, north-eastern *devakulikā*, south wall, eighth century, Osiā, Jodhpur, Rajasthan.

fig. 2. Harihara II, north-western *devakulikā*, north wall, eighth century, Osiā, Jodhpur, Rajasthan.

fig. 3. Harihara I, south-eastern *devakulikā*, north wall, eighth century, Osiā, Jodhpur, Rajasthan.

fig. 4. Details of *fig.* 1, Osiā.

fig. 5. Śiva Temple, south *jaṅghā*, early ninth century, Terāhī, Śivapurī, Vidiśā, Madhya Pradesh.

fig. 6. Gadarmal Temple, west face *jaṅghā,* Badoh Paṭhārī.

fig. 7. Gadarmal Temple, east face *jaṅghā,* Badoh Paṭhārī.

fig. 8. Caturmukha Mahādeva Temple, south-east view, *c.* eighth century, Nachnā–Kuṭhāra, Madhya Pradesh.

fig. 9. Ghaṭeśvara Mahādeva Temple, general view, first half of the ninth century, Badoli, Koṭā, Rajasthan.

fig. 10. Temple 6, general view, early eighth century, Roḍā, Himmatnagar, Gujarat.

fig. 11. Nīlakaṇṭha Temple, *maṇḍovara,* general view, first half of tenth century, Kekind, Rajasthan.

fig. 12. Sun Temple, west face *jaṅghā*, *c.* CE 900-25, Bodādit, Koṭā, Rajasthan.

fig. 13. Kṣemaṅkarī Temple, west face *maṇḍovara*, early eighth century, Chittorgaṛh, Rajasthan.

fig. 14. Ambikā Temple, general view, CE 960, Jagat, Udaipur, Rajasthan.

fig. 15. Śiva Temple, general view, early ninth century, Kotai, Kutch, Gujarat.

fig. 16. Śiva Temple, south face, second quarter of the tenth century, Nohṭā, Damoh, Madhya Pradesh.

fig. 17. Śiva Temple, view from west, second quarter of tenth century, Marai, Satnā, Madhya Pradesh.

fig. 18. Lakṣmaṇa Temple, south wall near *kakṣāsana, jagatī* and *jaṅghā* sculpture, mid-tenth century, Khajurāho, Madhya Pradesh.

fig. 19. Temple 1, Khirniwālā (group 7), west face, *c.* tenth century, Kaḍwāhā, Guṇā, Madhya Pradesh.

fig. 20. Ṭoṭeśvara Temple 1 (Group 1), general view from west, *c.* eleventh century, Kaḍwāhā, Guṇā, Madhya Pradesh.

fig. 21. Ṭoṭeśvara Temple 1, general view west face, *c.* eleventh century, Kaḍwāhā, Guṇā, Madhya Pradesh.

fig. 22. Udayeśvara Temple, general view, CE 1059-80, inscribed, Udaipur, Vidiśā, Madhya Pradesh.

fig. 23. Sūrya Temple, north face, mid-tenth century, Tusā, Udaipur, Rajasthan.

fig. 24. Mīrā Temple, general view, north side, late tenth century, Ahāṛ, Udaipur, Rajasthan.

fig. 25. Mīrā Temple, *maṇḍovara*, west wall, late tenth century, Ahāṛ, Udaipur, Rajasthan.

fig. 26. Rānī Vāv, *devāṅgnā*s, south buttress wall of the *kuṇḍa*, mid-eleventh century, Pāṭan, Gujarat.

fig. 27. Viṣṇu Temple, south face, general view, tenth century, Nāgdā, Udaipur, Rajasthan.

fig. 28. Harṣanātha Temple, *devāṅganā* blowing a conch, CE 956-73, Harṣagiri, Sīkar, Rajasthan.

fig. 29. Bajramaṭha, western face, *c.* tenth century, Gyāraspur, Vidiśā, Madhya Pradesh.

fig. 30. Bajramaṭha, north face, Gyāraspur, Vidiśā, Madhya Pradesh.

fig. 31. Temple 2, west wall, *c.* tenth century, Sūrwaya, Śivapurī, Madhya Pradesh.

fig. 32. Temple 2, south wall, *c.* tenth century, Sūrwaya, Śivapurī, Madhya Pradesh.

fig. 33. Mohajamātā Temple, view from north, *c.* tenth-eleventh centuries, Terāhī, Śivapurī, Madhya Pradesh.

fig. 34. Ṭoṭeśvara Temple, *jaṅghā* sculpture, west wall, Kaḍwāhā.

fig. 35. Ṭoṭeśvara Temple, *jaṅghā* sculpture, west wall, Kaḍwāhā.

fig. 36. Sun Temple, south wall, early eleventh century, Moḍherā, Gujarat.

fig. 37. Śyāma Sundara Temple, *mūlaprāsāda*, south *jaṅghā* sculptural frame relate with Osiā and Moḍherā, *c.* late ninth century, Atru, Koṭā, Rajasthan.

fig. 38. Temple 2, *maṇḍovara*, south wall, ninth century, Amvan.

fig. 39. Someśvara Temple, general view, west face, mid-eleventh century, Kirāḍu, Bāḍmer, Rajasthan.

fig. 40. Viṣṇu Temple, general view, mid-eleventh century, Kirāḍu, Bāḍmer, Rajasthan.

fig. 41. Saccīyamātā Temple, *maṇḍovara* sculpture, south wall, *c.* CE 1025, Osiā, Jodhpur, Rajasthan.

fig. 42. Śiva Temple, general view, *c.* twelfth century, Sander, Mehsānā, Gujarat.

fig. 43. Śiva Temple, general view, mid-eleventh century, Sunak, Mehsānā, Gujarat.

fig. 44. Navalakhā Temple, general view, *c.* twelfth century, Sejakpur, Saurāṣṭra, Gujarat.

fig. 45. Śaraṇeśvara Temple, general view, *c.* twelfth century, Ābhāpur, Antarsuba, Gujarat.

fig. 46. Kumāravihāra, view from west, mid-twelfth century, Achalgaṛh, Sirohī, Rajasthan.

fig. 47. Animal, woman and tree motif on ring stone, third century BCE, Murtaẓāgañj, Bihar.

fig. 48. Woman and tree, detail, ring stone, *c.* third century BCE, Murtaẓāgañj, Bihar.

fig. 49. Egyptian vase, inscribed drawing, Nut as tree goddess with the sun disk, Bronze vessel, *c.* 600 BCE, Louvre, Paris.

fig. 50. Egyptian stone relief, veneration of the tree goddess, XVIII dynasty, Kestner Museum, Hanover.

fig. 51. Egyptian painted ceiling relief, Goddess Nut, fertility connotation, temple of Hathor, Dendera, Roman period, source unknown.

fig. 52. Goddess as Flower Maiden, Stone, Eleusis, Roman period, Museum Eleusis.

fig. 53. Terracotta relief, Hellenic Period, Museo Nationale delle Terme, Ceres, Rome.

fig. 54. Astarte, Gold plaque, *c*. thirteenth century BCE.

fig. 55. Railing upright, Chulakoka Devatā, first century BCE, Barhut, Indian Museum, Kolkata.

fig. 56. *Śālabhañjikā*s flanking the *toraṇa,* Jaina *stūpa*, *āyāga* stone, second century CE, Kaṅkālī Ṭīlā.

fig. 57. *Toraṇa śālabhañjikā*, eastern gate, *stūpa* 1, first century BCE, Sāñcī.

fig. 58. *Śālabhañjikā-prasādhikā*, *gavākṣa*, first century BCE, Amarāvatī.

fig. 59. *Śālabhañjikā*, *gavākṣa*, first century CE, Amarāvatī.

fig. 60. *Aśokadohada*, man supporting the woman to entwine her leg around a tree trunk, second century CE, Bodh-Gayā.

fig. 61. *Śālabhañjikā*, bracket figure, Śuṅga period, first century BCE, Jamsot.

fig. 62. Early Indian mother goddesses, Mauryan and Kuṣāṇa periods, source unknown, Mathurā.

fig. 63. *Śālabhañjikā*, engraved drawing, resting against *makara-toraṇa*, first century CE, Nāgārjunakoṇḍa.

fig. 64. *Prasādhikā*, *mithuna* couple, Nāgārjunakoṇḍa.

fig. 65. *Prasādhanā*, *mithuna* couple, Nāgārjunakoṇḍa.

fig. 66. *Prasādhanā*, *mithuna* couple, Nāgārjunakoṇḍa.

fig. 67. *Keśanistoyakāriṇī*, *mithuna* couple, Nāgārjunakoṇḍa.

fig. 68. *Markaṭaceṣṭā*, *mithuna* couple, Nāgārjunakoṇḍa.

fig. 69. *Prasādhikā*, second century CE, Saṅghol, National Museum, New Delhi.

fig. 70. *Śuka-sārikā*, parrot nibbling the *mekhalā* knot, second century CE, Mathurā, Lucknow Museum.

fig. 71. *Vīrā khaḍgadhārī*, second century CE, Mathurā Pratihārī.

fig. 72. *Toraṇa-yoṣitā*, first century CE, Kaṅkālī Ṭīlā, Mathura Museum.

fig. 73. *Śālabhañjikā*, Kuṣāṇa, second century CE, Soṅkh, Mathura Museum.

fig. 74. *Śālabhañjikā* holding the branch of the tree, second century CE, Soṅkh, Mathura Museum.

fig. 75. *Stambha-yoṣitā, nṛtyābhinaya*, second century CE, Mathurā, Giridharpur, Mathura Museum.

fig. 76. Lady with a rattle, second century CE, Saṅghol, National Museum, New Delhi.

fig. 77. *Puṣpabhañjikā*, lady seen from the back, second century CE, Mathurā.

fig. 78. Lady holding lotuses, second CE, Saṅghol, National Museum, New Delhi.

fig. 79. River goddess, entrance doorway, lintel, *c.* fifth century, cave 1, Ajantā.

fig. 80. Lady with *viṭa,* Cave 4, Ajantā.

fig. 81. *Śālabhañjikā-nadīdevatā,* detail of left side of door-frame, upper part, Cave 5, Ajantā.

fig. 82. *Śālabhañjikā-nadīdevatā,* detail of right side, Cave 5, Ajantā.

fig. 83. *Śālabhañjikā* with *viṭa,* doorway, Cave 14, Ajantā.

fig. 84. *Śālabhañjikā-nadīdevatā* with a parrot, door-frame of a side shrine, second half of fifth century, Cave 27, Ajantā.

fig. 85. *Nāyaka-nāyikā* with *viṭa*, theatrical scene, Khilchipura pillar, ninth century, Mandsaur, Madhya Pradesh.

fig. 86. *Śālabhañjikā* with *viṭa*, pillar bracket, note the palm tree, sixth century, Jogeśvarī, Mumbai.

fig. 87 *Śālabhañjikā* with *viṭa,* antechamber, Cave 1, Ajantā.

fig. 88. *Śālabhañjikā* with *viṭa,* Cave 20, Ajantā.

fig. 89. Avalokiteśvara, with *yakṣa* Maṇibhadra (*viṭa*)?, Cave 1, Auraṅgābād, Maharashtra.

fig. 90. *Viṭa* with Tārā and attendant female groups, identified as *yakṣa* Maṇibhadra, seventh century, Cave 7, Auraṅgābād, Maharashtra.

fig. 91. *Śālabhañjikā* with *viṭa,* Cave 17, Ellorā, Auraṅgābād, Maharashtra.

fig. 92. *Śālabhañjikā* with *viṭa*, pillar bracket, *c.* seventh century, Cave 21, Ellorā, Auraṅgābād, Maharashtra.

fig. 93. *Śālabhañjikā* with *viṭa*, pillar bracket, *c.* seventh century, Cave 21, Ellorā, Auraṅgābād, Maharashtra.

fig. 94. *Śālabhañjikā* with *viṭa*, pillar bracket, left, south wall, *c.* seventh century, Cave 21, Ellorā, Auraṅgābād, Maharashtra.

fig. 95. Gaṅgā on *makara*, *viṭa* dangling on the creeper oozing out of *makara* mouth, fifth century, Śāmalājī, Baroda Museum.

fig. 96. *Mithuna*, lady in *śālabhañjikā* pose with *viṭa,* Lakṣmaṇa Temple doorway, seventh century, Sirpur.

fig. 97. *Vasanabhraṁśā devāṅganā* with *viṭa*, pillar capital, temple 6, *c.* eighth century, Roḍā, Gujarat.

fig. 98. *Vr̥kṣikā* leaning against the tree trunk, doorway, left side, upper portion, Cave 4, Ajantā.

fig. 99. *Viṭa-vr̥kṣikā* on pillar capital, Cave 1, Auraṅgābād.

fig. 100. Gaṅgā, holding mirror, Kaṅkālīdevī Temple, fifth century, Tigowā, Madhya Pradesh.

fig. 101. Yamunā, *śālabhañjikā* pose, with *gaṇa*, Kaṅkālīdevī Temple, fifth century, Tigowā, Madhya Pradesh.

fig. 102. Doorway with river goddesses, Pārvatī Temple, fifth century CE, Nachnā, Madhya Pradesh.

fig. 103. Gaṅgā with a dwarf and lotus flower, Khilchipura pillar, fifth century, Mandsaur.

fig. 104. Gaṅgā, with *chatra* and attendants, site unknown, Madhya Pradesh.

fig. 105. Doorway, with Gaṅgā on *makara* no Yamunā distinction identifiable, late fifth century, Cave 21, Ajantā.

fig. 106. Doorway, Cave unknown, Ajantā.

fig. 107. Shrine doorway, Cave unknown, Ajantā.

fig. 108. Shrine doorway with river goddesses, *c.* second half of fifth century, Cave 1, Ajantā.

fig. 109. River goddesses, outer doorway, *c.* second half of fifth century, Cave 26, Ajantā.

fig. 110. River goddesses, central doorway of *caitya*, second half of fifth century, Cave 26, Ajantā.

fig. 111. Buddist sene with *vr̥kṣkā* standing on *makara.*

fig. 112. Water nymph or river goddesses with food dishes standing on *makara*, first century CE, Coomaraswamy, pl. 19, Amarāvatī.

fig. 113. River goddess holding lotus standing on lotus pedestal, pillar upright, first century CE, Sāñcī.

fig. 114. Representation of *gīta-vādya-nr̥tya*, early fifth century, Cave 19, Udayagiri, Vidiśā, Madhya Pradesh.

fig. 115. Doorway, river goddesses under rich foliage, early fifth century, Cave 19, Udayagiri, Vidiśā, Madhya Pradesh.

fig. 116. Gaṅgā seated on *makara*, with a waterpot, terracotta, Berlin Museum.

fig. 117. River Goddess Gaṅgā, holding a water pot, *c.* CE 600 lower Kosala area, Rājim.

fig. 118. River Goddess Gaṅgā on *makara*, holding a pearl stick, *c.* CE 600, Rājim.

fig. 119. Doorway, Daśāvatāra Temple, *c.* fifth-sixth century, Deogaṛh.

fig. 120. *Vr̥kṣikā* near the doorway, Saccīyamātā Temple, tenth century, Osiā.

fig. 121. *Sadyasnātā*, Harihara I, ninth century, Osiā.

fig. 122. Doorway with *vr̥kṣikā* holding mirror, Ābanerī, Bharat Kala Bhavan Museum, Varanasi.

fig. 123. *Vr̥kṣikā* in *sva-stana-sparśā* pose, second half of fifth century, Cave 19, Ajantā.

fig. 124. *Sva-stana-sparśā*, second century, National Museum, New Delhi.

fig. 125. *Sva-stana-sparśā*, second century, collection unknown, Mathurā.

fig. 126. *Sva-stana-sparśā* standing on water pot surrounded by foliage, National Museum, Mathurā.

fig. 127. *Sva-stana-sparśā*, Gurgī fragment, tenth century, Rewa Kotwali, Rewa.

fig. 128. *Sva-stana-sparśā*, Ambikā Temple, south wall, Jagat.

fig. 129. *Paribhogadarśinī,* Kandarīya Mahādeva Temple, Khajurāho.

fig. 130. *Sva-stana-sparśā* touching the sole of the foot in *pr̥ṣṭhasvastika* pose, eleventh century, Gurgī, Rewa Kotwali.

fig. 131. Precursor of *sva-stana-sparśā*, fragments of the figure of Goddess Beltis, stone, Susa, seventh century BCE, from Hollander, Aeskulap und Venus, p. 206.

fig. 132. Primordial goddesses, *sva-stana-sparśā*, Cyprus, clay, *c.* 2500 BCE (Neumann pl. 8), British Museum.

fig. 133. Goddess, terracotta, Crete, from a cave near Lapethos (Neumann pl. 13), British Museum.

fig. 134. Isis Hathor, Suckling Horus, bronze, Egypt, seventh-sixth centuries BCE (Neumann, pl. 44), Louvre, Paris.

fig. 135. *Toraṇa* pillar, *sva-stana-sparśā* with *āmralumbī*, tenth century, Rewā Mahārāja's palace, Gurgī.

fig. 136. *Sva-stana-sparśā,* Saccīyamātā Temple, Osiā.

fig. 137. *Sva-stana-sparśā,* Śiva Temple, standing in *baddhācārī*, *c.* CE 900, Kodal, Damoh, Madhya Pradesh.

fig. 138. *Paribhogadarśinī,* Lakṣmaṇa Temple, Khajurāho.

fig. 139. *Keśanistoyakāriṇī*, Saṅghol, National Museum, New Delhi.

fig. 140. *Keśanistoyakāriṇī,* Temple 6, pillar capital, Roḍā.

fig. 141. *Keśanistoyakāriṇī,* Ambikā Temple, south wall, Jagat.

fig. 142. *Keśanistoyakāriṇī* and *sva-stana-sparśā*, south buttress wall, Rānī Vāv, Pāṭan.

fig. 143. *Keśanistoyakāriṇī* and *vasanabhraṁśā,* Nīlakaṇṭha Temple, Kekind.

fig. 144. *Keśanistoyakāriṇī*, *vasanabhraṁśā,* Sās Temple, Gwalior.

fig. 145. *Keśanistoyakāriṇī,* Gurgī fragment.

fig. 146. *Keśanistoyakāriṇī,* Śiva Temple, Kodal.

fig. 147. *Keśanistoyakāriṇī*, Viśvanātha Temple, Khajurāho.

fig. 148. *Keśanistoyakāriṇī*, *c.* tenth-eleventh centuries, Rani Durgavati Museum, Doni, Jabalpur.

fig. 149. *Maṇḍovara*, Ambikā Temple, eleventh century, Suhāniā, Madhya Pradesh.

fig. 150. *Putravallabhā* with waterjug and *āmralumbī,* Suhāniā.

fig. 151. *Putravallabhā* from back view, Kandarīya Mahādeva Temple, Khajurāho.

fig. 152. *Putravallabhā* with Varuṇa, south wall, Saccīyamātā Temple, Osiā.

fig. 153. *Putravallabhā,* Gurgī fragment.

fig. 154. *Putravallabhā,* ceiling, Sūrya Temple, Tusā.

fig. 155. *Putravallabhā*, Sūrya Temple, south wall, Indra panel, 1st quarter of eleventh century, Moḍherā, Mehsānā, Gujarat.

fig. 156. *Sva-stana-sparśā*, *putravallabhā*, *madhupānā,* Saṅghol.

fig. 157. *Putravallabhā,* Hārīti, pillar capital, Cave 3, Auraṅgābād.

fig. 158. *Putravallabhā* with *viṭa-kuṭilaka*, pillar fragment, tenth century, Jhalawar Museum, Jhālarāpāṭan.

fig. 159. *Kanduka-krīḍā*, pillar upright, second century, Mathurā.

fig. 160. *Ghaṭa* balancing, same pose as above, second century, Saṅghol.

fig. 161. *Kanduka-krīḍā* with *viṭa*, pillar capital, Temple 6, eighth century, Roḍā.

fig. 162. *Kanduka-krīḍā*, *pr̥ṣṭha-svastika,* Ambikā temple, south wall, Jagat.

fig. 163. *Kanduka-krīḍā*, same pose as above, accompanied by *viṭa,* Sūrya Temple, north wall, Tusā.

fig. 164. *Kanduka-krīḍā*, *ūrdhvajānu* pose, Rānī Vāv, buttress wall, Pāṭan.

fig. 165. *Kanduka-krīḍā*, *ūrdhvajānu vivr̥tta karaṇa,* Ādinath Temple, north wall, Āhaṛ.

fig. 166. *Kanduka-krīḍā*, *ūrdhvajānu vivr̥tta karaṇa*, Nāgdā, Rajasthan, fourth century, National Museum, New Delhi.

fig. 167. *Vasanabhraṁśā*, Bhūteśvara, pillar upright, second century, Mathura Museum.

fig. 168. *Vasanabhraṁśā* in a niche, Gadarmal Temple, south wall, Badoh-Paṭhārī.

fig. 169. *Vasanabhraṁśā* and *markaṭaceṣṭā,* Harṣad-Mātā Temple, pillar capital, Ābaneri.

fig. 170. *Vasanabhraṁśā* with a scorpion, *sva-stana-sparśā,* Kandarīya Mahādeva Temple, Khajurāho.

fig. 171. *Vasanabhraṁśā,* Ṭoṭeśvara Temple, Kaḍwāhā.

fig. 172. *Vasanabhraṁśā* and *markaṭaceṣṭā*, pillar fragment, *c.* ninth century, Rani Durgavati Museum (Damoh), Doni, Madhya Pradesh.

fig. 173. *Vasanabhraṁśā* with *kharjūra* and a *mithuna* couple, Devī Jagadambī Temple, Khajurāho.

fig. 174. *Sadyasnātā*, *keśanistoyakāriṇī* and *vasanabhraṁśā*. Note *viṭa* with *kuṭilaka*, Lakṣmaṇa Temple, Khajurāho.

fig. 175. *Vasanabhraṁśā,* Devī Jagadambī Temple, Khajurāho.

fig. 176. *Vasanabhrṁśā,* detail, Ambikā Temple, Suhāniā.

fig. 177. *Devāṅganā* alternate with *dikpālas* and consorts. *Vasanabhraṁśā* pose like Bhūteśvara, Scorpion visible, Rānī Vāv, south wall, Pāṭan.

fig. 178. *Vasanabhraṁśā* with a scorpion, *baddhācārī,* Rānī Vāv, north wall, Pāṭan.

fig. 179. *Vasanabhraṁśā* with scorpion, *baddhācārī, c.* twelfth century, Nīlakaṇṭha Temple, north wall, Sunak.

fig. 180. *Vasanabhraṁśā, markaṭaceṣṭā,* Nīlakaṇṭha Temple, north wall, Sunak.

fig. 181. *Markaṭaceṣṭā, maṇḍapa,* pillar, ninth century, Ghaṭeśvara Mahādeva Temple, Badoli.

fig. 182. *Markaṭaceṣṭā, nāyikā* represented from the back, Khajurāho area, site unknown, eleventh century, National Museum, New Delhi.

fig. 183. *Antarāla, devāṅganās, markaṭaceṣṭā, mithunas,* Lakṣmaṇa Temple, south wall, Khajurāho.

fig. 184. *Markaṭaceṣṭā,* interior pillar bracket, Devī Jagadambī Temple, Khajurāho.

fig. 185. *Markaṭaceṣṭā,* with *vyālas,* Gurgī, near *toraṇa,* left jamb, Rewā Mahārāja's Palace, tenth century, Rewā, Madhya Pradesh.

fig. 186. *Markaṭaceṣṭā,* west *jaṅghā,* Virāṭeśvara Temple, twelfth century, Sohāgpur, Shahdol, Madhya Pradesh.

fig. 187. *Markaṭaceṣṭā,* south wall, Ambikā Temple, Jagat.

fig. 188. *Markaṭaceṣṭā,* frontal view, *nāyikā* in *ūrdhvajānu* pose, Saccīyamātā Temple, Osiā.

fig. 189. *Markaṭaceṣṭā* in *ūrdhvajānu* pose, twelfth century, Śiva Temple, Sander.

fig. 190. *Khaḍgadhārī vīrā* or *pratihārī,* pillar upright, Mathurā.

fig. 191. *Khaḍgadhārī vīrā, pratihārī,* pillar upright, Mathurā.

fig. 192. *Vīrā* with a sword, Ambikā Temple, south wall, Jagat.

fig. 193. *Vīrā devāṅganā,* Urvaśī or Gaurī aiming a bow, arrow at a lion, twelfth century, Śaraṇeśvara Temple, east wall, Ābhāpur, Antarsuba, Gujarat.

fig. 194. *Khaṭvāṅgadhārī* holding fish-plate, *ūrdhvajānu* pose, accompanied by a drummer, Rānī Vāv, south buttress wall, Pāṭan.

fig. 195. *Khaṭvāṅgadhārī* with a bowl, *ḍamarū* and *muṇḍamālā* wearing *jaṭābhāra*, accompanied by a dog, Saccīyamātā Temple, Osiā.

fig. 196. Nude *devāṅganā* with serpent entwining her body, performing a nocturnal ritual?, south buttress wall, Rānī Vāv, Pāṭan.

fig. 197. Serpent goddess, Faience, Crete, middle Minoan III period, British Museum.

fig. 198. *Toraṇa* pillar, *yoginī*, with knife, *kapāla*, *jaṭābhāra* and *muṇḍamālā,* Mahādeva Tèmple complex, Ghaṭeśvara Badoli.

fig. 199. *Yoginī* with *kartāra* wearing yogic costume, Śiva Temple, west wall, Sander.

fig. 200. North *jaṅghā* upper register shows numerous demonic figures, Mohajamātā Temple, Terāhī.

fig. 201. Details of *fig.* 200.

fig. 202. Kubera and Kirāti, or *vīra devāṅganā* with bow, arrow, matted hair (left), Vāyu and *devāṅganā* with *āmralumbī* (right), Saccīyamātā Temple, Osiā.

fig. 203 *Darpaṇā*, first century BCE, collection: Unknown, Bharhut.

fig. 204. *Darpaṇā,* Ṭoṭeśvara Temple, south wall, Kaḍwāhā.

fig. 205.Same as above *prasādhikā,* Jagat.

fig. 206. *Devāṅgnā* applying *āltā* on her foot, eleventh century, Kandarīya Mahādeva Temple, Khajurāho.

fig. 207. *Devāṅganā* painting the foot and forehead, *pṛṣṭha-svastika,* Ambikā Temple, south wall, Jagat.

fig. 208. *Devāṅganā* applying *āltā* on foot, tenth century, Lakṣmaṇa Temple, Khajurāho.

fig. 209. Drawing of the same *devāṅganā* by Ratan Parimoo, 1958.

fig. 210. *Prasādhikā* painting foot lifted at the back, *vivṛtta kaṭi* Saccīyamātā Temple, Osiā.

fig. 211. *Alasā*, pillar upright, second century, Saṅghol, National Museum, New Delhi.

fig. 212. *Alasā* with *viṭa,* Temple 6, pillar capital, Roḍā.

fig. 213. *Alasā* standing next to Viṣṇu, tenth century, Lakṣmaṇa Temple, Khajurāho.

fig. 214. Drawing of the same *devāṅganā* by Ratan Parimoo, 1958.

fig. 215. *Alasā,* south wall, Ambikā Temple, Jagat.

fig. 216. *Alasā* in *pratiratha,* south wall, Nīlakaṇṭha Temple, Kekind.

fig. 217. *Maṇḍovara, mūlaprāsāda,* western *juṅghā,* early tenth century, Sūrya Temple, Tusā, Udaipur, Rajasthan.

fig. 218. *Alasā* and *kanduka-krīḍā* flanking Āditya, denoting time, space and movement (details of *fig.* 215), Tusā.

fig. 219. *Alasā,* Ambikā Temple, Suhāniā.

fig. 220. *Alasā, vasanabhraṁśā* and *markaṭaceṣṭā,* Temple 1, Khirniwālā, gorup 7, Kaḍwāhā.

fig. 221. *Alasā, prasādhikā,* Śiva Temple, Kodal.

fig. 222. *Nartakī* in *karihasta* pose, north wall, Śaraṇeśvara Temple, twelfth century, Ābhāpur, Gujarat.

fig. 223. *Nartakī, ūrdhvajānu,* Udayeśvara Temple, CE 1056, Udaipur, Madhya Pradesh.

fig. 224. *Nartakī, pṛṣṭha-svastika* pose, twelfth century, Jamsot, Allahabad Museum.

fig. 225. *Nūpurapādikā, ūrdhvajānu* pose, Pārśvanātha Temple, Khajurāho.

fig. 226. *Nūpurapādikā,* Saccīyāmātā Temple, Osiā.

fig. 227. *Nūpurapādikā,* Rānī Vāv, well portion, Pāṭan.

fig. 228. *Saṅgītavādinī,* second century, Saṅghol, National Museum.

fig. 229. *Saṅgītavādinī,* tenth century, Harṣanātha Temple, Harṣagiri, Sīkar, Rajasthan.

fig. 230. Flautist, bracket figure, Viśvanātha Temple, Khajurāho.

fig. 231. Vārāhī Mātṛkā, sixth century, Vaḍaval, Museology Department, M.S.U. Baroda, Gujarat.

fig. 232. Indrāṇī in dancing mode, *kṣiptā, kuñcitā, kaṭisamā,* seventh century (*in situ*), Karvan.

fig. 233. Mātṛkā Indrāṇī, dancing mode, eigth century, Kanauj.

fig. 234. *Dvārapāla,* eleventh century, Atru, Kota Museum, Rajasthan.

fig. 235. Lady holding lotus, fragment, Atru, Kota Museum, Rajasthan.

fig. 236. *Sva-stana-sparśā,* Saccīyamātā Temple, Osiā.

fig. 237. Mātr̥kā with broken arms, Nīlakaṇṭha Temple, Kekind.

fig. 238. Capital pillar *in situ*, *devāṅganā* with flower garland, *viṭa*, note similarity with Roḍā, ninth century, Ābanerī, Rajasthan.

fig. 239. Śeṣasāyī Viṣṇu flanked by *devāṅganās*, well buttress wall, mid-eleventh century, Rānī Vāv, Pāṭan, Gujarat.

fig. 240. Śeṣasāyī Viṣṇu, Rānī Vāv, Pāṭan.

fig. 241. Wooden door-jambs with carved figures of *devāṅganās*, in continuation of *devāṅganā* imagery in timber architecture, eighteenth century, L.D. Institute Museum, Ahmedabad, Gujarat.

fig. 242. Pillar representing *devāṅganā* imagery all around it, Ghaṭeśvara Temple, Badoli.

fig. 243. Large *naṭa-maṇḍapa*, late tenth century, Kirāḍu, Rajasthan.

fig. 244. *Maṇḍapa* with ornately carved pillars, CE 1043, Pārśvanātha Temple, Kumbhariā.

fig. 245. *Raṅgamaṇḍapa* ceiling, *apsaras*, *devāṅganās* and Kāmadeva placed on *hastimuṇḍī*, mid-tenth century, Sūrya Temple, Tusā, Udaipur, Rajasthan.

fig. 246. Ceiling (detail), Kāmadeva, Sūrya Temple, Tusā.

fig. 247. *Gūḍha-maṇḍapa* ceiling, *devāṅganās* placed on the ceiling supported by Vidyādhara, 1059-80 inscribed, Udayeśvara Temple, Udaipur, Vidiśā, Madhya Pradesh.

fig. 248. Pillar brackets, interior of the *maṇḍapa*, *vyāla*, *devāṅganā* alternate, Devī Jagadambī Temple, Khajurāho.

fig. 249. West *mandāraka* ceiling, dance and music, procession, VS 1288-96, CE 1232-40, Lūṇa Vasahī, Paṭṭaśālā, Sirohī, Mt. Ābu, Rajasthan.

fig. 250. Entrance gate pillar, decorated with *devāṅganā* imageries in *rathika* frames, Gurgī, Rewā Mahārāja's palace.

fig. 251. Entrance gate pillar, detail showing *alasā devāṅganā*, *bhāravāhakā*, *vyāla,* etc., Gurgī, Rewā Mahārāja's palace.

fig. 252. Details of *fig*. 250, tāntric sexual rites, group orgy.

fig. 253. Doorway, eleventh century, Śiva Temple, Nohṭā, Madhya Pradesh.

fig. 254. *Garbha-gṛha* doorway *vṛkṣikā-nalinī* on lintel, early ninth century, Śiva Temple, Terāhī, Śivapurī, Madhya Pradesh.

fig. 255. Sanctum doorway, *devāṅganā* on doorway, *c.* eighth century, Rāmeśvara Temple, Amrol, Gwalior, Madhya Pradesh.

fig. 256. *Hiṇḍolā, toraṇa, maṇḍapa,* northern architrave, south face, *vṛkṣikā, vasanabhraṁśā,* CE 1011, Gyāraspur, Vidiśā, Madhya Pradesh.

fig. 257. Doorway, *darpaṇā, vasanabhraṁśā* and *mithuna,* Sūrya Temple, Kauśāmbī, Allahabad Museum.

fig. 258. Doorway, *devāṅganā darpaṇā* on the lintel, *c.* tenth century, Chandwasa, Mandsaur, Madhya Pradesh, Indore Central Museum.

fig. 259. Doorway, *apsaras* flanking Ādityas, *c.* tenth century, Bajramaṭh central Sūrya shrine Gyāraspur, Vidiśā, Madhya Pradesh.

fig. 260. Āditya flanked by *devāṅganā* Padminī, south wall, Sūrya Temple, Tusā.

fig. 261. *Garbha-gṛha,* Āditya flanked by *devāṅganā*s, *kaṅduka* and *alasā,* south wall, Sūrya Temple, Tusā.

fig. 262. *Maithuna* couple flanked by *devāṅganā*s, *antarāla* wall, mid-eleventh century Kandarīya Mahādeva Temple, Khajurāho, Madhya Pradesh.

fig. 263. Bahū Temple *maṇḍapa*, pillars represent dancing figures at the base eleventh century, Gwalior, Madhya Pradesh.

fig. 264. Bahū Temple, interior view, eleventh century, Gwalior, Madhya Pradesh.

fig. 265. *Vṛkṣikā*, with drummer, Harṣanātha Temple, Harṣagiri, Sikar.

fig. 266. *Alasā* on pillar, *raṅgamaṇḍapa*, Viṣṇu Temple, late tenth century, Kirāḍu, Rajasthan.

fig. 267. Faizabad, *Stambha-yoṣitā* with food basket and a jug, second century, Bharat Kala Bhavan, Varanasi.

1

Introduction

A rigourous training in the twin disciplines of Bharatanāṭyam and History of Art has moulded my vision to explore areas of learning still neglected and lacking in scholarly rigour. Having settled upon field-based research, I found Gujarat, the state where I was born and grew up, the most accessible. I visited a number of architectural sites in Gujarat and Rajasthan to make first-hand observations since the 1980s. Eventually, I widened the scope of my research to include adjoining areas of Rajasthan and Madhya Pradesh, which have close cultural affinity with Gujarat.

For two decades I have been concerned with tripartite comparative analysis of dance text, its representation by an artist in painting or sculpture and its recreation in dance by a performer. At one stage, I had confined myself to Gujarat and Orissa,[1] while the textual references focused on *nṛttahasta*s, *sthānaka*s and *cārī*s from various texts.

The present concern is an outcome of the above focus on sculptures of the *surasundarī*, *apsaras* and *alasākanyā* that gradually became the most engaging, intriguing and challenging subject of my study. The more I saw them, the more elusive they became. This book is a holistic inquiry into their imagery, their evolution on various Indian monuments and the cultural connotations associated with their placement and meaning. In attempting this, I am focusing mainly on the "content" analysis as Panofsky (in Western art history) has demonstrated, without overlooking formal and stylistic analysis of the sculptural form. Most monuments discussed in this book are from the eighth to twelfth century CE, since the major efflorescence of *devāṅganā* imagery appeared on the temple architecture during these four centuries.

I have used the term *devāṅganā* to refer to the so-called *surasundarī*, *apsaras* and *alasā kanyā* figures, because this term was originally used in *Vṛkṣārṇava*, an architectural text from Gujarat and it is the only term in my view which is devoid of any erotic or sexual prejudice. It denotes divine beauty or a beautiful divine female. Terms like *surasundarī*, *apsaras*, *madanikā*, *alasā kanyā* refer to their amorphous and amorous characters; they are created and dissolved at will to allure the mankind with the power of their beauty.

Some are often spoken of as the dancers of Indra's court, while some bear the connotation of divine courtesans and prostitutes. The *naṭī*, *nartakī* or *nāyikā* imply they are dancers or characters of a play. In the light of my interpretation, the erotic connotation or the aspect of beauty and eroticism has been overridden by an urge to explore more dynamic meanings in the light of human cultural consciousness, "the power of the female", which is not necessarily religious, erotic or anything trivial. Instead, I have tried to focus on their image typology, its programming and placement on the temple wall. I urge the reader to visualize what is the role of the *devāṅganā* sculptures in the cultic context, what role would a chief priest or chief *sthapati* play in the planning of the iconographic arrangement on a temple wall. Were there specific rules and injunctions laid down by the *sthapati* or, were the sculptors free to use their creative and innovative ideas in configuring the images of the *devāṅganā*s? — these are some of the questions I have raised and tried to answer. Did sculptors specialize in carving *devāṅganā* figures or would the same sculptor carve a *devāṅganā*, a Viṣṇu and a Śiva statue? Since many of the Śilpa texts are dated later than the temples, one would imagine that they record a prevailing practice and continuing oral tradition and not theoretical prescriptive rules.

Below is an attempt to enumerate a critique of the writings of significant scholars on the topics of *śālabhañjikā*, *surasundarī*, and *apsaras* which has received some attention but not warranted a full-length book, which is why I feel this book shall fill some gaps. Using the field research material and various methodologies of the Western and Indian scholars such as Vogel, Coomaraswamy, Stella Kramrisch, V.S. Agrawala, Motichandra, C. Sivaramamurti, M.A. Dhaky, Kapila Vatsyayan, Pramod Chandra, Wendy Doniger O'Flaherty, Ratan Parimoo, Darielle Mason, Vishakha Desai, Vidya Dehejia, and others, I expand upon the existing interpretations and explore new avenues. The theories of "Iconology" and "Semiotics" of Erwin Panofsky and Roland Barthes respectively, along with psychoanalytic approach of Freud and Jung have also lent sufficient insight into the "contextual" interpretation of a work of art. Writings of Ernst Cassirer[2] regarding symbol formation and the philosophy of Human Culture have been a path breaker. I have tried to absorb some relevant concepts from their theoretical writings to analyse the *devāṅganā* imageries in the context of Hindu-Buddhist and Jaina architecture and the evolution of their imagery from the earlier forms of primordial mother goddess figurines, *śālabhañjikā* — *vr̥kṣikā* — *yakṣī*, river goddess — *nadī-devatā*s to *devāṅganā*s. The theory of evolution of imagery can also be observed in the structured manner in which the American Institute of Indian Studies has produced its *Encyclopedia of Temple Architecture*. This methodology of Dhaky and Meister has provided a framework for observing comparative trends within one motif or iconographic construct or regional sculptural or architectural styles. Drawing attention to the placement of the *devāṅganā* imagery on temple walls and their relation with other sculptures on the same wall and the entire edifice in the manner of Stella Kramrisch has taken my study to another plane — it has become a structured approach to deconstructing their meaning and reconstructing their function in a dynamic process. Following the trail of Kramrisch and Dhaky, I launch on this exploratory and interpretative journey armed with multiple tools from Indian and Western traditions.

Before critiquing the existing literature and unfolding my methodological concerns, I wish to state that the present thesis attempts to perceive the *apsaras/devāṅganā* sculptures as a continuation of the *yakṣī* sculptures found on Buddhist and Jaina monuments and further afar into the imageries in the Vedic texts of primordial mother goddesses such as Rākā, Sīnīvālī and Aditi. In sculptural representation of these celestial figures, one can notice that not only *yakṣī*s and *śālabhañjikā*s, but even *nadī-devatā*s (river goddesses) and *nāyikā*s (heroines) played an important role in the development of their iconography. This can be observed at many sites such as Ajantā and Ellorā in Maharashtra, Jagat and Mt. Ābu in Rajasthan, Badoli and Khajurāho in Madhya Pradesh and Roḍā, Rānī Vāv and Moḍherā in Gujarat. There are some obvious iconographical representations which are found with staggering regularity on most of the Nāgara style temples such as *darpaṇā* (holding mirror), *alasā* (longingly waiting), *vasanabhraṁśā* (removing the lower garment), *kanduka-krīḍā* (playing with a ball), *keśanistoyakāriṇī* (bathing beauty), *putravallabhā* (holding a child), *sva-stana-sparśā* (touching her breast), *markaṭaceṣṭā* (being disturbed by a monkey), *vīrā* (holding a weapon), *naṭī-nartakī* (dancing) and *prasādhikā* (doing make-up). Some architectural texts from Gujarat *Vṛkṣārṇava* and *Kṣīrārṇava* (fourteenth-fifteenth centuries) mention a list of 32 *devāṅganā*s suggesting that the details relating to this group of images was circulated within *sthapati* families and was known orally in many regions. I will elucidate on these *devāṅganā*s, their typology and how in a synchronic and diachronic way they coalesce into a vision of ever-changing cyclic order towards asceticism, eroticism, creativity and annihilation. It is the "continuity" and "constancy" in imagery and form of the entire corpus of the *devāṅganā* imagery in totality, that constitutes the *raison d'être* of my inquiry.

Critique of Earlier Writings

The concept of the feminine energy personified in Indian culture, thought, art and literature, is irrevocably immersed in the Indian psyche. In the course of the present research I found that the representation of the female, other than the goddesses *per se*, contained connotations of beauty, fertility, eroticism and asceticism that broadly oscillate between "material" *versus* "spiritual" polarities. In the process of collecting observations and interpretations of earlier scholars, I noticed that the subject of *śālabhañjikā* or *apsaras* has engaged the interest of many earlier scholars, but surprisingly their probing and interpretations have remained unidirectional.

Vogel[3] proposed the concept of *śālabhañjikā* in literature and art to understand the evolution essentially of the "woman and tree" motif. From a seasonal festival to an allegory of fertility — the standardization of its posture, is shared by Māyādevī in the birth-giving pose on Buddhist monuments. He also noted the continuation of this motif from a community festival to an architectural motif wherein any type of imagery is classified under the term *śālabhañjikā*. Thus the term is conceived very broadly and the imagery is left fluid. Vogel enumerates literary data from Sanskrit texts, prose and verse literature like *Nāṭyaśāstra*, *Mahāvaṁśa*, *Buddhacarita* and *Siṁhāsanabattīsī*. Vogel's interpretation has been repeated by Coomaraswamy, B.M. Barua and R.N. Misra in their researches on *yakṣa* cult and Bharhut sculptures. Since the scope of their research was specific, they did not delve deeper into the wider connotation of the *śālabhañjikā* motif, its related imagery and its continuation in later architecture.

But Coomaraswamy[4] rightly observed that the *yakṣī*s (carved on Bharhut, Sāñcī, Mathurā) give rise to three iconographically identical motifs, albeit differently interpreted: the Buddha's nativity, "the *aśoka dohada* motif in classical literature", and the "river goddesses of medieval shrines". He also distinguished between the *gandharvī*s, *apsaras,* etc. and pointed out that it was incorrect to call them merely dancing girls. Although indirectly, Coomaraswamy was probably the first ever to hint at the continuation of *yakṣī-śālabhañjikā* imagery in later sculptures of *surasundarī,* on temple architecture. I believe that the continuation or recalling of similar motifs on different monuments after a long lapse of time does not mean these had been erased from the memory of artists' visual vocabulary of motifs and images. They may have survived in other forms to be recalled back at an opportune time when an appropriate function on an appropriate monument may have emerged.

The contribution of V.S. Agrawala[5] to the study of *yakṣī-śālabhañjikā-vṛkṣikā* motif in the light of the Sanskrit literary data is extremely insightful. In his work, begun in the 1940s on Mathurā sculptures, he identified the imagery of a number of female sculptures such as *śukasārikā*, *keśanistoyakāriṇī*, *veṇīprasādhanā*, *aśoka dohada*, *putravallabhā*, *kanduka-krīḍā* and *padminī*. He also brought to light the numerous references from Sanskrit, Pāli and Prākṛt sources, parallel motifs or imageries of *nāyikā*s as described by the poets and dramatists like Kālidāsa, Bāṇa, Aśvaghoṣa, Rājaśekhara, Bhoja and others. A whole range of *krīḍā*s such as *udyāna-krīḍā*s and *jala-krīḍā*s are mentioned by him with literary references to show the cultural context from which the imagery of a number of *yakṣī*s on Mathurā pillars was derived. He has given only stray references to *alasā kanyā* and others on later temple architecture. Agrawala does not observe any parallels or evolution in any single imagery type, e.g. *keśanistoyakāriṇī*, through the centuries from *stūpa* architecture to temple architecture. The book *Indian Art*

(1965) treats the topic of Kuṣāṇa *śālabhañjikā* at great length. The development of the motif in the post-Gupta and the medieval period has been left out.

C. Sivaramamurti,[6] in his enormous study on Amarāvatī sculptures (1942), brought to light a number of references to *yakṣī* in architectural contexts from epic and classical Sanskrit literature like the *Rāmāyaṇa*, *Mahābhārata*, *Mahābhāṣya* and *Raghuvaṁśa*. He also noticed the overlapping meanings shared by the imagery of *yakṣī*, Śrī and *nadī-devatās*, i.e. bestowing prosperity and abundance. In his subsequent book, *Sanskrit Literature and Art: Mirror of Indian Culture*[7] (1955), he devoted one section to *śālabhañjikā* and *stambha puttalikā*, which are very brief and do not provide much insight.

References to *apsaras* in the writings of indologists and iconographers have been found much before art historians began to study them in earnest. *Vedic Mythology* of A.A. Macdonell[8] (1898) and A.B. Keith[9] (1925) contain enormous information from the Vedic and Purāṇic sources on *apsaras*. An extensive study of iconography with supportive discussion on parallel manifestations through the ages done by T.A. Gopinath Rao[10] (1914-16) and J.N. Banerjea[11] (1956), have brought to light one significant observation on associating Bharhut *apsaras* Misakosi, Alambuṣā and others with the sculptures of later day Gaṅgā and Yamunā on Hindu temple architecture. Banerjea justifiably observed that the imagery of Gaṅgā–Yamunā could be traced to the Bharhut prototypes (*apsaras*) even though they are not depicted in dancing postures. Thus the "continuity" of the visual imagery and form from *yakṣī–apsaras* to *nadī-devatās* was hinted at by Banerjea in 1941 in his *Development of Hindu Iconography*, but a systematic study was still wanting. The identification of dance postures had to wait for Kapila Vatsyayan's[12] research on *Classical Dance in Literature and the Arts* (1968), which was conducted during the 1950s. Now we know that every sculpture, standing or seated, of human figures, could be identified as a *sthānaka* or a *cārī* conforming to the *Nāṭyaśāstra*. The above book has contributed greatly to my training and analytical approach to the study of sculpture and literature and the inseparable, almost "symbiotic" relationship, shared by the visual, literary and performing arts in India. A number of sculptures of hitherto classified *apsaras*, *yakṣīs*, *devāṅganās* and *surasundarīs*, have been discussed by her from the context of their dance postures.

The *apsaras*, *śālabhañjikā* concepts in literature and the arts have been dealt with independently by two scholars, namely Projesh Banerjee[13] (1982) and U.N. Roy[14] (1979), which harks back to the method of the 1940s and 1950s although they belong to the 1970s. These are the recent researches of specialized nature and contain larger compilation of references from the Vedic, Purāṇic and classical Sanskrit sources. Projesh Banerjee also brings in *devadāsīs* as the "daughters of the celestial *apsaras*" and extends the interpretation to temple ritual, but fails to project any formidable conclusions. U.N. Roy in his study on *śālabhañjikā* refers mainly to the Kuṣāṇa period, and rounds off the Gupta period summarily. Although he mentions the continuation of this motif in *nadī-devatās*, he has made no efforts at elaborating and establishing the links. Motichandra[15] (1973), in his book *The World of Courtesans* refers to *apsaras* as courtesans and reduces them to the level of divine prostitutes and misses the point about their auspiciousness and profuse procreative power. The book incorporates photographs of *apsaras* interpreted as courtesans.

At this juncture, I pause with some questions — what are the *apsaras* or *devāṅganās* doing on a temple? What role do they play in the architectural and sculptural programming (plan and layout) of the temple? What is the meaning of their action? Does their iconography have any meaning? Why are certain types of *devāṅganā* repeated on many monuments across different regions over several centuries?

By far the most brilliant interpretation of *surasundarī* and *apsaras* sculptures in conjunction with temple architecture in the light of the above questions and in the larger context of the temple's iconographical programming, has been attempted by Stella Kramrisch way back in the 1940s, followed by Alice Boner in the 1950s.

The *Hindu Temple* by Kramrisch[16] (1946) has equal clarity, depth and vision on every aspect of the temple. In the last section dealing with Śakti, she has given a chapter on "Feminine Power", the most suitable nomenclature for denoting the world of *apsaras*, *surasundarī*s and *yakṣī*s, who are the protective energies of the ultimate Śakti and share a portion of her spirit. They are a part of the integrated exposition of the meaning of the *prāsāda*.[17] Mostly formulating her views on the basis of Āgamic and Tāntric sources, she explains the *vyāla* and *devāṅganā* juxtaposition on the temple architecture as an illustration of Śakti infusing "contemplative and passive" natured *śārdūla* to activate the power of *Brahman*.[18] She compares the temple draped with images of *dikpāla*s, *devāṅganā*s, *vyāla*s and the deities with a *yantra* of Śrī, on which *yoginī*s are placed at various positions. Their energies proceed inward to the Mahāśakti placed in the *garbhagṛha* or the centre. They are the *paricārikā*s or *dūtī*s (maids) of the transcendental power. They carry *mudrā* (gesture), raiment, mirror and various vessels.[19] The celestial beauties on the walls of the temple, serve man, the devotee, they satisfy his response to them so that increased in power, released from their attractions and transformed, he proceeds in his devotion towards god in the innermost sanctuary, of his heart and in the temple. They help man towards reintegration with god. Such a didactic explanation may have to be altered now, since *apsaras* are not completely religious nor philosophical in that rigorous sense. They do play a supporting role to the main deity but they do have an identity of their own as well. Their interpretation could be left open-ended. *Apsaras* and *yakṣiṇī*s are the *dik nāyikā*s or *āvaraṇa devatā*s and they embody movement: *apsaras* is the movement in the atmosphere, *yakṣiṇī* is the movement in vegetation and *nāṭakā* is the body of the man, as is shown by a dancer.[20] Thus Kramrisch zooms in on the philosophical meaning supposedly implied by these images, which encompass the *ahaṁkāra* (ego), and suggests her own reading of it through the beauteous images of the celestial women.

Alice Boner[21] in the "introduction" to her joint research with Sadasivarath Sharma on *Śilpa Prakāśa* (1966), the medieval Orissan Sanskrit text on Temple Architecture, has observed sixteen types of *alasā kanyā* which she contends pay homage to the femininity of the Śakti, who is lavishly decorated with tender voluptuous female figures. They represent in their playful liveliness nothing but liveliness. With their different attitudes, gestures and expressions they are all composed on one and the same *yantra* (1.391-480). As a house without a wife, as frolic without a woman, thus, without female figures the monument will be of inferior quality and bear no fruit (1.392-393), claims the text. Boner and Sharma illustrate each of the *kanyā*s (virgins) with their description and supportive drawings.

M.A. Dhaky,[22] in his series on *vyāla, gaṇa, praṇāla* and *toraṇa* has effectively demonstrated "genre" based research, picking up motifs, tracing back their origin and marking their evolution over a considerable time-frame and analogous regions. Thus cutting across periods, sites and sculptural typologies he brings forth syncretic and multi-layered conclusions that bring together collective information which creates an opportunity to read meanings using comparative analysis. For the research on *vyāla*s, identification of their imagery type from architectural texts like *Samarāṅgaṇa Sūtradhāra* and *Aparājitapṛcchā* and a stylistic analysis of their form, stance and organic structure and the larger context of these motifs on temple architecture have been put together by Dhaky like a scientist. A similar approach can be seen in his study of *vitāna* which deals with the ceiling types from Gujarat temples. He has, for the first time, brought to light textual data on architecture and illustrated it with actual temples as examples.

Adopting the methods of Alois Reigl (German art historian) Dhaky and Parimoo[23] (1980s) have followed up the study of the decorative repertoire of the temple wall with its distinct architectural components and the transmission and dissemination of decorative motifs on some Nāgara (north Indian) temples. Parimoo has evolved an approach of writing on Art Historical problems, which is more from the point of view of the artist, the image-maker and not so much from the onlooker's. The significant role of the artist as the observer and creator of form is usually highlighted. Parimoo's monograph on *Sculptures of Śeṣasāyī Viṣṇu* is more relevant to mention here since it is a study on one imagery type, its literary references, regional distribution of its manifestations in sculpture and painting and the various modes of representation. It has a humanistic extensiveness rather than being a mere iconographical compilation. Methodologies of Dhaky and Parimoo have contributed greatly to my own investigation and writing.

I have observed with much interest how authors of monographs on temple sites surveying their history, architectural structure and style, sculptures and iconography have dealt with the imagery of the *devāṅganā*. The attention given to them is only peripheral and mostly limited to description or an appreciation of their erotic gestures. Wibke Lobo[24] (1982), in her book on Moḍherā temple, describes the entire temple and its sculptures, unit by unit. She even tabulates the iconography of Dvādaśagaurī based on *Aparājitapṛcchā* and as programmed on Moḍherā *maṇḍovara devakoṣṭha*s. But such a specialized study on the *devāṅganā/apsaras* imagery is refrained from. The same can be observed of Kirit Mankodi's[25] (1990) impressive and extensively produced book on *The Queen's Stepwell at Pāṭan*. Although an enormously descriptive book, the author hardly discusses the imagery of the *devāṅganā*s in totality, just as he does those of Viṣṇu's *daśāvatāra*s or the *dikpāla*s, etc. Illustrated photographic captions refer to *apsaras*, *alasā kanyā*, *yoginī* and so on but the term *devāṅganā* has not been used at all even though this term is found in architectural texts of Gujarat. Even the dance-like postures have not been identified as depicting some classical *karaṇa*s. Hence, Mankodi opts for a clinical approach to enumerate the iconographies but does not enter into any specialized interpretation of the *devāṅganā* forms. R. Nath,[26] D. Handa[27] and R.N. Misra[28] in their independent monographs on *Khajurāho*, *Osian* and *Sculptures of Dahala and Dakṣiṇa Kosala* respectively, have attempted explaining the range of *devāṅganā* imagery, their textual references and functions. In their analysis of the *devāṅganā* imagery which are often referred to as *nāyikā*, *surasundarī*, *śālabhañjikā*, *alasā kanyā*, etc. the allusion to the texts like *Śilpa Prakāśa* or *Kṣīrārṇava*, attempts to distinguish the iconography of one from the other, are discernible. But, as the scope of such books does not allow them to explore the *devāṅganā* imagery and its development any further, their discourse on them is very limited.

On the other hand, authors like Kanwarlal[29] and many others on Khajurāho temples try to create an impression that they represent

Epicurean, materialist, sensualist society of India. The *apsaras* have been either portrayed by them as "seductresses" or as objects for deriving pleasure and titillation. Such limited views will be clearly overshadowed in the following chapters.

In the early 1990s, research conducted by Darielle Mason and Vishakha Desai[30] on the sculptures of the analogous regions of Gujarat, Rajasthan and Madhya Pradesh was published in an exhibition catalogue organized by the Asia Society in New York in 1993. This exhibition "Gods, Guardians and Lovers: Temple Sculptures from North India AD 700-1200" for the first time examined the sculpture and architecture of the region as an integrated phenomenon along with social, political and cultural perspectives that may have led to their making. Desai clearly outlines the scope of this exercise as an attempt to understand the sculptures as "individual parts of a greater whole". Contributions by many scholars in the volume are insightful. The catalogue of sculptures written most sensitively by Mason is most pertinent to our research as she discusses many figures of *apsaras* and talks about their form, the way artists conceived them, how they relate to the various gods they flank and their generalized depiction repeated often on Jaina and Hindu temples alike. "It is likely that, in their original architectural context, these dancing *apsaras* would have been found in such an attendant location, honouring the god in the central niche as the female dancers in the employ of the temple (*devadāsīs*) honoured the god within the sanctum."

At another place in the same catalogue Mason mentions:

> Although no two *apsaras* show precisely the same posture, the activities in which women engage fall into categories relating to favourite types in contemporaneous literature. The placement of a type within any designated location, however, seems more motivated by aesthetics than by meaning.[31]

The statement surely needs more reflection and the imagery of the *apsaras* a lot more intensive study; hence our attempt in this book would be to unravel those multiple levels that contribute meaning to these celestial women who are certainly not mere aesthetic appendages decorating a temple wall.

K.K. Handique[32] clearly connects the *apsaras* tradition with *devadāsī* tradition citing inscriptions, Purāṇic and literary references from Sanskrit literature and history. From Śiva, Viṣṇu and Durgā temples, from Kashmir to Kanyakumari and from Somanātha to Tezpur, *devadāsī*s were dedicated to the service of the main deity of the temples patronized by the royalty. Even queens and princesses were *devadāsī*s and danced before the deity, underscoring the fact that they belonged to high caste and class and were not obscure women of disrepute.

Interpreting the Devāṅganā Motif: Methodologies and Strategies

In this section, I have tried to formulate a methodology and examined several strategies from many disciplines. I assimilate them here to unravel the meaning of the *devāṅganā* motif and how temple architecture and sculpture have evolved to incorporate this motif. Thus using historical and sociological, formal and stylistic, semiotic and iconological methods of interpretation, emphasis on "meaning" has been squarely laid.

Iconology, semiology and psycho-analysis, all contribute to the understanding of the *devāṅganā* motif, individually as well as generically speaking. The motif of *devāṅganā* lends itself to be interpreted from the perspective of feminist intervention allowing different insights into the history of temple architecture and sculpture. Looking at close ties between sculptural and literary expression in Indian classical arts, I have not ignored what could be culled from the perspective of Indian aesthetics to understand the *devāṅganā* representation. There are ample theoretical bases in Indian aesthetics which I have tried to apply to understand the *devāṅganā* motif, thus *dhvani* (meaning) and *alaṁkāra* (figure of speech) are interpretative strategies that could be applied to *devāṅganā* figures. Here again, "meaning", its construction using representational methods, either using figural or visual images has been explored. This supports the view that all the arts are interrelated and they need to be viewed as a cultural process rather than a sporadic expression.

Besides meaning and form, I have also tried to explore what is "medieval quality" in Indian sculpture and architecture that is reflected in the sculptural efflorescence and the philosophical leaning of the temple design. Thus there is a fair balance in dealing with the formal and stylistic development of architecture and sculpture while focusing on the motif of *devāṅganā* figures thematically.

Erwin Panofsky's[33] formulation in *Studies in Iconology* (1939) paved the way for content analysis in visual arts in the larger context of history, period, class, religion and culture. Between this book and *Meaning in Visual Arts* (1955), Panofsky has demonstrated that study of content is not a mere description or an aesthetic appreciation of a work of art. He evolved the theory of iconology which is a method of interpretation arising from synthesis rather than analysis. The iconological method operates on three levels — (i) pre-iconographical description, (ii) iconographical analysis, and (iii) iconological interpretation.

Besides the above categories, Panofsky states that the above process is indivisible and integrated. He elaborates interpretation based on linear cognition and its interpretation. The primary and secondary levels are the most obvious. When a spectator learns factual, allegorical and symbolic imageries as represented by the artist, he also learns the intrinsic meaning through imagery. But it is the iconographical interpretation which requires knowledge of literary sources and the spirit of the age, *Weltanschauung* during which the artwork was produced, as no art is free of its contemporaneous connotations. Panofsky lays stress on the history of tradition which applies to any artistic tradition of any age. There are three aspects to the history of tradition, i.e. style, typology and historical conditions.

(i) History of style (insight into the manner in which, under varying historical conditions, objects and events were expressed by forms).

(ii) History of types (insight into the manner in which, under varying historical conditions, specific themes or concepts were expressed by objects and events).

(iii) History of cultural symptoms or "symbols" in general (insight into the manner in which, under varying historical conditions, essential tendencies of the human mind were expressed by specific themes and concepts).

At this point, I would like to introduce the theory of meaning in the spoken word according to the Indian tradition of poetic expression and its aesthetic appreciation by Ānandavardhana, the eleventh-century Sanskrit scholar from Kashmir. The concept of *dhvani* put forward by Ānandavardhana encompassed the earlier theories of *sphoṭa* to explain how the power of the linguistic symbol enriched the potential of poetic language to convey meaning. Pondering deeply on the imagery of the *devāṅganā* sculptures individually and in totality as the representation of the feminine power within the physical and experiential space of a temple, I feel tempted to apply the *dhvani* concept to unravel meaning in visual language in general and to the *devāṅganā* imagery in particular. The poetic language has double potential: literal (*vācya*) and implied (*pratīyamāna*). Such a poetry in which words and their literal meanings occupy a subordinate position and suggest some charming sense (an idea, a figure of speech or an emotion) is called *dhvani*[34] (*yatrārthaḥ śabdo vatam artham upasarjani kr̥tasvarthau vyaṅktaḥ kāvyaviśeṣaḥ dhvanir iti sūribhiḥ kathitaḥ*).

According to *dhvani* theory the poetic word has three powers: denotative (*abhidhā*), indicative (*lakṣaṇā*) and suggestive (*vyañjanā*). Ānandavardhana's basic postulate is that utterances possess a literal meaning, and can also convey a further meaning such as the socio-cultural meaning. This includes everything other than the literal meaning (the primary and the metaphorical senses). Ānandavardhana did not confine to the words and sentences as indicators of meaning; he included all the contextual factors, the intonation. The social and cultural meanings, which fall within the domain of intonation, is the power of *vyañjanā*.[35]

Understanding *devāṅganā* imagery according to *dhvani* and the iconological interpretation is like looking at the linguistic symbol which denotes on the primary level an image of a beautiful woman engaged in activities of different kinds, e.g. playing with a ball, looking into the mirror, touching her own breast, or discarding a scorpion from her lower garment. But on indicative or *lakṣaṇā* level some of the *devāṅganās* reveal metaphorical meanings which invite the spectator to transcend beyond their physical form and actions to the conceptual, philosophical, biological, erotic, poetic, ritualistic and esoteric meanings generated by their presence on the *maṇḍovara* (wall), pillar, bracket and on the ceiling of the temple. Their placement is not a decorative appendage to the body of the temple but organically integral to the physical, ritualistic and philosophical function of a place of worship.

The meaning of their action or attribute, seen individually or as a group, will emerge slowly by examining their imagery from temple to temple within geographical regions, over a period of time. One would then notice the continuity of a motif and its placement on the *maṇḍovara* or *vitāna*. This impression left by repeated examination and previous study would urge an aesthete's mind to discern the implied meaning behind the charming and alluring physical beauty of the female form, which metaphorically suggests a higher, transcendental phenomenon or truth of life.

The *lakṣaṇā* or metaphor operates by transference of meaning from the symbol by *tatsiddhi* (accomplishment of purpose), *jāti* (same origin), *vaiparītya* (contrareity), *sārūpya* (similarity), *praśaṁsā* (praise), and *abhidheya-sambandha* (relation with the literal meaning). These are the basic rules of interpretation explained by Mīmāṁsakas to explain the Vedic passages with metaphorical transfer of meaning that could be applied to the *devāṅganā* imagery.[36]

One more type of *lakṣaṇā* called *gauṇī vṛtti* has also been pointed out by Mīmāṁsaka Kumārila Bhaṭṭa and followed by Mammaṭa, Viśvanātha and Hemacandra. It refers to qualitative transfer, if the relation between the referent and reference is that of similarity, but if it is based on cause and effect, part and whole, measure and measured then it is called pure *lakṣaṇā*.[37] It is this *gauṇī vṛtti* that applies to the metaphorical aspect of some *devāṅganā* images, just like *siṁho devadattaḥ* (Devadatta is a lion) where *siṁhatva* — the universal character of courage, is present in Devadatta that justifies calling him a lion. The *sva-stana-sparśā* or *aśoka dohada* type of imagery in *devāṅganā* sculptures implies *gauṇī vṛtti*, the quality of fertility invoking power. Thus the female form is a potent generative vessel which implies fertility, a character shared with nature.

Ānandavardhana's division of *lakṣaṇā* (*avivakṣita vācya*) is further divided into *atyanta tiraskṛta vācya* (literal sense completely set aside) and *arthāntara saṁkramita vācya* (literal meaning shifted, pregnant use of words). Under the former category we can put *kanduka-krīḍā*, but *putravallabhā* holding mangoes will fall in the latter category.

In case of *vyañjanā* which lays stress on *vyaṅgya* or suggestivity, the distinct categories are *asaṁlakṣyakrama vyaṅgya* (stages of knowing the suggested sense are imperceptible) and *saṁlakṣyakrama vyaṅgya* (stages of knowing the suggested sense are perceptible). *Devāṅganā* imageries under the first category are *sarpadhārī*, *vasanabhraṁśā*, *markaṭaceṣṭā*, which have overtones of eroticism while *yakṣī*, *vṛkṣikā*, *śālabhañjikā*, *alasā*, *nartakī* refer to the second category. More details about the various *devāṅganā* types will be discussed in the chapters on individual *devāṅganā*s.

The *sphoṭa* or the concept of linguistic sign is analogous to the terminology of Saussure: signifier and signified, that which means and that which is meant, *śabda* and *artha*, form and content.[38] With this parallelism cited by Kunjunni Raja, our own attempt at a semiological analysis of the *devāṅganā* imagery as a social/cultural motif gets strengthened. Semiology is a theory of linguistics put forward by Saussure, Roland Barthes and others, which has been applied more significantly to literature than to the arts.

In Indian art, just a few scholars have attempted to explain the narrative structure in art and poetry, while at the same time to uncover the import of the allegorical meaning hidden behind the seemingly simple narration.[39] The interrelationship of the word and meaning is what is implied by *sāhitya* and the method of analysis attempted by semioticians. Taking the *devāṅganā* sculpture as a semiotic unit, one begins to uncover the meaning signified by this potential signifier, whose realm pervades cultural, social and artistic traditions. Since structuralist analysis is heterogeneous, one has to keep in view factors based on temporal and spatial contexts. This has been observed by scholars of living performing traditions such as Traditional Theatre and Devadāsī Tradition in south India.[40] One agrees that myths, complex rituals, colourful customs and festivals aim at a form of cultural transmission that is not based on analytical rationalism, but on imagination and poetic feeling. Hence a subject of inquiry such as *devāṅganā* sculptures needs to be probed from multiple perspectives which satisfy cultural, ritualistic and aesthetic needs. On the historical or chronological axis, this phenomenon is supported by the sculptural evidence recurring on temples whereas the synchronic axis supports its cultural relevance. The synchronic evidences encompass the Vedic and Purāṇic literature, historical information, through inscriptions, Sanskrit *nāṭya* and *kāvya* literature, ritual traditions of temples, evidences of *devadāsī* practice and Vāstuśāstra literature. (See Diagram in Chapter 8.)

The chapter on literary sources in this book conforms with "knowledge of literary sources" which Panofsky underscores in his iconological approach. The mother goddess, *vṛkṣikā*, *śālabhañjikā*, and *yakṣī* antecedents conform to the "history of cultural symptoms" or "symbols". Extensive analysis of the *devāṅganā* imagery follows the "history of types" thus to arrive at "intrinsic content" and the iconological interpretation of the *devāṅganā* imagery is through this route.

Understanding meaning of *devāṅganā* imagery using psychoanalysis is another methodological tool that I observe scholars are using and successfully analysing certain cultural practices and the spirit of the age, *Weltenschauung*. The post-Formalism methodological standpoint developed by Panofsky with regard to "iconology" for visual arts and Saussure, Barthes and others of semiotics for literature and the human sciences, have paved the way for an in-depth study of "content" based on "contextuality". The world of "meaning" and "reading an image" has widened the range of subject matter and the analytical study related with it. An extension of the content study in art and literature also came about with Sigmund Freud and C.J. Jung and their study related to psychoanalysis. More than Freud, it is Jung's work that is more potentially applicable to art and it has been demonstrated with the help of application of concepts such as "the collective unconscious" and the "archetype" to pre-historic and early historic art by Eric Neumann[41] and Seigfried Gidion.[42]

The theories of "iconology" and "semiology" offer the method of applying analytical tools to arrive at an interpretation, whereas Neumann and Gidion have demonstrated it on such universal phenomena and art manifestations which have universal applicability. Explaining the archetype, Neumann says it refers not to any concrete image existing in space and time, but to an inward image at work in the human psyche. The symbolic expression of this psychic phenomenon is to be found in the figure of the "Great Goddess" represented in the myths and artistic creations of mankind.[43] The effect of this archetype may be followed through the whole of history for we can demonstrate its workings in the rites, myths, symbols of early man and also in the dreams, fantasies and creative works of the sound as well as the sick human beings of our own day.

An archetype can have its emotionally dynamic components, its symbolism, its material component and structure. The symbolism of the archetype is its manifestation in specific psychic images, which are perceived by consciousness and which are different for each archetype, e.g. the terrible aspect and the life-giving "friendly" aspect of the female archetype. The structure of the archetype is the complex network of psychic organization which includes dynamism, symbolism and sense content and whose centre and intangible unifier is the archetype itself.[44] The "primordial archetype" according to Jung is a structural concept signifying "eternal presence".[45] Thus, the "eternal presence" of the archetype has symbolic multivalence. Gradually, the innumerable symbols get linked with the figure of the "great mother" as attributes and form the wreath of symbols that surrounds the archetypal figure and manifests itself in rite and myth. This wreath of symbolic images surrounds not only one figure but a great number of figures of "great mother", who as goddesses and fairies, female demons and nymphs, friendly and unfriendly, manifest the one "great unknown", the "great mother", as the central aspect of the "archetypal feminine" in the rites and myths, the religions and legends of mankind. It is an essential feature of the primordial archetype that it combines positive and negative attributes and groups of attributes. This union of opposites is the primordial archetype, its ambivalence, is characteristic of the original situation of the unconscious which consciousness has not yet dissected into its antithesis. Early man experienced this paradoxical simultaneity of good and evil, friendly and terrible, in the godhead as a unity, while as consciousness developed, the "good goddess" and the "bad goddess", usually came to be worshipped as different beings.[46] Neumann[47] has demonstrated this by constructing a schema in a circular order assigning the lower zone to the negative and the upper one to the positive. The positive zone contains, Isis, Mary, Sophia, Muse (Lakṣmī, Aditi, Sarasvatī, Durgā, Māyā, Ambikā can be thought of in the Indian context) whereas the lower-negative zone contains Astarte, Lilith, Circe, Hecate, Gorgon (Hārīti, Kālī and Cāmuṇḍā in Indian context). The same concept can be identified with the ambivalent imagery of the *devāṅganā*s which combine the features of both "kindness" and "terribleness". Thus, on a single monument some of the *devāṅganā*s are *śṛṅgāra* type while some others are *vīra* type. Their fertility connotation apart, they can also be identified as *vīra nāyikā*s (brave and fearsome heroines) and *śṛṅgāra nāyikā*s (sensuous heroines affected by love).

I have tried to expand upon the idea of "primordial archetype" following the concepts of dynamic symbolism, symbolic multivalence and its combination of positive and negative attributes. The evolving "concept of the feminine" is understood as a dynamic process of evolving imagery, evolving symbolism over a period of thousand years, which even in its changed form allude in some ways to its original form and meaning. The evolving imagery has dialectic, erotic and ascetic, creative and hostile overtones. In the *devāṅganā* imagery, the concept of the "feminine" has an inherent ambivalence that goes back to the time of the formation of the archetypal image. I have tried to analyse the *devāṅganā* imagery and plotted their attitudes and attributes according to their actions and characteristics using a cyclics circular schema.

Following the "universality of the archetype", Gidion has suggested the concept of "constancy and change" in the symbolism of the visual form and the function of the symbolism. He observes how constancy and change have seldom been so interwoven as in the sequence from symbols of fertility to symbols of venerable animal to the goddess. The different stages are so closely intermingled that one can scarcely be distinguished from the other.[48]

The only shortcoming in the application of these theories to the *devāṅganā* imagery is that they refer to pre-historic and early historic art, their authorship and patronage is shrouded in mystery while these sculptures range from the historic to medieval periods. Although the main focus is only on the temple sculptures of four centuries (viz. eighth to twelfth) we have to fall back upon the earlier sculptures to trace the origins of the *devāṅganā* imagery. Thus, I have excavated the imagery of mother goddess, *yakṣī*, *vṛkṣikā*, *śālabhañjikā*, *diśākumārī* and *nadī-devatā* to understand the "element of constancy and change" in *devāṅganā* imagery.

Notably, semiological analysis is like deconstruction or decoding of a history, philosophy, imagery motif, mythology, character or emotion, by which process an "archaeological excavation" is attempted from the present, through layers of the past to uncover various kinds of changes, interpretations and influences. The "enunciative analysis" and structural interpretation of the present text (*devāṅganā* imagery) is a process of reassessment of the entire "oeuvre" of the "feminine concept and form", dealt with at several levels of historic periods and in adjacent fields of Indian art, literature and thought. Such a discourse does not confine itself to Indian art alone and could be expanded to the arts of the early West Asian and Occidental cultures. This will be elaborated in the chapter on sculptures of *devāṅganā* where I have compared images of Egyptian tree goddess Nut, Greek Astarte and Roman Ceras. The "archaeology" of our "discourse" deals with such documents which are not transparent but opaque, which have to be pierced to reach to the depth of the essential meaning, which are pregnant with metaphor and allegory.

The evolving concept of the "feminine" can be described as a "tree of enunciative derivation" in Foucauldian sense; at its base are the primordial concepts and forms of the "feminine principle", that extend to its summit, and after a number of branchings are the statements of forms that put into operation the same regularity but more delicately articulated, more clearly delimited and localized forms.[49] This point can be illustrated with the help of major *devāṅganā* images which have the mother goddess figurines at their base. The Indus Valley and the West Asian examples denote fertility by holding breasts for nourishment. The same psychology continues in the Kuṣāṇa *yakṣī* figures and the *sva-stana-sparśā devāṅganā*s from Jagat and Rānī Vāv, spanning more than thousand years.

The imagery evolves from direct allusion to fertility towards a more stylized representation continuing on the lines of fertility and nourishment tinged with erotic fervour. Thus the *sva-stana-sparśā devāṅganā* is an offshoot of the primordial mother goddess where nourishment has been superseded by eroticism. The process vouches for the "original" departures made in the order of the "regular", which in turn expands the "oeuvre" and the scope of the discourse itself. The discourse on the "concept of feminine" by the virtue of its multiplicity in form and the homogeneity of its motif, through various fields of human expression, does not limit itself to art history or religion, strictly. In other words, the present attempt is to reassess certain artistic material (symbolic representation in sculptural form) of various historical periods in a new order, the "psycho-historical" one, which refers to the various stages in the development of the human psyche. The Foucauldian approach to the "excavation of knowledge" perpetuated from past centuries, but veiled and erased from immediate memory, could be applied to uncover the various stages and layers in the development of *devāṅganā* imagery on medieval temple architecture.

But while recollecting the *devāṅganā* imagery, the "primordial archetype" according to Jung, a structural concept signifying the "eternal presence" of the "concept of feminine" manifests in the "great mother" which I now demonstrate develops into the great goddess concept while the *devāṅganā*s remain semi-divine and ambivalent. The number of analogous concepts like water, vegetation, earth, air, etc. form a wreath of symbolic images and surround the number of figures of the *devāṅganā*. What compels us to probe their imagery is the idea of recurrence, their dynamic meanings and their appearance in conjunction with other gods on the walls and ceilings of Hindu and Jaina temples.

The concept of symbolic structures in a metaphysical sense, dealt with by Cassirer, offers another insight into looking at structures and their symbolic values, thus offering a distinct way of looking at the *devāṅganā* imagery and the "concept of feminine" centred around life. In Cassirer's summation, both life and myth are subjective elements; life is completely subjective, and myth is attached to this subjectivity at its origin. Myth does not hold life at a distance; instead it is intertwined with it. All symbolic forms possess the subjective elements of life to some degree, and all arise from myth. Cassirer says that life's motion "consists in their creation of ever new forms, *gestalts,* and in their destruction" and that each form's function "embraces this process within its own characteristic motion, within its own characteristic shaping and changing shapes". Life's process of change is passed on to the symbolic forms in their production. Explicating further on symbolic forms he says that:

> symbolic forms are centred in spirit through objectification. The objectivity is the result of spiritual activity. Through symbolic forms, the human being makes a world of objects that stand apart from spatial and temporal experience and that can be shared in culture. Moving from metaphysics to fine arts, Cassirer explains that whereas language objectifies through naming, art objectifies through embodying and shaping. Different in kind, both art and language represent and discover the world; neither merely reproduces an already given world. In these two forms, objectification is the stabilizing, defining, individuating and humanizing of reality.

Talking more specifically in the context of art and its depiction of reality, Cassirer says that:

> art produces reality through representation; representation here occurs in images. The images of art are not replicas of a given world of things, the form of art is an entire way of thinking. Art produces and thereby discovers reality.

Linking symbolic forms to reality, Cassirer further says that:

> symbolic form of historical consciousness determines reality through recollection. Historical reality is always based on a historical consciousness, a continual turning inward towards the past. Historical reality is not an absolute object but a recollection pertaining to the perspective of a particular historical consciousness.

In sum, cultural reality is the set of possibilities that the human being can make. These possibilities depend on spirit's power of objectivity, on spirit's ability to stabilize objects or events and form various meanings of them. The formation of these possibilities also depends on subjectivity; life's temporality causes the human being to form culture as a development in time. The real is ultimately the totality of symbolic forms as produced through the dialectic of spirit and life.

Devāṅganā Imagery and Feminist Analysis of Gendered Representation in Indian Art

The last and the most recent tool focusing on the feminist approach has been attempted here since way back in the mid-1980s when my research was being formulated and I wrote my doctoral thesis, application of feminist intervention in Indian art was still in its infancy. It had just begun to be noticed with regard to the Western art and in academic circles limited to the study and research of contemporary practice, women as producers of art. From the vantage of contemporary practice it entered the discourse of traditional art history and began to be applied at the level of postgraduate study as a perspective to examine art. Now of course, it is an accepted tool in the armoury of an art school-trained Indian art historian.

Using a term "feminist interventions in the history of art" Griselda Pollock[50] begins the argument in its favour from the standpoint of social construction, a broad matrix of cultural practice within which art history as a discipline falls and extracts the position given to women artists as an example of paradigm shift, because of which today we look at the production and consumption of art in social, economic, political, religious and ideological spheres, interconnected and not just admire it for its aesthetic value and artistic calibre of its producer. These factors condition our existence and insist upon its recognition naturally. Using Marxist, psychoanalytic, semiotic and deconstructionist approaches, she argues about place for women artists, their portrayal and how feminist intervention in art history would change the manner in which we negotiate art.

Application of the Western feminist concerns of gender, class and psychoanalysis when applied to Indian art has its own limitations and should be viewed from the Indian perspective. Vidya Dehejia[51] in her edited volume, *Representing the Body: Gender Issues in Indian Art* amply emphasized this realignment which is culture, history, body and psyche-specific. In the case of Indian art, where not only Sanskrit, Prākr̥t and other vernacular texts but also colonial translations and interpretations are constantly contested, forming any conclusive theories would be disastrous. Applying theories of "gaze and spectatorship" for instance, she states:

> A sacred monument where such an application of spectatorship proves to be irrelevant is the early Buddhist *stūpa* of Bharhut belonging to around 100 BCE. . . . The heavy sensuality of one and the provocative thrust of the limbs of the other might suggest at first glance, that they were created to delight male viewers. To locate these images in an appropriate context, however, it is necessary to consider the patronage of these works of art, the audience who viewed them, and the function which these images fulfilled.

From the study of their inscription it has been found that many of these figures were dedicated by nuns and female worshippers. These were displayed in public spaces, and both men and women, young and old would have gazed at them while visiting the *stūpa* for worship. Dehejia concludes:

> One may then affirm that sensuous female images, including those carved against the Bharhut railing, were not produced to satisfy the viewing pleasure of men. Whatever the actual position of women in society during the first century BCE such imagery is likely to have sent out a positive message and been viewed by women as a powerful affirmation, and a sign of affirmative engenderment. As twentieth-century views, inundated with exploitative female imagery, we perhaps tend

> to overlook the ambiance, and the relative "state of innocence" prior to the mechanical reproduction of visual images.

She further expands on the conflicting information about the position of women in ancient India and the position of goddesses in the pantheon of male Hindu gods; the role of women artists in ancient India and the use of gendered language in official documents in ancient and medieval India. It is important to note that although Dehejia has concerned her observations based more on spectatorship than on creative representation, the whole process of image-making in my opinion needs further exploration.

There are some basic pertinent issues here which have been missed. What concerns my study and what I labour to interpret is the nature of the female imagery of semi-divine beautiful *yakṣī*s, *apsaras* and *surasundarī*s (who are not accorded uncontested power as Durgā for instance, which makes it doubly difficult to place them in the hierarchy of Hindu gods and what they symbolize on a monument) which I generically call *devāṅganā*s. I would try to employ feminist intervention to interpret how the imagery developed by asking the following question: who formulated it — philosophers, *sthapati*s, religious teachers, patrons or the sculptors who carved the figures? They could either be men or women. This aspect of the engenderment of the *devāṅganā* imagery has not been unravelled by Dehejia who has also quoted texts such as *Śilparatna, Tantrasāra, Viddhaśālabhañjikā,* etc. to explain the motif of woman touching the tree with her foot in the manner of the Bharhut *yakṣī*s and the female images on the walls of Khajurāho temple which she illustrates. The aspect of representation of the image of the *yakṣī* and the production of this image has gone through many stages of contemplation and discussion. What I would like to emphasize here is the theorization on these aspects, even if there is no information available on the making of such magnificent monuments such as Sāñcī and Bharhut, to say the least. I also would like to stress here that the same conceptualization would have happened some 1,200 years later at great monuments of Khajurāho and Bhubaneswar temples, the planning and placement of figures, iconographic symbolism of the whole monument, the relation of its parts to the whole need a discourse or strategy that could either be, dialectic, structuralist, holistic or otherwise.

A pertinent approach to what I have indicated above, without yet attempting the feminist intervention, has been aptly formulated by Annapurna Garimalla[52] in the following passage in the context of *Engendering Indian Art*:

> Art production as practice, as object, as text, needs to be historicized to the point that generalizations rendered in gendered language cease to hold water. For example, why did specific courts sponsor eroticized representation in art and to what ends? Who rendered and negotiated these representations? What architectural texts did they produce and with what kinds of meaning? Leaving aside art production sponsored by courts, what kind of representations were made outside of this ambit? Even in monuments where information is only available through elite texts, scholars need to read against the grain to imagine alternative histories. If this process proves an impossibility, that impossibility needs to be theorized and an absence acknowledged in order to create a presence.

In my attempt to interpret *devāṅganā* imagery, absence of data has been acknowledged, new interpretation of well-known images which views *devāṅganā*s as powerful celestial figures, not as mere hand-maidens of the great goddesses or decorative appendages to their retinue, but dynamically pulsating forms of female principles, ever auspicious, balancing effects of good and evil that manifested collectively, but were never accorded definite recognition thus far. In this attempt, I have inquired "text", "representation" and "practice" all of which when brought together reveal greater understanding of the female representation and sexuality, gaze and spectatorship, questioning the litany of the major gods on whose monuments these *devāṅganā* figures appear as well as underscore the "image making" principles that led to the making of those images in the first place. Even historicizing the *devāṅganā* sculptures and the context in which monuments were constructed based on inscriptions to understand the relationship between the iconography of the monument, patron's aspirations and the artists' rendering of the imagery. This "reading between the lines" includes folklore as well as classical sources.

References

1. "A Study of Nṛttahastas in Indian Dance" — A dissertation submitted to the Department of Dance, Faculty of Performing Arts, M.S. University of Baroda, in 1985-86 (unpublished).
2. Introduced to me by my *guru* and mentor Ratan Parimoo, retired Professor of History of Art, M.S. University of Baroda.
3. J.Ph. Vogel, "The Woman and Tree, or Śālabhañjikā in Indian Literature and Art", *Acta Orientalia*, VII, Leiden, 1929, pp. 201-31.
4. A.K. Coomaraswamy, *Yakṣas* I, Smithsonian Institute, Washington, 1928.
5. V.S. Agrawala, (a) *Handbook of Curzon Museum of Archaeology*, 1939; (b) "Mathura Museum Catalogue", *JUPHS*, 1951; (c) *Indian Art*, Varanasi, 1965.
6. C. Sivaramamurti, "Amarāvatī Sculptures in the Madras Government Museum", *Bulletin of the Madras Government Museum*, New Series, vol. IV, Madras, 1942.
7. C. Sivaramamurti, "Sanskrit Literature and Art: Mirrors of Indian Culture", *Memoirs of the Archaeological Survey of India*, no. 73, New Delhi, 1955.
8. A.A. Macdonell, *Vedic Mythology*, Strassburg, 1898.
9. A.B. Keith, *The Religion and Philosophy of the Vedas and Upaniṣads*, Harward Oriental Series, 1925.
10. T.A. Gopinath Rao, *Elements of Hindu Iconography*, 4 vols., Madras, 1914-16.
11. J.N. Banerjea, *Development of Hindu Iconography*, Calcutta, 1941, revised 1956.
12. Kapila Vatsyayan, *Classical Indian Dance in Literature and the Arts*, New Delhi, 1968.
13. Projesh Banerjee, *Apsaras in Indian Dance*, New Delhi, 1982.
14. U.N. Roy, *Śālabhañjikā*, Varanasi, 1979.
15. Motichandra, *The World of Courtesans,* New Delhi, 1973.
16. Stella Kramrisch, *The Hindu Temple*, Calcutta, 1946.
17. Ibid., p. 318.
18. Ibid., p. 338.
19. Ibid., p. 339.
20. Ibid., p. 340.
21. Alice Boner and S.R. Sharma, *Śilpa Prakāśa*, Medieval Orissan Sanskrit text on Temple Architecture by Ramachandra Kaulacharya, Leiden, 1966, pp. 46-53.

22. M.A. Dhaky, *The Vyālas on the Medieval Temples of India*, Indian Civilisation Series II, Varanasi, 1965.
23. Ratan Parimoo, (a) *Essays in New Art History*, vol. I, Studies in Indian Sculpture: Regional Genres and Interpretations, New Delhi: Books & Books, 2000; (b) "Some Aspects of Decorative Repertoire of Gujarat Temple Architecture", *Decorative Arts of India*, Salarjung Museum Seminar Papers, ed. M.L. Nigam, Hyderabad, 1987, pp. 91-108; (c) "Khajurāho: The Candella Sculptor's Paradise", *K.V. Saundararajan Felicitation Volume*, New Delhi; (d) *Sculptures of Śeṣasāyī Viṣṇu*, M.S. University Press, Baroda, 1983.
24. Wibke Lobo, *The Sun Temple at Moḍherā*, Munchen, 1982.
25. Kirit Mankodi, *The Queen's Step-well at Pāṭan*, Bombay, 1990.
26. R. Nath, *Khajurāho*.
27. Devendra Handa, *Osia: History, Archaeology, Art and Architecture*, New Delhi, 1984.
28. R.N. Misra, *Sculptures of Dahala and Dakṣiṇakosala*, New Delhi, 1987.
29. K. Kanwarlal, *Erotic Sculptures of Khajurāho*, New Delhi, 1970.
30. Vishakha Desai and Darielle Mason (eds.), *Gods, Guardians and Lovers: Temple Sculptures from North India AD 700-1200*, New York: The Asia Society Galleries and Ahmedabad: Mapin Publishing Pvt. Ltd., 1993, p. 155.
31. Mason, 1993, p. 160.
32. K.K. Handique, *Apsarases in Indian Literature and the Legend of Urvaśī and Pururavas*, 2001.
33. Erwin Panofsky, (a) *Studies in Iconology*, Oxford University Press, 1939; (b) *Meaning in Visual Arts*, New York, 1955.
34. K. Kunjunni Raja, *Indian Theories of Meaning*, Madras, 1963, p. 284.
35. Ibid., p. 281.
36. Ibid., p. 236.
37. Ibid., p. 241.
38. Ibid., pp. 121-23.
39. Ratan Parimoo, (1) *Uncovering the Meaning of the Picture Puzzles of Bihari Satsai painted by Jagannath: A Semiotic Study, East & West;* (2) "Adaptation of Folk Tales for Buddhist Jātaka Stories and their depiction in Indian Art: A Study in Narrative and Semiotic Transformation", *Journal of M.S. University of Baroda*, Humanities Number, 1991-92; Vidya Dehejia.
40. Kapila Vatsyayan, *Traditional Indian Theatre*, New Delhi, 1980; Saskia Kersenboom Story-Nitya Sumangali, *Tradition of Devadāsī in South India*, New Delhi, 1987.

41. Eric Neumann, *The Great Mother: An Analysis of the Archetype*, New York, English tr., 1955.
42. Seigfried Gidion, *The Eternal Present*, 1964.
43. Eric Neumann, 1955, p. 3.
44. Ibid., p. 4.
45. Ibid., p. 8.
46. Ibid., p. 12.
47. Ibid. chapter 7 on "The Phenomenon of Reversal and the Dynamic of the Archetype".
48. Seigfried Gidion, 1964, p. 74.
49. Michael Foucault, *The Archaeology of Knowledge*, tr. A.M. Sheridan Smith, 1972, 1st published in Editions Gallimard, p. 147.
50. Griselda Pollock, "Feminist Interventions in the Histories of Art: An Introduction, pp. 1-17", *Vision and Difference: Femininity, Feminism and Histories of Art*, London: Routledge, 1988.
51. Vidya Dehejia (ed.), *Representing the Body: Gender Issues in Indian Art*, New Delhi: Kali for Women in association with The Book Review Literary Trust.
52. Annapurna Garimella, "Engendering Indian Art", p. 38 in ibid.

2

A Medieval Historical Backdrop

Disintegration of a systematic administration under a single dynastic rule in the post-Gupta–Vākāṭaka era was for some time put into order by Harṣa of Kannauj CE 606-47. After Harṣa, the conditions in India from the time of the arrival of the Hūṇas, to the period of Muhammad of Ghore, seems to be distraught with parochialism, rivalry and anti-nationalism. Many scholars of history subscribe to the view that the medieval period, which follows the post-Gupta, i.e. the eighth to the twelfth century and pre-Mughal times, was by and large degenerative and reflects the dissipation of values and systems. Geo-politically speaking, smaller geographical regions were further divided into principalities, and a number of ruling dynasties sprang up which controlled, over-ran and annexed neighbouring territories. It is difficult to assess whether the concept of "nation above self" meant anything at all at that time, but in the areas of religion, literature, art and architecture, "cultural" continuity could still be perceived. Rulers' initiatives and imperial patronage do translate into great artistic periods of creativity, but on the contrary it is also true that rulers may come, rulers may go, development of culture continues unhampered. Thus it needs to be probed as to how far can political history support cultural history, and what inference could be drawn from their links. This difficulty makes the entire exercise of bridging cultural links and substantiate them with political data purely hypothetical and postulation of a pattern of political events purely conjectural. Nevertheless, the least it does is to provide a context and a situational scenario to view the circumstance under which a temple was constructed, the religious and social affiliation of its patron and *sthapati* and the various renovations it may have undergone.

What is a Medieval Phenomenon?

It is assumed (from a largely Western perspective) that there was a Classical period of grandeur, sophistication and an urbanized, centralized structure of power from which the Medieval period of the Indian civilization has emerged as a phase of decadence referring to the political and social structures and their impact on the arts and culture as a whole. Replete with regionalism and feudalism, the period under study especially the post-Harṣa period was largely feudal and hierarchical where the monarch wielded token power while the vassals exercised the actual power.[1] The kingdoms were decentralized and segmental and the kings were simply symbolic figures. Power rested in so-called "ethno-agrarian micro-regions".[2] It is also to be noted that the social and religious conditions under which monuments such as Sāñcī, Amarāvatī or Sārnāth were built were quite different from the conditions under which Udayeśvara, Moḍherā, Osian or Dilwāṛā were built. Chattopadhyaya rightly explains that the urban milieu was missing and thus art activity depended largely on rural aristocracy.[3] It was also a period where many dynasties sprang up from tribal origins who validated their origin by identifying themselves with a sage or having emerged from *agnikuṇḍa* (inscription at Udayeśvara of the Paramāras). Patronage to temples in this case played an important role as well as to the following of esoteric cults; thus folk elements crept into the so-called Purāṇic Hinduism.[4]

B.D. Chattopadhyaya identifies elements of medievalism that can be broadly seen as a pattern emerging from the eighth to the twelfth century, that could be observed as variable in opposition to the early historical order of the so-called "Classical period". Political decentralization and the emergence of landed intermediaries, or landholding fiefs (including brāhmaṇas and other castes) who wielded enormous power, self-sufficient village production and change from market economy to ruralization, characterize the transition. Other observable features are the subjection of peasantry to forced labour, immobility and enforcement of revenue payment at very high rates. Even the proliferation of castes was much more intense during this period than ever before which led to *varṇasaṅkara* of a complex kind. In the sphere of religion, the *bhakti* ideology was very popular which drew its inspiration from the feudal culture of master–servant relationship translating into deity–devotee relationship. Loyalty and devotion are hallmarks of feudalism which were highly prevalent during this time. The new agrarian structure created a leisurely culture among the feudal society that led to the indulgence in degenerate Tāntric cults.[5]

In the following pages, I have collated information on temple architecture and literature (Sanskrit, Prākṛt, Apabhraṁśa) including from treatises on poetics, texts on architectural theory; literature dealing with politico-historical, social and mythological themes including inscriptions that will highlight the affinity, parallelism and mutual influences between the various seamless regions of Gujarat, Rajasthan and Madhya Pradesh. The attempt is to visualize the cognate regions of Gujarat, Mālwā and Rajasthan, despite their difficult political allegiances as a "socio-cultural" unit, sharing literary, architectural and sculptural styles, iconography and literary material. Sometimes the political allegiances and enmities support the idea of "intra and interrelationships", e.g. Pratihāra–Paramāra, Pratihāra–Candella and Paramāra–Cāḷukya relationships. Much of the stylistic affinity and uniqueness in sculpture, its iconography and architectural styles, can be explained on the basis of stylistic symbiosis based on dynastic alliances. Royal patronage and its record through the inscriptions brings to attention the contribution and achievements of kings like Nāgabhaṭṭa II, Mahendrapāla and Mahipāla of the Pratihāra dynasty; Bhoja and Udayāditya of the Paramāra dynasty; Siddharāja and Kumārapāla of the Solaṅkī dynasty; Dhaṅga and Yaśovarman of Candella dynasty, to name a few. Through political and cultural interactions, I intend to support the phenomenon of iconographic parallelism in the representation of the *devāṅganā* imagery and the movement of artists' guilds and architectural styles throughout the western and central Indian regions.

The regions under discussion here are traditionally known as Mālwā, Dahala, Jejākabhukti, Gopagiri, and Cedi in Madhya Pradesh; Medapāṭa, Sapādalakṣa, Uparamāla, Marumaṇḍala, Arbudā, in Rajasthan; and Ānartta, Surāṣṭra in Gujarat. This chapter is not a listing of genealogies of the kings of the medieval period of the modern-day Gujarat, Rajasthan and Madhya Pradesh but an attempt to understand the political ambience of the region.

Pratihāras

The Pratihāras were geographically and politically connected with Mālwā, Marusthalī and Mahodaya, i.e. Kannauj; the last became their capital from the time of Bhoja I. The kingdom was periodically weakened by the onslaught of the Rāṣṭrakūṭas of Mānyakheta during the reigns of Indra III and Kṛṣṇa III. According to the Cambay plate of Rāṣṭrakūṭa Govinda IV, his father Indra III had "completely uprooted the city of Mahodaya", probably some time about CE 915-18. Pratihāras regained their lost power by allying with their feudatories like the Guhilots, the Candellas of Jejākabhukti and the Cāhamānas.

A Cāhamāna inscription of Bhartravaddha, who was a ruler of Lāṭa, found from Hansot in Gujarat, dated VS 813 = CE 756, reveals that this prince owed allegiance to the Pratihāra king, Nāgāvaloka identified as Nāgabhaṭṭa I. Other Cāhamānas ruling from Pratāpgaṛh in south Rajasthan, namely Mahāsāmanta Indrarāja and Govaka I of the Śākambharī line, about CE 915, owed allegiance and acknowledged the suzerainty of Mahendrapāla II (CE 945-46) and Nāgabhaṭṭa II respectively.[6]

The Pratihāra power had reached its summit at the time of Mahipāla I, who had ruled between *c.* CE 912-42 and during whose time the empire had extended to its maximum. Rājaśekhara, the court-poet of Mahipāla, in his book entitled *Bālabhārata*, had eulogized his master as the "pearl jewel" of the lineage of Raghu and the Mahārājādhirāja of Āryāvarta. The Pratihāra power had reached a climax from the time of Bhoja I who had transferred his capital to Kannauj.[7]

The Cāhamānas appear to have acknowledged the overlordship of the Pratihāras until about CE 973. Doom was precipitated by the campaign carried out by Sultan Mahmūd when the Pratihāra ruler Rājyapāla was probably on the throne.[8] According to Utbi, Mahmūd, in course of his march through north India during CE 1018, devastated Bulandshahr and Mathurā and reached Kannauj which was protected by "seven district forts washed by the Ganges, which flowed under them like the ocean". Many sources converge on the issue of Rājyapāla's feeling on the arrival of Mahmūd and the enraged Vidyādhara, a Candella king of Jejākabhukti, slaying him for abandoning Kannauj. The Dūbakuṇḍa stone inscription of the Kacchapaghāta ruler, Vikramasiṁha (CE 1188), states that his great grandfather Arjuna "being anxious to serve the illustrious Vidyādhara Deva had fiercely slain in a great battle the illustrious

Rājyapāla". Another Candella inscription found from Mahobā, states that "Vidyādhara had caused the destruction of the king of Kannauj". Thus the final blow was given by the Candellas around CE 1018-19 to the Pratihāra rule who were by then quite a strong power in central India.

It is possible that the only branch of Pratihāras known to Candellas had settled at Mandor near Jodhpur, but it was not the one from the imperial Kannauj line, which originated from Mālwā.[9] After the fall of Kannauj, only this line continued until about the fourteenth century. Hence the regions associated with the Pratihāras of the main and the subsidiary branches, range from Mālwā to Kannauj to Mārwāṛ. The significant implication of this political phenomenon on styles of sculpture and the architectural programming under the Pratihāra rule will be discussed in Chapter 4.

Paramāras

From Padmagupta's *Navasāhasāṅka Carita*, written in honour of its patron Sindhurāja, during his reign between CE 995-1010, the reference to the first Paramāra king, Upendrarāja, is found.

The earliest grants of the dynasty traceable from *Saṁvat* 1005, i.e. CE 949, found at Harsola in Ahmedabad district in Gujarat, records the origin of the dynasty from rulers bearing the name Amoghavarṣa and Akālavarṣa, *alias* Pr̥thvīvallabha *alias* Śrīvallabha. The names Amoghavarṣa and Akālavarṣa and epithets like Pr̥thvīvallabha, were to be found among the celebrated Rāṣṭrakūṭa rulers of Mānyakheṭa, and this may well be taken as a conclusive proof of the fact that the Paramāras had descended from the Rāṣṭrakūṭa lineage. They were Mahāmāṇḍalika Cūḍāmaṇi of the Rāṣṭrakūṭas and had descended from the same stock. The principal branch of the Paramāras had produced great kings in their lineage like Siyaka, who though called a Mahāmāṇḍalika Cūḍāmaṇi, had assumed the title *mahārājādhirāja*. His son was Vākpatirāja, whose son was Sindhurāja, the father of Bhoja; the most celebrated among the Paramāra rulers of Ujjayinī. The dynasty had held sway in Ujjain and Dhāra till as late as CE 1305, when Ein-ul-Mulk Multani, a general of Ala-ud-din Khalji had defeated the ruler of Ujjain and had put an end to the Hindu rule.[10]

A branch of Paramāras controlled the regions around Mt. Ābu, Jālor (ancient Jāvālipura in Jodhpur), Kirāḍu (ancient Kirātakūpa also in Jodhpur state), during the period from VS 1099, i.e. CE 1022 (mentioned in Vasantgaṛh inscription of Pūrṇapāla, ruler of Arbudā Maṇḍala).[11] The Cāhamānas who had ascended to gain considerable power in Rajasthan had wielded this power till their glory was eclipsed by the conquest of Muhammad Ghorī in CE 1192 ousting Paramāras from the above regions.

The Udayapur and the Arthuṇā *praśasti* (inscriptions) eulogize Bhoja's military talents. Under his sway were most of Mālwā and Gujarat.

The Arthuṇā inscription of Paramāra Cāmuṇḍarāja of VS 1136, mentions

> the illustrious Bhoja was as sublime as the high peaks of the great mount Meru, who had caused the three worlds whitened by his fame, causing fear and destroying his enemies such as the Lords of Koṅkaṇ, Cedi, Gujarat, Lāṭa, Karṇāṭa.[12]

The Dhāra *praśasti* of Arjunavarman, glorifies Bhoja's empire with the title of Sārvabhauma. In Ganguli's opinion the kingdom of Bhoja extended until Chittor, Bāṅswāṛā, Ḍūṅgarpur, Khandesha, Koṅkaṇ and upper courses of Godāvarī.

Paramāras had an old enmity with Cāḷukyas of Gujarat, and Sindhurāja invaded Anahilawāḍa, which was ably resisted by Cāmuṇḍā. Cāmuṇḍā's son Durlabharāja, came into conflict with Bhoja, because of the *svayaṁvara* of Mahendrarāja of Nadol's daughter Durlabhadevī, when her choice fell upon Durlabharāja. This enraged Bhoja and the relations of Paramāras with the Cāḷukyas strained further. The river Sābarmatī remained an unbroken frontier between the Cāḷukyan domain and the kingdom of Bhoja.

Bhoja's military career began with Lāṭa, which extended up to modern Surat and up to the kingdom of the Śilāhāras of northern Koṅkaṇ. Since Bhoja wanted to control the Nasik-Bulsar passes, he had to first vanquish the Lāṭa king and the Cāḷukyas of Gujarat as well as Kalyāṇī.

According to the Surat grant of Lāṭa king, Kīrtirāja, dated CE 1018, it is evident that he was no match for the powerful armies of Bhoja, and being hard pressed by the latter, Kīrtirāja left the kingdom and the capital at the mercy of the invader. The literary and epigraphical evidences such as *Prabandha Cintāmaṇi*, the Kalyāṇa plate and the Udayapur *praśasti*, record Bhoja's victory over Lāṭa. But the annexation of Lāṭa by Bhoja did not last long.

Bhoja subsequently pushed his arms further south. During the ninth and tenth centuries, the Śilāhāras of northern Malabar Coast were feudatories of Rāṣṭrakūṭas of Mānyakheta and later of the Cāḷukyas of Kalyāṇī. Around CE 1020, the Koṅkaṇ region was swept by Bhoja, since the Thānā plates of Arikesarī mention him to be ruling in CE 1017. Control over the whole of Lāṭa and Koṅkaṇ may have prompted Bhoja to overcome natural enemy Jayasiṁha II (CE 1015-42) of the Western Cāḷukya dynasty of Kalyāṇī. Bhoja entered into an alliance with Rajendra Coḷa I and Kalacuri Gāṅgeya to consolidate his military strength. Unfortunately they met with defeat. The CE 1088 inscription of Jayasiṁha II glorifies him with glowing success against the allied forces, and further records "he (Jayasiṁha) routed the elephant squadron of the Coḷa king, Gāṅgeya and Bhojarāja".[13]

Bhīma I of Gujarat played an important role in the downfall of Paramāra Bhoja. Vaḍanagara *praśasti* of Kumārapāla records Bhīma's victory over Bhoja. Someśvara in *Kīrtikaumudī* also states the defeat of Bhoja by Bhīma. While the Vastūpāla–Tejapāla *praśasti* states it as proper that upon his attack, the goddess of wealth left Bhoja's heart, goddess of learning left his mouth and the swords left his hands.[14]

After the defeat of Bhoja by Bhīma, both the houses may have come to a compromise. Merutuṅga in *Prabandha Cintāmaṇi* gives the reference of one Dammara, who was Bhīma's ambassador at Bhoja's court. There were many military conquests between Anahilawāḍa and Dhāra. But when Bhoja died, Dhāra was sacked by Karṇa of Kalacuri and presented a golden *maṇḍapikā* to Bhīma, which is testified by the *Dvyāśraya Kāvya*.[15]

After Mahmūd's departure from India, Bhoja attached the kingdom of Candellas of Jejākabhukti, which bordered the north-eastern territory of the Paramāras. In the middle of the tenth century CE the Candella Yaśovarman was fighting with the Paramāras of Mālwā. Yaśovarman was followed by Dhaṅga (CE 950-99) and Gaṅda (999-1024), who was succeeded by Vidyādhara (1025-40) — known for his bravery and said to have defeated and killed the Pratihāra king Rājyapāla of Kannauj. The Kalacuri Gāṅgeyadeva of Dahala had also to yield to his military force. The Mahobā inscription of the Candellas records "Bhojadeva together with the moon of the Kalacuris (Gāṅgeyadeva) worshipped, full of fear, like a pupil (this) master of warfare (Vidyādhara)".[16]

H.C. Ray thinks that Vidyādhara even helped Kīrtirāja, the Kacchapaghāta ruler of Gwalior in defeating Bhoja. One Kacchapaghāta of Dūbakuṇḍa called Prince Arjuna, helped Vidyādhara Candella to defeat and kill Rājyapāla Pratihāra. Thus Arjuna remained a feudatory of the Candellas.[17] But after Arjuna, his son and successor, Abhimanyu, accepted the vassalage of the Paramāras instead of the Candellas. From the Dūbakuṇḍa (Gwalior) inscription of Kacchapaghāta Vikramasiṁha dated (VS 1145), H.C. Ray suggests that Bhoja, taking advantage of Vidyādhara's weak successors, may have extended his influence in the north until Dūbakuṇḍa. Ray also opines that Bhoja possibly succeeded in extending his influence in the Kullu Valley by taking advantage of the weakness of the Vidyādhara's successors.

Solaṅkīs

The Cāḷukya/Solaṅkī dynasty was established by one Mūlarāja, whose father hailed from somewhere around Kannauj and married the Cāpotkata princess by exhibiting his valour. Mūlarāja usurped the throne and established himself around CE 937 and ruled until CE 994. He encountered his contemporaries of Sapādalakṣa, the Cāhamānas of Śākambharī, Vigraharāja and the Cāḷukya king Tailapa of Telaṅgānā.

At this stage the Pratihāras were in power from Gujarat to Bengal and while they remained engaged in war with the Arabs, the

Rāṣṭrakūṭa Indra III of Mānyakheta, defeated Pratihāra Mahipāla, some time around CE 915. This weakened the Pratihāra control over the western Indian Territory and Mūlarāja snapped the chance to establish himself. A Candella epigraph found at Khajurāho claims that the contemporary Candella ruler, apparently a feudatory vassal of the Pratihāras had placed Kṣitipāla after his defeat at the hands of Indra III, to be restored to the throne. The opportunity of weakening of the power of the Pratihāras had undoubtedly facilitated Mūlarāja to expand his power eastwards, and establish himself firmly in Gujarat.[18]

Mūlarāja encountered the Cāhamānas of Rajasthan but before both could consolidate their own powers Mahmūd of Ghazni, the Turkish invader, overran them. When Bhīma I encountered Mahmūd who had plundered Somanātha, Thānesara, etc. his army could not sustain, but slowly the Solaṅkī collected their might. Bhīma II who ruled between CE 1178 and 1238 forcefully repulsed the attack of Muhammad of Ghore. The Solaṅkīs ruled over Gujarat right till CE 1304, when the Turkish tide in the form of Ala-ud-din Khalji swept the Solaṅkī power which was then in the hands of Karṇadeva II.

Bhīma I consolidated his kingdom and conquered Ābu from Paramāra Dhandhuka, annexed Bhīnmāl, but could not assert his supremacy over southern Mārwāṛ. He also allied with Kalacuri Karṇa and defeated Bhoja of Mālwā.[19] Many land grants are noted in his reign. He had two queens, namely Udayamatī from whom he had a son, Karṇa, while he also got attracted by the chastity of a *gaṇikā*, Caula Devī or Bakulādevī, whom he married and a son Kṣemarāja or Harīpāla was born (*Prabandha Cintāmaṇi*). The important monuments associated with the reign of Bhīma I are the Rānī Vāv, Pāṭan built by his queen Udayamatī, Sūrya temple of Moḍherā (CE 1027) and the Vimala Vasahi, Mt. Ābu (CE 1031).

Jayasiṁha Siddharāja (*c.* CE 1094–1144)

The most illustrious king of this dynasty is Jayasiṁha, the son of Mīnaladevī (Mayanallā) who was coronated at the age of three. Merutuṅga writes eulogizingly about him in *Prabandha Cintāmaṇi*. He reduced the might of Rākhengāra of Saurāṣṭra, and the Girnār inscription of CE 1120 informs that Sajjana, the governor of Jayasiṁha Siddharāja, was governing that area. The Cāhamānas of Naḍḍula were feudatories of Jayasiṁha, as notified by the Bali inscription of Asarāja which was issued in CE 1143 but with the Śākambharī branch the relations were more complex. Merutuṅga in *Prabandha Cintāmaṇi*, and Someśvara in *Kīrtikaumudī*, mention that Jayasiṁha defeated Arṇorāja, and Someśvara says that the only difference between Jayasiṁha and the Hindu God Viṣṇu was that Viṣṇu took the daughter of Arṇorāja (Ocean) as wife, while he (Jayasiṁha) gave his daughter in marriage to Arṇorāja. This information is supported by *Pṛthvīrāja Vijaya*, which says one of Arṇorāja's queens came from Gujarat.[20] Arṇorāja helped Siddharāja against the Paramāra Naravarman.

In the military career of Jayasiṁha, the victory over Yaśovarman of Mālwā was the greatest. He knew various forms of black magic, and various *yoginī*s and *kirāta*s helped him. He reached Ujjain and captured Dhāra and tied-up Yaśovarman like a sparrow. With this act he subdued the whole of Avantī and returned. Vaḍanagara *praśasti* mentions that Jayasiṁha "frightened all the rulers of the earth by the manner in which he fettered the proud king of Mālwā". Even Vastūpāla–Tejapāla *praśasti* mentions the victory of Jayasiṁha Siddharāja over the king of Mālwā.[15] He has been conferred the proud epithet "Avantinātha" in the Gala inscription of CE 1137. By the conquest of Mālwā the frontiers of the Cāḷukya kingdom were extended, bringing it into contact with those of Kalacuris and Candellas. According to Someśvara, king of Mahobā became frightened on hearing of the destruction of Dhāra, submitted to Siddharāja. The story given by Jina Maṇḍana and an inscription from Kālañjara Fort supports the instant defeat of king of Gurjara as Kṛṣṇa defeating Kaṁsa.[21] Except from the Candellas, Jayasiṁha never faced a defeat. He issued a number of stone inscriptions recording his victory over several regions, which testifies the fact that he really captured those areas. The extent of his kingdom ranged from the whole of Saurāṣṭra with its towering Girnār to southern Rajasthan (Asurāja's territory) and Śākambharī or Sapādalakṣa of Cāhamānas, to the Paramāra kingdom of Mālwā including Ujjain and Dhāra.

Siddharāja is considered a great patron of literature, religion and temple construction. The famous Rudramahālaya and the Sahasraliṅga Lake at Pāṭan were constructed by his orders. He patronized Śaiva and Jaina philosophy and practice. The great Jaina scholar, Hemacandra, was his contemporary.

Siddharāja was followed by Kumārapāla (CE 1144-74) and he too was a great builder. He replaced the Phase II shrine of Somanātha at Prabhāsa built by Bhīma I. He built *kumāra vihāra*s at Pāṭan, Girnār, Śatruñjaya, Prabhāsa, Ābu, Khambhāṭ, Tharad, Idar, Jālor, Div, Maṅgrol and a shrine dedicated to Ajitnātha at Tāraṅga and so on.[22]

According to *Prabandha Cintāmaṇi*, Kumārapāla was coronated in VS 1199. He wielded power over the Cāhamānas of Śākambharī, Paramāras of Mālwā and some parts of Mārwāṛ. Allaṇadeva acknowledged this supremacy and donated a village to a Śiva temple in Chittor (CE 1151), in Kirāḍu (CE 1153), Someśvara in Kirāḍu (CE 1162). Inscriptions at Pāli in Mārwāṛ (CE 1153-60) and Udayapur in Mālwā (CE 1164-66) also acknowledge his supremacy.[23]

An allegorical play *Moharājaparājaya* of Yaśapāla was written during his reign. He renovated the Somanātha temple (CE 1169). Hemacandra wrote *Dvyāśraya Kāvya*, *Kumārapāla-Carita*, *Triṣaṣṭiśalākāpuruṣa-Carita*, on the request of Kumārapāla.

Another important Solaṅkī king is Bhīma II (CE 1179–1242) who is also associated with great building activity. Nīlakaṇṭha Mahādeva Temple, Miani dated CE 1204 is the earliest example. His ministers Vastūpāla and Tejpāla built the famous temples at Mt. Ābu, Lūṇa Vasahī (CE 1231). Thus the literary and religious circles that developed around the Solaṅkī kings in the two centuries speak volumes for the cultural interaction between the fine minds of the neighbouring regions. The contribution towards the temple design, sculptural imagery, symbolism and literary development by the royal patrons can be justifiably conjectured.

Cāhamānas

The Cāhamānas or Cauhāns were a formidable power, can be learned from the great *kāvya*, *Pṛthvīrāja Rāso* in Apabhraṁśa, by the poet

Cānda Bardāī, in fourteenth and fifteenth century. This poem delves into the life and exploits of Pṛthvīrāja III, as an episode of absorbing interest from the point of history, medieval chivalry, heroism and humanity, as a model hero belonging to a tradition of long and abiding sustenance.

After the disappearance of the Pratihāras, the Candellas had succeeded in gaining remarkable power in the east of the central part of the subcontinent, while the Cāhamānas had emerged as a viable power further west, expanding their rule into Rajasthan, Punjab and Haryana. They are associated with Sapādalakṣa, but it is difficult to trace if they originally belonged to this region or came to settle there from elsewhere. There were Cauhān houses of Bharuch, Śākambharī, Naḍḍula, Jālor, Raṇathambhor, etc. of which the Naḍḍula had the upper hand and they contested with Paramāra and Cāḷukya and exercised their command over them.[24] The Naḍḍula king, Ahila, is claimed in the Sunda hill inscription to have defeated Bhīma I, the Solaṅkī king of Anahilawāḍ Pāṭan (*c.* CE 1022-64).

The earliest of the Cāhamāna rulers of Śākambharī of some consequence had been Vigraharāja II whose name is known from the Harṣa stone inscription, found upon the wall of a temple dedicated to Mahādeva situated near a village called Haras in Śekhāwatī area of the old state of Jaipur. The inscription is dated VS 1030, i.e. CE 973 and gives the entire genealogy of the family from a ruler named Guvaka I. Both the Cāhamānas and the Cāḷukyas had been the feudatories of the Pratihāras, and Vigraharāja won over Mūlarāja of Cāḷukya dynasty.[25]

Much of the energy of the Cāhamāna rulers went in repulsing the attacks of the invading Muslims, namely Mahmūd of Ghazni and Muhammad of Ghore.

The Cāhamānas were run over by the Paramāra Bhoja of Avantī (*c.* CE 1010-55) who killed Vīryarāma, the son of Vākpatirāja II.[26]

Cāhamānas were great patrons of literature. Even their inscriptions were composed by great poets, who used masterly language and set the verses to various *chanda*s, metres, and wrote with literary flourish. Of the Cauhān kings, Ajayapāla, Vigraharāja

IV and Pṛthvīrāja III, were lovers of good literature. Somadeva was the court-poet of Vigraharāja IV and wrote *Lalita Vigraharāja*.[27] Jayamaṅgala, the writer of Sunda inscription, used *sārdūlavikrīḍita, sragdharā, mandakrāntā, mālinī, śikhariṇī* and *hāriṇī* metres. During this time, writings on Jaina religion, philosophy, theology, etc. were simultaneously patronized in Prākṛt and Apabhraṁśa languages. The poets of this time were familiar with Alaṁkāra Śāstra and made full use of their favourite *alaṁkāras*. When it comes to building activity related to architecture, it is learned that Vākpatirāja built temple of Śiva at Puṣkara. His son Siṁharāja overthrew the Pratihāra yoke and became an independent ruler. He granted a number of villages to the temple of Harṣanātha, which was built in CE 956 in a village about 7 miles south of Sīkar. Vigraharāja II built a temple dedicated to Goddess Āśāpurī near Bhṛgukaccha.[28] It is difficult to characterize the Cāhamāna style of architecture or sculpture except for the fact that Harṣanātha temple has some of the finest sculptures of the *devāṅganā*s engaged in dance, music and other activities.

Guhilas

The Guhilas or Guhilots of Mewāṛ and later Sisodiās, are the most illustrious dynasty to have ruled over Mewāṛ. The Guhila rule was concentrated upon from Chittor, Nāgdā and Āhaṛ, the major centres of economic and political power in the Medapāṭa region. The Atpur inscription of Śaktikumāra, dated in the year CE 977 and an inscription of Naravāhana, the grandfather of Śaktikumāra, dated in VS 1028 (CE 971) mention the name of Bappaka as the ruler of Nāgahrada and as a moon among the princes of the Guhila family.[29]

Guhilas entered into a marriage alliance with Rāṣṭrakūṭas when Bhartṛpaṭṭa married Mahālakṣmī, and this emboldened the Guhilas from throwing the yoke of the imperial Pratihāras. An inscription of Allaṭa (son of Śaktikumāra) found in Sāraṇeśvara temple at Āhaṛ, gives an elaborate account of the administration of Allaṭa, who is mentioned as a Medinīpati, who has under him an *amātya*, a *sandhivigrahika*, two *akṣapaṭalikā*, a *vandīpati* and a *bhiṣagādhirāja*. After Allaṭa the successors of the Guhilas were not very strong, which made it easy for the Cāhamānas of Śākambharī,

Paramāra of Mālwā and Cāḷukyas of Gujarat, to make headway into the Guhila territory. It becomes evident that some time later the Cāḷukyas of Anahilawāḍ had gained occupation to quite some area of Mewāṛ since inscriptions indicating grants of land by the Cāḷukya ruler Kumārapāla, about CE 1050, would testify. The issue of a land grant by Kumārapāla (CE 1144-73), recorded in a temple at Chittorgaṛh, proves that the area around Chittor had been under the royal authority of the Cāḷukyas at this time. Kumārapāla had undertaken military campaigns against the Cāhamāna ruler Arṇorāja and this accounts for a number of land grants made by this ruler in Rajasthan, but there is no account of Kumārapāla having come into conflict with the Guhilas.

The temples associated with the Guhilas are the famous Ambikāmātā Temple at Jagat, which bears an inscription of Śaktikumāra of CE 956. Another inscription of CE 977 (VS 1034) of the same ruler is found from Āhaṛ, which refers to his wife establishing a village called Harṣapur, a long genealogical list and the economic conditions.[30] At Nāgdā on the Viṣṇu temple an inscription has been found, dated CE 1026 (VS 1083) which starts with a veneration to Puruṣottama. The king's name is defaced. It is significant to note the contiguous nature of Guhila and Solaṅkī territory and the architectural similarity shared by the temples of Moḍherā and Sunak in north Gujarat, Koṭai in Kutch and Jagat, Āhaṛ, Nāgdā, and Ekaliṅgajī in the Mewāṛ region.

Cultural Overview

It is very clear that despite the infighting between rulers of neighbouring regions, art, architecture and literature did flourish during the four hundred years just discussed above. It also underlines the possibility of exchange of ideas, styles and iconography through contemporary practices which in many ways is self-explanatory. The Encyclopedic *Samarāṅgaṇa Sūtradhāra* of Paramāra Bhoja, written around the first half of the eleventh century CE testifies that enormous tradition of building activity and rituals connected with Vāstuśāstra and iconography, iconometry, *hasta*s and *sthānaka*s, etc. had been underway, which were codified and actively practised. This text is not an isolated example of architectural codification, but is followed by *Pramāṇamañjarī* of Malla, son of Nakula, favourite king of Mālwā, Bhānu (rising Sun) of the dynasty of Śrī Muñja and Bhoja, i.e. Udayāditya Paramāra written in the late eleventh century; *Aparājitapṛcchā* of Bhuvanapāla of Pāṭan, written in the thirteenth century; *Dīpārṇava*, *Kṣīrārṇava*, *Vṛkṣārṇava*, written in the fifteenth century, all hailing from Gujarat.[31] The influence of *Samarāṅgaṇa Sūtradhāra* on the later texts and the burgeoning of active architectural programmes in Mālwā, Gurjaradeśa, Arbudā, Medapāṭa, Marū–Sapādalakṣa and Uparamāla regions, are phenomena which need to be studied simultaneously. These texts also enlist the features like the spread of a particular architectural style, such as the *bhūmija*, that originated at Mālwā and spread to Gujarat and Maharashtra. Therefore in totality, the corpus of architectural texts, when studied together, provide not only prescribed or traditionally accepted norms but also critical and analytically processed data on contemporary phenomena/manifestations.

In the field of literature we have the writings of poets, dramatists, aestheticians and philosophers which were at once universal and regional in character. In the previous sections, an attempt was made to juxtapose the historical and chronological events that linked the Pratihāras, Paramāras, Solaṅkīs, Cāhamānas and Candellas, during the two decades from the tenth century onwards. Most kings overran the territories of their neighbours, in order to establish their supremacy, but could not annex the captured territory to their kingdoms for long. Vassalage was the only political tool to administer the outlaying areas. But the fitting corollary to such political skirmishes is the interaction of the cultural material at human or spiritual levels. Simultaneously, in all the above areas there existed styles of sculpture, painting (degeneration of mural and beginning of palm leaf) poetry, drama, dance, music, which were at once universal and regional in character. There existed parallel stylistic and formal concepts. These trends in different art forms not only decided the character of the form itself, but also led to the mutual mutation, each trend fertilizing the other. The phenomenon of juxtaposition can only strengthen the idea that mutation is possible in visual and literary arts, which can lead to total morphological changes that can generate a totally new style.

As discussed in the introduction, the literary theories of *dhvani* and *alaṁkāra* are especially thought-provoking and developed at the same time as the period in question. Thus I try to juxtapose the *devāṅganā* imagery and the "meaning" evolving from it, in relation to the temple's sculptural programming, with the help of Indian aesthetic theories of "meaning". Devangana Desai mentions it largely in the context of Vaiṣṇava iconography and erotic sculptures with reference to the Lakṣmaṇa Temple at Khajurāho.[32] In my view if we understand the significance of *dhvani* and *alaṁkāra* in the temporal and spatial context of the medieval period literature, art and architecture, then it facilitates and enriches the scope for interpretation of meaning of the *devāṅganā* imagery.

Another significant parallel is the theory of *rīti,* which also corresponds with the regional styles of sculpture, and characterizes the various morphological and structural features that distinguish one style from the other. This role of individual creativity at individual level or at regional level, rising up to a high degree of sophistication, has been pointed out by Ratan Parimoo.[33] Recognition of regional styles was already noticed by Stella Kramrisch in her book on Pāla–Sena sculpture and by U.P. Shah in his Śāmalājī and Akoṭā sculptures.[34] Parimoo enumerates the *vṛttis*, *guṇas* and *rītis* from *Nāṭyaśāstra* onwards, stated in the context of drama, and applied it to sculptural styles that evolve from graceful to vigorous. Distinguishing *vaidarbhī* as *agrāmya,* i.e. sophisticated and cultivated as different from *gauḍī*, which lacks *saukumārya* (tenderness) and *mādhurya* (beauty), he identifies these elements in the styles of post-Gupta sculpture.

Rājaśekhara's *Kāvyamīmāṁsā* (eleventh century CE) is the first text of literary criticism in which a lot of cultural data is found, which throws light on the regional, and ethnic qualities of people's language, lifestyle and beauty. He also attempted through his travels, which earned him the title of *yāyāvarīya*, to bring a national awareness among the people.[35] Rājaśekhara was a court-poet of Pratihāra Mahendrapāla and his son Mahipāla. He was called "Bālakavi" in the court of Mihirabhoja. Two of his plays *Bālabhārata* and *Viddhaśālabhañjikā*, seem to have been performed in the court of

Kalacuri Yuvarājadeva, the latter refers to the coronation ceremony in which the heir prince is named Keyūravarṣa. *Viddhaśālabhañjikā* is a play in four parts and it was written between CE 908-12 at the Kalacuri court. His other works are *Karpūramañjarī,* a *śataka* in Prākṛt; *Bālarāmāyaṇa*, a play based on *Rāmāyaṇa* in ten parts, *Bālabhārata* or *Pracaṇḍa Pāṇḍava*, based on *Mahābhārata* in the form of an epic play, and *Kāvyamīmāṁsā*, a text on poetics, specializing on various aspects of Alaṁkāra Śāstra. His contemporaries like poets Dhanapāla, Soḍḍhala and even Kṣemendra, have appreciated Rājaśekhara for the delicacy of his compositions, intense expression of emotions, and a reflection of poet's individuality, *kavipratibhā*.[36]

References to *Kāvyamīmāṁsā* are found in Bhoja's (CE 1018-56) *Kāvyānuśāsana*. This interrelationship of aestheticians' views and the movement of literary ideas from central India to western India, testifies to the sharing and parallelism in literary thoughts and concepts between Gujarat and Mālwā.

Before we turn to the works of Daṇḍin, Vāmana, Ānandavardhana, Dhanañjaya, Mammaṭa and others, a note needs to be taken of *deśī*, the rise of the vernacular or colloquial language. It is difficult to exactly trace the origin and development of Prākṛt and Apabhraṁśa literature, but the writings of Avantīsundarī's *Deśī Śabdakośa* and Hemacandra's *Deśī Nāmamālā*, point out the rise of regional modes of expression. Parallel phenomenon can be observed in *Saṅgīta-Ratnākara* of Śāraṅgadeva of thirteenth century CE, which distinguishes *mārgī* and *deśī* styles of *āṅgikābhinaya* and expression through body movements.

Dhanañjaya, who wrote the *Daśarūpaka*, was the court-poet of king Muñja of Dhāra (CE 974-94). This has a very significant and specialized codification of the types of dramas that were written at that time. The examples of *saṭṭaka* (*Karpūramañjarī*), *bhāṇa* (*Caturbhāṇī*), *prahasana* (*Mattavilāsa*), *pratīka nāṭaka* (*Prabodhacandrodaya*), were extant at that time, and Dhanañjaya rightly wrote a classifying text on structure, style and form, of all types of dramas for posterity. Especially the allegorical plays draw our attention because (although they are not part of the *Daśarūpaka*), they throw some light on the ability of a trained audience, reader, aesthete to understand the meaning behind the symbolism. *Devāṅganā* imagery, as I propose, is after all to be perceived as a symbolic "construct" and it had to be observed as a potential embodiment of abstract values. The medieval literary tradition seems to have prepared the ground for understanding meaning in all the arts with the widest possible interpretative potential. For this, Alaṁkāra Śāstra played a key role and stimulated aestheticians to write on the intricacy of language and the potential relation, *sāhitya*, between *śabda* and *artha*.

In the post-Gupta period, the importance of *alaṁkāra* is raised by Bhāmaha in his *Kāvyālaṁkāra*, which showed the significance of *vakrokti,* which in the beginning of the eleventh century, Kuntaka developed to its ultimate form in *Vakrokti-Jivīta*. Mahimbhaṭṭa, his contemporary in *Vyakti-Viveka* clarifies *aucitya* in *Doṣa Prakaraṇa*. Alaṁkāra Śāstra refers to the methodology of poetic expression and its earlier name was "Kriyākalpa".[37] Vāmana brought it to the intrinsic level and declared that *alaṁkāra* is not external ornament of a poem but *śarīrin* integral to the form itself. This data is applicable to the sculptures of *devāṅganā*s on temple architecture, which some scholars call *āvaraṇa devatā*s. They are in my view the most integral to the temple and its iconographic symbolism, even though the original inspiration of its imagery may be secular.[38] Rudraṭa also belongs to the *alaṁkāra* school. *Dhvanyāloka* of Ānandavardhana and *Dhvanyāloka Locana* and *Abhinavabhāratī* of Abhinavagupta in the early eleventh century, brought about concepts like *rasa, dhvani, alaṁkāra, sādhāraṇīkaraṇa, vāsanā,* etc. and explained the whole creative experience at the human level.[39] The following aestheticians took *dhvani* and *alaṁkāra* to explore the potential of *upamā, rūpaka, lakṣaṇā* and *vyañjanā* — they are Kṣemendra (*Aucitya Vicāracarcā*), Mammaṭa, contemporary of Bhoja (*Kāvyaprakāśa*); Ruyyaka (*Alaṁkāra Sarvasva*) and Hemacandrācārya (*Kāvyānuśāsana*).

With the above observations I have attempted to encapsulate a literary world-view, simultaneous to the period of development of *devāṅganā* imagery in temple architecture, between the eighth and twelfth centuries in western India, to propose collateral phenomena in art, literature and culture at large. It also provides a notion of literary criticism and how the conceptual framework for unravelling meaning existed in medieval period in the light of *rasa*, *dhvani* and *alaṁkāra*. It also provides an interesting insight on Mālwā as a cultural thrust area, so also Dasārṇa Cedideśa, where Rājaśekhara, who stimulated the literary tradition in the rest of western India, flourished.

References

1. *Gods, Guardians and Lovers, Temple Sculptures from North India* AD *700-1200,* ed. Vishakha N. Desai and Darielle Mason, New York: The Asia Society Galleries, 1993; article by B.D. Chattopadhyaya, *Historiography, History and Religious Centres, Early Medieval North India, circa* AD *700-1200,* p. 36.
2. This term used by Burton Stein in *Peasant, State and Society in Medieval South India,* Oxford University Press, 1980 quoted by Michael D. Willis in *Religion and Royal Patronage in North India*, p. 53, *Gods, Guardians and Lovers*, ibid.
3. Chattopadhyaya, op. cit., pp. 36-37.
4. Ibid., p. 41.
5. *The Making of Early Medieval India*, Oxford University Press, 1994, pp. 9-14.
6. K.K. Ganguli, *Cultural History of Rajasthan*, Delhi, p. 31.
7. Ibid., p. 32.
8. Ibid.
9. Ibid., p. 34.
10. Mahesh Singh, *Bhoja Paramāra and his Times*, New Delhi, 1984, p. 27.
11. Ibid.
12. Ibid., p. 36.
13. Kulenur Inscription, *Epigraphia Indica*, XV, p. 330.
14. Vastūpāla-Tejapāla *Praśasti*, v. 13.
15. *Dvyāśraya Kāvya*, sarga IX and *Vikramāṅkacarita*, sarga X.3, v. 97.
16. Ibid.
17. H.C. Ray, *Dynastic History of North India,* New Delhi, 1973.
18. *Epigraphia Indica*, II, pp. 233-38, lines 17-18.
19. K.K. Ganguli, op. cit., p. 28.
20. A.K. Majumdar, *Cāḷukyas of Gujarat: A Survey of the History and Culture of Gujarat, from the Middle of the 10th Century to the end of 13th Century, of Bombay,* 1956, pp. 70-71.
21. Ibid., p. 72.
22. Ibid., p. 77.
23. Ibid.
24. (a) M.A. Dhaky, "The Chronology of Solaṅkī Temples of Gujarat", *Journal of the Madhya Pradesh Itihasa Parishad*, no. 3, 1961; (b) U.P. Shah, "Some Medieval Sculptures from Gujarat and Rajasthan",

Journal of the Indian Society of Oriental Art, Western India, 1966, ed. U.P. Shah & K.K. Ganguli, p. 70; (c) Rasiklal Parikh & Hariprasad Shastri (eds.), *Solaṅkī Kāla: Gujarat no Rājakiya ane Sānskrutik Itihās* (Guj.), vol. 4, Ahmedabad, 1976.

25. *Solaṅkī Kāla*, 17(c), p. 62.
26. Ganguli, op. cit., p. 43.
27. Ibid., p. 39.
28. Ibid., p. 40.
29. Dasarath Sharma, *Early Cauhān Dynasties* (AD *800-1316*), New Delhi, 1956, Chapter XXIV.
30. Gopinath Sharma, *Rājasthan ke Itihās ke Srota*, Jaipur, 1973, p. 66 (Hindi).
31. M.A. Dhaky, "The Problems on Pramāṇamañjarī", *Bharatiya Vidya*, vol. XIX no. 1-2, pp. 25-31.
32. Devangana Desai, "Sculptural Representation on the Lakṣmaṇa Temple of Khajurāho in the Light of Prabodhacandrodaya", National Centre for the Performing Arts, *Quarterly Journal*, Special issue, vol. XI, no. 324, 1982, pp. 99-107.
33. Ratan Parimoo, "The Myth of Gupta Classicism and the Concept of Regional Genres: Historical and Cultural Overview I & II", *New Quest*, November–December 1990, January–February 1991.
34. (a) Stella Kramrisch, *Pāla–Sena Sculptures*; (b) U.P. Shah, (i) *Sculptures of Shāmalāji and Rodā*, Baroda, 1961, (ii) *Akoṭā Bronzes*.
35. R.P. Pandey Sharma, *Rājaśekhara aur unakā Yuga*, Patna, 1977.
36. Baldev Upadhyay, *Sanskrit Sāhitya kā Itihāsa*, part I, *Kāvya Khaṇḍa*, Varanasi, 1947, 10th edn., 1978.
37. Ibid., p. 600.
38. Ibid., p. 604.
39. Ibid., p. 608.

3

Apsaras Imagery from Sanskrit and Prākṛt Sources

In the persona of a *devāṅganā*, I see an amalgamation of diverse attributes stemming from various genres. They are embedded within the Indian psyche and lend flavours at once secular, religious and philosophical to the personality of the *devāṅganā*. The present chapter is a compilation of many sources (which reflect that Indian psyche) from Vedic, Purāṇic, Prākr̥t, Kāvya and Nāṭya literature and technical texts. This exercise is undertaken with a view to create an awareness of the various perceptions and characteristics from which the *devāṅganā* imagery has drawn its iconography. It will also demonstrate how closely it was linked to everyday life in ancient and medieval societies in pre-Islamic India. From the Vedic goddesses such as Rākā and Sīnīvālī to the Purāṇic *apsaras* such as Urvaśī to *naṭīs*, *devadāsīs* and *pratihārīs* have been studied in this chapter keeping chronological progression and synchronic appearance of these female concepts and characters as the focus of inquiry.

Goddesses in Vedic Literature

Conceptually speaking, the feminine principles of nourishment, plenty and fertility are symbolized by different names in the Vedas, e.g. the concepts of Puraṁdhī (plenty and activity) and Dhīṣaṇā (abundance). Unfortunately, this principle does not develop beyond the Vedic literature. Iḷā (nourishment) and Br̥haddivā (mother), are mentioned more than once in the *R̥gveda*.[1] *R̥gveda* also mentions Rākā, a rich and bountiful goddess along with Sarasvatī and Iḷā. Sīnīvālī is referred to as a sister of the gods, broad-hipped, fair armed, fair fingered, prolific, a mistress of the family, and is implored to grant offsprings. In the *Atharvaveda* (8, 46.3) Sīnīvālī is called the wife of Viṣṇu. The later Saṁhitās and Brāhmaṇas also mention Goddess Kuhu, a personification of the new moon. Rākā and Sīnīvālī are in the later Vedic texts connected with phases of the moon, the former being the presiding deity of the actual night of full moon, and the latter of the first day of the fortnight of new moon.[2] It is significant to note that these goddesses exist individually and not as consorts of any male deities. This emphasizes their power and individual significance addressed in feminine gender and imagery which to a certain extent is anthropomorphic.

There is no further reference to these goddesses coming into their own, but as often observed, the highly developed concepts of Umā, Pārvatī, Durgā, Lakṣmī, etc. have close association with the Vedic fertility goddesses such as Sarasvatī, Puraṁdhī, Aditi, etc. It is only in the final stage of development of religious imagination that the divinity is conceived as "All Mother" — an abstract conception.[3] In my view, the divine and benevolent concepts of Durgā and Lakṣmī developed by the amalgamation of attributes of the above-mentioned Vedic goddesses, to which were conferred the attributes of procreation, regeneration and sustenance of "life". This conceptual vision took physical form as feminine figure on temple walls. This yearning to create beautiful imageries of female divinities to reassure, fulfil the desire and invoke love, found form in *apsaras* and *gandharvas*. When concepts of Śakti, Durgā and Lakṣmī began to assume esoteric and sacred nature, minor female divinities, auspicious yet approachable, representing the sphere of the profane continued to fulfil similar functions. The imagery of the *apsaras* is not only effusive, illusive, alluring but certainly fulfilling, sustaining and entertaining. Most of all, they seemed accessible even though their appearance was illusive. As concepts, these goddesses, *apsaras*, *yakṣīs*, etc. emerged out of the attitude of veneration for nature in which earth, sky, water, vegetation, sun, moon and air are all interlinked. Hence their attributes and functions are not only connected but transferable and therefore mutative. Hence the concepts of Vedic goddesses, *apsaras* and *yakṣīs* are not diametrically opposite but deeply interconnected.

The goddesses and *apsaras* developed in the Vedic literature did not find any visual representation, while the principle of *yakṣī* through its absorption in Buddhist art acquired a visual imagery which when compared with the *apsaras* and other goddesses appears to have analogous meaning. I can observe traces of Puraṁdhī in the Bharat Kala Bhavan *yakṣī* (*fig.* 267) holding a jug and a food basket, Iḷā in the *yakṣīs* from Mathurā and Saṅghol (*fig.* 126) — who are represented squeezing their breasts, a motif which appears even in medieval architecture at Jagat and Rānī Vāv temples, Bṛhaddivā in *putravallabhā*, the *devāṅganā* carrying a child. I also observe similarity in the representation of *yakṣīs* from Dīdāragañja and Sāñcī, with Goddess Sīnīvālī from the *Ṛgveda*.

The sheer continuation of generic female divinities and their visual representation in the art of Kuṣāṇa period suggests their secular impact and demand. The visual imagery has distinct gestures, postures and attributes which connect various forms of similar goddesses from different periods all the way.

Even the concept of *vāc* (speech) conceived in feminine gender and form, accompanied all the gods, supported Mitra–Varuṇa, Indra–Agni, Aśvins and bent the bow of Rudra against the unbeliever in the *Ṛgveda*. She has a place in the waters, besides encompassing all beings. In the Brāhmaṇas she is referred in the legend of Soma, which is procured from the *gandharvas* by the *devas* with the help of a woman, Vāc. She tempts the *gandharvas*, makes them surrender the Soma and returns it to the *devas*. Vāc is equated with thunder and the development of human speech.[4]

Stella Kramrisch identified the sculptures of *surasundarī* and *vyāla* juxtaposed on the temple architecture as symbols personifying *vāc* as *prakṛti*, activating the dormant *puruṣa*.[5] This *vāc* is also connected with Sarasvatī in the Brāhmaṇas (*ŚB* 3.9.1.7; *AB* 3.1.10) and in the post-Vedic mythology Sarasvatī becomes the goddess of eloquence — wisdom, who is invoked as a muse and regarded as the wife of Brahmā.[6]

Exploring nature worship as a germinal phenomenon in the development of the *apsaras-devāṅganā* imagery, the waters and rivers also play a significant part. The waters are personified as mothers, young wives, and goddesses who bestow boons and come to the sacrifice. They are celestial, as well as flowing in channels, and have the sea for their goal (*ṚV* 7.49.2). It is implied that they abide where the gods are and the seat of Mitra and Varuṇa is (*ṚV* 10.10). King Varuṇa moves in their midst, looking down on the truth and falsehood of men (*ṚV* 7.49.3). Here the rain water is implied and not the oceans. Agni is dwelling in the waters and as mothers they produce Agni (*ṚV* 10.91.6; *AV* 1.33.1). The waters cleanse and purify guilts and sins, and heal, bestowing wealth, strength and immortality. *Atharvaveda* refers to the installation of *pūrṇakumbhanārīs* (*AV* 3.12.8).[7] A number of rivers like the Sarasvatī, Sarayū, Sindhu, Gaṅgā, Yamunā, Śutudrī and Paruṣṇī, are mentioned in the *Ṛgveda,* out of which Sarasvatī is much celebrated than any other river. She performs the attributes of waters mentioned above. Over and above, she bestows vitality, offspring (*ṚV* 2.41.17) and is associated with deities who assist procreation (*ṚV* 10.184.2). She is bountiful, and in her terrible form she is a Vṛtra slayer (*ṚV* 6.61.3.7). This shows that the concepts of water are also closely linked with fertility and eroticism, while the upholding of ethical values and purification are also suggested. The connection between *nadī-devatā*s, *apsaras*es and later *devāṅganā*s is undoubtedly indicated here. Sarasvatī has a male correlative, Sarasvatī, who is invoked by worshippers desiring wives and offspring, protection and plenty. Here the male fertilizing water, semen is implied. Both regard him as a guardian of the celestial waters who bestows fertility.[8]

Soma is connected with waters and the moon for its quality to swell (*āpya*). In the *Ṛgveda* (1.91.16-18, 10.85.5) it is identified with the moon. It swells like a river or sea and is connected with waxing and waning of the moon. Soma produces waters and causes heaven and earth to rain (9.96.3). Soma is the embryo of the waters (*ṚV* 9.97.41; *ŚB* 4.4.5.21) or their child, for seven sisters as mothers are around the child, *gandharva* of the waters (*ṚV* 9.86.36) and waters are his mothers.

Soma is also called a bull (*ṚV* 9.7.3). Being a bull among cow waters, Soma is the fertilizer of the waters (*ṚV* 10.36.8). He is also an impregnator (*retodha*) (*ṚV* 9.86.39), an epithet applied to the moon in the *Yajurveda* (e.g. *MS* 1.6.1).[9] Hence he is a bestower of fertility (*ṚV* 9.60.4; 74.5). By drinking Soma, gods became immortal. Soma stimulates the voice and the speech. He is referred to as "Vācaspati" (*ṚV* 9.26.4; 101.5). Soma is also called the lord of the plants (*ṚV* 9.114. 2) and receives the epithet *vanaspati,* lord of the world (*ṚV* 1.91.6; 9.12.7).[10]

Soma is referred to as moon in *Ṛgveda* (1st & 10th *maṇḍala*) as well as *Atharvaveda* (*AV* 7.81.3-4; 11.6.7, etc.). *Chāndogya Upaniṣad*

(5.10.1) and even the Brāhmaṇas identify Soma with the moon. There is nectar in the moon, when gods feed on it, the moon wanes away. Soma is celestial and bright dispelling darkness and swelling in the waters and it is often called a drop, Indu (6.44.21). Thus Soma in the bowls is said to appear like the moon in the water (8.71.8).[11]

Therefore, Soma in water implies the male–female concept commonly shared by *apsaras–gandharva*, *apsaras–soma* (drink), *apsaras*–moon, cow–bull, water and drop of light, *apsaras–śālā* (tree and vegetation in general), a conceptualized natural phenomenon, explicitly depicted by the ever-auspicious *mithuna* pairs. In my view the element of suggestion (*dhvani*) of male--female principle is very subtly implied in this pairing. Further exploration of it in *devāṅganā* imageries of *keśanistoyakāriṇī*, *śālabhañjikā*, *madhupānā*, *prasādhikā* holding mirror or a bowl, is worth pursuing.

The representation of Śrī in early Indian art shares with our feminine forms the visual semblance in depiction of its postures and attributes, e.g. *śālabhañjikā* posture, lotus, *ghaṭam*-like brimming pot, elephant, rich foliage, etc. and conceptual function — bestowing of prosperity, abundance, progeny, good fortune and so on. The worship of Śrī as a popular goddess was prevalent in pre-Buddhist times along with the *yakṣa* cult, and the *yakṣī* was the model for the representation of her form. Śrī was associated with the northern quarter and Śrīmatī or Śrīmā with the southern one.[12]

In Śrīsūkta, Śrī is referred to as seated on a lotus, holding lotuses and being bathed by elephants holding water jars. The early sculptures at Bharhut, Sāñcī, Bodha-Gayā and Udayagiri conform to this description. The Vedic concept of Śrī as the "lady bountiful", bestower of garments, food and drink, is closely related to the Vedic concept of Aditi, the lady of Viṣṇu, the Vedic predecessor of the epic Bhūdevī. Early sculptures contain suggestions of some of these concepts. Thus the lady touching her breast in the Lucknow Museum (which I have identified as *sva-stana-sparśā*) and the lady carrying food and water, represented at both Mathurā and Amarāvatī, are sculptural echoes of the *Yajurveda* passages describing her as "rich in milk, the goddess . . . the lady of Viṣṇu" and "Śrī that brings garments, cows, food and drink".[13] Her association with lotus and her bounty in the bestowal of food and drink are brought together, as Coomaraswamy has pointed out in a sculpture from Sāñcī, which is the link between the *yakṣī* images from Mathurā and Amarāvatī and the lotus-inhabiting lady. Everything good and auspicious is believed to be the abode of Śrī who is *Maṅgaḷa*. Thus a good house, gateway, flowers, banners, parasole, seats, beds, gems, charming married women with their living husbands, fruits, grains, seeds, vessels, new clothes, cow, horse, elephant and host of other objects are the abodes of Śrī. Different concepts of Lakṣmī such as Dhanalakṣmī (goddess of wealth), Dhānyalakṣmī (goddess of corns), Bhāgyalakṣmī (goddess of prosperity), Bhogalakṣmī (goddess of pleasures), Rājyalakṣmī (goddess of royalty), Vīralakṣmī (goddess of valour) are all suggestive of the presence of Śrī in various auspicious things.[14]

Thus recapitulating the concept of goddesses personified as nature spirits and manifested as Rākā, Puraṁdhī, Sīnīvālī, Iḷā, not only lead to the concepts of Aditi (which is more abstract and generalized than the former) but also to the higher goddesses such as Śrī Lakṣmī, Durgā, Umā-Pārvatī, etc. on one hand and *apsaras*, *yakṣī*, *surasundarī*, *devāṅganā*, etc. on the other. This process is perennial and continues in temple architecture where it obtains a concrete form from the literary imagery. In one sense they are *alaṁkārikā*, they not only decorate the temple but also enrich the literary flourish with poetic imagination. It is very essential to visualize and consider the cognate nature of the Vedic goddesses, *apsaras*es, *yakṣī*s, river goddesses and later-day *devāṅganā*s.

Apsaras in Vedic Literature

Let us look at available references from the Vedic texts specific to *apsaras* and her nature. It has been observed that the nature and association of an *apsaras* have been changing from the *Ṛgveda* to *Atharvaveda* and the later Vedic literature. This provides a basis for the iconology of an *apsaras* motif through Vedic literature. The concept is both imaginary as well as ambivalent. The nature of *apsaras* as an aqueous nymph, also associated with trees, fertility and engaging in dance, song and play, tends to connect the *apsaras*es as the predecessors of the *devāṅganā*s represented in sculpture on temple architecture. In this section, I have brought together varied references and interpretations on *apsaras*es, posed them as analogous with the *devāṅganā* concept in order to try and see how both these concepts work as complementary and interfacing with each other.

Apsaras denoted a kind of nymph, referred to only five times in the *R̥gveda* as collated by Macdonell. She smiles at her beloved *gandharva* in the highest heaven (*R̥V* 10.123.5). *Apsaras*es of the sea are described as flowing of Soma (*R̥V* 9.78.3) with reference to the water which is mixed with the *soma* juice.

The long-haired ascetic with semi-divine powers, is spoken of as able to move on the path of the *apsaras*es and the *gandharvas* (*R̥V* 10.136.6). The *apsaras* is also meant by the aqueous nymph (*apyā yoṣā*), the wife of the *gandharva* in the waters (*R̥V* 10.10.4).

More light on *apsaras*es is thrown by the *Atharvaveda* as further explored by Macdonell. Their abode is in waters, whence they come and go in a trice (*AV* 2.2.3). They are besought to depart from the vicinity of men to the river and the bank of the waters (*AV* 4.37.3). The goddesses connected with *gandharva* Viśvāvasu are described to be connected with clouds, lightning and stars (*AV* 2.2.4). They are also known as wives of the *gandharvas* (*AV* 2.2.5) and their connection with the latter has assumed the character of a formula in the later Saṁhitās (*VS* 30.8; *AV* 8.9.9). In the *Śatapatha Brāhmaṇa* (11.5.1.4) the *apsaras*es are described as transforming themselves into a kind of aquatic bird (*atayaḥ*: *R̥V* 9.5.9). In the post-Vedic literature they are very often spoken of as frequenting forest lakes and rivers especially the Ganges, and they adorned Varuṇa's palace in the ocean. The etymological meaning of *apsaras* according to Yāska's *Nirukta* 5.13 is *ap-sāriṇī* "moving in the waters".[15]

From the early Vedic literature it can be discerned that the oldest conception of the *apsaras* is a celestial water nymph, and a consort of a "genius" named *gandharva*. In the later Saṁhitās the sphere of the *apsaras*es extends to the earth and in particular to trees. They are spoken of as inhabiting banyan (*nyagrodha*) and sacred fig trees (*aśvattha*), in which their cymbals and lutes resound (*AV* 4.37.4).

Elsewhere, the same trees as well as other varieties of the fig tree (*udumbara* and *plakṣa*), are said to be the houses of *gandharva*s and *apsarase*s (a group of lower deities) (*TS* 3.4.8.4). The *gandharva*s and *apsarase*s in such trees are entreated to be propitious to a passing wedding procession (*AV* 14.2.7). In the *ŚB* (11.6.1) the *apsarase*s are described as engaged in dance, song and play. Post-Vedic texts even speak of mountains, both mythical and actual, as favourite resorts of these two classes of beings. The *Atharvaveda* adds the traits that the *apsarase*s are fond of dice and bestow luck at play (*AV* 2.2.5). But they are feared especially as causing mental derangement, magic therefore is being employed against them (*AV* 2.3.5, etc.).

The love of the *apsarase*s, who are of great beauty (*ŚB* 13.4.3) is employed not only by the *gandharva*s but occasionally even by men (*ŚB* 10.95.9). A myth turning on such a union is related to at least one individual *apsaras* in the Vedic literature. The names of several other *apsarase*s are also mentioned. *Gandharva* and the aqueous nymph, are alluded to as the parents of Yama and Yamī (*ŚB* 10.10.4). They dwell in waters (*AV* 2.2.3; 4.37.12). The union of *gandharva* with the water nymph is typical of marriage. He is therefore connected with the wedding ceremony, and the unmarried maiden is said to belong to Soma and Agni (*AV* 10.85.40-1). The *gandharva* Viśvāvasu, in the first days of wedlock, is regarded as a rival of the husband, and the *gandharva*'s love of women is prominent in later texts (*HS* 3.7.3). The *gandharva*s and *apsarase*s thus preside over sexuality fertility and are prayed to by those who are desirous of an offspring (*PB* 19.3.2).

Originally, *gandharva* is a bright celestial being, sometimes thought of as dwelling in the waters with his spouse the *apsaras*. Various conjectures have, however, been made by different scholars. Some regard the *gandharva*s as wind spirits, representing the rainbow, or a genius of the moon, Soma, the rising sun or a cloud spirit.[16]

Yama lives in the other world delighting himself in the company of the *apsarase*s (nymphs) who are connected with Soma (*AV* 4.34.3). Thus *apsarase*s adorned the court of Yama and Varuṇa before getting associated with Indrasabhā in the Epic and Purāṇic periods.

Gandharvas and Apsarases

In the *Ṛgveda*, the word *gandharva* occurs 20 times, but only thrice in plural, from which it is fair to deduce that the nature of its "spirit" was originally conceived as one. He is the high being of the air in the sky, a measurer of space who stands erect on the vault of heaven. He is brought into relation with the sun, the sun-bird, the sun-steed and Soma, as also likened to the sun. He is also connected with the rainbow in a late hymn. He is especially connected with Soma, whose place he guards, standing on the vault of heaven. *Gandharva* is also connected with waters. Soma in the waters is said to be the *gandharva* of the waters: *gandharva* is the lover of the *apsaras*. The *gandharva* is further found in the marriage ceremony: the bride is claimed by him, and he is in the beginning of the marriage a rival of the husband. *Gandharva* has a fragrant garment and is wind-haired.

Keith observes that in the later Saṁhitās the account of the *gandharva* is more comprehensive, but not essentially different. They now form a class of demi-gods, their abode is in the heaven, they are mentioned with sun deities as Agni, Sun, Moon, wind and in the post-Vedic literature the Fata Morgana are connected with the *gandharva*s. *Gandharva*s guarded *soma* for the gods, but allowing it to be stolen, were punished by exclusion from drinking it. Gods manipulated the stealing of *soma* from the *gandharva*s through Vāc who in female form allured the *gandharva*s. In the *Atharvaveda*, *gandharva* knows plants, doubtless the *soma*, and that the odour of the earth rises to him, probably an idea due to folk etymology, with *gandha* (odour).

In the Brāhmaṇas, texts and rituals, the connection between the *apsaras*es and the *gandharva*s is especially close: the *gandharva* Ūrṇāyu sits among the *apsaras*es who swing themselves, and is loved by them (*PB* 12.11.10). In a rite, the priest may point to the young men and young maidens present, when he means to indicate the *gandharva*s and *apsaras*es (*ŚB* 13.4.3.7.8). They are besought to bestow progeny (*PB* 19.3.2; *SGS* i.19.2) and in the Buddhist texts, the being, which by the law of transmigration, enters the womb at the time of conception, is called a *gandhabba*.

For the nights immediately after the marriage, when the newly-wedded couple are not allowed to consummate the marriage, a staff which represents the *gandharva* Viśvāvasu, is placed between them and not until he is formally dismissed to the highest region, is the marriage completed (*ṚV* 10.85.22). A different and lower view of the *gandharva* is also found in the *Atharvaveda*, where the plant, goat's horn, is used to drive off the *gandharvas*, who are regarded as shaggy with half animal forms, and are said to ruin women in the guise of an ape, a dog, a hairy child or a fiend. Nāgārjunakoṇḍa reliefs showing *mithunas* in different actions and *markaṭaceṣṭā devāṅganā* could be cited to illustrate the above reference. (*fig* 64-66)

In the Buddhist text, *Saṁyutta Nikāya*, *piśācas* replace *gandharvas* in conjunction with the *apsarases* — which could be a development from the *gandharvas* of the *Ṛgveda*. *Gandharva*'s association with marriage leads to a secondary connection with the embryo. According to Keith, *gandharva* therefore is no longer an independent concept in the succeeding period of the Vedic religion: he is compounded of different and in essence disparate ideas. Different scholars interpret his nature differently — cloud spirit, rising sun, *soma*, a genius of the moon and a rainbow. To certain scholars he is a wind spirit developed out of the conception of the spirits of the dead as riding on the wind and passing therefore into wind spirits. The *gandharva* in his origin is a spirit of the heaven and is also associated with waters of the sky and the earth due to his association with the *apsaras*. The long-haired *muni* (ascetic) with magic powers, moves on the path of the *gandharva* and the *apsarases* (*ṚV* 10.136.6). Many temples examined here represent *muni* and *apsaras* on conjoints of the façade and sides of temples.

In the post-Vedic literature, parallel with the *apsaras*, the *gandharva* was also attributed to have the power of causing derangement or at least mental excitement, which is attested for in the Brāhmaṇa texts by the phrase "seized by a *gandharva*" while referring to a lady who is inspired (possessed) or demented.[17]

Rise of Individual Apsaras in Vedic, Epic and Purāṇic Literature

The *Atharvaveda* refers to three *apparases*, namly Ugrajīt, Ugrampaśyā and Rāṣṭrabhṛta (*AV* 16.118.1.2) while *Vājapeya Saṁhitā*, among others, speaks of Urvaśī and Menakā (*VS* 15.15-19). *Śatapatha Brāhmaṇa* (3.4.1.22) specifically recorded the name of Śakuntalā, the ancestress of the royal family of the Bharatas (*ŚB* 13.5.4.13) as well as Urvaśī (*ŚB* 2.51.1).[18]

According to *Nāṭyaśāstra*, the *apsaras*es were created by the powerful Brahmā from his mind, who were skilful in embellishing the drama and gave them over to Bharata in performance (*NŚ* 1.46-47). They are mentioned as *Nāṭyālaṁkāra*, the embellished support to drama. Their names in the *Nāṭyaśāstra* are as follows : Mañjukeśī, Sukeśī, Miśrakeśī, Sulocanā, Saudāminī, Devadattā, Devasenā, Manoramā, Sudatī, Sundarī, Vidagdhā, Sumālā, Santatī, Sunandā, Sumukhī, Māgadhī, Arjunī, Saralā, Kerala, Dhṛti, Nandā, Supuṣkalā and Kalabhā.[19]

Ṛṣi Kaśyapa is the father of the celestial nymphs who were delivered by his wife Ariṣṭā. They were thirteen *apsaras*es and four *gandharva*s. Alambuṣā, Miśrakeśī, Vidyutparṇā, Tilottamā, Rakṣitā, Rambhā, Manoramā, Keśinī, Subāhu, Surajā, Suratā, Supriyā, while the *gandharva*s are Hāhā, Hūhū, Atibāhu, Tumburū.[20]

Another theory prevalent in the Epic and Purāṇic literature about *apsaras*es and their origin is through the *samudra-manthana*. They were born out of the ocean, according to the myth describing the great cosmic event.[21]

Matsya Purāṇa[22] refers to the origin of *apsaras*es along with *ṛṣi*s, *gandharva*s and *kinnara*s from a common parentage, namely Kaśyapa and Ariṣṭā. A significant verse (*MP* 10.24) refers to a metaphorical comparison between the holding of a suckling infant by the *apsaras* (*dugdha vatsā*) with the aid of *gandharva*s and the smell and fragrance which is the inherent quality of the *padma-dala*. Therefore the creation of the suckling baby, Citraratha refers to the nourishing aspect of an *apsaras* character, where she is compared with the mother. By referring to *padma-dala gandha*, the intention is to underline the inseparability of the quality of nourishment from the *apsaras*.

Vāyu Purāṇa,[23] which is one of the older Purāṇas, has some most interesting verses referring to the nature of the *apsaras*, their creation and what they are responsible for. It refers to the origin of *apsaras* as a creation of Brahmā, who created moveable and immoveable objects along with groups of *yakṣa*s, *piśāca*s, *gandharva*s and *apsaras* (*MP* 9.55). Out of the many similar groups of *apsaras*, most of them were endowed with happiness, benevolence, protection, fragrance and purity (*VP* 30.87).

Moreover, each group of *apsaras*es contains fourteen boon-bestowing ones, who are called the beauty incarnates (*VP* 69.53). *Vāyu Purāṇa* clearly mentions them as the *mānasa kanyā*s of Brahmā who emerge from his mental creativity. They are endowed with the nature of energy, force and created from Agni and Ariṣṭā (*VP* 69.54). They are bright and resemble the long rays of the sun, they also bear nourishment from moon and benevolence (*VP* 69.55).

They are born of *yajña* and are called *śubha*, they also resemble the sound of *Ṛk* and *Sāma* recited before Agni. They are born of water and nectar and known as *amṛta* (*VP* 69.56). *Vāyu Purāṇa* also refers to them as born of the wind, and calls them as Śuddha, while the mundane ones are earth born, the lightning born are called Ṛcā, the death born are called Bhairava (*VP* 69.57). This verse is very significant because it characterizes the diverse origins, names, characters and affiliations of *apsaras*es. Some of them are boon-bestowing, nourishing, while some of them are fierce.

There is one amorous group of *apsaras*es who are referred to as beautifiers and they are fourteen in number. They are created to enhance the beauty of the Indra-Sabhā (*VP* 69.58). The Surāyana of Indra-Sabhā are bestowed with beautiful form and youth, and these celestial maidens are known by names such as Dhanurūpā, Mahābhāgā, Tilottamā. The illustrious divine beings are born in the circle of Brahmā and Agni (*VP* 69.59). Further on, *Vāyu Purāṇa* mentions a metaphorical verse in which one *apsaras*, called Vedavatī, is born from the altar of Brahmā's mental sphere bearing a great bright halo (*VP* 69.60).

The next verse refers to the daughter of Yama who is youthful and beautiful. This celestial maiden called Sulocanā is suffused with golden halo (*VP* 69.61). The range of these various groups of *apsaras* runs into thousands, some of whom are the wives of the *deva*s, and *ṛṣi*s while some are mothers (*VP* 69.62). This verse throws much light on the material aspect of the *apsaras*. It must be noted here that thus far we have not come across the nature of *apsaras* as a seductress, an enchantress, or a courtesan — the maligned position to which they were brought down in the later periods of the Epics and the classical literature is not implied in the *Vāyu Purāṇa*. Therefore the data gleaned from the *Vāyu Purāṇa* is very valuable in reviewing the character of the *apsaras* and for interpreting their sculptures.

Vāyu Purāṇa not only mentions the entire range of *apsaras*' imagery but also mentions their physical attributes along with their names. They are golden complexioned, suffused with fragrance and when they perform their chores, their orb intoxicates the onlooker without the aid of wine. Their touch alone enhances *ānanda* (*VP* 69.63).

This group of thirty-four *apsaras*es of the heaven are full of auspiciousness, water, and one of them, Surottamā, is specially loved (69.4). The list includes Miśrakeśī, Chasī, Varṇinī, Alambuṣā, Maricī, Putrikā, Vidyutparṇā, Tilottamā, Adrikā, Lakṣaṇā, Devī, Rambhā, Manoramā, Suvarā, Subāhu, Pūrṇitā, Supratiṣṭhitā, Puṇḍarikā, Sugandhā, Sudantā, Surasā, Hemā, Śaradvatī, Suvratā, Subhujā and Haṁsapādā — these are the popular *apsaras* known from the *munis* of yore (*VP* 69.5-8).

Brahmāṇḍa Purāṇa[24] also has a list of 24 *apsaras*es such as Miśrakeśī, Chasī, Parṇinī, Alambuṣā, Maricī, Sucibhā, Vidyutparṇā, Tilottamā, Adrikā, Lakṣmaṇā, Kṣemā, Divyā, Rambhā, Manobhavā, Asitā, Supriyā, Subhujā, Puṇḍarikā, Jagandhā, Sudalī, Surasā, and Subāhu. The list gives only 22 names and comparing it with the *Vāyu Purāṇa* list the names appear analogous, e.g. Sugandhā–Jagandhā, Sudantā–Sudalī, Putribhā–Sucibhā and so on. These *apsaras*es belong to the lower class of the auspicious heavenly beings, who are fair complexioned (Aruṇā) and harmless (*BP* 3.7.5). They are the attendants (Śaivyā) of the Devī (Lakṣmī) and out of the 1,016, the group of *apsaras*es consists of 14 of them (*BP*. 3 71.243). Brahmā once asked Indra to send some chosen ones from his palace to become the wives of Vāsudeva (*BP* 3.71.244). This connection of *apsaras* with Brahmā (as *mānasa kanyās*) reiterated by (*NŚ* 1.46-47) and with Kṛṣṇa (as *patnyartham vāsudevasya*) throws light on their acceptance into the pantheon of the higher gods (though only in secondary roles), right from the early classical period.

Viṣṇu Purāṇa: Dvitīya Aṁśa

Viṣṇu Purāṇa[25] mentions the *apsaras* as the attendants of Sūrya in the form of twelve Ādityas who are the harbingers of various seasonal changes and who dance to spread happiness. This iconography (which is given in a tabulated from on next page) throws further light to support the mainstream acceptance of *apsaras* in the Hindu pantheon in association with the major male gods. Their representation on Nāgara temples in the medieval period is a logical continuation of the same textual memory.

Parāśara says that between the extreme northern and southern points, the sun has to traverse in a year 180°, ascending and descending. His car is presided over by divine Āditya, *ṛṣi*s, heavenly singers and nymphs, *yakṣa*s, serpents and *rākṣasa*s (one of each being placed in it every month) (*VP* 2.10.1-2).

In this manner, Maitreya and a troop of seven celestial beings, supported by the energy of Viṣṇu, occupy during several months the orb of the sun. The sage celebrates his praise, and the *gandharva* sings, the nymph dances before him, the *rākṣasa* attends upon his steps, the serpent harnesses his steeds and the *yakṣa* trims the reins, the numerous pygmy sages, the *bālakhilya*s, ever surround his chariot. The whole troop of seven, attached to the sun's car, are the agents in the distribution of cold, heat and rain, at their respective seasons (*VP* 2.10.19-20).

Bhāgavata Purāṇa[26] reiterates the origin of *apsaras* from the churning of the ocean, they emerge after the *kalpavṛkṣa*. They were draped with beautiful robes and golden necklaces. These celestial nymphs were engaged in enticing by making sensuous movements and throwing amorous glances (*BhP* 8.8.7).

Table

Rise of the Individual Apsarases in Viṣṇu Purāṇa

Month	*Āditya*	*Ṛṣi*	*Gandharva*	*Apsaras*	*Yakṣa*	*Nāga*	*Rākṣasa*
Madhu or Caitra	Dhātṛ	Pulastya	Tumburu	Kratusthalā	Rathakṛt	Vāsuki	Heti
Vaiśākha or Mādhava	Āryamat	Pulaha	Nārada	Puñjikasthalī	Rathaujas	Kacanira	Praheti
Śuci or Jyeṣṭhā	Mitra	Atri	Hāhā	Menā	Rathasvāna	Takṣaka	Pauruṣeya
Śukra or Āṣāḍha	Varuṇa	Vasiṣṭha	Hūhū	Sahajanyā	Rathacitra	Rathacitra	Budha
Nabhas or Śravaṇa	Indra	Aṅgiras	Viśvavasu	Pramalocā	Śrotas?	Elaputra?	Elaputra
Bhādrapada	Vivasvat	Bhṛgu	Ugrasena	Anumlocā	Apūrṇa	Śaṅkhapāla	Vyāghra
Aśvin	Pūṣan	Gautama	Suruci	Ghṛtācī	Suṣena	Dhanañjaya	Vāta
Kārttika	Parjanya	Bhāradvāja	Viśvāvasu	Viśvāci	Senajit	Airāvata	Cāpa
Agrahāyana or Mārgaśīrṣa	Aṅśu	Kaśyapa	Citrasena	Urvaśī	Tārkṣya	Mahāpadma	Vidyut
Pauṣa	Bhaga	kṛtu	Urṇayu	Pūrvacitti	Ariṣṭanemi	Kārkoṭaka	Sphurja
Māgha	Tvaṣṭā	Jamadagni	Dhṛtarāṣṭra	Tilottamā	Ritajit	Kambala?	Brahmapeta
Phālguna	Viṣṇu	Viśvāmitra	Sūrya-varcas	Rambhā	Satyajit	Aśvatara	Yajñapeta

In another context *Bhāgavata Purāṇa* (12.8.16) mentions that Indra sent *gandharva*s, *apsaras,* Kāma, Vasanta, Malayanīla and Mada to the *āśrama* of Mārkaṇḍeya to disturb his penance. From the above references the amorous character of *apsaras* comes to the fore. They have been portrayed as agents of allurement, a stumbling block, to test the integrity of a sage or a mortal.

Beautiful women were created by Viṣṇu with his yogic powers. They were beautifully dressed and attended upon him. Looking at their Lakṣmī-like form and affected by their sweet smell, the subordinates of Indra lost their lustre. Then with a polite smile Viṣṇu selected an appropriate one from among them and embellished the heavens (*BhP* 11.4.12-13). At that time they also lauded Urvaśī as the best *apsaras*.

Viṣṇu Purāṇa mentions in the famous incident related with *samudra-manthana* how there arose the Goddess Vāruṇī, coral tree *pārijāta*, the jewel *kaustubha*, sacred cow *Kāmadhenu*, celestial *apsaras*es and the Goddess Lakṣmī who went to Hari (*VP* 1.9, 2.116). When the Goddess Lakṣmī arrived with vibrant beauty, the seers assembled there praised her with the Śrīsūkta and the *gandharva*s led by Viśvāvasu sang before her and the throngs of *apsaras*es led by Ghṛtāci, danced before her.[27]

One of the most fascinating imageries of *apsaras* ever found is in *Vāmana Sāromāhātmya* (10.33-66). When Vāmana shed his dwarf-like form, in a twinkling of an eye, he manifested the form which consisted of all the gods, his eyes were the moon and the sun, the sky was his head and the earth his feet, his toes were the *piśāca*s and his fingers the *guhyaka*s. The Viśvedevas were in his knees and the excellent deities, the *sādhya*s were in his skin. In his nails appeared the *yakṣa*s and in the contours of his body, the *apsaras*es.[28] This suggests that *apsaras*es have been associated with an aerial form — contourless, and changeable at will.

Emergence of the Most Significant Apsaras: Their Characteristics and Interpretation

In this section, we take a closer look at some of the most noted *apsaras*es to uncover their meaning and significance. This is necessitated by the uniqueness with which these *apsaras*es have been conceived in mythology and thus should be studied with special attention.

URVAŚĪ

Urvaśī is mentioned in the *Ṛgveda* as an *apsaras* to whom Vasiṣṭha is said to have been born (7.33.11-12). She is once invoked with the streams (5.41.19). She is also described as aqueous (*āpya*) as filling the atmosphere, traversing space, an expression which is applied to the celestial *gandharva* (in 10.139.5). She is said to have spent four autumns among mortals (5.16) and is besought to return (5.17); the request of Pururavas is granted with an entry into the heaven (5.18). Several verses of this hymn find their setting in a continuous story told in the *ŚB* (2.5.1) which fills in details partly based on a misunderstanding of the text of *ṚV*.[29]

Urvaśī is the abstraction of a subtle principle. She is the life-principle in matter (*prāṇāgni*) that requires a unit of *ghṛta* (clarified butter, literally) for its sustenance daily. *Ghṛta* is a form of Agni who in turn is nothing but the life-principle. It is then, this life-principle that is kept kindled by its daily share of sustenance that it receives from various sources. The crux of this all is that energy is sustained by energy and life is sustained by life — to continue for its full span of existence in the human body or on the material plane for a period of one hundred years. The measure of fuel which supports this life is symbolized by "one drop of *ghṛta*". The principle of *rajas* measures life and such is the function of Urvaśī as well (*ṚV* 10.95.17).

Urvaśī is most clearly a celestial nymph or *apsaras* (*amānuṣī*) who is wooed by immortal men (*ṚV* 10.95.8). She is the immoral lady of the heavens whom mortal man follows and possesses but for a while! Their mutual covenant is that she would have him if her daily share of *ghṛta* were to cease. She reveals her true nature in the *Ṛgveda* saying:

> I am like the first of the dawns; I move like the tempestuous wind difficult to hold or capture; I flash brilliantly as the falling lightning!

It is for Pururavas, the unique, separate manifestation of *prāṇa* that

Urvaśī has descended upon the Earth. She herself says:

> The birth had made me drink from earthly milch kine.
> —*ṚV* 10.95.11

According to the *Ṛgveda*, Urvaśī moves in a select band of six other nymphs making in all the seven sisters, which is analogous to the principle of the sevenfold female powers or mothers of creation. In addition to the condition of her daily portion of *ghṛta*, there were two other conditions that she imposed on King Pururavas. That her two lambs should be protected from any danger and that she should never behold the form of the king in a complete state of nakedness. The lambs symbolize the firm principles of *prāṇa* and *apāna* whose mingled energy is the lightning-like Urvaśī (*ṚV* 10.189.2). The veil over Pururavas is the physical body itself, the fabric of material form or corporeal modality which is essential as an element of life in matter; Urvaśī and Pururavas separate as soon as life leaves the mortal coil.

Urvaśī is a mental creation of Nārāyaṇa illustrated in a verse from *Viṣṇudharmottara* (3.35.2-4) which relates to a tale of the meditation of Nara and Nārāyaṇa in the Badarī grove. While they both were in deep concentration, celestial damsels were sent by Indra to disturb their peace. Nārāyaṇa took a fresh mango leaf and with its juice sketched on his thigh the most beautiful form of a nymph that at once sallied forth from it, appropriately styled Urvaśī. She put to shame everyone of the damsels by her superior grace and perfection of charm.[30]

The creation of *apsaras* from the thigh of a *ṛṣi* with the sap of a mango leaf presupposes a number of conclusions we are going to draw in the forthcoming chapters relating to eroticism, asceticism, fertility and creativity.

RAMBHĀ[31]

Rambhā in the Purāṇa is mentioned as an *apsaras* presiding over the month of Śuci (*BP* 12.11.36) and Ūrjā (*BP* 12.11.44; *IB* II.23.22; IV.33.18), whereas she is mentioned as the wife of Māyā (in *BṛP* 3.6.28, 7.7). In *Matsya Purāṇa* (136.11) Rambhā was created by

Brahmā, where she is described to be well versed in dancing (*MP* 24.28; *VāP* 69.6). She is supposed to have gone with the Sun sometimes (*IB* 126.23) while once she was seized by the *asuras* (*IB* 126.7, 133.9) in the *sabhā* of Hiraṇyakaśipu (*IB* 161.75). According to *Viṣṇu Purāṇa*, Rambhā accompanies Sūrya during the months of Phālguna and Āṣāḍha (2.10.18). The nature of Rambhā is snake-like in the month of summer, when she accompanies the Sun (*VāP* 52.6) whereas she along with other *apsaras*es was cursed by Aṣṭāvakra (*IB* 5.38.73.77).

In the Purāṇic literature, Rambhā is considered as one of the most beautiful of the *apsaras*es along with Urvaśī, Tilottamā and others. All these celestial women are considered to be daughters of Kaśyapa Prajāpati by his wife Pradhā. Ādi-Parva of the *Mahābhārata* Ch. 65 mentions that from the above parentage were born Alambuṣā, Miśrakeśī, Vidyutparṇā, Tilottamā, etc. Once Rāvaṇa raped Rambhā and her lover Nalakubera cursed him. Indra once killed an *asura* chief Māyādhara, and in the victory festival Rambhā danced before her preceptor, Tumburū.

ALAMBUṢĀ[32]

Alambuṣā is a celestial maiden born to Kaśyapa by his wife Pradhā. Alambuṣā entices sage Dadhīca, whose semen flows in the river resulting in the birth of child, Sārasvata. Then crops fail in the land resulting in a widespread famine. The brāhmaṇas flee the land and finally Sārasvata resuscitates the dying old order by reciting passages from the scriptures. Once, when Indra goes to see Brahmā, Alambuṣā also happens to be there, when her robes are displaced by the wind Vidhūma, who had accompanied Indra, is overcome by libido. The mutual passion of Vidhūma and Alambuṣā displeases Indra and Brahmā, who cursed them to be born as humans. Vidhūma is reborn as Sahasrānīka, an illustrious king of the Candra-vaṁśa; Alambuṣā is reborn as Mṛgāvatī, the daughter of King Kṛtavarmā and Kalāvatī. Sahasrānīka is invited by Indra to the heaven. The *apsaras* Tilottamā is sent with him to entertain, but Sahasrānīka is immersed in the love of Mṛgāvatī. He earns the curse of Tilottamā for having scorned her. She curses him to suffer the proverbial fourteen years of separation from his beloved. The child born of the union of Sahasrānīka and Mṛgāvatī is Udayana who is instrumental in bringing them together eventually.

Alambuṣā is said to have taken part in the birthday celebrations of Arjuna (*Mbh*, Ādi-Parva 65.49).

TILOTTAMĀ[33]

One of the more prominent celestial maidens, was born to Kaśyapa through his wife Pradhā. Kaśyapa was the grandson of Brahmā and the son of Mañci. Alambuṣā was one of the sisters of Tilottamā (Ādi-Parva 65). To cause a schism between the demons Śuṇḍa and Upaśuṇḍa, Brahmā creates her, backing the best (*uttama*) of both the animate and inanimate objects (Ādi-Parva 215). She is also said to have been created from small particles of diamond by Brahmā (Anuśāsana-Parva 141.1).

Śiva sees her circumambulating Brahmā and wanting to behold her constantly, he causes faces to form pointing towards all the four quarters. A similar situation results in the "many eyed" form of the king of the gods, Indra.

MENAKĀ[34]

A nymph of extraordinary beauty, taking instructions from Indra, enticed and shook the *tapas* of many sages destroying their powers of penance. Impregnated by a *gandharva* named Viśvāvasu, she bore a girl child whom she deserted on a river bank. Sage Sthūlakeśa brought up this girl as Pramadvarā who married King Ruru. Another source has it that Menakā unites with Viśvāmitra to give birth to Śakuntalā. Menakā's gift to Durvāsā leads to the churning of the Kṣīrasāgara. Menakā holds pride of place amongst the *apsaras*es along with Urvaśī, Pūrvacittī, Sahajanyā, Ghṛtāci and Viśvāci (Ādi-Parva 74.68). Menakā is said to have been present at Arjuna's *janmotsava* and is also said to have sung on the occasion (Ādi-Parva 122.64). She was a dancer in the court of Kubera (Sabhā-Parva 10.10). Menakā gave a musical performance in Indra's court to honour the archer, Arjuna (Vana-Parva 43.21).

Apsarā–Diśākumārī Interrelationship

While exploring the contents of the Vedic and the Purāṇic literature regarding the role of *apsaras* in ancient Indian psyche, I explored Āgamic and Prākṛt indexes as well, which yielded interesting results.[35]

The *apsaras* as we now understand is a charming and beautiful concept of aquatic origin which resides in air and shares intimate communion with Sūrya, Marut, Kubera, Kāma, Yama and of course Indra and Varuṇa. Personified *apsaras* appear on earth to charm mortal men. They are bestowers of luck, happiness, prosperity and progeny. As they adorn the *sabhā* of Indra in the heaven, they also adorn the earthly abode of the gods to add splendour and beauty to the monument. Conceived by the temple architects and sculptors these *apsaras*es (*devāṅganā*s) adorn all the four walls of the temple facing the four cardinal and the four subsidiary directions. An interesting concept of *diśākumārī*s is found in Prākṛt literature which indicates the presence of presiding directional deities who belonged to the Bhavana Vai class of gods.

It was observed that many of the *diśākumārī*s shared the same names as the *apsaras*, viz. Alambuṣā, Miśrakeśī, Vicittā, Vijayā, etc. These *diśākumārī*s preside over the four directions of the Ruyagga mountain. They are 56 in all and they are called *diśākumārī mahattarīyā*s. Each of them has a large retinue and mount Ruyagga is their main abode. Each of the four quarters has four divisions and each division has eight peaks. They are divided into those of the *adholoka* and *ūrdhvaloka*. Their character has been observed as sportive and they participate in the consecration ceremony of *tīrthaṁkaras*. The following list gives their names. The principal *diśākumārīs* of *adholoka* are Bhogaṁkarā, Bhogavatī, Subhogā, Bhogamālinī, Toyadharā, Vicittā, Pupphamatā, Aniṁdiā. They build a maternity hall for the expectant mother of a *tīrthaṁkara*, while the *diśākumārī*s of the *ūrdhvaloka* purify the maternity hall with artificial rain. They are known as Mehaṁkarā, Mehavatī, Sumehā, Mehamālinī, Suvacchā, Vaccamittā, Varisenā, and Balahavā.

The *diśākumārī*s of eastern Ruyagga mountain wait on the

expectant mother holding mirrors in their hands. They are Nanduttarā, Nandā, Ānandā, Nandīvadhanā, Vijayā, Vejayantī, Jayantī and Aparājitā. The western Ruyagga is adorned by Iḷādevī, Suradevī, Puhai, Paumarai, Egaṇasā, Navamiyā, Bhaddā and Sītā, who wave the fan. On the northern Ruyagga are placed Alambuṣā, Miśrakeśī, Puṇḍarikā, Vāruṇī, Hasā, Savvapabhā, Śrīdevī and Hīrī, who wave the *caurī*s. The southern Ruyagga is inhabited by Samahārā, Supainnā, Supabudhā, Jośaharā, Lacchimai, Sesavai, Cittaguttā, Vasundharā, who raise pitchers in their hands and all of them sing auspicious songs. Some more are also known, viz. Cittā, Cittakanāgā, Sutarā and Soyamaṇi, who belong to the sub-quarters and hold lamps while Ruā, Ruasiā, Ruagavai of the middle region perform the ceremony of severing the naval string of the newborn child.

Does the above data not throw light on the similarity of functions shared by *apsaras* and *diśākumārī*s? The aquatic association is clearly indicated by rain and other auspicious functions like holding lamps, fan, pitchers and fly whisks. Their presence during childbirth and with maternity in general itself suggests fertility connotation. It is very plausible to perceive the *diśākumārī*s analogous with the *devāṅganā*s sculpted on the temple *maṇḍovara* in four corners next to the *dikpāla*s. The *devāṅganā*s adorn the temple which is conceived as a Meru-prāsāda, the form of a mountain and the *devāṅganā*s in different imageries adorn the walls of the mountain just like the *diśākumārī*s.

The Āgamic tradition also has a concept of Vijjukumāra and Vijjukumārī *mahattarīyā*, who are the personification of light and they are supposed to hold lamps in their hands. This personified idea of nature could be transferred from iconography to physical representation of female forms on temple architecture. Jaina and Hindu temples alike have the representation of the *devāṅganā*s in all cardinal directions signifying auspiciousness. It is very likely that the original idea must have come to sculptors in the context of *diśākumārī*s to evolve from their imagery their visual representation. This phenomenon of identifying *devāṅganā* imagery within the *diśākumārī* genre, suggests a step beyond personification. Hence, *devāṅganā*s could be taken as embodiment in female form of natural phenomena personified in the forms of *apsaras*, *surasundarī*, *yakṣī* including *diśākumārī*. Their representation often follows their imagery because symbolically and conceptually, they are parallel. In primary *abhidhā* sense, they look alike because their visual representation is similar, but when probed for further meaning, one could unravel segments of parallel symbolism. This brings us back to noticing the significance of female energy and its role in religion, culture, life and philosophy.

Even Buddhist sources reveal the significance of protective directional guardian gods and goddesses. The four quarters of a Buddhist *stūpa* are protected by the *lokapāla*s known as kings or guardians of the four quarters, each quarter being represented by a quadrant of the railing. According to setting suggested in the *Atanatīya Sutta*, Dhṛtarāṣṭra is to guard the eastern quarter with the aid of Sūrya, seven constellations and eight *devakumārī*s. Virudhaka is to guard the southern quarter with the aid of Yama, seven constellations and eight *devakumārī*s; Virūpākṣa is to guard the western quarter with the aid of Varuṇa, seven constellations and eight *devakumārī*s, and Kubera is to guard the northern quarter with the aid of Maṇibhadra, eight constellations and eight *devakumārī*s.[36] It is difficult to verify if these directions have been strictly followed, says Barua. Here the *devakumārī*s are mentioned in every direction accompanying the *lokapāla*s of each direction. The above data tallies with *diśākumārī*s quoted by us in the Jaina context. The only difference is that their names and functions are not mentioned, but conceptually their presence as protective spirits is commonly shared in Jaina and Buddhist iconography art architecture. On Bharhut *stūpa* they appear in the form of *devatā*s and *yakṣī*s for the first time and continue to appear at many other *stūpa* sites.

II

In this section, I have examined literary sources dealing with the role of dance in social, literary, aesthetic and religious spheres. Tracing its development through the Vedic–Purāṇic to classical Kāvya and Nāṭya literature, it is clear that dance was integral to life. Dance was the most significant accomplishment of the *apsaras*, *devadāsī*s and the royal women who were expected to learn it as one of the sixty-four arts. But dance is also a mode of worship dedicating one's body and soul in honour of the deity. The tradition of temple dancers and temple dancing originated as a continuous process of thought and living. This also gives a thematic focus to our dance forms which are essentially religious in origin.

I am intrigued by the poetic imagery of dance and its comparison with the beauty of nature and the beauty of charming women. In this section focus is on the similies drawn from nature and feminine beauty, dance and nature's play with seasons and the various social events in which dance is integral to celebration.

The Concept of Feminine Beauty

Sensual charm of a woman has always engaged the attention of poets, writers, painters and sculptors from time immemorial. In Indian psyche, woman is not only a mother, wife, sister, courtesan or goddess — her representation in visual form is also always charming and beautiful. So, the image and the imagination both yield a beautiful form. And, when it comes to depicting an *apsaras*, *yakṣī* or a *surasundarī*, the epitome of beauty and ultimate charm of allurement, the artist puts his heart and soul into the creation of an ideal form. The ideal of Indian feminine beauty[37] can be traced from Mauryan times and the most bewitching examples of *yakṣī* and *śālabhañjikā* come from Dīdāragañja at Patna and Mathura museums as well as from Sāñcī. Another glorified *yakṣī* of the medieval period is the Gyāraspur *vṛkṣikā* of Gwalior Museum. The Āndhra, Kuṣāṇa and Gupta period *yakṣī*s, *nadī-devatā*s and other deities have always been recognized for the beauty of their supple bodies, youthfulness and accentuated sensuality. The conventions of drapery, *mekhalā*, *ekāvalī*, hair-do and ornamentation augment their resemblance. They provide a concrete evidence of an artist's vision of an ideal Indian woman, may she be a *dūtī* (attendant), Māyādevī, Lakṣmī, *apsaras*, *devāṅganā*, *vṛkṣikā*, *yakṣī*, queen or the Mother Goddess Durgā.

When invoking the imagery of a beautiful female body, allusion to nature denoting emotions, physical form and actions is constantly encountered in Sanskrit and Prākṛt literature. Thus, this illustrates the implicit parallelism between nature's forms and human form, nature's mood (e.g. seasons) and human mood (e.g. emotions) and a symbiotic relationship that exists between the two. This poetic imagination pervades the world of art as well, and as *dhvanikāra* or *ālaṁkārika*s would say, the best mood for illustrating is *vipralambha śṛṅgāra* and the most delicate symbol of appreciation is woman.

Poets and writers from Hāla, Aśvaghoṣa, Kālidāsa to Rājaśekhara and Jayadeva, have sung the glory of the feminine beauty. Although nature's forms are often cited as comparable examples qualifying feminine beauty, the woman's body bears all those qualities in totality which in nature exist but in parts. As *yakṣa* in *Meghadūtam* recalls the beauty of his beloved wife in nature around him on the Rāmagiri hill,

> In the *soma* vines I see your body, your glance in the gazelle's startled eye, the cool radiance of your face in the moon, your tresses in the peacock's luxuriant train, your eyebrow's graceful curve in the stream's small waves, but alas! O cruel one, I see not your whole likeness any where in any one thing. —*Meghadūtam*, 103[38]

Similes on Dance in Literature

From the *Buddhacarita* of Aśvaghoṣa we find that the *mṛdaṅga* was ornamented with golden bands and played by women "with the foreparts of their hands" (*nārī karāgrabhira hastaiḥ*). The ladies of the palace hold different musical instruments in their laps which the *bodhisattva* notices and then walks away from the palace. In another instance, Buddha's voice has been compared with the sound of the thundering clouds (*ghana dundubhi* VIII.53).

The ladies of the palace are endowed with alluring movements (*lalita bhāva*) while their eyebrows are arched (*bhruvañcitaiḥ*) and they cast on *bodhisattva* half-shut half-stolen glances (II.31). Amorousness is described by terms *lalita* and *añcita* occurring in *Nāṭyaśāstra*.

Kālidāsa in *Kumārasambhava* mentions the Sukumāra dance of Pārvatī, the graceful *abhinaya* of the trees, the dance of the peacocks, as also the grotesque dance of Bhṛṅgī on the occasion of the marriage of Śiva and Pārvatī (IX.48).

The graceful dancing of the earlier cantos is replaced by the dance of swords and men in the context of Kārttikeya's fight with Tārakāsura (XVI.48.49). The swords covered with blood dance like lightning in the battle field (XVI.15) and soon there is nothing but the dance of headless trunks of soldiers which the spirits of the soldiers watch from above.[39]

Meghadūtam and *Ṛtusaṁhāram* are more imaginative and the similes on nature's beauty resplendent with rhythm and grace are numerous in these two epic poems. The peacocks dance to the rhythm of thunder, trees dance to the rhythm of personified wind, while the thunderous clouds provide percussion like *muraja* accompaniment to the music in Alakāpurī.

The women of Alakāpurī have large eyes and with their *cakita netra* (curious eyes) and through their graceful movements they allure the cloud — messenger (*Pūrva Megha* 29). The *bhrū-vilāsa* is the amorous movement of the eyebrows which attracts the attention of the cloud. Kālidāsa has not missed noticing the graceful dance-like movement of a delicate part of the human body namely *bhṛkuṭi* and *kaṭākṣa*.[40]

In *Ṛtusaṁhāram*, Kālidāsa observes the gracefully gliding movement of the river as

> Prettily girdled by glittering minnows darting about garlanded by rows of white birds on the margins. With broad curving flanks of sandy banks, rivers glide softly like young women rapt in love.
>
> — *Ṛtusaṁhāram* III, Autumn, 3[41]

Dance and Drama Types: Krīḍā and Courtly Pastime

Here I have compiled references on "love sports" (*deśī krīḍā*s) which are performed by men and women together or by all women groups. Representation of courtly pastime is found in painting and sculpture from time to time in all the regions of India. Significantly, not only Kāvya and Nāṭya literature mention them, but even Śāstras mention them. Even in Prākṛt literature such references are met with. This signifies the cross-over between Sanskrit and Prākṛt and between *mārgī* and *deśī* literature, and the fluid nature of the themes like *aśoka dohada* and *kanduka-krīḍā*. Some of these *deśī krīḍā*s are mentioned in *Kathā-Sarit-Sāgara*, *Bṛhatkathā* and *Bṛhatkathā*

Mañjarī (folk tales), Hāla's *Gāhāsattasai* (Prākṛt), Bhoja's *Śṛṅgāra Prakāśa* and *Kāmasūtra* of Vātsyāyana (Śāstra), Bāṇa's *Harṣacarita* and Rājaśekhara's *Viddhaśālabhañjikā* (Nāṭya).

A light on the nature of the *krīḍās* unfolds a totally secular world. This is an aspect of Indian culture committed to abandon and celebration of youthfulness. Bhoja mentions them in *Sarasvatī-kaṇṭhābharaṇa* and *Śṛṅgāra Prakāśa*, under different headings of seasonal festivals, while Vātsyāyana calls them as *uddīpana vibhāva*, nourishing love.

References to *udyāna-krīḍā* (garden sports) are ample (*BKŚS* II.24, IV.55), known also as *mandirodyāna* or *bhāvanodyāna* in which the king ordered his ministers to arrange for an *apāna bhūmi*, a pavilion for enjoying drinks. Royal enjoyments in the palace garden consisted of several items: *puṣpa-krīḍā* (flower sport) and *salila-krīḍā* (water sport), *vastrābharaṇa maṇḍana*, *keśa saṁskāra* and *candanānulepana* (applying sandalpaste), *nṛtya* (dance), *saṅgīta* (music), *rativilāsa*, *pānagoṣṭhī* (gathering to enjoy wine), to which references are found in the *kāvya*s and the Purāṇas.[42] The drinking sessions were punctuated by dance and music and "all-women" theatre (*BKŚS* II.30-32).[43]

There are a number of *krīḍās* mentioned in *Śṛṅgāra Prakāśa*, *Kāmasūtra* and its commentaries, and *Bhāva Prakāśa*, that refer to the seasons in which they are celebrated. Bhoja's *Śṛṅgāra Prakāśa* written around CE 1050, has chapters related to celebration of love. In other *mahākāvya*s and *nāṭaka*s, references to love festivals like *Kaumudīmahotsava*, *Carcarī* dance are present. As an *aṅga* of the subject of *Kāmaśāstra*, a large number of these are mentioned by Vātsyāyana. Bhoja also mentions them in *Sarasvatī-kaṇṭhābharaṇa*, as a comparative study between *Kāmasūtra* and Jayamaṅgala's *Ṭīkā*.[44] *Kāmasūtra* (1.IV.42) enumerates twenty group sports or *sambhūya krīḍā*s, and some *deśī krīḍā*s (III.6.7). *Śāradātanaya* borrows from Bhoja, and makes slight amplifications by classifying them according to the six seasons (*Bhāva Prakāśa* VI, pp. 137, 138). *Sāhitya Mīmāṁsā* follows Bhoja, and gives some regional varieties also, while Vīrabhadra's *Kandarpa Cūḍāmaṇi* follows *Jayamaṅgalā* in his description of these sports.

During the season of Vasanta (spring), the following sports are known: Aṣṭamīcandra, Śakrārca, Vasantotsava, Madanotsava, Vakulavihāra, Aśoka Vihāra and Śālmalimūla Khelana.

Śakrārca or Indrotsava is a festival in honour of Indra, its antiquity going back to the Ṛgvedic times. References to Indradhvaja festival can be found from the *Rāmāyaṇa*, *Mahābhārata*, *Mṛcchakaṭika*, *Raghuvaṁśa*, *Buddhacarita* and also *Śilappadikāram* and *Maṇimekhalai*. The origin of Sanskrit drama can also be traced to this festival and in the *Pūrvaraṅga* this is absorbed in the form of a ritual. Indra's banner is represented by a high pole which when installed is followed by sword fights and wrestling. *Samarāṅgaṇa Sūtradhāra* mentions about the manufacture of divine staff, its erection and festival (*SS* XVII). People keep awake all night around it, singing, dancing and making merry (*SS* XVII.104.141-42, 191).

Vasantotsava is mentioned in the opening of *Ratnāvalī* while Bhoja calls it Suvasantaka. It occurs in Caitra when the mango trees are in blossom. Jayamaṅgala mentions that both these festivals are characterized by music and dance. Vasantotsava is also called Madanotsava in which Bhoja says Kāmadeva is worshipped by ladies, on the *Caitra Śīta Caturdaśī* (KS) wearing saffron-coloured dresses.[45]

They also play Ekaśālmali decked with flowers, and playing the blind man's buff. Raghavan gives a number of references to *aśokottamsika* and the use of these references to interpret the motif of *śālabhañjikā* in Indian sculpture. When beautiful damsels kick the *aśoka* tree with their delicate feet, decked with *alaktaka* paint and tinkling anklets, the tree bursts into blossom and the damsels deck themselves with fresh *aśoka* flowers. The act of *aśokadohada* is mentioned by Kālidāsa in *Mālavikāgnimitra*, the only place in a *nāṭaka* where it integrates with the plot of the play. It is believed that the tree requires *upacāra*s from the ladies before that gives forth flowers, such actions as spitting of chewed betel, half drunk wine, embracing, kicking and so on. The *aśokottamsika* of Bhoja is Aśoka Vihāra for Śāradātanaya. Thus we notice the woman and tree motif in literature and art even in the medieval period.

Another *krīḍā* is the *cūtabhañjikā*, plucking of fresh clusters of mango blossoms, offered as arrows to cupid and bedecking them. Kālidāsa in *Śākuntalā* also mentions this *krīḍā* in Act VI, whereas *Śṛṅgāra Prakāśa* mentions this as *sahakāra bhañjikā* among group sports (*saṁbhūya krīḍās*). Jayamaṅgala describes it as eating mangoes and not the blossoms. Raghavan observes that these kinds of amusements for couples and ladies in the gardens were mentioned as early as Pāṇini's times. They have also been found apt for the interpretation of the common sculptural motif of *śālabhañjikā* and other such images.[46]

Vasanta also calls for a play with water filled in syringes and spraying on each other. It is known as *udakasvedikā* by Bhoja and *sṛgakrīḍā* by Jayamaṅgala. The last two sports namely *cūtalatikā* or *navalatikā* will be discussed in Chapter 5 in support of the sculptures illustrating these *krīḍā*s.

The *vinoda*s mentioned for *grīṣma* (summer) are *salila-krīḍā* (water sport), *udyānayātrā* (visit to a park), *puṣpavācayikā* (playing with flowers), *navāmrakhādikā* (eating fresh mangoes), *cūtamādhavī, navasamāgama* and others.

The *varṣā* (monsoon) *vinoda*s are *śikhaṇḍilasya* and *navambuda abhyudāgama*, the enjoying of peacock dance and the welcoming of first rain clouds at hearing their rumbling noise. The game of *kadamba yuddha* is also mentioned by Bhoja and Vātsyāyana. The couples search for *kadamba* blossoms and subsequently a mock fight is enacted. In Śrāvaṇa month *ḍolovilāsa* is also performed.[47]

The *navapatrikā* of *śarada* (autumn) is mentioned by Bhoja in which men and women sit on the ground making merry, eat, drink and celebrate fictitious marriages. *Mṛṇālakhādika* is a game which is a water sport in which men and women eat the lotus stalks. Other sports are *kanduka-krīḍā*, *candrikātalana*, *haṁsalīlāvalokana*, *balikrīḍā*, *yakṣarātri*, *saritpulinakeli*, according to Śāradātanaya. Raghavan refers to *kanduka-krīḍā* very elaborately pointing to the dance form and various *cārī*s employed in this dance, *cūraṇapada*, *maṇḍalabhramaṇa*, *pañca-bindu-prasṛta*, *gatamārga*, *gomūtrikā*, etc. *Daśakumāracarita*, Chapter VI, mentions the daughter of King Tauṅgadhanva named

Kandukāvatī, who plays *kanduka-nṛtya* on *kṛttikā* of every month to propitiate Goddess Vindhyavāsinī. The commentary quotes a treatise on this dance game called *kanduka tantra*.

Yakṣarātri or Dīpāvalī, and Kaumudī Jāgaraṇa, in the month of Āśvin are celebrated by keeping awake whole night, and enjoying gambling, swing games and others in the moonlight. Some more sports like cock and ram fights, sun-bathing, drinking, and teaching pets to speak, while eating freshly roasted pulses in the fields with raw sugar cane, etc. are among the known ones.

Pratihārīs/Female Attendants, Kañcukins and Dancing Girls from Epigraphy and Literature

It is an accepted fact that dancing girls (among them *devadāsīs*) were dedicated to major temples (Śaiva, Vaiṣṇava, Śākta) of India (more so in south India but also to a notable extent in the north) all through the medieval period. Indian epigraphy can furnish authentic reference to the activity of dancing in temples, the proficiency of women at dancing and the socio-economic condition of many such families that dedicated themselves to the temple. Even Sanskrit literature furnishes enough evidence to the historicity of certain social/religious/cultural institutions like *devadāsī*, *kañcukin* and *pratihārī* systems in the medieval period.

The following references are collected from secondary sources assembled by historians and Indologists. The Harṣanātha Temple at Sīkar was presented with many maidens, so mentions the Harṣanātha Temple Inscription of the time of Vigraharāja II (VS 1030).[48]

An inscription found from Kālañjar of the Candella period mentions that the Mahāpratihāra Saṅgrāma Singh had a court dancer by name Padmāvatī. Many dance performances were organized in Nīlakaṇṭha Temple during this time.[49]

A fragmentary copper-plate inscription of Alhaṇa (VS 1205) records the arrangements made by various rulers for courtesans and musicians attached to the temples of Cāṇḍāleśvara and Tripuruṣadeva. The debate broke out when Rājā Jojaladeva of Nadol ordered the courtesans to join the royal processions in order to punish learned people, old men and others who tried to interfere with this time-honoured custom.[50]

While exploring the medieval cultural history, an interesting debate between the royal class patronizing the institution of prostitution and the resenting Jaina monks has come to light.

Among the puritanic Jaina monks, Haribhadra Sūri raised his voice against the above practice, including the Kharataras and others which led rulers like Jojaladeva to issue their edicts. Haribhadra's pupil Uddyotana Sūri wrote an allegorical story named *Upamitibhāvaprapañcakathā*, to carry the message in his own way to the people.[51]

It appears that the participation of monks in dance and music as part of the temple worship was a normal practice against which certain Jaina monks raised their voice. As part of Jinavallabha's anti-*caityāvāsa* (worshippers of the *caitya*) propaganda, *Saṅgha Paṭṭaka*, is a specimen of his writing which criticizes those monks whose life was interfered by singing of musicians, dancing of courtesans (in front of the deity) sounding of drums and crowding of spectators wearing garlands.[52]

Conversely, courtesans added magnificence to the glory of the ruler and were a major source of income to the state. The Bhīnmāl inscriptions of VS 1306, 1334, and 1345 convey elaborate arrangements which were made for the *pramadā-kūla* of the Sun Temple of Jagat Swāmin.[53] From *Moharājaparājaya* it is learned that Kumārapāla Cāḷukya tried to eradicate many social evils from his dominions, but for prostitution he says that nothing is lost or gained from its removal or continuance.[54]

According to *Kāvya Kalpalatā Vr̥tti*, a Jaina work of the thirteenth century, there is a general rule cited, in which the ruler should always be attended upon by courtesans in the royal court.[55] *Kādambarī* and *Priyadarśikā* of Bāṇa and Harṣa mention that the courtesans bathed the ruler and even accompanied him to the temple and danced in front of his favourite deity.

Jinadatta Sūri, the pupil of Jinavallabha (d. VS 1167) who propagated the *Kharatara-gaccha*, adopted Apabhraṁśa to popularize his ideas. His *Carcarī*, *Upadeśarasāyana* and *Kāla-Svarūpa-Kulaka*, were set to music and sung while dancing.[56]

Some epigraphical references from Bhoja Paramāra's time are collected here to understand the issues of the times and how the institution of dancing girls dedicated to temples may be understood.

The Sudi inscription of the reign of Someśvara I dated CE 1054, refers to dancing girls as members of the organizing staff of the temple.[57] Kalhaṇa refers to the *devadāsīs* in the temples of Kashmir and Merutuṅga in the Kumāra Vihāra in Somanātha Paṭṭana.[58]

Alberuni observed that the kings maintained the institution of *devadāsīs* for the benefit of their revenue even in the teeth of opposition by brāhmaṇa priests. Kings made these dancing girls as a source of attraction to their subjects for meeting the expenditure of the armies out of the revenue derived therefrom.[59]

This practice of maintaining *devadāsīs* in temples is as old as Kauṭilya, but there was no attempt before the eleventh century to pool together all dancing girls, attached to all the temples of a particular region, with a view to adding to the attraction of a particular religious festival. A tenth-century inscription from Rajasthan confirms the statement of Alberuni. It records the instructions of a chieftain to his descendants that if the arrangement that he had made about the services of the dancing girls at different temples was interfered with by ascetics and brāhmaṇas, they should at once be stopped.[60]

Merutuṅga in *Prabandha Cintāmaṇi* refers to hetaera poetess of Gujarat, who pleased the Paramāra king Bhoja.[61] He also tells the story of Cauḷa Devī of Paṭṭana, a courtesan who remained faithful to her lover during his long absence. The great-grandfather of Kumārapāla was born of this Cauḷa Devī.[62] Dancers thronged the temple courtyards and the palaces of the kings.[63] The above data has been supported by inscriptions from different parts of India. In the plan of a palace, Bhoja had included in his treatise, *inter alia*, the construction of a dancing hall, a theatre and a gymasium.[64] In the same chapter a reference to a music hall has also been given. The well-known architectural text — *Aparājitapṛcchā* as well describes the various kinds of dances with their main characters.[65]

The *Kuvalayamālā*[66] of Uddyotana Sūri describes that to the temples of Avantī were attached *vilāsinīs* who gave musical concerts, plied *morchals* (wind instruments) and held umbrellas. In one instance, the author describes the scene of heaven on earth in which some *vilāsinīs* hold pitchers, fans, fly whisks, mirrors, etc. while some *apsaras*es held *vīṇās*, *mr̥daṅgas*. Some moved langurously and danced. This implies that heavenly activities of the court were recreated in the temple courtyards where the *vilāsinī-devadāsīs* impersonated the roles of the heavenly *apsaras*.

In *Kuṭṭanīmattam*,[67] 563 there is mention about *devadāsīs* who carved their livelihood from the temple. In *Samayamātr̥kā*[68] of Kṣemendra, it is recorded that the *devadāsīs* received grains in exchange for their services. They performed only before the God. *Śr̥ṅgāra-Mañjarī*[69] cites an example of a beautiful courtesan known as Lāvaṇya Sundarī who danced only in front of the deity in the temple of Bhaillasvāmi at Vidiśā. The above reference has been interpreted by Moti Chandra who describes *devadāsīs* as some kind of courtesans on the basis of their proficiency in music, dance and the other 64 arts. In my view, a *devadāsī* and a *gaṇikā* should not be equated for their functions because their respective functions are targeted at two different categories of audiences. This distinction on microlevel is rendered insignificant by the esteemed scholar.[70]

Other types of female attendants need to be looked into as we get many figures of women holding weapons in temple and *stūpa* sculptures — are they *pratihārīs* or *apsaras*? It was interesting to observe that the sword of the king was generally held by a female attendant who would be called a *khaḍga-vāhinī*. She appears to be the female counterpart of the *asiggāhaka* of the Jātaka stories.[71] According to S.P. Tiwari, the characters employed in the roles of keeping charge of the king's sword or bow and addressed as Yavanīs in the Sanskrit dramas, as mentioned above are the same as the *khaḍga-vāhinīs*. From Kauṭilya's specific reference to them we may presume that they were Greek or of Amazonian origin.

Bāṇa's works are full of descriptions of personal attendants of royal courts, of which *Kādambarī* has an instance of King Śūdraka. Bāṇa says that when King Śūdraka after lunch reappeared in the audience hall, he was sitting with his feet resting on the foot stool, which were gently massaged by his sword bearer. She was doing this with her delicate hands after placing, for the time being, the long thin sword on her lap. She herself was seated on the floor of the audience hall. This shows that besides the *pratihārī* it was the *khaḍga-vāhinī* who was closer to the king and followed him everywhere and attended upon him as a *dāsī* shampooing his feet as well. In fact, if one begins to notice carefully, there are numerous sculptures from Mathurā, Amarāvatī, Ajantā and other early sites depicting the *khaḍgadhārī*. A detailed discussion on individual *devāṅganā* motif will be followed in Chapters 5 and 6.

The *Bṛhat-Kathā-Śloka-Saṁgraha* of Buddhaswāmi,[72] written in chaste Sanskrit some time in Gupta period, is a summary of the *Bṛhat-Kathā* of Guṇāḍhya. This collection of verses is divided into *lambhaka*s which revolve around the fact that the hero Sanudasa in each *sarga* contracts a new marital alliance. It throws light on female attendants of this kind. The female attendants of the royal palace were kept satisfied with drinks, ornaments, clothes, garlands and sweet words. These were the same as *antaḥpurika* (members of the women's quarters), chief of them were known as *dauvārika* or *vetragrahiṇī* (*BKSS* II.19) referring to their role as doorkeepers.

The rakes formed part of the royal entourage to which literature and art provide enormous proof. The *Bṛhat-Kathā* refers to *Viṭaśāstra*, i.e. the lore of Rakes (or ways of Rakes?) which the girls of the courtesan's quarters were expected to learn as part of their education. Attached to their quarters, was a shrine of God Kāmadeva, in which the deity was worshipped by offering a *pradakṣiṇā* (circumambulation) to him. In X.76-77, the actual *veśa* is described as having the appearance of a royal palace in which a number of hermaphrodites (*yosidvarṣavarapriyā*) were employed.

Besides the courtesans' quarters, mention of *prekṣaka kula* and *raṅgāṅganam,* i.e. auditorium and stage are found, on which the two *nṛtyācārya*s are said to have come and done *namaskāra* (XI.3). *Kañcukin* or chamberlain is the attendant of the women's apartment. Kauṭilya mentions his job, the designation and also the uniform, viz. the dress of a *kañcukī*. The *varṣavara*s (eunuchs) and other attendants of the *abhayagarika* are also mentioned in the *Arthaśāstra*. It describes the *kañcukī* as the chief, *kañcukoṣṇiṣṭa*, because they were all wearing *kañcuka* (a close jacket), and *uṣṇīśa* (the turban). *Kañcukī* would generally accompany the king everywhere, and being the king's attendant, would remain in the forefront of the palace activities. It is said that while Sītā was being brought out of the palace of Rāvaṇa, the attendants of the inner apartment, wearing *kañcuka* and *uṣṇīśa* and holding cane-sticks in their hands, cleared her way to the palanquin.[73] While dwelling on *abhayagarika*s, Bharata, in his *Nāṭyaśāstra*, offers details regarding not only the *kañcukī*, but also other attendants of the harem. *Kañcukī* knows the nature of the women of the harem and can keep them under his control. In one MSS of the *NŚ*, *kañcukī* is described as an expert in the art of controlling women.[74] *Kañcukī* appears prominently in the plays of Kālidāsa such as Latavya, the *kañcukī* of *Vikramorvaśīyam* who finds it difficult to handle the women of the harem in his advancing age. The reference to *vetra-yaṣṭi* in *Śākuntalam*, concerns the old *kañcukī*, whose cane staff which was once the mark of his office in the female apartment of the palace, has now become, in course of time, an indispensable object of support for him in his tottering old age.[75]

In the *Kādambarī*, Bāṇa takes up the description of the birthday celebrations of Candrāpīḍā and Vaiśampāyana describing the joyous abandon with which the ladies of the harem and their maids, were celebrating the happy occasion. Bāṇa says that their pranks did not spare even the old and the sober looking chamberlains. They were playing jokes upon the multitude (*kādambaka*) of ageing chamberlains, by tying the silken upper garments round their necks and dragging them.

The term *vidambi* could mean teasing, joking and pranking. The reference to playing of joke by tying the upper garment (*uttarīya*) is interesting, because even V.S. Agrawala refers to a term, *celukkhepa*, from Pāli which means the waving of the upper garment as a token of joy. A similar reference is made by Harṣa in *Nāgānanda*, where a *viṭa* pulls away a scarf thrown round the neck of the court jester, who wants to run away. *Amarakośa* mentions *kañcukī* and his synomyms, like *sauvidala*, *sthāpatya* and *sauvida*. These terms, as explained by the commentators of *Amara*, tend to mean one and the same thing, namely that a *kañcukī* was to look after the ladies of the harem. Figures of dwarfish males holding a crooked stick are found at many sites of Buddhist and Hindu art, leading to the above investigation.

Bāṇa in *Kādambarī* mentions *mahāttarikā*, the female official, in-charge of the bed-chamber called Kulavardhanā. She is called efficient by long experience in the service of the royal household. She is even well skilled in all the auspicious rites.[76] Tiwari differs with Agrawala in his comparison of *mahāttarikā* of queen Vilāsavatī, with the *pratihārī* of Indumatī, called Sunandā, because the lady attendant of the royal bed-chamber and an ordinary female doorkeeper are altogether different. According to S.P. Tiwari, in the *Vaijayantī Kośa* of Yādavaprakāśa, it is described that *mahāttarī* is an old lady-attendant of the harem who was well versed in all the auspicious rites. The above information on women of the palace has raised our general understanding about the complexity of roles played by the various courtly attendants and thus to conclude every *apsaras* or *devadāsī* as courtesan is a bit short-sighted way of looking at female characters in ancient Indian society. These literary images cited here tend to take on an archetypal role in interpreting the *devāṅganā* sculptures.

References from Architectural Texts for Devāṅganā Placement and Other Dance References

So far we have examined literary material, now we have collated verses from some architectural texts which refer specifically to the placement of *devāṅganā* figures. Since temple architecture is the main focus of this research, the references collated here elaborate upon the architecture of the temple alone and not the *stūpa*, *vihāra*, or *caitya*. The references to *śālabhañjikā* on *stūpa,* etc. will be taken up in the context of the evolution of the *śālabhañjikā* motif itself in the chapter on sculpture. The textual references collected here are not exhaustive and newer material is yet to come to light. The present information bears testimony to the tradition of placing *apsaras*, *kumārikā*, *śālabhañjikā*, *varāṅganā*, *surāṅganā*, and *devāṅganā* type of figures on the *vitāna*, *stambha*, *jaṅghā*, *śikhara* and such other parts of the temple. Curiously, only two texts refer to their number, names and imagery while the rest only suggest their generic names as listed above. Their ritualistic or religious purpose is seldom attested to, although they are generally invoked to protect, decorate, bestow peace and prosperity. Their cultic association with Śākta or Śaiva sects is absent since in texts and in practice, they are freely incorporated and represented. It appears that even though their iconography and individual names are seldom mentioned by the architectural texts before the fifteenth century, their representation in sculptures from western India to eastern India, retains staggering uniformity of form and imagery. Hence there must have been an oral exchange of ideas between sculptors of various regions, shared iconography of gods, goddesses and other semi-divine figures must have been common knowledge. Even in texts dealing with *Pratimā Lakṣaṇa* the iconography of Viṣṇu, Śiva, Devī, etc. are mentioned in detail, but the *apsaras* are generally not described (except for *Kṣīrārṇava* and *Śilpa Prakāśa*). It appears that information on *apsaras* may have circulated in the form of *deśī* literature in colloquial parlance and widely shared by authors of classical texts like Bhoja and Bhuvanadeva. The following passages are extracted from architectural texts focusing on *apsaras* and describe their placement on temples, palaces, courts, city gates, etc. The texts referred here are *Samarāṅgaṇa Sūtradhāra, Śilpa Prakāśa, Aparājitapṛcchā, Vaikhānasīya Atri Saṁhitā, Lakṣaṇa Samuccaya, Vāstusūtra Upaniṣad, Kṣīrārṇava, Vṛkṣārṇava.*

SAMARĀṄGAṆA SŪTRADHĀRA

It is a text written by Bhoja Paramāra around the middle of the eleventh century. Bhoja was a great builder and a learned scholar. His text on architecture is like an encyclopedia, referring to the architectural traditions in Mālwā region in particular, and northern Indian style (*Nāgara*) in general. In the section on Meru-prāsāda, he describes that the *toraṇa* should be adorned with *makara*, heads of elephants, leaves as well as groups of *apsaras*.[77] The pillar design contains an elaborate prescription using auspicious motifs for its decoration. The pillars should be many faceted and contain many sections. These should be decorated with painted design everywhere, auspicious signs, *candraśālā* along with *toraṇa* and beautiful *cāmaradhāriṇīs* (57, p. 404).[78] The placement of elephant heads, highly intoxicated and in playful mood is also indicated. The Vidyādhara couples should also be adorned here who are in playful mood (57, p. 404).[79] It should be surrounded by groups of *siddhas*, *gandharvas*, *yakṣas*, *devas*, *apsaras* and *kinnaras* holding *vīṇā* (57, p. 404).

In the *vimānāvalī* (dome of the roof), groups of divine *apsaras*es should be adorned, highly immersed in play continuously with beautiful swaying movements (57, p. 404). Even *nāgakanyā* and *kadamba* should also be used for adornment everywhere on every storey (57, p. 404).[80] It appears that the figures of *apsaras*, *nāgakanyās*, *kinnaras*, etc. should be placed in the *vitāna* as well as on the *bhūmis* of the *jaṅghā* and the *stambha*. But their detailed imagery and significance are not told by Bhoja explicitly. At the Paramāra and Solaṅkī temples in Gujarat, Rajasthan and Madhya Pradesh, all these features can be identified.

ŚILPA PRAKĀŚA

According to *Śilpa Prakāśa*, the Orissan temple architectural text,[81] the pillar should be decorated with *nāga-nāyikā* who is a giver of wealth, corn and good fortune (1.225, p. 32).[82] No further description of this is given. There is another section in this chapter called *āvaraṇa devatās* which include *dikpāla*, *mahāvidyās*, etc. (1.256, p. 35).[83] It is followed by a section on *alasā*, which in local terminology is referred to as *nārībandha* or *kanyābandha*, and it is indispensable in architecture. The main purpose of embellishment is indicated here — a house without a wife, as frolic without a woman, so a monument without (figure of) a woman will be inferior and bear no fruit (1.392).[84] *Gandharvas*, *yakṣas*, *rākṣasas*, *paññagas* (*nāgas*), *kinnaras* become enchanted on seeing the graceful postures of women (1.393).[85] Contemplated in various postures, she is known as *alasā* and it should be placed in *gavākṣa*, *śikhara*, walls and other parts of the *mukhaśālā* (1.394-395). The names given to them (recommended by the Śāstras) are Alasā, Toraṇā, Mugdhā, Māninī, Ḍālamālikā, Padmagandhā, Darpaṇā, Vinyāsā, Dhyānākarṣitā, Ketakībharaṇā,

Mātṛmūrti, Cāmarā, Gunthanā, Nartakī, Sukasārikā, Nūpurapādikā, and Mardalā.[86] These are the seventeen most important types of *alasā*. There is no sequence or order of placement indicated in this text. The *alasā* also does not have any relation with *dikpāla* or the major forms of the gods and their placement in the temple architecture seems to be independent and uncanonical, although we do observe that they are placed next to *dikpāla*s, *ṛṣi*s and major gods on temple walls. But *Śilpa Prakāśa* mentions a *yantra* to denote the posture of the indolent *nāyikā* with predominant oblique lines to indicate *tribhaṅga* posture. The text also indicates the position of the palms — *caṇḍita* (palms turned upwards), *spandita* (palms turned downwards) as the two movements prescribed for the *alasā*.[87]

The various *alasā kanyā*s are described thus denoting their actions and states of mind:

1. Alasā — indolent, make *caṇḍita* or *spandita* hand movements.
2. Toraṇā — leaning on a doorway.
3. Mugdhā — innocent and young.
4. Māninī — resentful or offended.
5. Dālamālikā — garlanding herself with a branch.
6. Padmagandhā — smelling the lotus.
7. Darpaṇā — holding a mirror.
8. Vinyāsā — having her mind fixed in meditation.
9. Dhyānākarṣitā — attracting other's attention.
10. Ketakībharaṇā — wearing flowers.
11. Mātṛmūrti — image of a mother.
12. Cāmarā — holding a fly whisk.
13. Gunthanā — hiding herself, showing her back holding drapery, flowers, fan.
14. Nartakī — dancer.
15. Śukasārikā — playing with a parrot.
16. Nūpurapādikā — wearing ankle bells.
17. Mardalā — drummer.

This attractive *nārībandha* should be placed on the *śikhara* and other parts like *gavākṣa,* etc. This list could be compared with the list from *Kṣīrārṇava* to find out how many of the *alasā*s correspond with each other and the sculpture representation on the whole. The texts from different regions do vary in details but not radically.

APARĀJITAPṚCCHĀ

It is written under the influence of *Samarāṅgaṇa Sūtradhāra* in the reign of Kumārapāla by Bhuvanadevācārya, during the later part of the twelfth and first half of the thirteenth century.[88] It says that on the *vitāna* place 8, 12, 16, 24, 32, 64 *vidyādhara*s and above them *varāṅganā*s (190.14).[89] They should hold string and leather instruments, and perform acting and dancing movements creating sounds of singing and music (190.15).[90] It also mentions that in the decoration of the house, village or town, make a *nṛtyaśālā* to the north of *ghaṭisthāna* on whose *vitāna śālabhañjikā* should be made along with *ghaṇṭā* (95.26).[91] The *jaṅghā* should be in 35 parts and it should have *stambha*, *nāsikā* and *phālanā*s on all the sides of the *sandhāra* (*prāsāda*). On the *mūlanāsā* and on all sides of the *stambha*s *gaja, siṁha, vyāla* and *makara* should be made (127.21-22).[92] On all the sides of the *karṇa*s eight *dikpāla*s should be placed in the *pradakṣiṇā* order. Naṭeśa facing the east, Andhaka facing the south and Caṇḍikā with canine teeth facing the north side. Compassionate *śāsanadevī*s should be placed in all the directions (127.23, 24).[93] On the *vārimārga munīndra* should be placed while ascetic figures should be in the *pralīna*.

The placement of decorative figures on gateways to a city is also mentioned by Aparājitā:

> On all the four corners make repeated decoration everywhere, after every 3,000 measures should be a pair of *vidyādharī* and a *yoddhā*.[94]
>
> While on the four sides of the royal court's exit place *yakṣī*s for decoration. Embellish each wall with gems in all the *dviśālā*s. On each *pratibhadra* of the *śālā* delineate lotuses which are the favourites of the kings. In the *vitāna* place unusual hanging *lūma*s from the centre while various forms of royal sports be represented in different shapes. On the upper part of the *stambha* place *śālabhañjikā* statues.[95]

It is only here that the term *pratimā* is denoted.

A number of references have been brought to light from the Āgama which enlighten us about the parts of temple architecture in which the *apsaras* should be placed.

Kāśyapa Śilpa Paṭala (chapter 48, 49-57) describes the form of the *apsaras* as very bright with long and heavy hair, decorated with various flowers and draped with silk clothes. Their thighs should be thick and touching each other, waist should be narrow, but face should be serene and slightly smiling, their bodies should be smeared with different fragrances. Arranged in groups they should be installed in interrelated movements on the *bhadrapīṭha* in *samabhaṅga* and they should be seven in number.

Vaikhānasīya Atri Saṁhitā (Samūrta Canadhikaraṇa 7.29) mentions the *maṇḍapa* as the place for pure and divine *apsaras* and five of them should be placed at five places in the *maṇḍapa*. It can be noted that the number varies from five and seven to sixteen which are all auspicious numbers. Even at Aṅgkor Vat in Cambodia, figures of *apsaras* in groups of five and seven are placed on temple walls, both in the interior as well as the exterior.

Lakṣaṇa Samuccaya (chapter 26, 9-11)[96] is more precise in stating the placement of the *kumārikā*s. The twenty-eight *kumārikā*s should be carved fully all around on the *stambha*s of the *bhitti* and not on the *kuḍya* (plaster on the relief wall). Referring to the *maṇḍapa*, which should be visible from all the four sides clearly and divided into thirty parts, four pillars in its centre should be installed with twelve *kumārikā*s. Further it states that on the corners, foreparts and sides of the pillars place *kumārikā*s. The figures of numerous such *kumārikā*s can be seen when walking into the *maṇḍapa*s of Kumbhariā and Mt. Ābu temples in Rajasthan.

According to *Vaikhānasa Kāśyapa Janakhaṇḍa* (chpater 32)[97] the temple wall should be decorated with *apsaras*, *yakṣa*, *gandharva*, and *nāga*, as if they have descended from the heaven in a playful mood. This group should be represented in a beautiful and enchanting way which should give pleasure to the eye.

VĀSTUSŪTRA UPANIṢAD

This is a text with a difference. Its attributed author, Pippalāda, has divided it into six *prapāṭhaka*s just like the *Praśna Upaniṣad* of the *Atharvaveda*.[98] It is known as *Vāstusūtra* and not *Śilpasūtra*, because it deals more with the layout, and composition of sculptures and not so much with modelling of forms. It proposes a fundamental grid structure for images which are created using geometrical and mathematical configurations. The *khilapañjara*, as it is known, indicates basic disposition and movement of figures in space. In the composition for an image of the main deity who occupies the central Brahma-Kṣetra the upper Daiva-Kṣetra is occupied by the *yakṣa*s, *gandharva*s and *apsaras*. The lower *kṣetra* is occupied by the adorers, human worshippers and the vehicles of the divinities (*VSU* 8. 9). The *apsaras* entertain the gods in diverse ways and through the representation of singers of praises, the images become particularly beautiful (*VSU* 25). Thus, details referring to composition and placement of minor figures such as *apsaras*es and *gandharva*s on temple walls is immensely significant.

PRĀSĀDA MAṆḌANA

This is written by Sūtradhāra Maṇḍana in the reign of Rāṇā Kumbhā of Chittor between CE 1433 and 1468. In the reference dealing with temple parts, he mentions that the *vidyādhara thara* should be seven parts broad and ten parts long. On this make beautiful dancing *śālabhañjikā*s. Decorate the centre of the *maṇḍapa*, *vitāna* with paintings and *devāṅganā*s in dancing mode along with the Paurāṇic themes (*PM* 7.32, 34).

KṢĪRĀRṆAVA/VṚKṢĀRṆAVA

Three texts were written during the fifteenth century in Gujarat, with information recycled from earlier architectural texts with new focus on images such as *apsaras* and *devāṅganā*s, namely *Vṛkṣārṇava*, *Kṣīrārṇava* and *Dīpārṇava*. Dhaky observes that *Vṛkṣārṇava* belongs to the first half of the fifteenth century, while *Kṣīrārṇava* (also known as *Nāradapṛcchā*) belongs to the beginning of the fifteenth century. *Dīpārṇava* derives from *Aparājitapṛcchā* and

Kṣīrārṇava while *Vāstuvidyā* is a sixteenth-century architectural text.

While describing the emergence of the *caturmukha mahāprāsāda*[99] the author of *Kṣīrārṇava* mentions the measurements of its parts and the placement of the figures on its *maṇḍovara*. The figures consist of *lokapāla*, *dikpāla* and *devāṅganā*, who should be placed in the *ratha-pratiratha* playing on musical instruments and dancing gleefully. Indra and other gods, with *āyudha* and vehicles, should also be made along with *gaṇa*s and attendants, as if celebrating some festive occasion. The dancing *devāṅganā*s should look with downcast eyes and aiming arrows or taking a step forward with the left foot. Some *devāṅganā*s should be shown dancing with left hand descending towards the left side as if demonstrating the left side of her body.

The following few verses throw light on the placement of specific *devāṅganā*s on certain directions conjointly with the *dikpāla*s. West is the place of Varuṇa, who is flanked by Rambhā holding bow and arrow; north-west is the territory of Vāyu, who is to be represented dancing in a circular manner some sort of *tāṇḍava nṛtya* holding a scarf. Mañjughoṣā is to be represented to his right. In Kubera's abode in the north direction, padminī *devāṅganā* is to be placed dancing in an amorous way with one hand above the head. In *īśāna* (direction of the north-east) install Menakā emerging from the heaven to descend

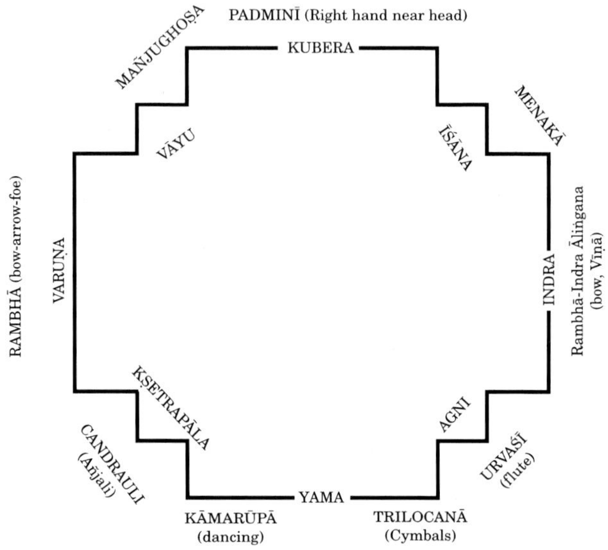

Details of *Devāṅganā*s and *Dikpāla*s based on Kṣīrārṇava.

on the earth. Even show Indra embracing Rambhā (in the east direction), who holds beautiful bow-arrow and *vīṇā* with her. Urvaśī should be shown playing a flute in the *agni-koṇa*, while in the south make Trilocanā with cymbals and Kāmarūpa to dance with Yama. In the south-west direction, place *kṣetrapāla* and *candraulī* holding *añjalī hasta*.

I have observed that the above description is not consistent with the temple sculptures and some of the *devāṅganā*s do not have a specific form, since only their names are given without reference to imagery. It is important to note that the use of the term *devāṅganā* in place of *apsaras* is unique to this text, suggestive of a regional preference such as *nārībandha* and *alasā* in Orissa.

Here, I compile another list of thirty-two *devāṅganā*s from *Kṣīrārṇava*, who according to the text should be placed in *pradakṣiṇā* order on the *jaṅghā* starting from the *īśāna* corner (north-east) with Menakā. The thirty-two *devāṅganā*s are: Menakā, Līlāvatī, Vidhicitrā, Sundarī, Śubhagāminī, Haṁsāvalī, Sarvakalā, Karpūramañjarī, Padminī, Gūḍhaśabdā-Padmanetrā, Citriṇī, Putravallabhā, Gaurī, Gāndhārī, Devaśākhā, Marīcikā, Candrāvalī, Candrarekhā, Sugandhā, Śatrumardinī, Māninī, Mānahaṁsā, Susvabhāvā, Bhāvacandrā, Mṛgākṣī, Ūrvaśī, Rambhā, Mañjughoṣā, Jayā, Vijayā, Candravaktrā and Kāmarūpā.

The text says,

> place all these *devāṅganā*s on *maṇḍovara* and *vitāna* of the temples of Brahmā, Viṣṇu, Śiva, Sūrya and Jina. Some of the *devāṅganā*s could be repeated more than once on the same temple.

Kṣīrārṇava describes how each of the *devāṅganā*s should be represented according to their prescribed iconography and description:

1. Menakā — holding bow and arrow, left leg raised.
2. Līlāvatī — amorously shunning laziness.
3. Vidhicitrā — holding mirror and putting *bindī*.
4. Sundarī — simply dancing.
5. Śubhagāminī — pulling out a thorn from the foot.

6. Haṁsāvalī — putting on *pāyala*, lotus-eyed.
7. Sarvakalā — dancing with *varada-* and *cintana-mudrā*.
8. Karpūramañjarī — dancing in nude while bathing.
9. Padminī — holding a stalk of lotus.
10. Padmanetrā — holding *abhaya-hasta,* a child stands by her side.
11. Citriṇī — dancing with left hand on the head.
12. Putravallabhā — one who has a baby on her side.
13. Gaurī — killing a lion.
14. Gāndhārī — a special one dancing with right hand aloft.
15. Devaśākhā — one dancing a circular dance.
16. Maricikā — aiming a bow-arrow and looking at the left side.
17. Candrāvalī — looking in front with *añjalī-hasta*, beautiful eyed.
18. Candrarekhā — writing a letter, her forehead is broad like the half-moon.
19. Sugandhā — dancing in circles holding the moon aloft.
20. Śatrumardinī — holding knives and dancing.
21. Māninī — holding flower garlands and dancing.
22. Mānahaṁsā — dancing with her back visible.
23. Susvabhāvā — one whose body is bent in *caturbhaṅgī*, leg is lifted and hands raised above the head.
24. Bhāvacandrā — one who is dancing with her hands and the feet are in *yoga-mudrā*.
25. Mṛgākṣī — dancing with full bloom and beauty.
26. Ūrvaśī — killing an *asura* with a *khaḍga* and pulling him by his *śikhā*.
27. Rambhā — holding knives in both hands and dancing with her right foot lifted up.
28. Mañjughoṣā — she dances in circles holding *khaḍga* in both hands.

29. Jayā — dancing with a water pot on her head.
30. Mohinī — dancing and embracing the male companion.
31. Candravaktrā — dancing gracefully by lifting one foot.
32. Tilottamā — either holding *mañjīrā* or *puṣpa-bāṇa* and dancing.

In this manner, *devāṅganās* should be represented in the *jaṅghā*, *vitāna* and the celestial places on the four sides of the *maṇḍovara* and the *maṇḍapa*, whereas the *munis*, *tāpas*, *vyāla* and others should be arranged in the *jalantara* or *salilāntara*.

P.O. Sompura, who has edited and translated this text and also designed new temples on ancient sites, such as Kāyāvarohaṇa and Somanātha in Gujarat, has incorporated these figures in his temple plan giving new significance to an age-old tradition, seldom elaborated to this extent prior to the writing of this text, thus giving a new lease of life to the *apsaras-devāṅganā* imagery.

References

1. A.A. Macdonell, *Vedic Mythology*, Strassburg, 1898, rpt., Delhi, 1981, pp. 124-25, most of the information below has been compiled based on Macdonell.
2. Ibid., p. 125.
3. S.K. Das: (i) *Śakti or Divine Power*, Calcutta, 1934, p. 741; (ii) *Indian Culture*, vol. VIII, p. 67; (iii) M.C.P. Srivastava, *Mother Goddess in Indian Art, Archaeology and Literature*, Delhi, 1979, p. 33.
4. A.B. Keith, *The Religion and Philosophy of the Vedas and Upaniṣads*, Harvard Oriental Series, 1925, p. 199.
5. Stella Kramrisch, *Hindu Temple*, Calcutta, 1946.
6. Macdonell, op. cit., 1898, p. 87.
7. V.S. Agrawala, *Indian Art*, Varanasi, 1965, p. 325.
8. Macdonell, op. cit., 1898, p. 88.
9. Ibid., p. 108.
10. Ibid., p. 112.
11. Ibid., pp. 112-13.
12. C. Sivaramamurti, "Amarāvatī Sculptures in the Madras Government Museum", *Bulletin of the Madras Government Museum*, vol. IV, new series, Madras, 1977, p. 82.
13. Ibid., p. 84.
14. C. Sivaramamurti, *Śrī-Lakṣmī in Indian Art,* New Delhi: Kanak Publications, 1982.
15. Macdonell, op. cit., 1898, p. 134.
16. Ibid., pp. 134-37.
17. A.B. Keith, *The Religion and Philosophy of the Veda and Upaniṣads*, Harvard Oriental Series, vol. 31, 1st edn., 1925, pp. 179-84, this section is compiled from data collected from Keith.
18. Macdonell, op. cit., 1898, p. 135.
19. Bharata, *Nāṭyaśāstra*, tr. Manmohan Ghosh, Calcutta, 1950.
20. (a) *Agni Purāṇa*, chapter 19 from Vettam Mani, *Purāṇic Encyclopaedia: A Comprehensive Dictionary with Special Reference to the Epic and Purāṇic Literature*, 1st edn. 1964 (Malayalam), 1975 (English); (b) *Mahābhārata*, Ādi-Parva, 67-83, Vettam Mani, 1975.
21. (a) *Vālmikī Rāmāyaṇa*, Bāla-Kāṇḍa, 45.32, from Keith, 1925; (b) *Viṣṇu Purāṇa*, H.H. Wilson, I.9; (c) *Agni Purāṇa*, Vettam Mani, 1975, chapter 3.
22. *Matsya Purāṇa*, Anandashram Series, no. 54, Poona, 1907.
23. *Vāyu Purāṇa*, Anandashram Series, no. 49, Poona, 1983.

24. *Brahmāṇḍa Purāṇa*, ed. J.L. Shastri, New Delhi, 1973.
25. *Viṣṇu Purāṇa*, Oriental Press, Bombay, 1889.
26. *Bhāgavata Purāṇa*, ed. J.L. Sastri, New Delhi, 1973.
27. Cornelia Dimmitt and J.A.B. Buitenen, *Classical Hindu Mythlogy*, 1st published 1978, Indian edn., New Delhi, 1983, pp. 74, 97.
28. Dimmitt and Buitenen, 1978, p. 82.
29. According to V.S. Agrawala, *Matsya Purāṇa: A Study*, Varanasi, 1963, p. 133.
30. C. Sivaramamurti, *Citrasūtra of Viṣṇudharmottara*, New Delhi, 1978.
31. V.R. Ramachandra Dikshitar, *The Purāṇa Index,* vol. III (Ya to Ha), University of Madras, 1955.
32. Vettam Mani, *Puranic Encyclopaedia* (f n. 20), New Delhi: Motilal Banarsidass, 1975 (English).
33. Ibid.
34. Ibid.
35. Mohanlal Mehta and K. Rishabha Chandra, *Āgamic Index*, vol. I, General Editor Dalsukh Malvania, Ahmedabad, 1970.
36. B. Barua, *Bharhut: Stone as a Story Teller*, Calcutta, 1934, 2nd edn., Patna, p. 54.
37. Heinrich Zimmer, *The Art of Indian Asia: Its Mythology and Transformations*, 1st published Princeton University Press, 1st Indian edn., New Delhi, 1984, vol. I, pp. 68-84.
38. Kālidāsa, *Meghadūtam*, tr. Chandra Rajan, *Kālidāsa: The Loom of Time, A Selection of his Plays and Poems*, New Delhi, 1989, p. 162.
39. Kapila Vatsyayan, *Classical Indian Dance in the Literature and the Arts*, New Delhi, 1968, 2nd edn., 1977, p. 195.
40. Ibid., p. 199.
41. Kālidāsa, *Loom of Time*, 1989, p. 116.
42. V.S. Agrawala, *Bṛhat Kathāśloka Saṁgraha: A Study*, Varanasi, 1974, p. 301.
43. Ibid., p. 302.
44. V. Raghavan, *Śṛṅgāra Prakāśa*, Madras, 1963, p. 648.
45. Ibid., p. 853.
46. Ibid., p. 652.
47. Ibid., p. 850.
48. D. Sharma, *Early Cauhān Dynasties*, New Delhi, 1959, p. 260.

49. Shishirkumar Mitra, *Early Rulers of Khajurāho*, Calcutta, 1958, pp. 178-79.
50. D. Sharma, op. cit., 1959, Appendix G (iii) and *Epigraphia Indica,* XI, p. 28.
51. Ibid., p. 222
52. Ibid., p. 224.
53. Ibid.; and Bombay Gazetteer, vol. I, part I, p. 469.
54. Ibid., p. 261; *Kumārapāla Carita*, VI.32, I.66-67.
55. Ibid., p. 261.
56. GOS XXXVI, p. I (Jinapala on Charchari) and D. Sharma, op. cit., 1959, p. 226.
57. *Epigraphia Indica*, XV, p. 85.
58. *Rājataraṅgiṇī*, VII, p. 858; P.C.C. Singhi, *Jain Mala*, p. 108.
59. Mahesh Singh, *The Paramāras*, 1984, p. 177.
60. *Epigraphia Indica*, XI, p. 28.
61. *Prabandha Cintāmaṇi*, IV, p. 93.
62. Mahesh Singh, op. cit., 1984, p. 214.
63. *Rājataraṅgiṇī*, VIII, 606, 928, 931, 944; *Prabandha Cintāmaṇi*, III, 35.37; *Inscriptions from Bengal* II, 35.41.
64. *Samarāṅgaṇa Sūtradhāra*, GOS, XV, Baroda, p. 18.
65. *Aparājitapṛcchā,* GOS, CXV, Baroda, 1950, 239, *Tāṇḍavādi Nāṭyalakṣaṇā,* p. 614.
66. Udyotanashri, *Kuvalayamālā*, ed. A.N. Upadhye, Bombay, 1957, p. 50.
67. Moti Chandra, *The World of Courtesans*, New Delhi, 1973, p. 57.
68. Kṣemendra, *Samayamātṛkā*, VIII, 83.
69. *Śṛṅgāramañjarī*, ed. Kalpana Munshi, Bombay, 1959, p. 57.
70. For a discussion on this point see critique section in the Introduction of this book.
71. S.P. Tewari, *Royal Attendants in Ancient Indian Literature, Epigraphy & Art*, New Delhi, 1987, p. 30.
72. Buddhasvami, *Bṛhat Kathā Śloka Saṁgraha*, ed. V.S. Agrawala, Indian Civilization Series, no. IV, Varanasi, 1974.
73. S.P. Tewari, op. cit., 1987.
74. *Nāṭyaśāstra*, M. Ghosh, 1950.
75. Monier-Williams vide Tewari, 1987.
76. Tewari, op. cit., 1987.

77. *Samarāṅgaṇa Sūtradhāra* (57, 46-47), ed. Ganapati Sastri, GOS, no. 25, Baroda, 1966.

78. *SS,* 57, p. 404.

79. Ibid.

80. Ibid. The above five verses are not numbered but they constitute the Meru section of the chapter 57, which covers Mervadiviṁsika *Prasāda Lakṣaṇā*. Besides Meru, the other type of *prāsāda* which contain *apsaras*, *kinnara*, *vidhyadharī*, *gandharva*s, *yakṣa*s and *śālabhañjikā* for decoration are *śrīdhara, puṣpaka, mahāvraja, ratideva, vimānam*.

81. Alice Boner and S.R. Sharma, *Śilpa Prakāśa*, *Medieval Orissan Sanskrit Text on Temple Architecture*, by Ramachandra Kaulacharya, Leiden, 1966, pp. 46-53.

82. *SP*, 1.225, p. 32.

83. *SP*, 1.256, p. 35.

84. *SP*, 1.392, p. 46.

85. *SP*, 1.393, p. 46.

86. *SP*, 1.394-95, p. 46.

87. *SP*, 1.407-481, pp. 46-53.

88. *Aparājitapṛcchā,* Bhuvanadevācārya, ed. P.A. Mankad, GOS, CXV, Baroda, 1950.

89. *AP*, 190.14.

90. *AP*, 190.14, 15. *vitāna varṇana*.

91. *AP*, 85.26: *gṛha grāma nagara śobhā*.

92. *AP*, 127.21-22

93. *AP,* 127.21-24: *nagara prāsāda vibhakti pramāṇa*.

94. *AP,* 70-21: *bhūdharādi brahma nagaram.*

95. *AP,* 77.7-11: *sabhāstakavedi nirṇaya*.

96. *Lakṣaṇā Samuccaya*, 26-9, 11. This and the above reference from *Atri Saṁhitā* were conveyed to me by M.A. Dhaky.

97. *Kāśyapa Śilpaśāstram*, ed. S.H. Ganapati Sastri, Anandashram Sanskrit Series, 1986.

98. *Vāstusūtra Upaniṣad*: *The Essence of Form in Sacred Art*, text, tr., ed. Alice Boner, S.R. Sharma, B. Bäumer, New Delhi, 1982.

99. *Kṣīrārṇava,* ed. P.O. Sompura, Palitana, 1967.

4

Weaving the Architectural Fabric

Morphology of Architectural Style and Placement of Devāṅganā Sculptures

Methodology

The architectural development of Nāgara temples in Gujarat, Rajasthan and Madhya Pradesh from the eighth to the twelfth centuries is examined in this chapter. The observations are drawn from "reading" the *maṇḍovara* patterns and the placement of various *devāṅganā* types on their facets. The exploration brings into focus only those temples which integrate figural ornamentation as part of their iconographic vocabulary, which is essentially a medieval phenomenon noted during the above period. This chapter examines various regional manifestations which are unique to those regions and enables us to formulate more accurate view of the architectural planning than a generalized opinion based on a few well-known sites.

There were two trends in *maṇḍovara* layout design and iconographic programming during the medieval period, viz. (i) one style in which no figures are placed in the *ratha*, *pratiratha*, while *bhadra* and *karṇa devakoṣṭha*s are invariably occupied by the manifestations of the presiding deity and the *dikpāla*s respectively. Even during the tenth century, this trend is observed on the *maṇḍovara* walls of sites such as Auwa, Lamba and Nāgdā, and (ii) the second trend, in contrast, brings into action a whole range of images which not only adorn every facet of walls with variety but also lend aesthetic beauty and richness of meaning. Sometimes even the recesses are occupied by *ṛṣi*s, *devāṅganā*s and many tiered sculptures.

The imagery of figures placed on the *maṇḍovara* includes aerial beings such as *gandharva*s and *apsaras*, fantastic composite creatures like *vyāla*s and *nāginī*s, terrestrial beings like *ṛṣi*s, *kanyā*s and *tapas*es; rallying in unison with other iconic deities — culminating into a pulsating vision of the cosmos. Notice this at Osiā Harihara temple group and Khajurāho — Lakṣmaṇa and Kandarīya Mahādeva temples. Therefore, it is the second trend that is relevant to my study here, because it hints at a geo-political region and dynastic time-frame during which the emergence of the *devāṅganā* imagery as part of the temple iconography becomes noticeable.

In the following sections, I have attempted to thread the

(facing page)
fig. 1. Harihara 1, north-eastern *devakulikā*, south wall, eighth century, Osiā, Jodhpur, Rajasthan.

(facing page)
fig. 2. Harihara 2, north-western *devakulikā*, north wall, eighth century, Osiā, Jodhpur, Rajasthan.

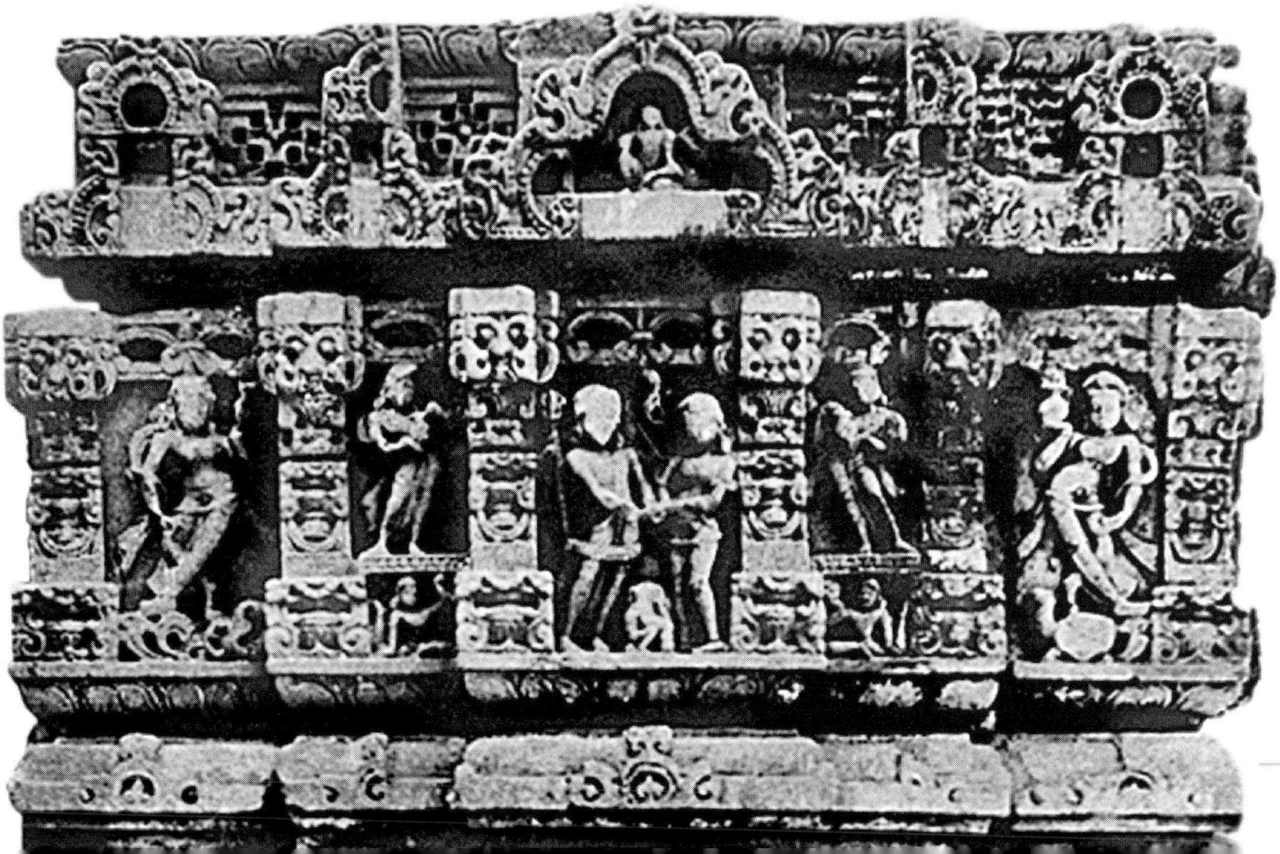

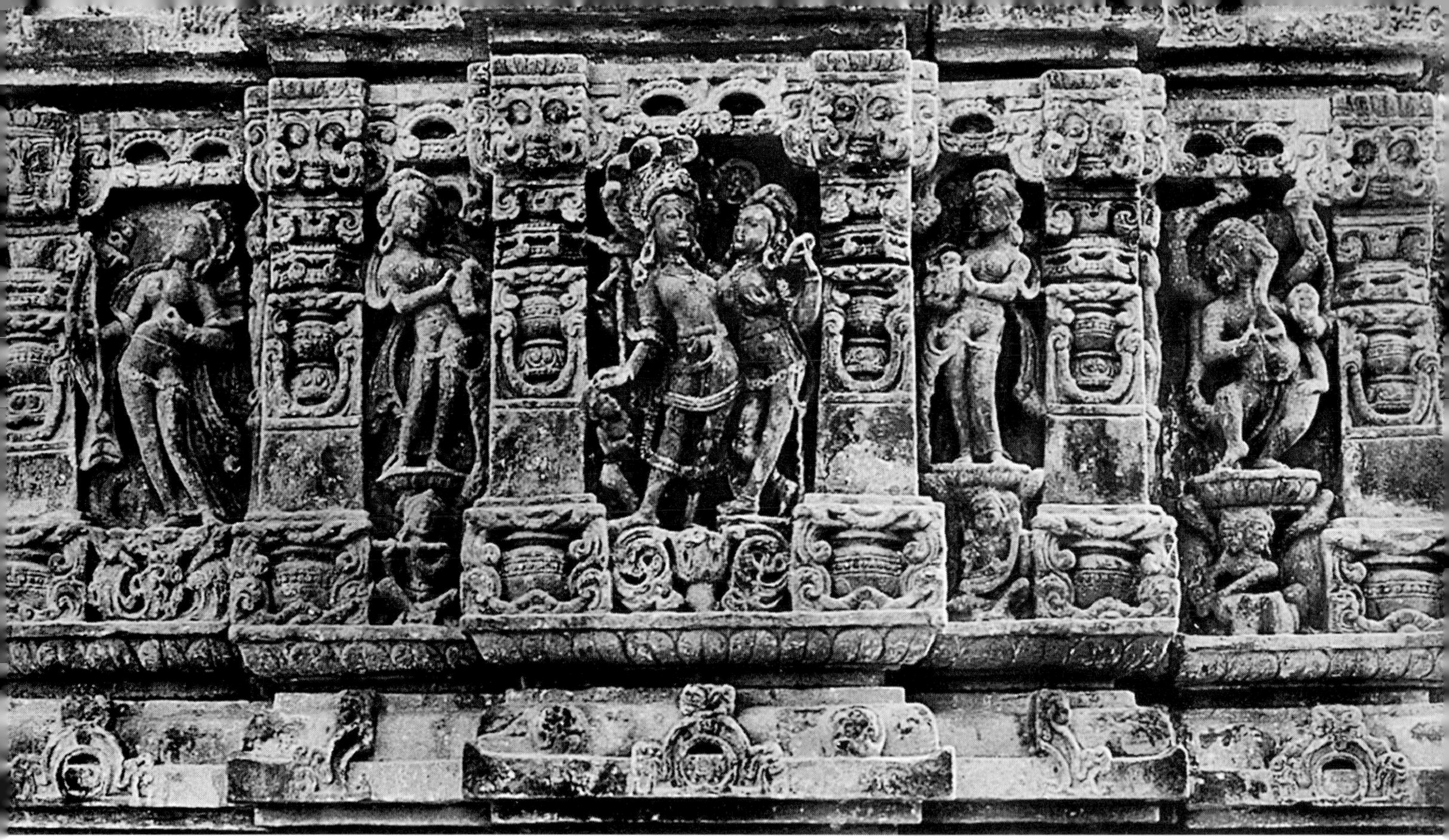

fig. 3. Harihara 1, south-eastern *devakulikā*, north wall, eighth century, Osiā, Rajasthan.

fig. 4. Details of *fig.* 1, Osiā.

development of individual image types and their preference during specific dynastic periods and frequent representation with its iconographic function preferred by a guild or prescribed by the *sthapati*, e.g. the aquatic connection is a very early phenomenon which goes back to the Gupta doorways; the post-Gupta Harihara group at Osiā is a case in point, where the river goddesses (Gaṅgā and Yamunā) appear in large size on the *karṇa* of the *maṇḍovara*, flanking the Kalyāṇasundaramūrti in the *bhadra devakoṣṭha*s. On the Harihara temple 2, in the north-west *devakulika*, they appear on the north wall. Their *makara* and *kūrma vāhana*s are distinctly visible (*figs.* 1-4). The river goddesses stand holding water pitchers with flowing garments striking *svastika cārī* and *kaṭyāvalambita* postures. At many other temples in Osiā, the *devāṅganā*s have been shown, but the aquatic connection is unique to this site.

In this manner, by analysing *maṇḍovara* patterns of a cross-section of temples, we arrive at a generic scheme recurrent in all the regions, as well as unique schemes peculiar to regional schools, e.g. Pratihāra, Kacchapaghāta, Candella, Guhila, Cāhamāna, Solaṅkī, etc. Keeping the chronological framework as a supportive guideline, the main focus will actually be on the regional stylistic exchanges of motifs, development of architectural parts and the overall temple plan. When more material on artist guilds dealing with the *devāṅganā* motif will be found, we will journey through the same old tracks on which this imagery must have once travelled from region to region with the skill and imagination of the master craftsmen. But for now, some basic assumptions will suffice.

Introduction

Devāṅganā/apsaras/surasundarī sculptures emerge on temple architecture in the post-Gupta phase. Hence, it is clearly an early medieval phenomenon. But at the outset, it has to be observed that in the past, architectural necessity had given rise to these motif types, which went into oblivion for some time and remerged when the aesthetic, social and religious functions called for their presence. In other words, neither the religious purpose nor the placement on temple wall, was prescribed as sacrosanct, and thus playing around with the various image types, was the privilege of the creative artists,

fig. 5. Śiva Temple,
south *jaṅghā*, early ninth century,
Terāhī, Śivapurī, Vidiśā,
Madya Pradesh

who fared unimaginably well at places, creating masterpieces of exquisite beauty and grace, since we have already looked at the architectural texts in the chapter on literary sources which specify the placement of decorative motifs at various places throughout a temple; here we shall look at actual examples and comment on regional variations.

The geo-political areas under discussion here are traditionally addressed as Marū, Gurjara, Marū–Gurjara, Dahala, Dakṣiṇa-Kosala, Gopagiri, Mālava, Arbudā and so on. The architecture that developed in these areas falls under the greater category of "Nāgara", but when minutely observed, each area has its own localized style, scale and motif type. Each region osmotically merged with the adjoining due to exchange of goods, ideas and persons. Morphologically speaking, M.A. Dhaky was able to give his insight into the unique as well as common features, shared by these regions which gave birth to a new amalgamated style in the late tenth century CE which he coined Marū–Gurjara.[1] This particular research has lent a new approach and dimension to the study of architectural morphology and structure, based on lines of biological species and the study thereof. What is even more significant, is the use of Sanskrit terminology and its introduction in describing the various parts of the temple; their typologies and their variations. The present study also takes into consideration the nomenclatures, stylistic groupings, cross-currents of influences and sharing of common motifs, as proposed by Dhaky, Michael Meister and Krishna Deva.[2]

Rightly observed by Dhaky,

> the style of Madhyadeśa, of contemporary Daśārṇa–Mālava, Cedideśa, of the Marū-Medapāṭa-Śākambharī complex, and of the Himalayan kingdoms, represent variants of one and the same style, which evolved in the pre-medieval period (the Pratihāra age) from the earlier, almost homogeneous, style that prevailed in the Gaṅgā–Yamunā Valley as well as in central India during the times of the Guptas.[3]

Krishna Deva has called the art and architecture of pre and early medieval times in central India and upper and eastern India, an "extension of Gupta art".[4] But elsewhere, Krishna Deva distinctly mentions the "common features" and "regional variations" and "local idioms" shared by the temples of the Pratihāra period in central India and Rajasthan.[5]

My architectural concern neither pertains to the originality of the Pratihāra style nor to the motifs developed by the localized guilds, but to the furtherance of the style itself; to its evolution and specifically to the development of the *maṇḍovara*. In order to do this, the *maṇḍovara* of the Pratihāra temples comes into focus, since our period of study starts with the beginning of the Pratihāra age and it has been the most widely influential style.

Krishna Deva identifies the Pratihāra style of central India as akin to that of Rajasthan, but its roots lie deeper in the soil of central India itself, with antecedents for a number of decorative motifs in the earlier temples of the Gupta period of the area; echoed by Dhaky in his study on *vitāna*s. This point remains undisputed.[6] Temples at Amrol (early eighth century CE) and Naresar (late eighth century CE), were constructed by the imperial Pratihāras after their shift from Marūmaṇḍala to Kannauj. The ninth century CE saw the rise of Jaina Temples at Deogaṛh and the Badoh Śiva Temple, Indore; Caturmukha Mahādeva Temple, Nachnā Kuṭhāra; the Jarai Mātā Temple, Barwāsāgar; the Sun Temple, Mānkheṛā; the Telīkā Mandir, Gwalior; the Gadarmal Temple, Badoh; Śiva Temple, Terāhī (*figs*. 5, 6, 7, 8); the Mālādevī Temple, Gyāraspur and Ghaṭeśvara Mahādeva Temple, Badoli (*fig*. 9).[7]

The eighth and ninth century temples of the Pratihāra age in Rajasthan are of the Osiā, Harihara group; the Kālikā Mātā Temple, Chittorgaṛh, the Kumbhaśyāma Temple, Chittorgaṛh; the twin temples of Śiva and Viṣṇu, Buchkala, were built by the Pratihāra king, Nāgabhaṭṭa II in CE 815. The Kāmeśvara Temple at Auwa (dating from the mid-ninth century) and the old Temple at Lamba, also fall into the early phase of this architecture.

The pre-Solaṅkī period architecture prevailing in Gujarat was of the Saurāṣṭra style, patronized during Maitraka and Saindhava rule. Resembling the Kālikā Mātā Temple at Chittorgaṛh and generally relating with the architecture of the Pratihāra age, are the Sun

fig. 6. Gadarmal Temple, west face *jaṅghā*, Badoh Paṭhārī.

fig. 7. Gadarmal Temple, east face *jaṅghā*, Badoh Paṭhārī.

Temple, Sūtrapāḍā, the Roḍā group of temples (*fig.* 10) and the Sun Temple, Bhīmnātha near Prabhās Pāṭan.[8]

The commencing of the tenth century brought about further development in temple architecture, not only in terms of structural complexity and expansion but also in intricacy of design, sculptural imagery and form. At the close of the tenth century, the styles of Marū and Gurjara were swept off their heels and they lost their individual provincial features giving birth to a new style, which is termed by Dhaky as "Marū–Gurjara". This confluence turned out to be a "passionate embrace" of styles, one exemplified by a masculine strength and structural monolithic firmness (Gurjara) and the other epitomized by grace, decorative beauty and delicacy of treatment (Marū). This style was patronized later by the Solaṅkī kings of Gujarat and it spread its influence to Maharashtra, Mālwā and the Cedi country.[9]

The "Mahā-Marū" and the "Mahā-Gurjara" are two distinct regional schools with their own sub-regional stylistic variations. The following sites indicate the development process, observed in the architecture of these two major regional styles by Dhaky, which I have mostly conformed to, in the present study concerning the placement of *devāṅganā* sculptures on the *maṇḍovara*s of the following temples:

The datable Mahā-Marū temples are Kālikā Temple (Sun Temple) and Kumbhaśyāma Temple (Śiva Temple) at Chittor, in all probability founded by the Grahapati king, Manabhaṅga, in the years between CE 644 and 743. The Mahāvīra I Temple, Osiā has a foundation inscription of VS 1013/CE 956, co-eval to the Pratihāra king Vatsarāja (*c.* CE 777-808). The Viṣṇu Temple at Buchkala was founded in the reign of his son, Nāgabhaṭṭa II, which is securely dated to VS 872/CE 815, while the Harṣanātha Temple at Sīkar, on the basis of its famous inscription, was constructed sometime

fig. 8. Caturmukha Mahādeva Temple, south-east view, *c.* eighth century, Nachnā–Kuṭhāra, Madya Pradesh

fig. 9. Ghaṭeśvara Mahādeva Temple,
general view,
first half of the ninth century,
Badoli, Koṭā, Rajasthan.

fig. 10. Temple 6,
general view,
early eighth century,
Roḍā, Himmatnagar, Gujarat.

fig. 11. Nīlakaṇṭha Temple, *maṇḍovara,* general view, first half of tenth century, Kekind, Rajasthan.

between CE 956-73.[10] The two sub-regional styles of Marū region are Marū–Sapādalakṣa and lower Medapāṭa–Uparamāla regions. The major temples taken for discussion here from Marū– Sapādalakṣa are the Harihara Temple, 1, 2, and its *devakulikā*s at Osiā; old temple at Lamba CE 775-800; Śiva Temple at Buchkala; Kāmeśvara Temple at Auwa; Mahādeva Temple at Bundānā CE 825-50; Nīlakaṇṭheśvara Temple at Kekind (*fig.* 11); and Harṣanātha temple at Sīkar CE 950-75.

The lower Medapāṭa-Uparamāla temples are Kālikā-Māta and Sūrya temples, Chittor CE 725-50; Sun Temple, Bodādit (*c.* CE 950) (*fig.* 12); and Kṣemaṅkarī Temple, Chittor (*c.* CE 825) (*fig.* 13).

The early Mahā-Marū temples essentially are *dviaṅga* or *triaṅga* plan shrines, with a *latinā śikhara* which bears transverse *latā*s. The *maṇḍapa* is not fully developed except for a small *mukhacatuṣkī*. The *madhyalatā* called *pañjara* is in rare instances flanked by a second, inner *veṇukośa*, which takes the place of the subsidiary *latā*s called *bālapañjaras*. The *raṅga-maṇḍapa*, when present, consists of a *vedikā*, *āsana paṭṭaka* and a *mattavāraṇa*. The pillars are of *ghaṭapallava* or *rūcaka* or *bhadraka* type. The *vitāna*s are also decorated and either follow *samatala* or *nābhicchanda* orders. The door-frames are either *triśākhā* or *pañcaśākhā*, containing *patraśākhā*, *nāgaśākhā*, *mālāśākhā*, *mithunaśākhā* and *rūpa-stambha,* etc. Gaṅgā–Yamunā are also present along with attendants on the *udumbara* level. Generic connections with the temples of the Gupta period on one hand, and the temples of Pratihāra age in Madhyadeśa and the Daśārṇa–Cedi–Mālava country on the other are borne out by these door-frames.[11]

fig. 12. Sun Temple, west face *jaṅghā*, *c.* CE 900-925, Bodādit, Koṭā, Rajasthan.

The *maṇḍovara* either remains plain, save for the *bhadra* niche containing a major manifestation of the presiding deity and the *karṇa koṣṭhas*, sometimes carrying the *dikpālas*. Some temples of Medapāṭa–Uparmāla region repeat the older style of the Marū–Sapādalakṣa of tall *udgamas* surmounting the sculptured niches of *bhadra* and *karṇa*. Rarely do these also cover the *pratiratha* sculptures of *devāṅganās* and *caurī*-bearers. Refer to the Bodādit Sun Temple and the Nīlakaṇṭheśvara Temple, Kekind (*figs.* 11, 12). Dhaky observes elongated *udgamas* as reminiscent of central Indian examples such as found at Barwāsāgar. The extensive sculpture material observed on the Mahā-Marū temples consists of *nāgas*, *vidyādharas*, *gandharvas*, *mālādharas*, foliage of different kinds, and decorative geometric designs as well.

fig. 13. Kṣemaṅkarī Temple, west face *maṇḍovara*, early eighth century, Chittorgaṛh, Rajasthan.

The Mahā-Gurjara style is represented in three regions namely, Ānartta, Arbudā and the lower Medapāṭa. The handful of dated temples are Durgā Kṣemaṅkarī Temple, Unwas (CE 960); Ambikā Temple, Jagat (CE 961) (*fig.* 14) and Lakulīśa Temple, Ekaliṅgajī (CE 972). An indirect reference dates the temple of Ghanerao to CE 954, to which its style also conforms.[12]

The Mahā-Gurjara temples have a *pīṭha* but the *jaṅghā* has shorter *udgamas* and practically no sculptural images save for the *bhadra* niches. The *pratiratha* is not articulated as a *ghaṭapallava* pilaster (which is of Gupta origin) but is reminiscent of the Rāṣṭrakūṭa style. The door-frames are quite elaborately carved but the *mithuna* and *nāgaśākhās* are absent while the Gaṅgā–Yamunā do not occupy the same prominent position as

fig. 14. Ambikā Temple,
general view, CE 960,
Jagat, Udaipur, Rajasthan.

they do at Mahā-Marū sites.[13] Rightly observed by Dhaky, the Mahā-Marū style has more inclination towards sculpturesque treatment of the *maṇḍovara* and doorway while the Mahā-Gurjara is essentially architectonic which emphasizes the structural strength and not decorative embellishment. The above observation leads to an inference which I would like to explore with definite examples and that is the placement of *devāṅganā* figures on the *maṇḍovara*, as a unique Mahā-Marū phenomenon and later its spread to the Mahā-Gurjara area in the tenth century CE. This phenomenon will be elaborately discussed elsewhere.

The Mahā-Gurjara style in its last phase, developed in the Arbudā–Medapāṭa region and introduced the *anekāṇḍikā-śikhara* and *samadala pratiratha*. With this change, the expansion of the Nāgara temple was possible and it began to develop from Jagat and Koṭai (*fig.* 15) in lower Medapāṭa and Ānartta to the central Indian Jejākabhukti and Cedideśa through the Cāhamāna channel.[14] The Lakṣmaṇa Temple at Khajurāho (*fig.* 18) exemplifies this development. The tenth century also saw the inception of the merging of Mahā-Marū and Mahā-Gurjara traits, which will be dealt with in the section III of this chapter.

Central India is replete with temples of the Gupta period, situated at Sāñcī, Eraṇ, Tigowā, Nachnā–Kuṭhāra, Bhumarā, Deogaṛh, among others. The Pratihāra age in central India kept the continuity of the Gupta tradition further by fusing the indigenous tradition of *maṇḍapikā* shrines with it. Krishna Deva has found a recognizable "cognate group of temples with very distinctive features" attributable to this period and calls it "the Pratihāra style of central India". This style has its offshoots in Rajasthan as well, represented by the group at Osiā.

The central Indian sites are Naresar and Baṭesar, near Gwalior; Mahādeva Temple, Amrol; Telīkā Mandir, Gwalior Fort, founded most probably in the reign of Pratihāra king Mihira Bhoja (CE 836-88); and Śiva Temple, Indore. Co-eval with the former are the Jarai Mātā, Barwāsāgar; Gadarmal Temple, Badoh (*figs.* 6, 7); Caturmukha Mahādeva Temple, Nachnā; Sun Temple, Mānkheṛā; Jaina Temple no. 12 and 15, Deogaṛh; and Mālādevī Temple,

(facing page)
fig. 15. Śiva temple, general view, early ninth century, Kotai, Kutch, Gujarat.

Gyāraspur; which bear similarity with the Śiva Temple at Kerakoṭ in Kutch.[15] Thus the Pratihāra temples of central India of eighth and ninth centuries have a simple plan and design, displaying some characteristic ornaments of the style including tall pediments, a frieze of loops of garlands on the top of the wall, a band of *nāga*s on the door-frame and rich carvings of vases and foliage, scrolls and *kīrtimukha*s, and a square, ribbed cushion capital to be found largely on the pillars.[16]

The temples of Dahala region included for our study are the Śiva temples at Nohṭā (*figs*. 16, 17), Marai, Sohāgpur, and Jañjagīr between the tenth and twelfth century belonging to the "Cedi style". Most of them possess a *maṇḍapa*.

The Jejākabhukti area, at Khajurāho, the medieval capital of the Candella monarchs, saw the raising of grand temples, namely the Lakṣmaṇa Temple (*c*. CE 954) (*fig*. 18); the Pārśvanātha Temple (*c*. CE 955); Ghantai Temple (late tenth century CE); the Viśvanātha Temple (*c*. CE 1001-02); the Devī Jagdambī and Citragupta temples (*c*. early eleventh century CE); the Kandarīya Mahādeva Temple (mid-eleventh century CE); the Vāmana and Jawarī Temple (late eleventh century CE); and the Duladeo Temple (early twelfth century CE). This chronology follows Krishna Deva. Dhaky and Krishna Deva have observed the presence of powerful Rājasthānī elements in the fabric of these temples, especially in the ceilings. The present study will subsequently show how the *devāṅganā* sculptures of Khajurāho bear the influence of the Rajasthan sculptures especially of Kekind and Jagat.

fig. 16. Śiva Temple, south face, second quarter of the tenth century, Nohṭā, Damoh, Madya Pradesh (facing page)

fig. 17. Śiva Temple, view from west, second quarter of tenth century, Marai, Satnā, Madya Pradesh

fig. 18. Lakṣmaṇa Temple, south wall near *kakṣasaṇa, jagatī* and *jaṅghā* sculpture, mid-tenth century, Khajurāho, Madya Pradesh

fig. 19. Temple 1, Khirniwālā (group 7), west face, *c.* tenth century, Kaḍwāhā, Guṇā, Madya Pradesh

The Kacchapaghātas of Gopagiri, ruling in the area where older Pratihāra temples exist, have a unique style. The transitional style temples are the Kaḍwāhā Temple 1, Khirnīwālā (group 7) and Ṭoṭeśvara Temple (*figs*. 19, 20, 21), Terāhī (Śiva temple) (*fig*. 5), and the ruined Viṣṇu Temple of Gyāraspur, while the fully developed temples are Padhavali Jain temple (late tenth century), Jhālarāpāṭan (*c*. end of tenth century) the great temple, Suhāniā (*c*. CE 1001-10); Viṣṇu Temple, Nohṭā (*fig*. 16) and the Sās-Bahū Temple, Gwalior Fort (*c*. CE 1094).[17]

The Paramāras of Mālwā took the lead in temple architecture from Ujjain and Dhāra in the eleventh century CE. The Udayeśvara Temple (*fig*. 22) erected in the time of Udayāditya (CE 1059-80) at Udaipur, is the finest example of Paramāra architecture in the Bhūmija style. Dhaky observes an influence of Karnāṭa-Maharashtra style, fused with the Kacchapaghāta style in the Paramāra architecture.

I

Pratihāra Period: Beginning of Devāṅganā Sculptures on Nāgara Temples — Rajasthan, Gujarat and Madhya Pradesh

The Pratihāras ruled during the eighth and ninth centuries CE over a vast region of the western and northern India and the identifiable style of architecture that they helped evolve has been recognized by scholars as the Pratihāra architecture. This style had its regional variations and local idioms, but most notably, it took on from where the Guptas left off. The Pratihāras extended the existing tradition by adding a full-fledged *maṇḍapa* to the single shrine temple types of the Gupta age and of the early Pratihāra period, e.g. Nāresar and Baṭesar. The *śikhara* also got elaborated and as a consequence, the *maṇḍovara* too got articulated into either the *triratha*, or the *pañcaratha* plan, e.g. Gadarmal Temple, Badoh–Paṭhārī, Śiva Temple, Kherat, etc.[18] The pioneering contribution of the Pratihāras to Nāgara temple architecture is the structuring and designing of the *maṇḍovara* wall, devising sculptures to decorate its erstwhile bareness and standardizing an iconography of *dikpāla*s, *devāṅganā*s and *vyāla*s, to drape the *garbha-gṛha* and the *maṇḍapa* walls.

(facing page)
fig. 20. Ṭoṭeśvara Temple 1, (Group 1)
general view from west,
c. eleventh century,
Kaḍwāhā, Guṇā,
Madya Pradesh

It being the most widely known architectural idiom, the Pratihāra architecture had its impact on far-off regions like Uttar Pradesh, Punjab and Himachal Pradesh. But the building activity patronized by the Pratihāras in north-western Rajasthan and central India before the Kannauj phase of sculpture and architecture, is more significant. They created new space concepts, structural and functional constructs, motifs, designs and figures together with aesthetic and iconographic norms.

Here we take a closer view of the earliest Pratihāra temples of Rajasthan and central India with analogous examples from Gujarat. The Harihara group 1 and 2 temples from Osiā (*figs.* 1, 3); Kṣemaṅkarī Temple from Chittorgaṛh; Viṣṇu and Śiva temples from Bundānā; Roḍā Temple from Gujarat; Śiva Temple, Terāhī; Gadarmal Temple, Badoh–Paṭhārī (*fig.* 6); and Telikā Mandir, Gwalior Fort from Madhya Pradesh, are some of the leading examples considered here. The Roḍā group in the Ānartta region and the Osiā group in the Marū–Sapādalakṣa region, bear witness to (i) *latinā śikhara* type of a humble size, (ii) and articulation of the *garbha-gṛha* walls into *bhadra*, *karṇa* and *pratiratha* projections, preceded by a small porch (*mukhacatuṣkī*) outside the main doorway. These temples have been securely dated between the last quarter of the eighth and the early ninth century by Dhaky.[19] Out of these temples, the Roḍā group bear niches for placement of sculptures in the *bhadra* while the rest of the wall remains plain. While at Osiā, *dikapāla*s are also introduced along with other forms of presiding deities, which are placed in the *karṇa*, at the Viṣṇu Temple, Osiā, and Roḍā Temple I. Buchkala and Bundānā also adhere to similar *maṇḍovara* designing, in which the size of the *bhadra* is slightly larger than the *pratiratha* and *karṇa*. Rāṇak Devī Temple, Wadhwān, and Maniyāra Mahādeva Temple at Dedadarā (early ninth century) also consist of plain bare walls with no embellishment, except for the niche in the *bhadra* and a garland circumscribing the temple; while the Roḍā Temple III of the late eighth century has *rūcaka* type pilasters with fluted cushion like capitals at the *pratiratha*, creating another facet for the *salilāntara*. Now a stage has come when the wall articulation is complete, but the figural sculptures have yet to be fashioned.[20]

(facing page)
fig. 21. Ṭoṭeśvara Temple 1, general view west face, *c.* eleventh century, Kaḍwāhā, Guṇā, Madya Pradesh

For this breakthrough, we will have to turn our attention to the Osiā group of temples in Marū–Sapādalakṣa and the earlier temples at Chittorgaṛh in the lower Medapāṭa–Uparamāla region and Kṣemaṅkarī temple *c.* CE 825 (*fig.* 13). The *maṇḍovara* of this temple is divided into *karṇa*: *pratiratha*: *bhadra*: *pratiratha*: *karṇa* in the ratio of 1:½:2:½:1 leading to unequal but rhythmic facets that correspond with the *śikhara śakhā*s, creating deep recesses leading to an articulated three-dimesionality. The *pratiratha* is treated more like a pilaster of the *rūcaka* type, topped by a *ghaṭapallava* capital with dense cluster of drooping foliage. The *pratiratha* contains the *cāmara dhāriṇī*s flanking the *bhadra* as is present above the *bhadra* and *karṇa* images of the *dikpāla*s.

The rider figure of possibly Revaṅta is flanked not by *camara dhāriṇī*s as in the case of Kṣemaṅkarī image, but by *devāṅganā*s who are shown holding a mirror and a bowl respectively. It is probably one of the earliest representations of *devāṅganā*s on the *maṇḍovara*, a position which they will firmly maintain during the forthcoming centuries. From the point of view of space organization on the *maṇḍovara*, the sculptors' hesitation in giving fuller growth to sculpture is self-evident. The *udgama*s cover large surfaces overbearing the plain wall spaces, preventing sculptures to emerge out. Gradually, within a century this design process will change. Note should also be taken of *vyāla* brackets supporting the *bhadra* niches which later will multiply and secure prominent position in the *salilāntara*s.

Devāṅganā sculptures (*fig.* 2) were introduced by Pratihāra sculptors on the *devakulikā*s or the subsidiary shrines and not on shrines of the presiding deities, i.e. the *mūlaprāsāda* at Osiā.[21] Hence, the main temples like Harihara 1 and 2, Sun temples and Viṣṇu temples do not represent *devāṅganā*s on the *maṇḍovara*s of their *mūlaprāsāda*s. One wonders, what could be the reason for this purposeful elimination. Conversely, the sculptors may have first experimented with this imagery on the

fig. 22. Udayeśvara Temple, general view, CE 1059-80, inscribed, Udaipur, Vidiśā, Madya Pradesh

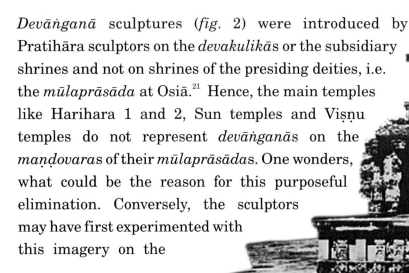

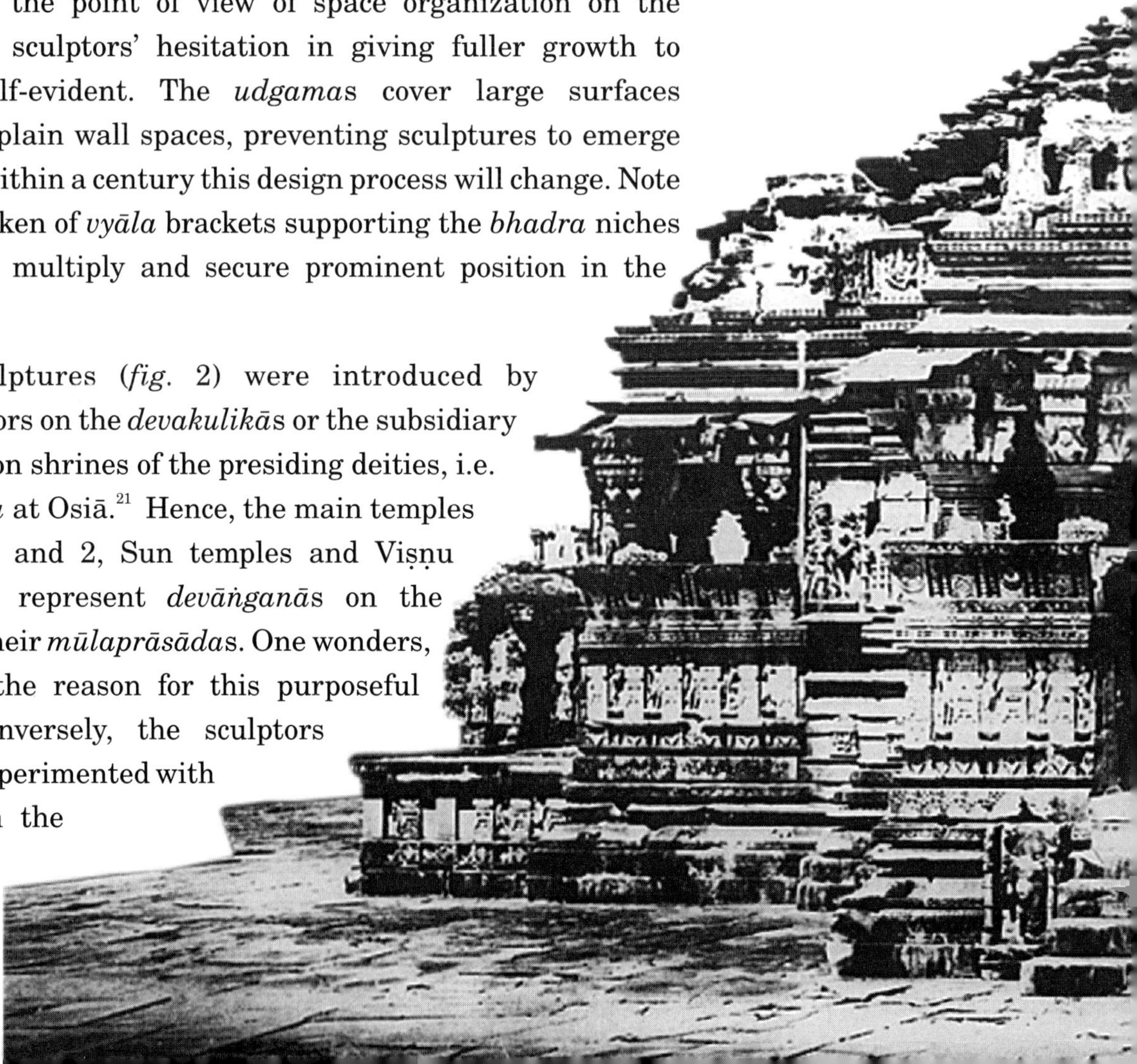

devakulikas and later on introduced it on the main shrine. However, at Osiā it is only in the Marū–Gurjara phase that *devāṅganās* return on the *maṇḍovara* of the Saccīyamātā Temple.

In the south-eastern *devakulikā* (north face) of the Harihara 1 group, the *maṇḍovara* is divided into five parts with the *bhadra* twice as big as the *karṇa* and the *pratiratha*. The *bhadra udgama* is well articulated, canopying the figures of Balarāma and Revatī; *karṇa* contains a six-armed Gaṇeśa and a lady with a bow, while river goddesses or ladies bearing water pitchers (*kumbha*) flank the central aqueous deity in the *pratirathas*. This scheme of rectangular composition is not complete without the *pūrṇa kalaśas*, *ghaṭapallavas* and *kīrtimukhas* to which are added musicians, who squat at the lotus pedestals supporting the figures above. Here, the *maṇḍovara* design is compact, decorative motifs and human figures are carved with equal sensitivity and spirit. They cover equal volumes and spaces without surpassing each other in prominence. The graceful *tribhaṅga* disposition of the sculptures lends an air of casualness to the form, and at this stage of iconographical development, the sculptors seem to have visualized the wall articulation gracefully (*fig.* 3).

Two more examples of Harihara group 1 and 2 will provide a clearer idea of the *maṇḍovara* design concept, which is analogous to the previous example and is often repeated at this site which goes to indicate its preference at Marū–Sapādalakṣa in general.

On the *maṇḍovara* of the north-eastern *devakulikā* of the Harihara group 1, one cannot fail to notice a *darpaṇa devāṅganā* holding a mirror and a lotus. This image is placed on the *karṇa*, a position accorded generally to *dikpālas*.[22] The *bhadra* niche proudly bears the Garuḍārūḍha Viṣṇu, who is flanked by female attendants, each holding a *cāmara* and a lotus. The *koṣṭha* at the bottom is occupied by *gaṇa* figures. This arrangement clearly distinguishes the *devāṅganā* figures from the mere attendants. From here, the *devāṅganā* imagery seems to take off on its own independent growth and has its own *locus standi* (*fig.* 2).

The second example refers to Harihara group 2, the north wall of

fig. 23. Sūrya Temple,
north face, mid-tenth century,
Tusa, Udaipur, Rajasthān.

the north-western *devakulikā*. The *bhadra* niche bears the Kalyāṇasundaramūrti flanked by attendants and the river goddesses, Gaṅgā–Yamunā distinguished by their *vāhanas*. The *karṇa* position is rarely given to river goddesses, who generally appear on the doorways of the Gupta–Vākāṭaka and the Pratihāra temples (*fig.* 1).

Pondering upon the question of origin of the *devāṅganā* motif in conjunction with development of the *maṇḍovara,* a possibility emerges that Marū–Sapādalakṣa could be one of the leading sites for the emergence of *devāṅganā* imagery? But on the other hand, the regions of Daśārṇa–Cedi and Mālwā are not lacking in development of the *devāṅganā* imagery that adorned pillar, *maṇḍovara* and doorway. At different sites, artists designed figures and motifs, with the aim of creating visual articulation, on the physical surface of the temple walls, by juxtaposing various iconographic imageries. This very articulation immensely contributed to the symbolic enrichment of a temple, imparting it a larger cosmic meaning.

Before leaving the eighth century, the major Mahā-Gurjara site of the Pratihāra age, namely the Roḍā group of temples in north Gujarat demands our attention. Most of the temples are in ruins and languishing for attention by scholars and conservationists alike. Other analogous sites in this group are Rāṇak Devī Temple, Wadhwān; Maniyāra Mahādeva Temple, Dedādarā; Brāhmaṇasvāmi Temple, Varman, etc. which do not bear any *maṇḍovara* figure sculpture and hence are eliminable. But the very fact that they do not bear any figural sculpture, signifies a different stylistic trend and an approach to design which has its manifestations in Kāmeśvara Temple, Auwa, Ghaṭeśvara Mahādeva Temple, Badoli and Sās-Bahū Temple, Nāgdā. The eight temples of the Roḍā group follow the stunted *śikhara* type *triratha* and *pañcaratha* plan with a small *mukhacatuṣkī* and a large śukanāsa, a prominently adorning its façade. Inscriptional evidence to support its patronage and date are still wanting. It has been dated to the last quarter of the eighth century by Dhaky and hence is contemporaneous with the Osiā group. The temple VI at Roḍā (*fig.* 10) interests me particularly not for its *maṇḍovara* articulation, but for the sculptures over the pillar capitals

(facing page)
fig. 24. Mīrā Temple, general view, north side, late tenth century, Āhaṛ, Udaipur, Rajasthan.

of its *maṇḍapa*. A complete range of *devāṅganā* imagery is found here framed by a small niche above the pillars. This is the first time one encounters the *devāṅganā* iconography in such detail in the pre-Marū–Gurjara phase. It is also unique for the placement *devāṅganā*s on pillars and not the usual *maṇḍovara* where one would normally expect them. From the example of Roḍā temple VI (*fig.* 97) one can infer two things — one that the *devāṅganā* imagery is not lost from craftsmen's guilds but it is making a comeback gradually from pillar capitals to *maṇḍovara* wall within a century. Further within a century, this motif and its entire range has been absorbed at the nearby Osiā region where one can notice full-fledged *devāṅganā* forms sculpted on the *maṇḍovara*, without hesitation (*figs.* 1, 2, 226).

The two temples from central India, namely Śiva Temple, Terāhī (*fig.* 5) and Gadarmal Temple, Badoh–Paṭhārī (*figs.* 6, 7) reveal yet another *maṇḍovara* morphology, which is in the process of evolving. The Terāhī Śiva Temple has a *triratha* plan without a *salilāntara*. *Bhadra* niches have a canopied *udgama* and a roof which covers the deity placed within it. The *karṇa* houses the *dikpāla*s as well as a very tall *udgama* of five tiers. The *pratiratha* appears in the form of a false pillar, containing two *ghaṭapallava*s, *āmalaka*s and brimming leaf motifs. The absence of *devāṅganā* is especially noteworthy.

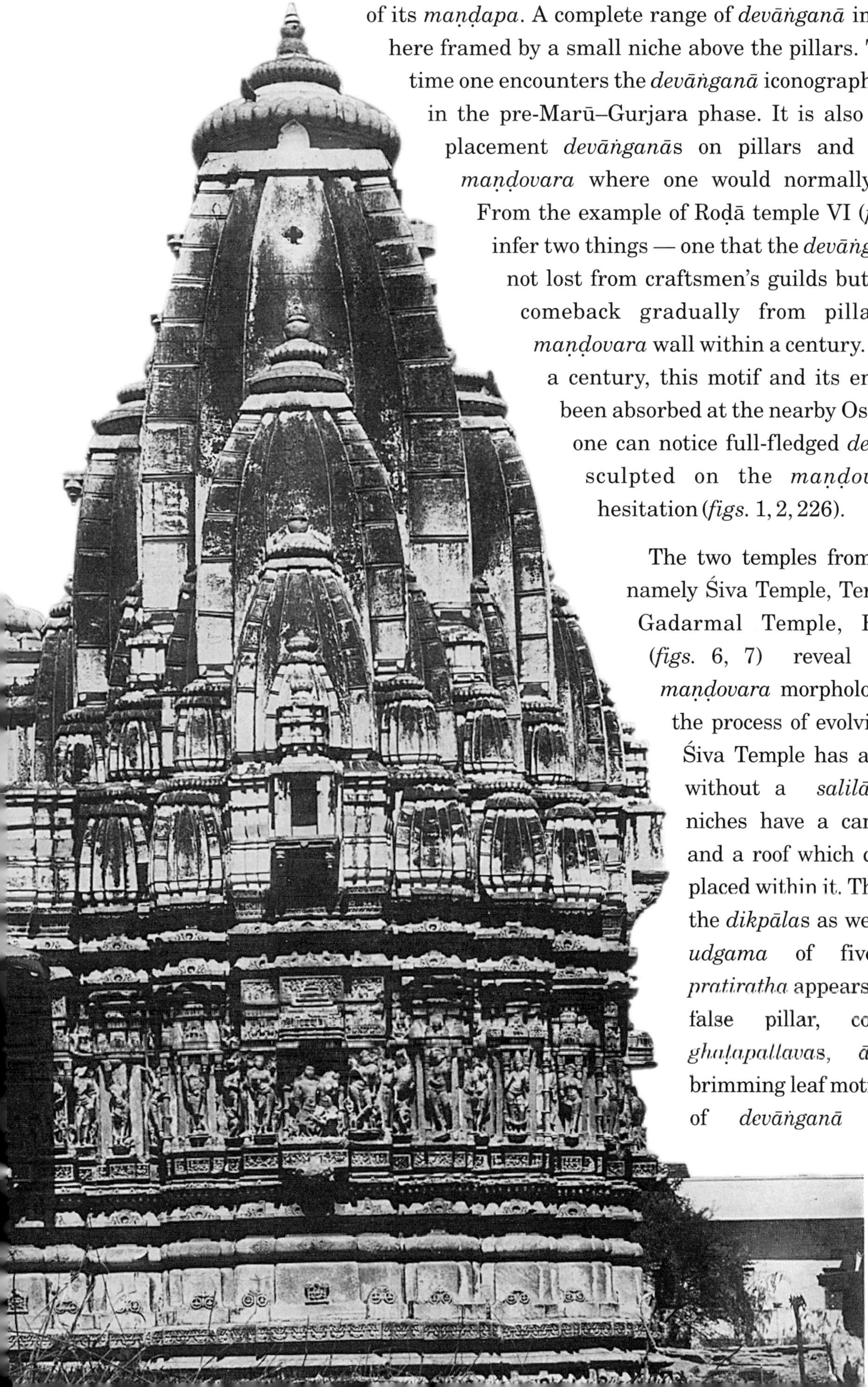

The Gadarmal Temple of Badoh–Paṭhārī is the most complicated of them all because the decorative motifs, niche windows and sculptures do not appear in a vertical arrangement of juxtaposition, but chequered all around the *maṇḍovara* wall. This temple is one of the first large-scale temples to appear in this age. It has to be viewed as a predecessor to the Khajurāho temples of the next century built by the Candellas. Its high plinth is the first connecting link with Khajurāho, while the second is the scale, and the third is the mode of dividing the *maṇḍovara* into two tiers. At the plinth level, no *thara*s (horizontal bands) like *narathara, gajathara,* etc. appear, except for a chequered pattern and an acanthus creeper motif pattern. The *maṇḍovara* is divided into two horizontal levels, both containing small niches with tiny figures and tall *udgama*s with *kīrtimukha*s. The ground plan of this temple is *triratha* and hence the highly-faceted surfaces are available for the sculptor to fill in the empty spaces. The *devāṅganā*s in this temple are placed in both the tiers of the *maṇḍovara*, surmounted by tall *udgama*s. Their placement on *pratiratha*, *karṇa* and even *nandikā* have been identified by me as *vasanabhraṁśā*, *nalinī*, *alasā*, *sva-stana-sparśā*, and *prasādhikā* (*figs.* 6, 7, 168). This unique feature of the Gadarmal Temple emerges as the earliest example of *devāṅganā* imagery designed to embellish temple architecture in central India. In the ninth century, this remains a significant experiment of *devāṅganā* imagery revived and retrieved since the Kuṣāṇa period.

The Ghaṭeśvara Mahādeva temple at Badoli (*c.* ninth century) in east Rajasthan has a *triratha* sanctum and *śikhara*. The *kapilī* joins the *mukhamaṇḍapa* which is surmounted by a *śukanāsa*. The *maṇḍapa* has a stepped roof which presupposes the *samavaraṇa* roof of Jagat. The *maṇḍovara* wall is plain, save for the *bhadra* niches containing Naṭarāja, Cāmuṇḍā, etc. The plinth is not very high at the sanctum base, but the *maṇḍapa* is almost at the ground level. The *maṇḍapa* pillars bear octagonal faces which are occupied by *apsaras* and *devāṅganā*s standing on lotus pedestals (*fig.* 9). Krishna Deva observes the resemblance of these figures with Khajurāho *apsaras* in postural details of dress and jewellery. This temple anticipates the Lakṣmaṇa Temple at Khajurāho (*fig.* 18) and appears to date roughly from the end of the ninth century.[23] The *devāṅganā* imagery represented on pillars include *vasanabhraṁśā*, *markaṭaceṣṭā* and some other. By the tenth century, this particular trend is continued at many more sites in Madhya Pradesh, namely Gurgī (now in Rewā Mahārāja's Palace (*figs.* 251), Sās-Bahū Temple, Gwalior Fort (*figs.* 263, 264) and in Rajasthan at *naṭa-maṇḍapa* of the Dilwāṛā temples, Ābu and Kumbhariā group of Jaina temples. In Gujarat, Sun Temple of Moḍherā provides the most leading example (*fig.* 36).

Thus, the above examples highlight two major trends in *maṇḍovara* decor — one favouring plain surfaces interspersed by decorative motifs, and the other favouring sculptural forms with a definite iconography and hierarchy of placement. The hesitation and experimentation of artists continue, and so *devāṅganā*s shift their placements from the capitals to the bases of the pillars, to small niches on the *maṇḍovara*, but seldom do they come on par in scale with sculptures of other divinities. With the onset of the tenth century, *devāṅganā* sculptures appear with certainty in the treatment of this imagery, and developed to its final culmination, when they surpassed the other sacred images of deities, in grace, charm and aesthetic beauty.

Tenth Century: Coming of Age with Koṭai, Jagat, Kekind and other Western Indian Sites

The tenth century brought about a new enthusiasm in temple architecture and replenished temples in western India with new motifs, sculptures and layout designs. Both the Mahā-Marū and the Mahā-Gurjara styles came to a point of final fruition. Any further growth beyond that was difficult to perceive. It was at this opportune moment of merging of both the contemporaneous styles, that the harmonious fusion of Maru with the Gurjara elements showed a fresh avenue of growth; the path traversed upon by these combined styles has come to be termed as "Maru Gurjara" by Dhaky. Further, had they been left uncrossed, the fate of each one of the two styles would have been not unlike that of the sedentary style of Jejākabhukti best exemplified at Khajurāho.[24] Still however, it is important to note that tenth century also brought about development in Dahala, Mālwā and Kosala regions. While viewing all these developments in totality, tenth-century temple architecture stands at the highest peak of the parabolic ascent after which medieval architecture slips into stagnancy.

The tenth-century Ānartta temples (region of Saurāṣṭra, western Gujarat) that I have discussed here are the Śiva and Sūrya temples at Kotai (*fig.* 15); Lakheśvara Temple, Kerakoṭ (*c.* CE 950); Muni Bāvā Temple, Thān (*c.* CE 975); and Bhadreśvara Temple, Añjār (*c.* CE 1000). While in the Medapāṭa (region of southern Rajasthan) are Mahāvīra Temple, Ghānerāo (CE 954); Ambikā Temple, Jagat (CE 960) (*fig.* 14); Sun Temple, Tusā (*c.* CE 950) (*fig.* 23); Viṣṇu Temple, Kirāḍu; Sās-Bahū Temple, Nāgdā; Mīrā and Mahāvīra temples, Āhaṛ (*c.* CE 1000) (*figs.* 24, 25).

In the Marū–Sapādalakṣa region, I have focused on the Nīlakaṇṭheśvara Temple, Kekind (*c.* CE 975) (*fig.* 11): and the Harṣanātha Temple, Sīkar (CE 956-73) (*fig.* 28) while the Sun Temple of Bodādit (*c.* CE 950) is significant from the lower Medapāṭa region (*fig.* 12).

The most prolific phase of the Mahā-Gurjara style at Ānartta and

fig. 25. Mīrā Temple, *maṇḍovara*, west wall, late tenth century Āhaṛ, Udaipur, Rajasthan.

Medapāṭa culminated at Koṭai and Jagat respectively, with the arrival of the *anekāṇḍikā śikhara*, multiple *śikhara* form. With the introduction of the *samadala pratiratha* plan, the designing of the *anekāṇḍikā śikhara* became possible. The *kumbha* of the *vedībandha* began to get decorated with figural sculptures, while the *jaṅghā* in most cases contained the full retinue of images — *dikpālas*, *apsarases*, *gandharvas* and *vidyādharas*, elephants and *vyālas*.[25]

In the Ambikā Temple at Jagat CE 960[26] the sanctum is *pañcaratha* with an *anekāṇḍikā śikhara*; it has a *kapilī* with stepped roof, a *maṇḍapa* with latticed windows in the lateral transepts, and a *mukhacatuṣkī* with balustrades (*fig.* 14). The humble scale and compactness of the structure is the unique quality of the Jagat Temple. Fortunately, the pristine purity and originality of the structure is well preserved. Save for some repairs, much of the structure appears complete. The *jaṅghā* section emerges on a very high *pīṭha* with several bands of *kumbhaka*, *kalaśa*, *antarapatra*, *kapotālī* and *mañcika*. The *jaṅghā* is draped with several sculptures that begin to integrate organically with the substance and form of the architecture. The Jagat Temple sculpture leave little space which is empty or devoid of ornamentation, while the articulation of the wall facets, creates a pulsating visual effect in unison.

It is with this century that figural sculpture takes the front seat in the design of the *jaṅghā* and other parts of the *maṇḍovara*. On the typical *pañcaratha* plan the *bhadra*, *pratiratha* and *karṇa* are interspersed with *salilāntaras*, as is also the case at Koṭai and Thān, besides a Jagat (*figs.* 14, 15). The *bhadra* and *karṇa* niches are prominently styled as *rathikas* with *udgama* and pillars, in which the presiding deities and *dikpālas* are placed. The images of *devāṅganās* are invariably placed on the *pratiratha* which is projecting forward as can be noticed at Koṭai, Thān and Jagat. But very often, the Jagat sculptors have placed *devāṅganās* as well, in the *salilāntara* along with *vyālas*, a feature that emerges gradually with the expansion of the *maṇḍovara* facets, due to which more space is made available for all kinds of figures. The *devāṅganās* are perched on a simple pedestal (Jagat) or a lotus-petalled pedestal with a stem alluding to the aquatic origin (Koṭai). On the sanctum *maṇḍovara* of the Koṭai Śiva Temple, and above the *jaṅghā* sculptures, *bharaṇī*, *antarapatra* and *kapotālī* are located; while on the *maṇḍovara* of the *maṇḍapa*, a *parikara* runs across the face of the entire wall, depicting some floral design just behind the head and shoulder of the images. Another group of seated figures is perched above the main images, involved in music, love play, performing a fire ritual, worshipping *Śivaliṅgam* or just conversing. At Jagat they appear only on the *salilāntara* and *pratiratha*, while at Koṭai they recur on all the facets of the *maṇḍapa*. The meaning of these figures has been discussed in Chapter 6.

The recurrence of some generic motifs, e.g. *dikpāla*, *devāṅganā* and *vyāla*, on the *maṇḍovara* seems to follow a system which remains more or less unchanged. As for instance, the *devakoṣṭha* on the *bhadra* contains Durgā Mahiṣāsuramardinī on the south wall, flanked by two *vyāla*s on the *salilāntara*s, which are immediately followed by *devāṅganā*s in the narrow *pratiratha*s, riding on elephants. The following *pratiratha* contains a *devāṅganā* again and is buttressed by a *karṇa* containing *dikpāla*s. Hence the *jaṅghā* division is as follows: d, c, c, b, a, b, c, c, d. This completes the *garbha-gṛha* unit.

The Koṭai (*fig.* 15) *maṇḍovara* programming differs slightly from the above in which the *bhadra* is immediately followed by a *vyāla* pair in two *salilāntara* on both the sides. This is followed by a pair of *devāṅganā*s in *pratiratha* projecting forward. Even the two lateral sides of the *pratiratha* wall contain sculptures of *devāṅganā*s. The next column is occupied by *vyāla*s in the *salilāntara*, which is completed by the *karṇa* containing *dikpāla*s. The corners are traditionally assigned to the *dikpāla*s and hence the guardians of both the coinciding directions stand adjacent to each other, but facing their own directions. Hence, they come in pairs around the central *bhadra* niche, a feature which will continue in the Marū–Gurjara and the Candella styles as well. This shows that sculpture developed analogous to the developments in architecture and as the articulation of faceted walls emerged, sculptures were developed to accommodate in the new spaces that were created. Centrality of the *bhadra* niche was amply emphasized and two sides of the faceted walls which bore two sculptures placed at right angle to each other.

On the Muni Bāvā Temple, Than, the pattern is d, b, c, a — a, b, c, b, d which conforms to the Koṭai pattern. Interestingly, the width of the *bhadra* in Thān Temple is two units that of *pratiratha* and *salilāntara* one unit each and the *karṇa* is one-and-half units.

While at Koṭai, the *bhadra* covers two units, *salilāntara*s half, and the *pratiratha* and *karṇa* one-and-half units. At jagat, the proportion varies totally — the *bhadra* occupies two, the *salilāntara*s one, the *pratiratha* a quarter and the *karṇa* two units respectively. Thus, the faceting of the wall follows an asymmetrical pattern, interspersed by a regulated division. It is quite evident from the above that each temple has its own unique layout and *maṇḍovara* planning, although stylistically they may resemble each other, but a closer look brings out their uniqueness.

From the central and southern Rajasthan, two temples from Koṭāh district need to be mentioned here, since they represent the *triratha* plan temples with a *kapilī* and a small *mukhamaṇḍapa* as an extension of the Pratihāra type plan. One is the Sun Temple from Bodādit (*c.* CE 900-25)[27] and the other is Amvan Temple 2 of *c.* ninth century CE. Both are in the Mahā-Marū style. The *udgama*s are very tall and elaborately carved. The *pratiratha*s contain the *devāṅganā*s, while the *karṇa*s contains the *dikpāla*s. The *devakoṣṭha*s of the Bodādit Sun Temple, are canopied by a roof which is supported by *stambhikā*s. The roof is supported by small figures of *vyāla*s. The later protrusion of the *bhadra* is also occupied by figures which appear to divide the *bhadra* into a triptych with the two-sided columns further divided into two. This particular division of the *jaṅghā* actually occurs first at Osiā, and from here, in my view, it was adapted on the Sun Temple, Moḍherā on a very large scale. The sculpture of Bodādit is much multilated but the *devāṅganā*s on the *pratiratha* depict *alasā* and *padminī nāyikā*s (*fig.* 12). The *jaṅghā* programming of the Amvan Śiva Temple also follows the same mode of representation of images of attending female figurines in two rectangular boxes around the *bhadra devakoṣṭha*; a feature which reappears at Bodādit, Moḍherā and Atru. This feature of the Marū convention will be taken up while studying the Marū–Gurjara architecture.

It appears to be an important feature of Guhila and Cāhamāna temples that the figural sculptures placed in the *jaṅghā* of the *maṇḍovara*, are given a special treatment and individuality. The sculpture for architecture comes into its own in the tenth century only with these sites. And therefore, even though Osiā may have taken the lead, the overall development of architecture and the placement of sculpture in it, were devised entirely by the Mewāṛ artists of the Cāhamāna and Guhila monuments, in their transition from Mahā-Gurjara to Marū–Gurjara. The concept of sculpture integrated with architecture, was entirely non-existent in Mahā-Gurjara, but for the transitional phase, when there was a sudden outburst of sculpture. This can be observed at the Tusā, Āhaṛ and Nāgdā temples, of course, besides Jagat. This however, need not be confused with the already existing sculpture of Mātr̥kās in western India of the seventh and eighth century hailing from Śāmalājī, Aṁjhara, Mandasaur, Sondhani, Koṭyārka, Jagat, Mt. Ābu, etc. These sculptures, most likely may have existed as individual entities for ritual worship. But whether the "body" of architecture was draped with the "raiment" of sculpture, is not known. The sensibility for integrating sculpture with architecture should have posed a different kind of challenge and this watershed century with its prolific examples invites us to probe into this issue.

The Sun Temple at Tusā in Udaipur district (*c.* CE 975) resembles the Jagat Ambikā Temple in a modest way (*figs.* 23, 14). It is smaller in size and less crowded than Jagat, but the sculptural style and *jaṅghā* decoration clearly reminds us of Jagat. The *bhadra devakoṣṭha* has an image of Sūrya, seated in his seven-horsed chariot surrounded by a tiny *udgama*. The *bhadra* is flanked by a *pratiratha* in which two *devāṅganās* are placed; one involved in *kanduka-krīḍā* and the other in *alasā* pose, lifting her arms aloft. They are held on lotus pedestals without *koṣṭha* frames, while above them are *mālādhara* couples. These *devāṅganās* are accompanied by *kuṭilaka* and dwarfish attendants. These *devāṅganās* bear an allusion to time through their poses metaphorically. Their occurrence in conjunction with Sūrya, who signifies eternal movement, enables us to extend the metaphor further, in interpreting the two adjacent figures of *devāṅganās* as symbolically alluding to the "up and down movement" of the ball and the *aṅgadāyī* of time, as suggested often in Bharatanāṭyam dance by a *viraha nāyikā*, in the posture as the one struck by the *devāṅganā* on the left (*fig.* 23, 217).

The *salilāntara* follows next, which is occupied by *vyāla*s, while the *karṇa* is occupied by the *dikpāla*s. This unit of the sanctum is quite compact, yet open, since none of the sculptures are bound by any frame. This allows the surrounding space to interact with the space occupied by the sculptures. This feature will be slowly absorbed for a more crowded *jaṅghā* organization in the following centuries. The *naṭa-maṇḍapa* of the Tusā Sūrya Temple also needs a mention, since it contains eight Vidyādevī (*devāṅganā*) figures in its *vitāna*, in keeping with the tradition suggested by the texts and confirmed by practice in Gujarat, Rajasthan and central India from the tenth century onwards.[28]

Dhaky has an interesting observation on the placement of *nāyikā*s on *vitāna*s and this is the first time in our discussion on *devāṅganā* in temple architecture, that the question related to *vitāna* is occurring.

> The provision for *nāyikā*s in the form of supporting brackets attached to the pillars is highly significant, in that here one sees the beginning of that well-known convention not known in that age anywhere else in western India.[29]

Hence, according to Dhaky, at the Kāmeśvara Temple, Auwa, the *nāyikā*s on the *vitāna* are seen for the first time while in the tenth and later centuries its occurrence is quite usual. In our second chapter the section dealing with architectural texts, portions from *Aparājitapṛcchā* and *Samarāṅgaṇa Sūtradhāra* are quoted which throw light on the components of the *vitāna* and placement of the *devāṅganā*s. There is an interesting conformation of the text to architectural practice here.

The Mīrā Temple at Āhaṛ (*c.* CE 990) is another interesting temple, bigger in height and width as compared to the Tusā temple of the Mahā-Gurjara style in Udaipur region. It is an *anekāṇḍikā śikhara* structure, *pañcaratha* on plan. The *maṇḍapa* and *śikhara* appear highly renovated but the *garbha-gṛha maṇḍovara* seems to be original (*figs.* 24, 25).

(facing page)
fig. 26. Rānī Vāv, *devāṅganā*s, south buttress wall of the *kuṇḍ*, mid-eleventh century, Pāṭan, Gujarat, .

The *bhadra* contains Viṣṇu–Lakṣmī or Śiva–Pārvatī images surrounded by two *devāṅganā*s in the *bhadra pratiratha*, which bears two more *devāṅganā*s in its lateral wall facets. The *salilāntara* bears ferocious *vyāla*s while the *pratiratha* and its lateral sides support two *devāṅganā*s on a pedestal. The *stambhikā*s are slender and contain two drooping *tamāla patra*s. The *devāṅganā*s are so placed as though they were looking down from a balcony above. This convention of organizing the *pratiratha rathikā*s continues at Moḍherā and Rānī Vāv in Gujarat, where the images are not bound by the frame and breathe the surrounding space with ease (*fig*. 26). The imageries of *devāṅganā*s range from *nalinī*, *cāmara-dhāriṇī*, *vīṇāvādinī* to *markaṭaceṣṭā*, *alasā*, *sva-stana-sparśā,* etc. Probably a number of stylistic features of the *devāṅganā* sculptures of Mīrā Temple, Āhaṛ relate on the one hand to those at Ambikā Temple, Jagat and on the other to the sculpture of Rānī Vāv.

One sees a shade of both these styles on the Ādinātha Temple, Āhaṛ (*c*. CE 1000) *maṇḍovara*s, which depict a profusion of *devāṅganā* sculptures. It was built slightly later than the Mīrā Temple. The plinth is very high in keeping with the Jagat character and the *jaṅghā* portion quite squeezed and

fig. 27. Viṣṇu Temple, south face, general view, tenth century, Nāgdā, Udaipur, Rajasthan.

fig. 28. Harṣanātha Temple, *devāṅganā* blowing a conch, CE 956-73, Harṣagiri, Sīkar, Rajasthan.

compact. The *bharaṇī* and *kapotālī* have been pushed up by adding another moulding to contain Jaina *tīrthaṁkara*s. The *devāṅganā*s are carved in the same manner as at the Mīrā Temple, projecting out of the *stambhika*, but at the background of all these figures a thick foliage in the form of a stylized lotus stalk is carved. This reminds us of *yakṣī*s and their vegetation connotation. To find *yakṣī*s on Jaina temples is not unusual, since an allusion to vegetation and *yakṣī* is integrated into Jaina iconography. The *devāṅganā* imagery of *nūpurapādikā*, *vīṇādhāriṇı*, *darpaṇā*, *markaṭaceṣṭā*, *keśanistoyakāriṇī*, *alasā*, *kanduka krīḍā* (*fig.* 165), *prasādhikā*, and *putravallabhā* are found on this temple. Almost the entire range of *devāṅganā* imagery has been presented here. It must be noted here that the reliefs depicting the *tīrthaṁkara*s on the *maṇḍovara* have not compromised the prominence of the *devāṅganā* images. If one notices carefully, the cult images are never given prominence, nor profusion, on the tenth-century temples. It is the *vyāla*s, the *devāṅganā* and the *dikpāla*s, who have reigned supreme. That the sculptures of the *gūḍha-maṇḍapa* are much later than those of the *mūlaprāsāda*, is quite evident. On the *apsaras* of the southern *bhadra* niche, an inscription is carved which mentions the name Padmāvatī.[30] The arrival of the eleventh century is actually proclaimed by the Ādinātha Temple at Āhaṛ, and Dhaky opines that the Viṣṇu Temple (Nāgdā) stands at the end of one tradition and the Jaina Temple at the beginning of the other. The difference between the two is due not so much to the time factor. Hardly a quarter of a century separates the two. It is due to a separate phenomenon that had happened precisely during that very interval, namely the fusion of the Mahā-Marū style of the upper Rajasthan with the Mahā-Gurjara style of the lower Rajasthan and Gujarat. The Āhaṛ temple reflects the impact of the art of the Marū land and hence its ideals and expression.

The Nāgdā temples known as the Sās-Bahū temples are Vaiṣṇavite in affiliation (*fig.* 27). Sculptures of these temples show strong stylistic affinities with those on Jagat, Tusā and Koṭai temples. The presence of the typical leaf and chain leitmotif along the upper edge of the wall, reminds us of the same feature which is in an identical position on the Lakulīśa Temple in the Ekaliṅgajī group. The walls of *garbha-gṛha* and *antarāla* are plain, while a host of sculptural figures are placed on the *maṇḍapa* exterior as well as the interior. In the *vitāna* of one of the temples, eight figures of *śālabhañjikā*s are found. The magnificence of decorative carvings in the interior, is balanced by the simplicity of the exterior.

The most magnificent and sculpturally excelling temples of the Cāhamāna times in Rajasthan are the Śiva Temple on the Harṣagiri Hill near Sīkar (CE 956-73) and the Nīlakaṇṭheśvara Temple at Kekind (CE 956) which are coeval.

Much of the Harṣagiri Temple[31] is dilapidated, hence it is not very convenient to study the programming of its *maṇḍovara* sculptures or the proportional relationship of the different parts of its *ratha*s. Nevertheless, out of the existing sculptural figures of *devāṅganā*s *in situ* on the sanctum wall, one is able to observe a range of imagery devised by the artists and to realize that this image type has now come into its own. The larger figures placed on individual lotus pedestals appear to sway in unison to the rhythm of the music they are engrossed in. Some of them are shown playing on a *vīṇā*, some blowing a conch, some holding flowers and garlands or standing with rapt attention, fixing their gaze on the horizon. Some are also decorating themselves or holding *cāmara*s. The *kṣipta* knee enhancing the curve of the body, or *svastika pada* inducing a dance-like movement can be observed in every figure. There is no stiffness in any of the figures; instead their movement adds dynamism to the otherwise stationary architecture (*fig.* 28). Only the *devāṅganā*s holding the *vīṇā* and possibly flute are accompanied by drummers and flautists and are made to stand below a densely foliate tree. Here, traces of vegetation connection can be deciphered. These *devāṅganā*s are actually seventeen in number and stand surrounding the sculpture of Gaurī or Pārvatī.

Interesting figures of *devāṅganā*s are also found in the doorway sculpture, *antarāla* panel and *kakṣāsana* balustrade, although this may not have been their original place. The doorway *mithuna*s merit special mention, since they seem to depict some *śṛṅgārika* events, a feature that was first observed at the Khilchipura pillars (referred to in the sculpture chapter), the origin of which goes back to the Mathurā pillars.[32]

Similarity in the treatment of the sculptural form of this temple sculpture, especially with that of the *devāṅganā*s of Jagat and Kekind, is striking, but they are coeval and might have exchanged ideas between them but the similarity with Khajurāho is even more striking.

They almost impose their presence upon the monument and stand there with grace and poise, as if to communicate with the onlooker. The sculptors of the tenth century go out of their way to decorate their temples with *devāṅganā*s so much so that at Nīlakaṇṭheśvara Temple, Kekind (*fig.* 11) the *devāṅganā*s are placed prominently in the *devakoṣṭha*s of the *pratiratha*s and also on the lateral facets, while the mother goddesses, the Sapta-Mātr̥kās are pushed into the *salilāntara*. The *karṇa* retains the *dikpāla*s and thus completes the programming. The uniqueness about Kekind is: (i) the incorporation of Mātr̥kās on the *jaṅghā*, a placement never offered to them before and (ii) the prominent placement given to *devāṅganā*s. But in terms of depiction of the imagery, the sculptor has truly excelled above our expectations. The disposition of the figures which are generally in *svastika* or *gatāgata* or *baddhācārī* posture, is extremely dynamic and full of vigour. Their outstretched arms in *uromaṇḍalī hasta* (*fig.* 216), despite mutilation, create an impression of verve and strength. The imageries of these *devāṅganā*s will be discussed in the sculpture section. Dhaky observes their stylistic similarity (especially of the headgear, coiffure and ornaments) with the *devāṅganā*s of Lakṣmaṇa Temple, Khajurāho (CE 954) in a generic way.[33] The pattern created by the placement of figures on the Śiva Temple, Kekind is d, b, c, c, b, a, b, c, c, b, that creates symmetry and rhythmic order on all the three sides of the sanctum.

Khajurāho and the Central Indian Contingent

This section has been specifically separated from the previous one in order to focus more closely on the central Indian temples of the tenth century and the role of sculpture in their architecture, which has a strong stamp of its own individual style and design organization. The Khajurāho sculptures have been extolled as the most glorious sculptures of medieval India but little has been done to probe into their antecedents, the Gurjara–Pratihāra phase.[34] The present

(facing page)
fig. 29. Bajramaṭha, western face, *c.* tenth century, Gyāraspur, Vidiśā, Madya Pradesh

section is an attempt to discuss at length Khajurāho and certain other temples of the tenth century in central India, which cannot be overlooked in the broad survey of *devāṅganā* sculpture on Nāgara temple architecture of the medieval period. Parimoo observes that the whole articulation of the temple wall changed by the tenth century, as the Candellas became the patrons in Bundelkhaṇḍ and the Solaṅkīs in Gujarat. As the articulation of the wall became more evolved, the role of the sculptor became more demanding. During the second phase of the medieval period however, the phenomenon of the collaboration between the architect and the sculptor became very dynamic. It is at Khajurāho that the sculptor emerges as the most eloquent, and the temple turns into a sculptor's paradise.[35]

The following temples of Madhyadeśa of the tenth century will be discussed here: of the Kaḷacuri–Cedi style in Dahala region, the

Mahādeva Temple, Nohṭā (Damoh district) (*fig.* 16); Śiva Temple, Marai (Satnā district) (*fig.* 17); Virāṭeśvara Temple, Sohāgpur (Shahdol district); Śiva Temple, Kodal (Damoh district); Bajramaṭha, Gyāraspur (Vidiśā district) (*figs.* 29, 30); and Pāli (Bilāspur district).

The group of temples of the Kacchapaghāta in the Gopagiri region Surwaya (Śivapurī district) (*figs.* 31, 32); Mohajamātā Temple, Terāhī (Śivapurī district) (*fig.* 33); Kakanmaṛh Temple, Suhāniā (Morena district); as also temples at Padhavali and Mitaoli, in the same district; Ṭoṭeśvara Mahādeva temples, Temple 1, Khirniwālā Group 7, Kaḍwāhā (Guṇā distirct) (*figs.* 19, 20, 21), Chorepura ruined temple (Śivapurī district); Sās-Bahū temples of Gwalior Fort; the temple of the Candellas of Jejākabhukti from Lakṣmaṇa (*c.* CE 954) to Duladeo (early twelfth century), from the Mālwā region under Paramāra sway, and Udayeśvara Temple of CE 1059-80 built by King Udayāditya (*fig.* 22).

fig. 30. Bajramaṭha, north face, Gyaraspur, Vidiśa, Madhya Pradesh

The Śiva Temple at Kodal (CE 900) is an interesting structure. The *śikhara* is *triratha* but the *garbha-gṛha* is *pañcaratha*, the *kapilī* has a broad *śukanāsa* at the top and the temple has no *gūḍha-maṇḍapa* or a *mukhacatuṣkī*. The *pīṭha* is broad and tall, which carries traces of Gurjara–Pratihāra elements, some contemporaneous and some of a century anterior, viz. the tall intricately carved *udgama*. The *jaṅghā* is clearly divided into two tiers by a *madhyapatra* — a floral motif. The upper section contains *vyāla*s and *gandharva*s and Śaiva *ṛṣi*s, while the lower section contains *devāṅganā*s placed in *pratiratha* and *salilāntara* with the *dikpāla*s on the *karṇa* and the main deity's form in the *devakoṣṭha*. The *devāṅganā* figures placed either on the *pratiratha* or the *salilāntara* merge with the outer space of the wall facets, are not bound by any *stambhikā* framework. This typical Mahā-Gurjara feature is also traceable at Jagat, Tusā and Koṭai but

fig. 31. Temple 2, west wall, *c.* tenth century, Sūrwaya, Śivapurī, Madya Pradesh

at Āhaṛ, Kekind and some other sites, the *stambhikā*-bound frames become an established convention. The imagery of the *devāṅganā* also draws our attention because the entire range is represented here with immense vigour and abandon. The highly dynamic figures, seem to bend and sway, striking ever-captivating sensual postures. The *devāṅganā* prototypes seen are the *prasādhikā*, *vasana-bhraṁśā*, *sva-stana-sparśā*, *alasā*, *keśanistoyakāriṇī*, *padminī*, *cāmaradhāriṇī* and *nartakī*. The preference for *baddhācārī* (*figs.* 137, 146), *nūpurapādikā*, *avaspanditā cārī*s and *āyata, avahita, tryasra, gatāgata, svastika, valita, moṭita sthānaka*s of dance, in the depiction of the *devāṅganā*s, can be observed. Many of these postures are used in *nāṭya* such as *āyata* and *avahita* and by the virtue of their being adapted for these images; the entire *maṇḍovara* appears to have been used as a theatrical arena by the sculptors.

Temples of the early tenth century pre-Khajurāho phase are Nohṭā in Damoh district and Marai in Satnā district. The *śikhara* is of the *latinā* type primarily with a *triratha* plan, but the presence of broad *salilāntara*s on the *maṇḍovara* have necessarily converted it

fig. 32. Temple 2, south wall, *c.* tenth century, Sūrwaya, Śivapurī, Madya Pradesh

into a *pañcaratha* ground plan. The temple is placed on a prominent *pīṭha* and the parts of it are highly developed. The *maṇḍovara* is divided into three tiers horizontally and a *madhyapatra* decorative creeper serves as the divider. The second tier contains *udgama*s which are placed above each image of *dikpāla*, *vyāla* and *devāṅganā*. The largest *udgama* is obviously above the *devakoṣṭha* which contains *varāha*. The third tier is separated by a *mañcika* and in the *devakoṣṭha* above *varāha*, a seated image of Sūrya is placed, while other sculptures represent *mithuna*s, *devāṅganā*s, dancing groups, etc. The temple also has a large-pillared *maṇḍapa* and a porch, but with no sculpture on this section. It is similar to the temple of Śiva at Maihar in Satnā district, dating from CE 960, which is locally known as Golmaṭh.

Marai has a ruined temple constructed on a high plinth. The *śikhara* has completely collapsed and so have the upper portions of its *maṇḍapa* and *mukhamaṇḍapa*. The *maṇḍovara* of the sanctum wall is divided into two tiers and contains highly graceful but heavily proportioned sculptures of *vyāla*s, *devāṅganā*s, *dikpāla*s on the lower

fig. 33. Mohajamātā Temple, view from the north, *c.* tenth-eleventh centuries, Terāhī, Śivapurī, Madya Pradesh

tier; and *vasus*, *devāṅganās*, and erotic couples on the upper tier. The *nūpurapādikā* and *markaṭaceṣṭā* are represented on the *pratiratha* around the *devakoṣṭha*. The *vyālas* are as large as the human figures (*fig*. 17).

The most developed among the Kaḷacuri temples are the Virāṭeśvara Temple of Sohāgpur and the Śiva Temple at Pālī, which are *c*. eleventh-twelfth-century temples. At Pāli, the *maṇḍovara* is highly ornate, the *jaṅghā* sculptures are placed in three tiers and each tier is supported by *bhāraputras*. The repertoire of the sculptural decoration is highly elaborate; one could say matching that at Khajurāho. *Vyālas* of various types in the *salilāntara* and *devāṅganās* in dancing modes, *śṛṅgārika* and *raudra* modes, are placed on each facet of the temple *pratiratha* walls. The sculptures have now become so profuse and activated, that the whole wall has become complex and replete with a varied imagery. The occurrence of cultic images is markedly much less, compared with iconographically less rigid motifs of *devāṅganās*, *vyālas* and their various manifestations. At this period, Nāgara temple architecture is a celebration of the sacred and the secular, without which the cosmic order could never have been complete. The sensuous, the ferocious and the erotic combine to form the secular repertoire of the temple's decor.

The Bajramaṭha Temple at Gyāraspur, is a less ornate Kacchapaghāta structure of the tenth century, which is triple shrined and hence its *maṇḍovara* is very broad and multifaceted. The much dilapidated *maṇḍapa* is supported on three rows of pillars which lend a lot of bay space to the interior. While watching the temple from the corners of the south-east or the northern sides, the tiered roof of the side shrines cusps at the centre to join the main *latinā śikhara*. Structurally a unique temple, Bajranātha also has some unique type of *devāṅganās*. Divided into two parts by a horizontal band of creepers, the *maṇḍovara* contains figures of deities, *dikpālas*, *devāṅganās* (*figs*. 29-30) but not of *vyālas*, etc. The upper tier is devoid of any sculpture. It is quite clear that empty spaces meant a lot at this stage but this gradually gave way to figural forms and exhibition of spatial organization and virtuosity. The unique type of *devāṅganā*

fig. 34. Ṭoṭeśvara Temple, *jaṅghā* sculpture, west wall, Kaḍwāhā.

fig. 35. Ṭoṭeśvara Temple,
jaṅghā sculpture,
west wall, Kaḍwāhā.

found at Bajranātha is a horse-headed lady dancing in *āyata maṇḍala*, one foot in *kuñcita*, holding a fish and a cup. Perhaps, it is a representation of Mātṛkā Vārāhī. The other Kacchapaghāta temples of the tenth century hail from Sūrawaya, Terāhī (Mohajamātā Temple); Suhāniā (Kakanmaṛh); Kaḍwāhā (Khirniwālā group) and Gwalior (Sās-Bahū temples).

Both Surawaya Temple II and Mohajamātā Temple at Terāhī are devoid of *śikhara*. The plinth is not very high and the *maṇḍovara* is not very tall. The *maṇḍapa* in front is supported on four pillars. The *bhadra* niche houses the Andhakāsuravadha Śiva (*figs.* 31, 32, 33) surmounted by a canopied *chatra*. The *udgama*s above the *bhadra* and *karṇa* are large, reminding us of the Gurjara–Pratihāra period temples of Badoh–Paṭhārī and Terāhī. The *devāṅganā*s stand on the *pratiratha* which has drooping foliage. The *devāṅganā*s are not bound by any frame and stand gracefully on their pedestals (*fig.* 33); on the west wall there is a noteworthy sculpture of a lady with her back towards us lifting her foot as if to pluck a thorn.[36]

The Mohajamātā Temple has an elaborate design of sculptural figures, occupying both the tiers and representing *devāṅganā*s, *dikpāla*s, *vyāla*s and *devī*s. Many figures are depicted striking *āyata maṇḍala* postures. The second tier of sculptures on the west, south and north walls are occupied by skeletal and demon-faced figures. On the lower tier Mātṛkās are arranged thus suggesting mother goddess worship and Tāntric ritualism (*fig.* 33).

The Chandalmaḍh Temple, Kaḍwāhā, belongs to the first half of tenth century; the second half is represented by a small Śiva Temple near Murayat of *c.* CE 975; and the Khirniwālā group represents the first quarter of the eleventh century. Murayat dates from *c.* CE 1075 closing the cycle towards the end of the eleventh century. At the Khirniwālā group temple I, one sees a compact treatment of the *maṇḍovara* in which the *devāṅganā*s and *dikpāla*s are placed in two horizontal bands. The sculptures remain mainly embedded into the stone surface but the postures are highly accentuated and create a great sense of movement. The *salilāntara* is broader than the *ratha-pratiratha*, which allows greater space for the sculptural forms. The lower band contains *devāṅganā*s, *vyāla*s and *dikpāla*s while the upper band in the *salilāntara* bears the forms of dancing *devāṅganās* instead of the *vyālas*.

The Ṭoṭeśvara Temple of *c.* eleventh century at Kaḍwāhā is a temple of singular beauty for its figural sculptures. The elongated figures, elegantly bent with accentuated grace are carved with great plastic facility. The ornamentation is rather understated with the result sensuality of the plastic form is accentuated. The sculptures are characterized by the highly attenuated proportions and both male and female figure types are slimmer even than the figures at Kekind. The *devakoṣṭhas* are now empty but the upper row contains figures of couples, *devāṅganās* and *dikpālas*. Most of the sculptures are mutilated but never fail to create an impact (*figs.* 20, 21, 34, 35). The noteworthy *devāṅganās* are *keśanistoyakāriṇī*, *kanduka-krīḍā*, *darpaṇā*, *prasādhikā*, *nartakī* and *alasā* which compare admirably well with the Lakṣmaṇa or Kandarīya Mahādeva Temple *devāṅganās* (*fig.* 262).

The two temples of Sās-Bahū at Gwalior mark the culmination of the Kacchapaghāta architecture. Both are Vaiṣṇava temples, the larger one was completed by Kacchapaghāta Mahipāla in CE 1093.[37] Its plan comprises a sanctum, *antarāla* and *mahāmaṇḍapa* with three entrance porches; the temple has grand dimensions and an impressive design showing a two-storeyed elevation for the *antarāla* and the entrance porch and a three-storeyed elevation for the *mahāmaṇḍapa* which has lofty *samavarṇa* roof. The roof has a circular ceiling supported on pillars, and therefore, there is not much of a *maṇḍovara* wall. There is only one recognizable *devāṅganā*, *keśanistoyakāriṇī* while the rest of the figures are of deities and their consorts. The *maṇḍapa* interior contains *alasā*, *vasanabhraṁśā*, *sva-stana-sparśā*, *putravallabhā,* etc. The smaller temple, which is like a *naṭa-maṇḍapa,* has a series of dancing figures girdling the pillars, suggesting a movement in unison.

The early temples of Dahala and Kacchapaghāta suggest the stylistic base for Khajurāho temples. Also the Kodal, the Kaḍwāhā, and the Nohṭā styles seem to have possibly blended together, to form the Candella idiom, and perhaps the sculptors too would have expanded their ideas, norms, forms and aesthetic sensibilities. The two-tiered *maṇḍovara*, high plinth, *anekāṇḍikā śikhara*, prominent *bhadra* niches, *vyāla*s placed in *salilāntara* some of the features which remain unchanged. The Candella style strikes its individual note with the sculptures of *devāṅganā*s and *nāginī*s, *mithuna*s and *vyāla*s on the *maṇḍovara* designed very intricately to fill the *ratha-pratiratha-salilāntara* facets. The basic decorative scheme followed by Khajurāho artists bears witness to precision in general as well as in its particular treatment of sculptural form and decorative motif. The manner in which sculpture and decoration pulsate the surface of the temple exterior is unmatched.

The Lakṣmaṇa Temple is considered the earliest temple constructed by the Candella Yaśovarman in *c*. CE 950. It is a Vaiṣṇavite temple of the *pañcāyatana* variety. The Pārśvanātha Temple appears stylistically closer to Lakṣmaṇa, having been built during early part of Dhaṅga's reign in *c*. CE 950-70. Despite its Jaina affiliation, it is adorned with Vaiṣṇava sculptures. Sculpturally and architecturally, the Śiva temple of Viśvanātha comes midway between Lakṣmaṇa and Kandarīya, and its importance lies in the fact that it anticipates in plan, design and ornamentation, Kandarīya that marks the culmination of central Indian architectural building style. Viśvanātha Temple (*c*. CE 1002), Devī Jagdambā, Citragupta, Vāmana and Ādinātha temples are notable for their excellent sculptures, including nymphs flaunting their voluptuous charms in an infinite variety of gestures and flexions. Duladeo is the most developed Saptaratha Temple, having a large closed hall with the ceiling embellished with twenty *apsaras* brackets grouped in bunches. It is datable to the twelfth century and marks the last glow of the remarkable vitality of Candella art.

On Lakṣmaṇa Temple, the river goddesses and *nāginī*s appear on the *salilāntara* and other *phālanā*s of the *maṇḍovara*, wearing hoods and standing either with folded hands or engaged in all the activities that the *devāṅganā*s do (*fig*. 18). They are *keśanistoyakāriṇī*, *darpaṇā*, *vasanabhraṁśā*, *nalinī*, *alasā*, *vīṇāvādinī*, etc. Some of them have five to seven serpenthoods above their heads, while the body is completely feminine. There is no tail and these females stand firmly on their feet. They are placed in the rain water recesses metaphorically by the artist to suggest their fluvial connection. They stand with folded hands as if venerating the deity and illustrating its abode. While not repeating this action, they are also given the attributes and actions of the *devāṅganās*; since they are all auspicious and boon-bestowing protective spirits. Their interchangeability, based on their aquatic connection, on various parts of the temple are noteworthy. On Kandarīya Mahādeva, *nāginīs* with folded arms are present only on *salilāntara* along with *vyālas* while at Viśvanātha they appear on the *karṇa kṣobhana* projection of the *bhadra*. They stand prominently adjoining the *bhadra kṣobhanas* engaged in actions of *keśanistoyakāriṇī*, *sadyasnātā* or *nalinī*, indicating vegetal and aquatic principles.

On Lakṣmaṇa, Viśvanātha and Devī Jagdambī temples, *bhadra* niche is converted into *kakṣāsana* balcony, thus sculptures are present only in the *antarāla* connecting *garbha-gṛha* and *gūḍha-maṇḍapa* and the other between *gūḍha-maṇḍapa* and *mukhamaṇḍapa*. This is a unique positioning for sculpture. The *vyālas* are present in *salilāntara* but the new form of *devāṅganā–nāginī* combine can be noticed in many temples in conjunction with the erotic sculptures on the conjoints of the *antarāla* and *maṇḍapa* sections. The entire range of *devāṅganā* imagery is present here and enfolds several times on one and the same monument. At Kandarīya Mahādeva, the *pratiratha* is further faceted into five *phālanās*, *karṇas* and *kṣobhanas*. *Devāṅganā* sculptures not only appear on these facets but they are also present on the *sandhāra* vestibule on the walls of the *garbha-gṛha* (*fig.* 262). They reveal women in sensuous poses captured in intimate activities, as if seen by their lovers or seen by the adepts in spirituality whose goals are way above the world of sensuality. At Khajurāho temples in general, due to variety and multiplicity of form, the identification of *devāṅganās* and *nāyikās* is completely blurred, thus finding meaning

fig. 36. Sun temple, south wall, early eleventh century, Moḍherā, Gujarat.

becomes ambiguous and futile. Individual *devāṅganā* imagery, however, has been discussed in the special chapters on *devāṅganā* imagery and meaning.

The culmination of the decorative sensibility of the tenth century is the celebration of the sculptor's virtuosity with the depiction of human figures and a glorification of the temple as the Cosmos in stone. This is seen in all its splendour in the tenth century on the Lakṣmaṇa Temple at Khajurāho. The high plinth lends soaring height and an expanding breadth bequeaths an unprecedented majesty to these temples (*fig.* 18). It would not be an exaggeration to say that the Khajurāho temples are as exquisite as a finely-cut diamond, as delicate as a smoothly finished silk, as intricate as filigree — an epitome of perfection in nature, could they have been created by men or gods?

Marū–Gurjara Temples

The merger of the Marū and the Gurjara styles led to a great efflorescence in temple architecture in western India. Great temples were built at Kirāḍu, Moḍherā, Pāṭan, Mt. Ābu and Osiā, charged with the new vitality and dynamism sparked by the composite style. The mid-tenth-century temples of Jagat, Kekind, Auwa and Koṭai were already showing signs of change but the actual Marū–Gurjara decorative opulence came about only by the eleventh century CE.

The Sun Temple at Moḍherā in Mehsānā district is a structure of very fine proportions and heavy embellishment (*fig.* 36). At the Moḍherā Temple site, there is a *kuṇḍa* with shrines on all four corners that date from the beginning of the eleventh century while the temple proper is after CE 1026 (Bhīmadeva I phase) while the dancing hall, gateway, main temple from *mukhamaṇḍapa* till the *garbha-gṛha* are executed in the third quarter of the eleventh century.[38] Although Marū–Gurjara style leads to heavy embellishment, the sculpture itself loses plasticity and naturalism in favour of stiffness and exaggerated bends. Fortunately at Moḍherā, the state of dullness has not arrived. In fact, the monument pulsates with diverse handling of *maṇḍovara* and *jaṅghā* sculptures which is uniquely different from that at Jagat, Kirāḍu or Koṭai but carry on from Osiā, Atru and

Bodādit to suggest a connecting link. It has the unique convention of designing a *devakoṣṭha* which is occupied by the figural image in the centre and its *kṣobhana*, buttresses which are divided into two, the upper one occupied by a decorative motif, a figure or a *vyāla,* while the lower one contains *apsaras*, *devāṅganā*, *ṛṣi,* etc. framed by a *stambhikā*. The *vyāla* is also used as a bracket to support the canopy above, on which a tall *udgama* is carved. In my observation, the Sun Temple, Bodādit; Śyāma Sundara Temple, Atru and Temple II, Amwan form the stylistic inspiration for Moḍherā *maṇḍovara* design (*figs*. 12, 37, 38).

fig. 37. Śyām Sundar Temple, *mūlaprāsāda*, south *jaṅghā* sculptural frame relate with Osiā and Moḍherā, *c.* late ninth century, Atru, Koṭā, Rajasthan.

At Moḍherā, the sculpture porgramming on the *maṇḍovara* wall is quite unique and elaborate. The presence of Ādityas, Gaurīs, *dikpālas*, *ṛṣis*, *mātṛkās*, and *apsaras*es on the *maṇḍapa* and *garbhagṛha* walls maintain a logic of their own (*fig.* 36). The Devīs or Gaurīs

fig. 38. Temple 2, Mandovar, Southwall, ninth century, Amvan.

are twelve in total, and six each are placed on either side of the *maṇḍapa* wall projections, i.e. the south and the north sides. The Ādityas are also twelve and they are placed on either side of the *garbha-gṛha* wall facets, six on each side. The *dikpāla*s are placed on the *karṇa*s of the *garbha-gṛha*, *antarāla* and *maṇḍapa,* which make them ten in total.[39] Looking at the arrangement of Ādityas and *devāṅganā*s, one is tempted to look for some pattern in the arrangement of these figures but has to admit that their placement is arbitrary and does not conform to any logical sequencing. Thus artists have taken liberty to arrange the figures in close vicinity of the Ādityas, but not necessarily adding any metaphoric meaning. Hence, any semiotic analysis does not seem plausible.

Kirāḍu, north-west of Bāḍmer, has one Vaiṣṇava and four Śaiva temples, dating from the first half of the eleventh century. According to Dhaky, the Viṣṇu temple at Kirāḍu is the first definite landmark

attesting to the stylistic fusion of Marū and Gurjara styles, that were to appear about a generation later (*figs.* 39, 40).

fig. 39. Someśvara Temple, general view, west face, mid-eleventh century, Kirāḍu, Bāḍmer, Rajasthan.

The Viṣṇu temple at Kirāḍu has a stylistic affinity with the Dilwāṛā temple, Mt. Ābu as rightly pointed out by Dhaky with reference to its sculptures and grooved *udgamas*. This would suggest that the guild working at Kirāḍu had possibly more immediate relations with Mt. Ābu rather than with Medapāṭa, Ānartta or Mālwa.[40] Dating from somewhere between second half of the tenth century and first half of the eleventh century, this temple bears some very significant features; the presence of a true *narathara* and *gajathara* on the *pīṭha* and the presence of *mañcika*, and it also has the first full-fledged *samavarṇa*. There is a *rūpapaṭṭikā* above the *vedībandha*, not found before in Gujarat, at this position. For the junction between *maṇḍapa* and *śikhara*, the *pratikarṇa* is formed for coupling, because of which the *śikhara* in profile assumes a sort of pseudo rotundity. This convention is not found on Solaṅkī temples of Gujarat. The *raṅga-maṇḍapa* is twice in ratio to the sanctum and thus, too broad for the size of the shrine as a whole. Although this region was not under the Solaṅkīs, its stylistic affinity as well as the imagery of *devāṅganās* finds close connections with the neighbouring Solaṅkī regional temples.

The *mūlaprāsāda* of the Someśvara Temple at Kirāḍu has *caturaṅga*, and the *bhadra kṣobhanas* contain *caurī*-bearers attending on the deity in the *bhadra* niche. Followed by *devāṅganās* in the *pratiratha*, *dikpālas* in the *karṇa*, the fourth *aṅga* called *nandika*, contains one more pair of *devāṅganās* in the profile, which is a feature hardly repeated in the Solaṅkī temples (*fig.* 39).[41] The *rathikas*, which contain the sculptures of *devāṅganās* and the *dikpālas*, are surmounted by *udgamas*, which look like the Kekind ones and so do the sculptures, which stylistically relate with the Kekind Mātṛkās and *devāṅganās*. Despite much damage, the sculptures of *devāṅganās* holding a bow and arrow or involved in *vasanabhraṁśā* act are visible. A representation of a *vīra nāyikā* holding a *khaṭvāṅga* and wearing *muṇḍamālā*, is seen on the south wall near Andhakāsuravadha Śiva. The figure appears to be in a mood of great dynamism and would swing into action any moment. There are

fig. 40. Viṣṇu Temple, general view, mid-eleventh century, Kirādu, Bāḍmer, Rajasthan.

devāṅganās on the lateral *phālanās* as well. The *salilāntaras* are occupied by the *vyālas* as well as *r̥ṣis*.

The large open-pillared *maṇḍapa* near Viṣṇu temple bears *devāṅganā* sculptures carved on their pillar-bases looking closely akin to the Badoli pillar *devāṅganās*. Their actions, postures and the manner in which they jut out into the space enliven the Badoli grace. The same convention appears at Gwalior, Gurgī, Ābu, Alwar, Moḍherā, Kirāḍu, and many other sites. Hence, the study of pillar sculptures also emerges as an important case study for *devāṅganā* figures (*figs*. 181, 266). The *keśanistoyakāriṇī*, *alasā*, *markaṭaceṣṭā* and some more imageries are identifiable while the rest are badly mutilated.

Rānī Vāv at Pāṭan and Kumbhariā in north Gujarat and Mt. Ābu in southern Rajasthan are important sites for stylistic homogeneity. The Jaina and Śaiva temples at Kumbhariā of the early eleventh century anticipate the Dilwāṛā group of Vimala Vasahī and Lūṇa Vasahī of CE 1031 and 1230, commissioned by Vimala Shah and Vastūpāla–Tejapāla, the ministers of the Solaṅkī dynasty who were Jainas. They bear memorable figures of *vidyādevīs*, *apsarases*, dancers, musicians, etc. on pillars, ceilings and *maṇḍovara*.

The Saccīyamātā group of temples at Osiā (*c*. CE 1025) have a fine structure in which the *jaṅghā* sculptures and the entire *maṇḍovara* design, resemble the Solaṅkī style of the Marū–Gurjara phase (*fig*. 41). It bears an inscription dated CE 1178 referring to repairs done by one Sādhu Gayapāla. The placement of *devāṅganās* on its *maṇḍovara* will be discussed in the sculpture section.

In the final phase of architectural development at Osiā, one comes across the Marū–Gurjara features on the Saccīyamātā Temple, dating back to around *c*. CE 1025. The *maṇḍovara* is well preserved and the temple rests on a high plinth which has a *gajathara, narathara,* etc. clearly defined. The *jaṅghā* portion is very narrow and contains sculptures in *rathikas*, which have inverted leaves on both their *stambhikas*. The *bhadra* niche contains gods with their consorts. Its *stambhikas* with *vyāla-makara* brackets support a large *udgama* and sloping roof. This convention is originally a Mahā-Marū

fig. 41. Saccīyamātā Temple,
maṇḍovara sculpture,
south wall, *c.* CE 1025
Osiā, Jodhpur, Rajasthan.

feature found at Osiā, Chittor and Kekind. The *salilāntara*s contain *ṛṣi*s while the *vyāla*s are completely absent. The *devāṅganā*s are prominently placed and their hierarchical position has remained intact for four centuries. On the *jaṅghā* of the western *devakulika*'s north wall, *devāṅganā*s like *sva-stana-sparśā*, *markaṭaceṣṭā*, *yoginī* (holding *kapāla*, wearing *jaṭābhāra* and *muṇḍamālā*) are quite noticeable *(fig.* 41). On the east *devakulika,* on the north side are *putravallabhā*, *alasā* and *nūpurapādikā devāṅganā*s (*figs.* 152, 226). The *ratha*s are proportionately organized based on a ratio of 1:5:1:2:1:1:5 from *karṇa* to *pratiratha* to *bhadra*, on each directional facet. The presence of *yoginī* and *kirātī* type of *devāṅganā*s at Kirāḍu and Osiā will be studied more closely in the sculpture section.

Eleventh and Twelfth Centuries: The Final Phase

Majority of the temples in this section are a continuation of the Marū–Gurjara idiom, which came into vogue and spread like wild fire between Gujarat and adjoining areas of Rajasthan and Madhya Pradesh. The attempt is to enlist those temples which still employ the *devāṅganā* sculptures in the *salilāntara*s, *vitāna*s and on the pillars.

The temples listed here, corresponding to the phase of the Solaṅkī period rulers, help to identify the stylistic features better: (Bhīmadeva I Phase, CE 1022-66) — Limbojīmātā Temple, Delmal; Someśvara Temple, Gorad; Śiva Temple, Sander (Karṇadeva Phase, CE 1066-94) (*fig.* 42) — Nīlakaṇṭha Mahādeva Temple, Sunak (*fig.* 43); Śāntinātha and Mahāvīra temples, Kumbhariā (Siddharāja Phase, CE 1094–1144); Pārśvanātha Temple, Kumbhariā (*fig.* 244); Navalakhā Temple, Sejakpur (*fig.* 44) (Bhīmadeva II Phase, CE 1178–1242); Navalakhā Temple, Ghumlī.

The Delmal Temple is *dviaṅga*; its *raṅga maṇḍapa* is compact and connected with the main shrine by a *kapilī*. The *jaṅghā* sculptures contain the *devāṅganā*s and *dikpāla*s along with *ṛṣi*s but not *vyāla*s. In profile, the images project out from their niches and pedestals. But plasticity seems compromised for stiffness in forms, the monumentality of the sculpted form is compromised altogether.

Sculptures on all the eleventh/twelfth-century temples are marked by exaggeration and accentuation. Notice the Śiva Temple at

fig. 42.
Śiva temple,
general view,
c. twelfth centuries,
Sander, Mehsānā, Gujarat.

fig. 43. Śiva temple,
general view,
mid-eleventh century,
Sunak, Mehsānā, Gujarat.

Kumbhariā, which is *triratha* in plan; even the lateral facets contain sculptures making the walls pulsate with action. The sculptures of *devāṅganā*s are bent, twisted and turned around their axis, the *madhya sūtra*. Each lateral facet is distinguished by deep *salilāntara*s. This interplay of spaces articulates the visual beauty of the *maṇḍovara* form in total. This is a new feature of the mature medieval period sculpture where *devāṅganā*s are not only multiplied but also reposed with expressive dancing postures. What should not surprise in their representation, is the aquatic association that is still noticed in the lotus pedestal on which they stand. This allusion to their original form as the vegetal–aquatic personifications in nature are still extant.

At Sander, on the main temple with a *samavaraṇa maṇḍapa*, the plinth is very tall and the *jaṅghā* sculptures occupy very little space at a very high level (*fig.* 42). The conventions of designing are the same as in Delmal, Gorad, etc. but the quality of carving is such that the sculptures do not really project out. The *salilāntara*s contain *ṛṣi*s in different postures of penance which lend a punctuation to the projecting rhythm of the *jaṅghā* design. Dhaky observes an appearance of an *upabhadra* here, which is an advancement over Koṭai or Moḍherā; indicating the beginning of the tendency towards further elaboration. The circular ceiling has the eight *nāyikā*s still in their position.[42]

Taking a global view of the eleventh-twelfth-century temples in Gujarat and Madhya Pradesh, one notices that at Khajurāho for instance, the height increases dramatically, so also the multiplicity of the *phālanā*s and *ratha*s. Thus, both linear as well as transverse accent is noticeable. Whereas, in the ninth- and tenth-century temples, it was possible to grasp the shapes and forms of the *jaṅghā* sculptures, but with the subsequent period, each individual decorative motif, human or divine figure and form, lost their individuality. This change in the syntax of the architecture and sculpture is clearly represented. This could be labelled as the "Baroque" phase of temple décor and design in which the work of art gets charged with momentum and dynamism, swirling around the compositional axes in almost all directions. There is no empty space

(facing page)
fig. 44. Navalakhā Temple, general view, *c.* twelfth century, Sejakpur, Saurāṣṭra, Gujarat.

left disallowing one's eyes to focus on one thing but enabling a "helicopter view".

The Gujarat temples do not increase in height like the Khajurāho ones, but the intense vertical faceting of the structure is present in both the structures. The *jaṅghā* of Khajurāho temples is divided into three tiers, while providing *kakṣāsanas* and *garbha-gṛha* and *gūḍha-maṇḍapa* positions. Gujarat temples peculiarly retain their Mahā-Gurjara design, without much dramatic changes, except for more figural articulation to their wall facets and *śṛṅgas* to the *śikhara*.

The Sunak Temple of Nīlakaṇṭha Mahādeva (*fig.* 43) which Dhaky dates to the later half of the eleventh century, shows a number of flaws in alignment, proportions and plumb line, but it contains some of the finest *devāṅganā* sculptures. Not only the lateral walls of each of the *rathas* but the *salilāntaras* also have *devāṅganās*. The multiplication of this motif is indeed charming and gracefully exploited for decoration.

The Navalakhā Temple at Sejakpur (*fig.* 44) has a *maṇḍapa* that reminds us of Moḍherā, smaller in dimension and lacking in lateral porches. Its plan is based on octagonal shape and since it contains as many as five *phālanās*, it creates an illusion of

(next page)
fig. 45. Śaraṇeśvara Temple, general view, *c.* twelfth century, Abhapur, Antarsuba, Gujarat.

vṛttasaṁsthāna.[43] Dhaky and Sankalia date this temple to the twelfth century, closer to Ghumlī than to Sunak.[44] The sculptures of the Sejakpur temple are highly stiff and stereotyped. The form begins to lose plasticity and becomes ornately decorated.

The Sāraṇeśvara Temple at Ābhāpur (*fig.* 45) near Antarsuba in Gujarat is an example of *caturmukha mahāprāsāda*, comparable only with the Rudramahālaya in Gujarat. It has *kakṣāsana*s on all the four sides and it is a double-storeyed temple. The *devāṅganā*s appear in the *salilāntara*s and *pratiratha*s on both the storeys in highly imaginative postures. The sculptures are lacking in plasticity and gradually become devoid of it.

The sculptures of the Navalakhā Temple at Ghumlī in Saurāṣṭra also fall into the same category. The iconographies of the *devāṅganā*s get perpetuated for more than four centuries only to become stylistically degenerated and repetitive. But for the decorative beauty of the Marū–Gurjara style, the final phase of culmination is marked by this architectural brilliance which is attained at the cost of sculptural plasticity.

One last category of temple structures, the Bhūmija temples need to be recorded here which are highly ornate and accommodate a number of *devāṅganā* sculptures. To name a few remarkable ones here: Nīlakaṇṭha Mahādeva Temple, Udayeśvara (CE 1058-80) (*fig.* 22); Kumāravihāra, Achalgaṛh (*c.* CE 1165) (*fig.* 46); Sun Temple, Jhālarāpāṭan (*c.* CE 1075). There are different trends with sculptural representations on Bhūmija temples whereas some are completely devoid of them. Under the influence of the Marū–Gurjara temples, the representation of sculpture enters on the *maṇḍovara* of these temples. One other area in which this study could be expanded is to include regions such as Karṇāṭa, Kaliṅga and Draviḍadeśa after which a pan-Indian conception of the *devāṅganā* sculptures will emerge. As these are beyond the purview of the present book, the above understanding of medieval temple architecture, its complexities and manipulation of its sculptures will suffice.

(facing page)
fig. 46. Kumāravihāra, view from west, mid-twelfth century, Achalgaṛh, Sirohī, Rajasthan.

References

1. M.A. Dhaky, "Genesis and Development of Marū-Gujara Architecture", in *Studies in India Temple Architecture,* ed. Pramod Chandra, Bombay: American Institute of Indian Studies, 1975.
2. M. Meister, M.A. Dhaky and Krishna Deva, *Encyclopaedia of Indian Architecture*, Varanasi: American Institute of Indian Studies.
3. Dhaky, op. cit., 1975, p. 116.
4. Krishna Deva, *Seminar on Indian Art History*, New Delhi, 1962, p. 12.
5. Krishna Deva, *Temples of North India*, New Delhi, 1969, p. 21.
6. J.H. Nanavati and M.A. Dhaky, "The Ceilings in the Temples of Gujarat", *Bulletin of Baroda Museum*, vol. XVI, XVII, Baroda, 1963, p. 3.
7. Ibid., p. 4.
8. Krishna Deva, op. cit., 1969, p. 44.
9. Dhaky, op. cit., 1975, p. 120.
10. Ibid., p. 139.
11. Ibid., pp. 141-42.
12. R.C. Agrawala, "Khajurāho of Rajasthan: The Temple of Ambikā at Jagat", *Arts Asiatiques*, X, 1964, pp. 43, 65 and Dhaky, op. cit., 1975, p. 146.
13. Dhaky, op. cit., 1975, p. 149.
14. Ibid., pp. 150-51.
15. Krishna Deva, op. cit., 1969, p. 23.
16. Ibid., p. 26.
17. Nanavati and Dhaky, op. cit., 1963, p. 6.
18. Krishna Deva, op. cit., 1969, p. 21.
19. Dhaky, op. cit., 1975, pp. 144-65.
20. For illustrations refer Dhaky, op. cit., 1975.
21. Pointed out to me by Jayaram Poduwal.
22. For this example see Kṣemaṅkarī Temple, Chittorgaṛh and small Śiva Temple, Kirāḍu.
23. Krishna Deva, op. cit., 1969, p. 34.
24. Dhaky, op. cit., 1975, p. 153.
25. Ibid., p. 150.
26. R.C. Agrawala, op. cit.
27. Krishna Deva, op. cit., 1969, Kacchapaghāta Temples, *The Researcher*.
28. Nanavati and Dhaky, op. cit., 1963.

29. M.A. Dhaky, "The Old Temple at Lamba and Kāmeśvara Temple at Auwa", *Journal of the Asiatic Society*, Calcutta, vol. VIII, no. 3, 1966, p. 147.
30. Dhaky, 1961, *JMPIP*, p. 53.
31. V.S. Srivastava, *The Ancient Shiva Temple*; M. Harsha, "Sikar: An Early Chauhan Monument", *The Researcher,* Journal of Rajasthan Department of Archaeology, vols. V & VI, pp. 17-32.
32. Pointed out to me by Ratan Parimoo.
33. M.A. Dhaky, op. cit., *JOI*, vol. XXII no. 3, pp. 397-408.
34. Ratan Parimoo, *Khajuraho*: *The Chandella Sculptor's Paradise* — Is there a Chandella Style of Medieval Indian Sculpture? Its Sources and Characteristics — Indian Archaeological Heritage, ed. Margabandhu, pp. 503-10. Expanded version in Ratan Parimoo, *Essays in New Art History, Studies in Indian Sculpture*, Delhi, 2000.
35. R. Parimoo, ibid., p. 505.
36. An appraisal of the back view has been done by Parimoo in the above article, p. 507.
37. Krishna Deva, *Kachchapaghata Temples*, Researcher, pp. 5-9.
38. M.A. Dhaky (a) "The Date of the Dancing Hall of the Sun Temple, Moḍherā", *Journal of the Asiatic Society of Bombay* (New Series), Bhaudaji Volume, ed. P.V. Kane, vol. 38, Bombay 1964, pp. 211-22; (b) "Modhera, Modha-Vaṁsa, Modha-Gaccha and Modha-Caityas", *Journal of the Asiatic Society of Bombay*, Bhagavanlal Indraji Memorial Volume, ed. Devangana Desai, vols. 56-59, 1981-84, Bombay, pp. 144-58; (c) Wibke Lobo, *The Sun Temple at Modhera*, Munchen, 1982, p. 145.
39. Wibke Lobo, op. cit., 1982, p. 60, fig. 24.
40. M.A. Dhaky, "Kiradu and the Marū–Gurjara style of Temple Architecture", *Bulletin of American Academy of Benaras*, vol. I, Varanasi, 1967, p. 39.
41. Dhaky, op. cit., 1975, p. 55.
42. M.A. Dhaky, "The Chronology of the Solanki Temples of Gujarat", *Journal of the Madhya Pradesh Itihas Parishad*, no. 3, 1963, pp. 32-33.
43. Ibid., p. 53.
44. Ibid. and H.D. Sankalia, *Archaeology of Gujarat*, p. 105.

5

Devāṅganā Sculptural Image Study I

Emergence and Evolution of Individual Motif Types

Methodology

In this chapter I have tried to establish the antecedents of the sculptural imagery of the *devāṅganā* motif and how it evolves in an evolutionary order on Indian religious architecture for several centuries. Here the emergence of the motif in feminine form and the "concept of the feminine" will be explored from the prehistoric "mother" figurines and the "woman and tree" seals of the Indus–Sarasvatī cultures, to the *yakṣī–śālabhañjikā* motif of the Kuṣāṇa period. The analytical approach, according to Iconology as demonstrated by Erwin Panofsky, helps to study the individual sculptural forms, their attributes, gestures and postures and the meaning signified by their actions in general, as well as in particular. The iconological analysis of meaning in a work of art operates in three stages: primary meaning — understanding the iconographic and formal configuration; conventional meaning — identification of motifs and attributes of the images, stories and allegories; and finally the intrinsic meaning or content, which is apprehended by ascertaining those underlying principles which reveal the basic attitude of a historical period, a class, a religious or philosophical persuasion, unconsciously qualified by one personality and condensed into one work, the *devāṅganā* imagery.

The sculptural examples for this chapter have been freely selected, irrespective of their religious connotations from Buddhist, Jaina and Hindu architectures. To establish the origin and development of the *yakṣī–śālabhañjikā* motif, one has to take into account a number of other sculptural forms and subjects for discussion. Therefore, the "text" of this "discourse" is diachronic in axis and based on "polysemy" of diverse meanings which enable us to arrive at a concrete meaning of *devāṅganā* sculptures on the medieval temple architecture, which already existed in various prototypes in the earlier periods. The present analysis and juxtaposition of the sculptural form, both synchronically and diachronically points out the visual semblance on the basis of similar attributes, thereby arriving at the implicit similarity of meaning. It is by now obvious that the vegetation motif of "woman and tree" evolves via *śālabhañjikā* and river goddess motifs, into full-fledged *devāṅganā* with diverse imageries. This semiotic process not only goes into the depth of each individual *devāṅganā* and its earlier possible origin, but also explores when the *yakṣī-śālabhañjikā* connotation ceases and where (and when) the gamut of *devāṅganā* imagery germinates and blooms.

Further, the association and exploration of the Indus–Sarasvatī and the West Asian material brings to light a conceptual classification by Eric Neumann based on Jungian psychology. From the universal concept of the primordial mother based on the fertility, fecundity, vessel connotation, the concept of the "Great Mother" is developed. This concept transcends to expose sexuality and eroticism. The main principle behind this formation is the cycle of Uroboros: it bears, begets and devours, suggesting a process that is ever evolving.[1]

While re-assessing certain artistic trends (symbolic representation in sculptural form) of various historical periods in a new "psycho-historical" order, one which refers to the various stages in the development of the human psyche, we begin to notice the development of archetypes. Taking the development of consciousness as the decisive phenomenon of human history, we arrive at an arrangement of the phenomenon that does not, to be sure, coincide with the usual sequence of historical events, but makes the psychological orientation we require.[2] This "training of the eye for the archetype", helps to examine the archetype-conditioned development of consciousness and the dominance of particular archetypes in the context of *yakṣī*, *devāṅganā*, *apsaras* and what they stood for in their own period context.

Origin and Development of the Feminine Concept

THE PRE-KUṢĀṆA DEVELOPMENT OF THE LATER YAKṢĪ–ŚĀLABHAÑJIKĀ AND DEVĀṆGANĀ MOTIFS

The Foucauldian approach to the excavation of knowledge that perpetuated from the past centuries but remained veiled and erased from immediate memory, referred earlier in the chapter on methodology helps to uncover various layers and stages in the development of *devāṅganā* imagery.

The other approach that can help initiate the exploration of this motif from the larger world context of the female principle, is the psychoanalytical one in which female figurines and representations of female sculptures with similar attributes, will be juxtaposed in order to reassess the existing interpretations of the so-called "goddesses" or "mothers", which lead to the higher divine female concepts of the Devī or Śakti. But what I like to explore is the set of connotations and attributes of the widespread spontaneous folkloristic culture in most of the early civilizations, which slowly gets absorbed in the higher religious order. What has so far been interpreted by scholars in a narrowly religious context, could for once be seen from my perspective with an open-ended approach, i.e. in the larger world civilization context of attributing the concept of the female, parallel with that of nature — an all powerful, richly endowed, personified with attributes. These female principles are distinct from the higher and developed concept of the "Great Mother" and its various shades. Hence, the "archetypal mother" concept need not necessarily be linked with the highly canonized, mystified and codified "Mother Goddess" concept. Instead it could be taken as a product of the "collective unconscious", which weaves around the archetypal mother, the varied attributes of the feminine, of which some grow into the higher religious connotations of the Great Mother, while the others continue to multiply at the elemental level, the symbols of auspiciousness, fertility, abundance, sexuality and theatricality.

Let us now proceed on to the Panofskian path to "re-study" the sculptural representation of the archetypal "concept of the feminine" of various historical periods and to uncover the various layers of meaning and function, constructs and attributes generated by the artists and the contemporary milieu, keeping in view the gender perspective as well.

Not only do the female terracotta from West Asia, Haṛappā and the Mauryan

fig. 47. Animal, woman and tree motif on ring stone, third century BCE, Murtaẓāgañj, Bihar.

period connect well with each other through their affinity of content, but also bridge the Haṛappan and Mauryan forms of female divinities.[3] They represent the nude female form with stunted and simplified outstretched arms and legs. The female attributes like the breasts and pudenda are made prominent. Sometimes they are heavily adorned with girdles, necklaces and flower-decorated headgears. The Mauryan "Baroque ladies" remind one of the Indus Valley ones, due to the presence of the rosettes and the full and bulky forms. Comparable with this are the mother goddess figurines depicted on the ring-stones or stone discs (*figs*. 47, 48) and on a gold-leaf plaque found from Laurīya–Nandangaṛh, Murtaẓāgañj and Piprahwā. The broad pelvic region of the nude goddesses suggests their procreative power. Their presence on ring stones along with animals and vegetation connotes the larger context of fertility of woman and nature. Here both the terms "divinity" and "goddess" are misleading, the original context for the making and worshipping of these images may have been purely mysterious and symbolic.

According to Irene Gajjar, the association of the mother goddess type with discs apparently associated with fertility on the one hand and with Buddhist remains on the other, reveals that the cult was versatile and adaptable to both primitive as well as relatively more developed religions. They may have served a votive or cultic purpose. The associated ritual and myth is unfortunately not available. Even then it suffices to say that a collective unconscious was at work in the formation of this votive image.

INDUS–SARASVATĪ CULTURES

The archetype of fertility extant during the Indus–Sarasvatī civilizations can be seen on the seals found from Haṛappā, Mohenjo-Dāro and Kālibaṅgan, ranging from the period between 3000 and 2000 BCE. The following seals as represented by

fig. 48. Woman and tree, detail, ringstone, *c*. third century BCE, Murtaẓāgañj, Bihar.

Pupul Jayakar in Earthen Drum are of importance because they deal with the representation of fecundity, fertility, transformation and metamorphosis of feminine–masculine energies. Some relevant imageries are cited below:

1. Seal showing a plant sprouting out of the womb of an inverted figure, Haṛappā.
2. Seal showing a priest worshipping a female deity within a tree, attended upon by seven other deities, Haṛappā.
3. Seal showing a tree, woman and a tiger in a dialogue, Moheṅjo-Dāṛo and Kālibaṅgan.
4. Woman transforming into an animal developing horns, hoofs and tail, provoking a tiger.
5. Woman and tiger united and metamorphosed into a unique organism, Moheṅjo-Dāṛo and Kālibaṅgan.

The sprouting plant with five leaves or petals represents the genesis of nature from mother-earth, who is manifest in the inverted figure of a woman in the birth-giving position. The earth is the great *yoni* and the woman is the earth-bound root, the fecundating source. The rampant tigers, guardians of initiation, protect the mysteries and the immense magic of creation.[4] The reverse side of this seal shows a seated figure with dishevelled hair, perhaps in the form of the branches of a plant, approached by another figure with a bow and a sickle. The representation may be read again as that of a sacrifice offered to the symbol of the earth goddesses. The script on the seal consists of the same set of letters on both the obverse and reverse sides, but fails to shed light on the semantics of the seal.

The other representation is that of a "tree spirit" with horns and a pigtail placed within the *aśvattha* tree which is shown as a womb-like vessel. The vessel is circumscribed at its base. There is a kneeling figure with outstretched arms adoring the tree spirit, while a large human-headed long-horned goat looks on. In the foreground are placed seven figures with pigtails adorned with feathery headgear and tendril-like tiny leaves growing out on the hair and the arms. The tree spirit also has a similar representation. The adoring figure appears to be a female due to the pigtail. Due to the presence of the fish above the goat, Pupul Jayakar thinks it establishes the sexual nature of the imagery and links the rituals portrayed to rites of union, birth and transformation.[5] The fish is a recurrent female symbol in the Indian tradition of the aphrodisiac and was later identified with Bhaga, as the female divinity. As Jayakar rightly observes, the seven pigtailed virgins of the rural symbology represent the vegetal and water nymphs found throughout India, the *sāta saheliāṅ* of the northern river valleys, the *sapta kannigai*s (the seven virgins) of Tamil Nadu, the *sāta apsaras* (the seven *apsaras*) of Maharashtra — seven forms fusing into a composite image, held within a single field, water divinities invoked at times of drought, protectors of tanks and water dams, the essences that make the earth fertile. I feel that the seal represents the propitiation of the feminine tree spirit, i.e. nature in the womb vessel to unite with the masculine force, represented by the goat which is attended upon by the seven virgins. Could it be a spirit of *yakṣī*?

The most interesting representation on the Moheṅjo-Dāṛo and Kālibaṅgan seals is that of a tree woman and a tiger, who are represented in stages of transformation and fusion of principal energies. It represents the intimate relationship shared by the early man with vegetation, earth and animals. The ritual scenes project a fluid movement and a free changeability of form and identity between plant, animal and human. The magician priests of the Indus Valley must have had access to the secrets of a highly developed plant chemistry and alchemy.[6]

In the seal, a tree spirit or an *apsaras* perched on the tree (her lithesome body matches the slender branches of the tree), is summoning the tiger, who attentively looks at her. In the continued dialogue, the second seal represents the tiger in a more agile posture lifting his forelegs up, and responding to the lady who has transformed herself by developing a tail, horns and hoofs. Her feminine figure seems fleshy and round.

The tree, the buffalo lady and the tiger, have established contact. They move in rhythm in that still moment of magic. The movement of mutation has commenced.

In the last representation, both the buffalo woman and the tiger have become one. Here, the lady rides the tiger which has adopted the linear form of the woman. Now the mutation is complete.

Instead of interpreting these seals as representing a magical ritual of alchemy as Jayakar does above, I would like to stress the mutual interdependence of nature and humans for fertility, worship and their symbiotic relationship. Later on, the same spirit will formulate the sculptural representation of the *aśokadohada* and *śālabhañjikā* motifs. What is even more noteworthy is the germination of the symbol of the female in association with the tree, i.e. the female archetype and its perpetuation in plastic medium as a symbol of the collective unconscious. As has rightly been observed by Jung, archetype in the form of a symbol is firstly a figure of speech. Thus *aśoka dohada* and *śālabhañjikā*s are firstly figures of speech, drawing immene inspiration from literary sources and figuratively lending a dynamic meaning to their symbolic value.

Let us now examine some parallels from Babylonia, Egypt and Crete. According to Eric Neumann, the tree plays many roles, birth-giving and nourishing. Like the primeval hill, the uroboric serpent, the lotus blossom, and Horus, the Sun-child, rise up from the primeval ocean as births and rebirths of the luminous principle. Ocean and the earth as generative principles that stand close together, and like the ocean, blossom and tree are archetypal places of mythical birth.

fig. 49. Egyptian vase, inscribed drawing, Nut as tree goddess with the sun disk, Bronze vessel, *c.* 600 BCE Louvre, Paris.

The goddess as the tree that confers nourishment on souls, as the sycamore or date-palm, is one of the central figures of

fig. 50. Egyptian stone relief, veneration of the tree goddess, XVIII dynasty Kestner Museum, Hanover.

fig. 51. Egyptian painted ceiling relief, goddess Nut, fertility connotation, Temple of Hathor, Dendera, Roman period source unknown.

Egyptian art. The motherhood of tree consists not only in nourishing, it also suggests transformation, and the tree goddess gives birth to the sun.[7]

As goddess of the earth and fertility, of the sky and rain, whose priestess was originally the repository of rain magic, the "Great Goddess" is everywhere the ruler over the food that springs from the earth, and all the usages connected with man's nourishment are subordinated to her. She is the goddess of agriculture. For this reason the "Great Goddess" is frequently associated with a vegetation symbol (*figs.* 49, 50, 51) in India and Egypt with the lotus, as Isis, Demeter; as tree spirit nut, or later the Madonna with the rose. Flower and fruit are among the typical symbols of the Greek Mother, Daughter, Goddess. The ear of grain is the symbol of the goddess of Rasshamra, of Ishtar and Demeter, of Ceras and Spes, and of the Madonna, who in her character of the Earth Mother is the "Madonna of the sheaves" (*figs.* 52, 53).

Apples, pomegranates, poppy seeds and other fruits or boughs are symbols of fertility. According to Neumann, branch and sprout were already related to the "Great Goddess" in Sumer, and with innumerable images of Ishtar and the Cretan goddess (*fig.* 54). Branches and flowers appear as cult objects of the Great Mother. And we still encounter such tree worship in the cult of Dionysus, as well as later in Rome, and in the pagan rites of medieval peasants. In India too, the tribal rituals and fertility rites are associated with tree worship.

Originally human life was strongly connected by its participation mystique with the outside world, so much so that stone, plant, man, animal and star, were all bound together in a single stream. One form could always transform itself into another. Men and gods are born of trees and buried in trees, men can turn into plants, the two realms are so close together that one can merge with the other at any time. Man has achieved little independence and is still close to the maternal womb. This proximity to the womb is not only the cause of the frequent mythical transformations of men into plants but also of the magic by which human beings — at first precisely woman — attempted to influence the growth of plants.

The bond between woman and plant can be followed throughout all the stages of human symbolism. The mythical psyche as lotus, lily and rose, the virgin as flower in Eleusis, symbolize the flower-like unfolding of the highest psychic and spiritual developments. Thus, according to Neumann, birth from the female blossom is an archetypal form of divine birth, whether we think of Ra or Nefertem in Egypt, of the Buddhist "divine treasure in the lotus" or, in China and the modern West, of the birth of the self in the Golden Flower.[8] Here, the connotation of Śrī Lakṣmī and Sarasvatī with lotus, needs to be pointed out; Lakṣmī as a parallel to Nut, Demeter, Astarte, Ceras and Sarasvatī to Sophia, who share the same attributes and similar visual representations (*figs.* 51, 52, 53).

(facing page)
fig. 52. Goddess as Flower Maiden, Stone, Eleusis, Roman period Museum Eleusis.

fig. 53. Terracotta relief, Hellenic Period Museo Nationale delle Terme, Ceres, Rome.

The representation of Demeter and Kore, as the mother–daughter pair of Greek art, represented by fruit and flower as their attributes, reflects their maiden and mature woman connotations. In the case of Aphrodite, there is transformation of the figure of the "Great Mother" as "Lady of Plants and Animals", into the young and seductive goddess (*fig.* 133). But Neumann feels that it is not the transformative "anima" character of the Feminine that Aphrodite gloriously represents, but the world-governing individual/dual love principle and sexual principle of life.

Does this explanation not remind us of the *yakṣī-śālabhañjikā* motif found in early Indian art, that governs the "concept of the feminine" from a vegetation goddess, *sālābhañjikā* to a fertility inducing *dohada krīḍā* performer on Buddhist and Jaina architecture to exhibiting sexuality as a *devāṅganā* on later temples? (*fig.* 167). I will elaborate upon this point in this chapter.

fig. 54. Astarte, Gold plaque, *c.* thirteenth century BCE.

Origin and Development of the Yakṣī-Śālabhañjikā Motif in Literature

From different references it is learnt that *śālabhañjikā* adorned gateways, temples, pavilions, carts and chariots. They were also carved or painted on walls and pillars. Vogel suggests that Aśvaghoṣa was probably the first writer to use the term *śālabhañjikā*.[9] Earlier than him it is from *Mahāvaṁśa* (XXX.91, XXX.99) that the motif is known as *pupphasākhādhara*.[10] The connotation in both the cases is either of holding the branch of a flowering tree or breaking it. The motif is also known from *Kāmasūtra*, which connects it with festivals of eastern India (Kāśikā VI.2.74), *prācyam krīḍā* (Pāṇini 6.2.74). Hence it is quite probable that from a spring sport of a profane kind this motif entered into the sphere of religious imagery, first of the independent *yakṣa* cult and later got absorbed in Buddhist art.

V.S. Agrawala mentions that *śālabhañjikā* was a spring sport and in Buddha's lifetime it was celebrated at Śrāvastī. Several people gathered there to play and make merry and gather the blossoms.[11] *Nidānakathā* describes the *śālabhañjikā* festival celebrated in the Lumbinī garden in which Māyādevī had delivered Buddha (as Siddhārtha) standing in the *śālabhañjikā* pose.[12]

As referred to earlier, *Kāmasūtra* mentions some more *deśya-krīḍā* (local sports), e.g. *sahakāra-pañjikā*, *abhyuṣa-khadikā*, *udaka-kṣvedikā*, *ikṣu-khadikā*, *aśokottainsikā*, *puṣpavācayikā*, *cuta-latikā*, *dāmanabhañjikā*, *ikṣubhañjikā*, etc.[13]

By post-Gupta period in *Harṣacarita*, this motif is connected with Madanotsava, the festival connected with the arrival of the spring. In *Mālavikāgnimitra* it is associated with *dohada*, the desire during pregnancy.[14] Hence the *śālabhañjikā* and the *aśokadohada* are interconnected, indirectly implying the fertility of the tree and the woman. The strong vegetative connections imply fecundity of the earth and the woman. The fecundating power of the woman, who is identified in the *śālabhañjikā* pose, is the *yakṣī* who is the boon-bestowing type. She is a female counterpart or spouse of *yakṣa*.

The *yakṣa* cult was a creation of the forces that were latent and operating silently in the substratum of the early Vedic religious life.

These forces created out of a "word concept", viz. a "sentient being" and a "cult" developed around it, with a body of rituals and practices. *Yakṣa* is considered mysterious, not clearly definable, dreadful and unfriendly. He is considered to be an honorific of Varuṇa, looked upon as a primordial, chthonic deity or a god. This ambivalence later became the twin aspect of his nature, benevolent and malevolent.[15] *Yakṣī*s also have both these aspects to their nature.

Yakṣa cult was absorbed into Buddhism because of mysticism and *bhakti* in its mode of worship. Since it lacked cultic force from within, it slowly wilted away under the pressure of higher cult gods. Later the Tāntric mode of *yakṣa* worship also entered, which evoked better response due to the magical power attached to it. The warding off of charms and controlling them to obtain desired wishes, were the two purposes for which Tāntric practices were offered to them, says Misra.

It is from the *Mahābhārata* and *Vāyu Purāṇa* that *yakṣiṇī*s were regarded as creatures of great beauty. Misra observes that a *gandharva kanyā*, Suyaśā, the wife of Pracetas, gave birth to five *yakṣa*s and four *apsaras*es (*VP* 69.10-13). It is worth noting that *apsaras* and *yakṣiṇī* are treated as one and the same, so also *śālabhañjikā* and *yakṣī* as equivalent interchangeable terms. There seems to be a bit of ambiguity in the usages of the term *yakṣī*, *śālabhañjikā* and *apsaras*. A discussion on this will be taken up in the section on river goddesses.

Misra mentions that Tantra had already come to grips with the *yakṣa* cult in the fourth century CE, and in the *Kathā-Sarit-Sāgara* we have a number of instances of *yakṣiṇī*s controlled by magic and charms to serve as wives of the person practising them. It also mentions a cannibal *yakṣī*, who was a Pāśupata devotee.[16]

*Yakṣa*s were attracted by fragrance and their habitats were usually fragrant with jasmine and lotus perfumes. This characteristic is also shared by *apsaras*. They relished honey and liquor. They enjoyed dance, song and music (*Mahābhārata* XIII.101-60). Bharata says a particular instrumental melody, *mārgasaritā*, pleased them (*NŚ* V.47, V.20). Daughters of Kubera were excellent dancers and *nāṭya* came into being only to relieve people from obsession with *yakṣas*. It is also said that *yakṣas* were great actors because they could change their whole image,[17] i.e. impersonate.

Surprisingly, these references remain at the level of literature, religious practice and faith, but do not enter the illustrated world of Buddhist art as much as the various aspects of the so-called *yakṣīs*. Thus literary imagery is more developed than the visual imagery at this stage.

A reference from *Jātaka* (*J* II.254) refers to the celebration of Kārttika festival, making the start of the sowing season, in the presence (of an image) of Yakkha Cittarāja. Apparently, this *yakṣa* must have been regarded as the promoter of crops.[18] But the vegetation connotation in art is implied by the *śālabhañjikā* motif and not the *yakṣa* Cittarāja.

According to Misra, Tāntric literary sources dealing with the controlling of *yakṣīs* are *Guhya-Samāja-Tantra, Mañjuśrī Mūlakalpa* and *Jayākhyā Saṁhitā*. After the rites are performed, they appear either as mother, sister or wife and fulfil the wishes of their devotees (*JS,* p. 295; *MMK* II.293, III.720). One of the things offered to them is *guggula*, with chanting of *mantras*. In the *Atharvaveda*, *apsaras* are known by the term *guggula*, *pila*, *nalādi, aukṣagandhī, pramardinī,* etc. which indicate smells (*AV* IV.37.3) produced by different herbs. Such ephemeral imagery is useful to understand at the outset as we try to grip the *apsaras–devāṅganā* imagery.

There are elaborate ceremonies involved in *yakṣī* worship; there is a passage *yakṣiṇī sādhanam* from *Jayākhyā Saṁhitā* and *Mañjuśrī Mūlakalpa*, which indicates their names, forms, modes of propitiation and the objects to be offered to them.[19]

By offering before a picture of *yakṣiṇī* incense and *guggula* for one week at midnight, she would appear before the devotee on the seventh day, amidst the chanting of the charms. The *vaśīkaraṇa* of the *yakṣī* could be obtained by offering of wood of banyan tree, curd, honey, ghee or *kumkum*, juice of *dhatūrā arkakṣīra*, *lakṣarasa*, *mṛgamada*. From another Tāntric work *Bhūtaḍāmaratantra* the names of *yakṣiṇīs*, who could be brought under control by the above means, are mentioned as Surāsundarī, Manohāriṇī, Kanakamatī, Kāmeśvarī,

Ratipriyā, Padminī, Naṭī and Anurāgiṇī. All these names suggest erotic, mystical and theatrical connotations.

A *yakṣī* worship involves the drawing of her picture on different objects such as wooden panel for Naṭī, *paṭa* for Tamasundarī, wooden panel, silk or wall for Guhavāsinī, silk for Naravīrā, who should be shown as resting against the *aśoka* tree, birch bark for *yakṣī* Kumārikā, who should be represented as holding a citron in the right hand and branch of *aśoka* tree in the other. These *yakṣī*s satisfied the devotees by bestowing upon them, immortality, nectar, riches, food, clothing, sexual pleasure and the normal birth of a child.[20]

Dehejia has suggested that there is an underlying connection between the *yoginī*s and *yakṣiṇī*s who are associated with trees and fertility.[21] *Yakṣiṇī*s were believed to reside in forests and their touch could cause a tree to blossom or produce fruit (an ability extended poetically to all women). Dehejia refers to *Kulārṇava Tantra* which mentions *kulavṛkṣa*s in which *yoginī*s reside. There are eight varieties of this tree, which should be approached with respect. Their fruits or leaves should not be plucked and one should not sleep under such a tree (*Kulārṇava*, 11.66-68). Dehejia rightly observes that Coomaraswamy, without looking into the Kaula texts, had believed that the sixty-four *yoginī*s must originally have been *yakṣiṇī*s (1928-31, pl. 9). References to *yoginī* Padmāvatī, as being originally a *yakṣī*, are cited by Dehejia with further information on the *prayoga* and *siddhi*. Thus, *yakṣī* is not only a literary motif but a part of *yakṣa* worship and Tāntric ritual. This evolution of the concept envelops all of desires that can be fulfilled by the propitiation of the feminine energy. Here the simple connotation of fertility and eroticism have been replaced by mystical power and insight, adding a further layer to the complex personality of the *yakṣī*. Let us see how the same concept has been visualized by the sculptors of the early Indian art.

Origin and Development of the Yakṣī–Śālabhañjikā Motif in Sculpture

Our survey through the plastic arts exploring the representation of the "lady of the plants" (Neumann) "Woman and tree motif" (Coomaraswamy) has entered a phase of great variety and multiplicity in visual forms and imageries. This makes the "training of the eye to look for an archetype" more focused, since the data is not only challenging but evocative as well.

Yakṣī or *yakṣiṇī*, as they are often known, are essentially tree spirits associated with sacredness, auspiciousness and prosperity. They can be evil as well as good characters. But in visual representation of this "woman and tree" motif the good character is generally portrayed.

The word *yakṣa* is perhaps of indigenous non-Āryan origin and the tree spirit concept is originally non-Buddhistic but got absorbed in Buddhist iconography.[22] Out of the four Vedas, it is the *Atharvaveda*, which contains elements incorporated from the original non-Āryan sources. It is perhaps also significant (in view of possible Sumero–Draviḍian connections) that in the Babylonian tradition, immortality and productiveness are original functions of the Tree of Fortune.[23] We have already referred to this in the earlier chapter.[24] But in the *Ṛgveda* and also in the *Atharvaveda* the trees and tree deities play but an insignificant part; here they are connected with human life and productivity through the spirits of *gandharva*s and *apsaras*es residing in the trees.

An early observation by Coomaraswamy should be mentioned here in connection with the representation of the imagery of *yakṣī* on a Buddhist monument.[25] The *vṛkṣikā*s of the railing pillars are properly to be described as *yakṣī*, is proved by the inscriptions accompanying the similar figures at Bharhut.[26] *Vṛkṣikā*, is of course, legitimate, but hardly more than a descriptive term. Some with musical instruments should perhaps be described as *gandharvī*s, or even *apsaras*es, but none are represented as actually dancing, and to call them dancing girls is certainly an error. Here, Coomaraswamy not only points out the range of the imagery of these female figures but also clarifies the pitfalls in the interpretation of this motif as that of a dancing girl.

This motif occurs in early sculptures of Bharhut (*fig.* 55), Jaggeyapeṭa, Kaṅkālī Ṭīlā (*fig.* 56), Sāñcī (*fig.* 57), Amarāvatī (*figs.* 58, 59), Bodha-Gayā (*fig.* 60), Mathurā, etc. They appear on pillars, gateways, the *āyāga-paṭṭa*s and other narrative slabs, as railing

fig. 55. Railing upright, Culakoka Devatā, first century BCE, Barhut, Indian Museum, Kolkata.

uprights, brackets supporting the architraves or as punctuating decorative motifs in between two narrative frames. They are represented as full-bodied, voluptuous beauties, alluring and inspiring the viewer. They wear broad *mekhalā*s, large anklets, bangles, *kuṇḍala*s and necklaces. The diaphanous treatment of their drapery renders them as almost nude. The sensuous beauty of the breasts, like full urns, and the fleshy pudenda, signify their generative power and feminine charm. They sometimes stand on *vāhana*s like *makara* (*fig.* 61), elephant or the *yakṣa*. Very often they hold with one hand a branch of the tree under which they stand, sometimes one leg is twined round the trunk of the tree (an erotic conception, for *latā* is both "creeper" or "wine" and "woman").[27] Sometimes they are also shown with the child holding the branch of either *aśoka* or mango tree. Rightly observed by Coomaraswamy, these *yakṣī*s give rise to three iconographically similar motifs, differently interpreted: the Buddha Nativity, the *aśoka dohada* motif in classical literature, and the so-called river goddesses of medieval shrines.[28]

fig. 56. *Śālabhañjikā*s flanking the *toraṇa*, Jaina *stūpa*, *ayāga-paṭṭa* stone, second century CE, Kaṅkālī Ṭīlā.

Following the lead casually but keenly suggested by Coomaraswamy already mentioned above, let us examine the diverse attributes and actions of these voluptuous female forms, generically

fig. 57. *Toraṇa śālabhañjikā*, eastern gate, *stūpa* 1, first century BCE, Sāñcī.

fig. 58. *Śālabhañjikā-prasādhikā*, *gavākṣa*, first century BCE, Amarāvatī.

fig. 59. *Śālabhañjikā*, *gavākṣa*, first century CE, Amarāvatī.

fig. 60. *Aśokadohada*, man supporting the woman to entwine her leg around a tree trunk, second century CE, Bodh-Gayā.

(facing page)
fig. 61. *Śālabhañjikā*,
Bracket figure, Śuṅga period,
first century BCE, Jamsot,

fig. 62. Early Indian mother goddesses,
Mauryan and Kuṣāṇa periods
source unknown, Mathurā.

called *yakṣīs*. A closer scrutiny of their imagery will help us to formulate a relevant nomenclature for these sculptures. It will also enable us to have a better clarity of their imagery and purpose in relation with the monument on which they occur. Even by themselves, these images have a connecting thread which on formal and thematic levels maintains a continuity in time and space. Our exploration might lead us to observe that what had been so far called a *yakṣī*, could also be an *apsaras* and the texts also support this. Hence, the watertight compartments distinguishing a *yakṣī* from an *apsaras* would have to be reviewed. Let us proceed with the classification of the imagery types on Bharhut, Sāñcī, Mathurā (*fig.* 62) and Amarāvatī–Nāgārjunakoṇḍa (*fig.* 58, 59, 62).

BHARHUT

This is the earliest site on which *apsaras*es, *devatā*s and *yakṣī*s are represented. Probably the first-ever visual representation of *yakṣī*s in human form can be seen here. They act as potent symbols or metaphors signifying vegetative energy and sensual agility in nature. Most of them are represented on the inner side of the railing uprights in high relief. They are full-bodied and sensuously disposed but the carving being elementary, their volume and dynamism appear under-developed. Even then the corporeality of the incorporeal form flashes forth. The Bharhut sculptures are inscribed and therefore it is easy to understand the imagery of some of these figures.[29] Sirimā Devatā is represented by a lady holding lotus flowers in *samabhaṅga* stance (Barua pl. 7a, 78), while Candra *yakṣī* (on northern gateway along with Kubera), Culakoka Devatā (Kṣudrakoka Devatā) (*fig.* 55), Madhyamakoka Devatā (Barua pl. 73, 75, 76), are represented in the pose of a *vṛkṣikā* or later *śālabhañjikā*, entwining one of their legs around the tree trunk and clasping the branches of the blossoming tree with the upraised hand in *uromaṇḍalī*. They stand on a composite animal, elephant and horse respectively. The interrelationship between the vegetation and the female form enhances the idea of the "Woman and Tree" motif. It is noteworthy that both *yakṣī* and *devatā* imageries share common imagery and attributes. Agrawala observes that *cula* and *mahā* signify small and big, while *koka* refers to either a lizard, goose, wolf or frog. In that case these figures could be interpreted as analogous to goddess and lizard represented on the Mauryan ring stones.[30]

From the point of view of dance, these figures could be observed as employing *kuñcita* and *svastika pada*, whereas it is not possible to call them as dancers. "Woman and Tree" motif has engaged the attention of many scholars from the beginning of the twentieth century, but the erotic meaning is read in them for the first time by K. Rama Pisharoti,[31] suggesting that *dohada śālabhañjikā* should be adopted, as the Indian technical term to denote all these popular artistic devices, represented "both in Indian literature and sculpture".[32] The idea in *dohada* is that some plants, trees and creepers would blossom in the off-season, when lovely women are directly or indirectly touching, kicking or embracing and spitting, singing, laughing, talking or dancing in front of them. Rightly observed by Pisharoti in the *ālaṁkārika* terminology, these features are like *uddīpana vibhāva*s of *śṛṅgāra rasa*, especially of the *saṁbhoga* variety. Barua questions this justification in reading an erotic meaning into all of such devices, particularly at Bharhut.[33] Barua is also convinced that in interpreting them, we must consider them along with other motifs in which the *yakṣiṇī*s, *devatā*s and *devakumārī*s are represented either as female devotees or as actresses. They are collecting flowers, offering them, adoring the deity, or performing dance and gymnastic acts. They are present in miniature form on edges of the uprights as well. All the ascetic and erotic literature see woman as all sex or lust, and in every gesture, posture, movement and activity, lustfulness is indicated.[34]

Our alternative suggestion is to see in this range of female motifs at Bharhut and such other sites a visual representation of fertility archetype continued since Indus and Mauryan periods, in an altered form encompassing vegetation and extending eroticism with male partner symbolized by animals. Thus, the fertility archetype absorbed from nature extends to nature and induces erotic feeling in the onlooker. In that sense the female images act as symbols transcending above their physical form. It is not the sensuous form that matters but the higher and wider concept of generative power implied. The erotic implication is a development in the imagery which will connect *yakṣī*, river goddess and *devāṅganā*. *Yakṣiṇī* by the name Sudarśanā (Barua pl. 74) and Alakanandā (Barua pl. 72) are also represented on the upright pillars. Sudarśanā holds a *tarjanī-mudrā* pointing upwards, standing on an aquatic composite animal, while Alakanandā holds a bunch of flowers and stands on a *bhāravāhaka yakṣa*. The *devatā*s, *yakṣiṇī*s and *koka*s are all fertility spirits. Sirimā Devatā or Śrī holding lotus blossoms, is represented several times at Bharhut, a motif which eventually evolves into the concept of Gajalakṣmī. The *Lalitavistara* and *Mahāvastu* versions of the *Atantīya Sutta* mention four types of this goddess, Śrīmatī, Lakṣmīmatī, Yaśaprāptā and Yaśodharā, they belong to the southern quarter and stand as prototypes of ideal housewives.[35]

The *makaravāhinī* Gaṅgā (Barua pl. 77) is also found at Bharhut and in *Vimānavatthu*; she may be called *padumaccara* (Barua 81) or lotus nymph. Barua surprisingly observes that at Bharhut it stands for Sarasvatī, the goddess of aesthetic culture. It is significant to note that Śrī is considered as one among the *devakumārī*s. The above listing of imageries and attributes brings to light the commonality of motifs which will re-emerge and merge on the doorways and pillar brackets at Ajantā, Ellorā and early Nāgara temple doorways of Gupta architecture. The motif of tree woman and river goddess will be evolving at this stage sharing, changing or interchanging their attributes. Lotus is an emblem of beauty, purity and moral sensibility. Lotus is identified with earth, waters, birth place of Agni; hence tree and lotus signify similar spirits of creation or existence or space. Even Nalinī or padminī *devāṅganā*s are prominently placed on Lakṣmaṇa Temple at Khajurāho.

At Bharhut, the *apsaras*es are also represented on the Prasenajit Pillar in dancing mode, with their names inscribed (Barua pl. 34). Alambuṣā *achara*, *Miśkosī achara*, Padumavatī *achara*, Sabhadā *achara*. It also mentions *sadika sammadam turam devānām*, meaning the music of the gods, joyous with dance. The performance is taking place under a tree which is partly broken. Under the tree sits a group of musicians and singers in a circular manner, engrossed and attentive, while the dancers strike poses keeping arms in *caturasra, uromaṇḍalī, ūrdhvamaṇḍalī* and *lolahasta nṛtya hasta*s. This depiction appears more like an *udyāna-krīḍā* than a heavenly court dance. The reference to *saṭṭaka* is supportive too. Another noteworthy scene depicting dance is *cūḍāmaha* (Barua pl. 39), the hair lock festival. The scene is depicted in two registers with place and the canopy covering the hair lock occupying the upper register, and the four dancers and musicians in the lower register. One of the dancers holding *patākā caturasra hasta*, stands in *kṣipta* position, while the rest are either in *sama* or *svastika* position.

The Prasenajit pillar relief is interpreted by Irāvatī as an early representation of "all-women's" theatre.[36] The association of *apsaras* with Indra's court as inscribed here links Bharhut imagery with Purāṇic concept of Indrasabhā and its *apsaras*.

Thus, Bharhut represents a significant juncture of continuation and extension of meaning emerging out of similar imagery, but offers limited "violation". It marks a significant beginning with respect to *yakṣiṇī-śālabhañjikā* and the river goddess motif.

There is an unidentified goddess or *yakṣiṇī* found from Bharhut (Barua 68, 25) in which the lady is shown holding a mirror and adjusting her make up. This imagery will continue to develop as *darpaṇā* in later sculptures on medieval temple architecture (*fig.* 204). This is a singular motif that develops uninterrupted.

SĀÑCĪ

While going around the great *stūpa*, the railing uprights become visible. Compared to Bharhut, Sāñcī pillars appear very simple. Instead of *yakṣa*s and *yakṣī*s, there are medallions carved with lotus motifs. This reminds us of the *padmavara vedikā* reference pointed out by V.S. Agrawala,[37] which is the decorative scheme prescribed for a *stūpa* monument in *Rāyapasenīya Sutta*. Barring a few representations of female figures (*yakṣī* or *padmaccara*) surrounded by lotus stalks and blossoms (Marshall Pl. LXXVI-12b, 15a, LXXVIII-

(facing page)
fig. 63. *Śalabhañjikā*, engraved drawing, resting against *makara-toraṇa* first century CE, Nāgārjunakoṇḍa.

fig. 64. *Prasādhikā*,
mithuna couple,
Nāgārjunakoṇḍa.

fig. 65. *Prasādhanā*,
mithuna couple,
Nāgārjunakoṇḍa.

22a) there are no representations of *yakṣīs* in life size on the pillar uprights. There is an interesting figure called Māyā according to Marshall,[38] standing in the middle of the arch surrounded by creepers oozing out of the navels of the *kumbhāṇḍakas*. Below her stands another lady on a half rosette inside a medallion holding a long lotus stalk and the hem of her scarf looking like a supportive beauty of Mathurā, as Marshall rightly observes. Vogel has also made a similar observation.[39]

But the most celebrated sculptures of the Sāñcī *yakṣīs* are the *toraṇa śālabhañjikās*, the round full-bodied sculptures of women bending the branch of a tree with gay abandon. They are placed as curvaceous brackets connecting the architraves with pillars and with the upper registers. Most of them are represented in diaphanous dress revealing their nudity wearing *mekhalās* and leg rings. They appear like rustic beauties, the kind one finds among the tribal people of central India today.

The *yakṣīs* placed on the northern gateway of *stūpa* 1 lean against the richly foliate tree trunk, their legs are now broken. One of the arms is placed on the waist. Their hair-do is highly intricate and large. Both the brackets appear as though hanging from the architraves. The upper two registers also show *yakṣīs* in *śālabhañjikā*

fig. 66. *Prasādhanā*, *mithuna* couple, Nāgārjunakoṇḍa.

poses, while the one on the rear upper register entwines her leg and arm almost embracing the tree. Such a representation almost presupposes *dohada* action.

The right side bracket on the eastern gateway represents yet another significant *toraṇa śālabhañjikā* of a later date. It rests its weight on the prominent contraposto of the *svastika pāda* and the raised arm in *uromaṇḍalī* holding the branch above. She embraces the tree but does not take its support like the one on the northern gateway. Her lush hair are kept open at the back while some of the hair are tied in a top knot (*fig.* 57). Another *yakṣī* is placed on the upper architrave who leans against the tree in an oblique way resting the weight of the body on the bent leg in *daṇḍapādācārī,* supporting the tree. The arms are raised up caressing the fruits. This posture will be seen again on the Ajantā Cave 4 doorway, in the representation of the river goddesses in which the abundant foliage lingers on (*fig.* 98). Some more examples of Sāñcī *śālabhañjikā* are found in the following museum collections, viz. Indian Museum, Kolkata; British Museum, London; Heeramanek Collection, Museum of Fine Arts, Boston and many other Indian collections.

A reference to *śālabhañjikā* has been cited in the *Buddhacarita,* which was referred to by Sivaramamurti, in which the lady holding the side of the window stands flexing her beautiful body like a bow and with her pearl necklace dangling looks like a carved decorative figure on the *toraṇa* gateway[40] (*Buddhacarita* V.52, V.35, IV.35). Vogel has also found references to *toraṇa śālabhañjikā* from *Nāṭyaśāstra*.

AMARĀVATĪ–NĀGĀRJUNAKOṆḌA

The sculptures of Amarāvatī offer scant examples of *śālabhañjikā* motif, whereas Nāgārjunakoṇḍa is prolific. Since most of the railing pillars, horizontal bars, *stūpa* slabs and gateways have been brought to various museums, it is difficult to obtain a complete view of the original structure and placement of the *yakṣī* figures. When studied closely, the *śālabhañjikā* sculptures and other related motifs appear on the horizontal architraves of the doorway; often they are placed on the two ends of a horizontal slab bearing a scene from Jātakas or Buddha's life. These figures are made to stand on fantastic *vyāla*-like animal, a cross between *makara*, lion and deer in their characteristic posture. The sensuous *yakṣī* steals our heart by holding the branch in *uromaṇḍalī hasta* and standing in *svastikacārī* or *daṇḍapādācārī*. This motif repeats at three places in Nāgārjunakoṇḍa, while the postures struck by the *yakṣī* using extreme *tribhaṅga* in *svastika* and *daṇḍapada*, have occurred at Sāñcī before and will be found at Ajantā later. But neither Amarāvatī nor Nāgārjunakoṇḍa have large size *yakṣī*s represented on the upright pillars as in Bharhut. An unusual engraving of a *śālabhañjikā* supporting an architrave, standing next to a pillar is quite unique (*fig.* 63).

There are two *śālabhañjikā* figures represented on *caitya gavākṣa*s from Amarāvatī and an engraved line drawing representing the *toraṇa śālabhañjikā* from Nāgārjunakoṇḍa (*figs.* 58, 59). One of them stands firmly planted in the *svastika cārī* while arms are in *karihasta* (one in *lolahasta* and the other bent at the elbow) embracing the tree trunk. The figure is slightly turned to one side which saves the figure from striking an uninteresting frontal pose. Such oblique thrusts are often found in Āndhra art, thanks to the sensitivity of sculptors and the pliability of the soft stone. The thick foliage at the back is predominant in both sculptures. The second *yakṣī* is engaged in putting on an earring into her large split earlobe. She too is bent to one side due to the shift of weight in her contraposto.

The occurrence of *mithuna* couples engaged in *śṛṅgārika* love sports, is for the first time found at Nāgārjunakoṇḍa, out of which some imageries of *yakṣī–devāṅganā*s will evolve later. At Mathurā and Saṅghol, similar *yakṣī* images can be seen, where the iconography is similar with the Andhra figures. The *nāyaka* is shown fondly accompanying the *nāyikā* who is engaged in *prasādhana* (putting on make up) (*figs.* 64, 65, 66), *keśanistoya* (drying hair) (*fig.* 67), playing with a *śuka* (parrot or pet bird) or simply standing in amorous poses (*fig.* 68). At Mathurā the same imagery will reappear and the *nāyaka* figure will be dropped from the pair. Hence, this is the only site where the *mithuna* couple is represented and the *nāyikā* is engaged in activities that will continue as the imagery of *yakṣī* later on. These couples are possibly placed as profane punctuations in between the didactic narratives of Buddhist lore. Later on *mithuna*

fig. 67. *Keśanistoyakāriṇī*, *mithuna* couple, Nāgārjunakoṇḍa.

fig. 68. *Markaṭaceṣṭā*, *mithuna* couple, Nāgārjunakoṇḍa.

couples will be adopted in the decoration of *dvāraśākhās* of the Nāgara temple architecture in a standardized manner (*fig.* 253, 255). There possibly was a psycho-religious or magical purpose in representing couples on a monument, an autochthonous tradition which was embraced by Hindus, Buddhists and Jainas alike.

There are two instances of *keśanistoyakāriṇī* where the *nāyikā* stands in a languid pose holding the wet hair, the *nāyaka* holds her by the waist and the swan catches the droplets of water in its beak. The *śukasaritā* is the representation of *nāyikā* holding the parrot in one hand near her shoulder, as if talking to her, while the *nāyaka* looks on. The woman's shyness and hassled expression is revealed through her stance in *svastika cārī*, while the ruby held in the other hand indicates what she is about to do and why. A verse from *Amaruśataka*, aptly illustrates the mood:

> Having heard the words of love whispered by the couple at night, the parrot began to reel them off in elder's presence, next day! The shy young bride took off a ruby from her eardrops, and thrust it into its beak.

Even *Gāthā Saptaśatī* has a verse (*GS* 6.52):

> O aunt, won't you take this parrot cage away from here, my bed chamber? He keeps repeating to all what others should not know![41]

The *mithuna* couple also engage in *prasādhana* (make up) where the *nāyaka* plaits the hair while the *nāyikā* holding a *darpaṇa* fondly looks on. This gentle depiction of a couple immersed in their own world is sensuously represented first by the Nāgārjunakoṇḍa masters. The sensuous grace is also achieved by the plastic modelling and organic naturalism of the form. Both Sāñcī east gate *yakṣī* and Nāgārjunakoṇḍa figures, pulsate with excessive softness of feminine beauty that urges one to think of the similie of creeper clinging to the tree trunk. They invoke in the onlooker an avalanche of eagerness to have a tactile experience.

I have noticed the presence of *markaṭaceṣṭā* (monkey harassing the woman) represented on Nāgārjunakoṇḍa sculptures (*fig.* 68). The *āyāga* cornice stone of *stūpa* 3 represents in between narrative frames from scenes of the Buddha's life, couples engaged in *madhupāna* and *prasādhana*. This theme is very lyrically captured by the artist representing the lady lifting up her feet in *kuñcita* and leaning towards the *nāyaka*, who holds her firmly, by planting his other arm on the frame (Longhurst, pl. XXXVII).[42] This is a significant sculpture because the *markaṭaceṣṭā* motif continues to develop in the *devāṅganā* imagery on the temple architecture, note Badoli and Khajurāho examples (fig. 181, 182).

MATHURĀ AND SAṄGHOL

The nature of the imagery that one confronts at Mathurā and Saṅghol, is so diverse and mind-boggling that one will immediately try to list the varieties and classify them under common groups. Over and above the *vr̥kṣikā-śālabhañjikā* motif there are *aśokadohada-krīḍā*, *sadyasnātā* (bathing under a waterfall), *keśanistoyakāriṇī* (squeezing water from the hair), *prasādhikā* (putting on ornaments) (*fig.* 69), *śukasārikā* (*fig.* 70), *khaḍgadhārī* (holding a sword) (*fig.* 71), *vasanabhraṁśā* (her garment slipping inadvertently) (*fig.* 167), *dugdhadhāriṇī* (gently touching the breast maternally) (*fig.* 125, 126), *putravallabhā* (lifting a child), *naṭī* (dancer or actress), *paribhogadarśinī* (enjoying looking at one's love marks), *yakṣārohī* (sitting on the back of a dwarf *yakṣa*), *darpaṇadhāriṇī*

fig. 69. *Prasādhikā*, second century CE, Saṅghol, National Museum, New Delhi.

fig. 70. *Śuka-sārikā*,
Parrot nibbling the *mekhalā* knot,
second century CE, Mathurā,
Lucknow Museum.

(holding a mirror), *kaṅduka-krīḍā* (playing with a ball), *madhupānā* (drinking liquor) and *alasā* (standing in an erotic pose).[43] The Kuṣāṇa period monuments especially from the Mathurā region have taken the lead in diversifying the vocabulary of the imagery of the so-called *vṛkṣikā* and for the first time, one is faced with the problem of how to identify them. One must admit that a number of scholars have already written about their beauty, their graceful actions and the *krīḍā*s they depict. Even then a lot still needs to be said regarding their function conjointly with the architecture they drape and the pan-Indian cultural consciousness, reflected through their imagery. This "cultural consciousness" is commonly shared in literature, painting, sculpture and dance, which forms the substratum of thematic background of all the Indian arts. Through this thematic structure evolves the metaphorical imagery, which beautifies the language of all the arts and suffuses these with enormous charm and brightness. Hence, the *vṛkṣikā* sculptures allude to poetic imagery and transcend their physicality and feminine charm.

Taking stock of the *vṛkṣikā* placement and occurrence on *stūpa*s of the Buddhists and Jainas in the Mathurā region during the Śuṅga–Kuṣāṇa period, one finds that

Bhūteśvara and Kaṅkālī Ṭīlā have brought to light the best examples. Jaina *stūpas* at Kaṅkālī Ṭīlā and Buddhist *stūpa* at Bhūteśvara of Huviṣka's time, present the *vṛkṣikā-śālabhañjikā* sculptures on the uprights of the railings and the supporting brackets of the architraves of the *stūpa* gateways[44] (*fig.* 72). Other well-known sites near Mathurā, such as Soṅkh (*figs.* 73, 74), Mehraulī, Narolī, Jamālpur, Govindnagar, Kumrahāra, Faizabad, Giridharapur Ṭīlā (*fig.* 75), Lakṣmaṇagaṛh Ṭīlā, Mahāban, have also provided more sculptures of diverse imagery types. The recently discovered Saṅghol (Punjab) material has contributed still further in enriching this subject (*fig.* 76). Even from Begram (ancient Kapiśā) in Gandhāra region, some ivory plaques have been found depicting many more types of *śālabhañjikās* and ladies engaged in various *krīḍās*. Hence, the entire northern and north-western region during Kuṣāṇa period was sharing the common vocabulary of female motifs engaged in various activities including the *vṛkṣikā-śālabhañjikā* motif; only a few out of these are *yakṣīs*.

Much has been written about Kuṣāṇa *yakṣīs*. Here are some observations made by the past scholars. Some accept them as *yakṣīs* (superhuman spirits), *vana-devatās* (forest deities),[45] *vṛkṣikās* (tree goddesses), nymphs, dryads and dancing girls. It has also been observed that these figures were derived from the early terracottas representing the nude goddess.[46] V.S. Agrawala is of the opinion that they possibly represent the taste of the donor and that neither donors nor sculptors were completely religious minded, and so to make the monument more popular they had to make the monument to adjust to the taste of the contemporary society.[47] Agrawala has brought to light a reference from *Rāyapasenīya Sutta,*[48] which explains the making of a *vedikā* for *stūpa* decoration containing numerous types of lotuses called *padmavara vedikā*. As time went by, the non-figurative organic language of decorative motifs got altered with the representation of divine damsels, that presented a

fig. 71. *Vīrā khaḍgadhārī*, second century CE, Mathurā Pratihārī.

fig. 72. *Toraṇa-yoṣita*,
first century CE, Kaṅkālī Ṭīlā,
Mathura Museum.

glimpse of the profane human activities of sensual pleasure. Agrawala refers to one more verse from *Rāyapasenīya Sutta*,[49] which prescribes the making of "16 *śālabhañjikā parivādi*" who should be decorated with ornaments and be made to stand on the doorway in graceful poses, slender waisted, eyes with red corners and black curly hair, standing under *aśoka* trees and holding their distended boughs, stealing the hearts of the gods as it were, with their soothing glances and, teasing as it were with the play of their eyes. Agrawala observes that on the Bharhut *stūpa* railing there were sixty-four pillars which confirm the *Rāyapasenīya*'s prescription.

The frequency of the "woman and tree" motif, i.e. *vṛkṣikā* or *śālabhañjikā*, is followed by the *aśokadohada* motif and the *dugdhadhārī* and *puṣpapracāyikā* motifs on Mathurā railing pillars. The *śālabhañjikā* action of bending the branch of the *śāla* or mango tree is invariably depicted by the *vṛkṣikā* or *yakṣī* in the *svastika pāda* position while one of the arms is *kaṭisama*. This gives rise to sensuous *tribhaṅga* of the torso and the waist is either in *prasārita* or *vivṛtta* movement.[50] This lends a rhythm and verve to the body of the lady which merges with the rhythm of nature signified by the tree. She either represents the action of a garden sport, *śālabhañjikā*, or the tree spirit, *yakṣī*. She generally stands on a human dwarf who is her *vāhana*. But there are some types of *śālabhañjikā–aśoka-dohada* representations in which the *vāhana* is not shown, then such sculptures cannot be identified as *yakṣī*s, instead they can be referred to as *udyāna-krīḍā*s (ladies engaged in various sports)[51] (Czuma pls. 31, 34).

The *yakṣī*s represent a tree spirit who is endowed with procreative powers that from the early animistic cults, was so successfully adapted to new religious orders. Mackay observes it as one of the manifestations of the Mother Goddess. She is easier to worship and she is the guardian of the house and the village, she presides over child birth and takes a more human interest in people's needs.[52] In their malevolent moods they can cause violence and destruction, so they were frequently

fig. 73. *Śālabhañjikā*,
Kuṣāṇa, second century CE,
Soṅkh, Mathura Museum.

fig. 74. *Śālabhañjikā* holding
the branch of the tree,
second century CE,
Soṅkh, Mathura Museum.

worshipped more ardently than other idols. It is difficult to agree with the above interpretation of worship and goddess connotation ascribed to the *yakṣīs*. They were probably psychologically satisfying symbols and not objects of worship on Buddhist or Jaina monuments. Before *yakṣa-yakṣī* cult got absorbed into these religions, they had separate sanctuaries, but when they got absorbed into these two expanding cults, they became part of a larger religious affiliation. The common man's mind could not reconcile with the new religions without the earlier concepts of chthonic principles like water, wind, earth, vegetation and other spirits. Here, a detailed analysis of the *yakṣī* imagery is called for.

The most important example of *śālabhañjikā* as bracket sculpture is found from Soṅkh (Mathura Museum) (*fig.* 73, 74) in which the body of the *yakṣī* is bent echoing the curve of the bracket. The infectious smile on her face intensifies the eroticism implied by her langurous posture.

Two examples from Kaṅkālī Ṭīlā also need to be mentioned, since one of them is a slightly crude sculpture carved in front and back like the Sāñcī *toraṇa śālabhañjikā*, while the other is represented on a Jaina *āyaga-paṭṭa* relief standing on small railing, flanking the gate. These *yakṣīs* stand in the typical *śālabhañjikā* pose leaning against the votive *stūpa* behind them. There is no tree present here.[53]

The *aśokadohada-krīḍā* enhances the concept of fecundity in which the act of striking the tree with the left foot of the lady stimulates the tree to blossom. Kālidāsa's *Mālavikāgnimitra* is an example of classical Sanskrit *nāṭya* adapting this theme as the major part of the plot around which the romance of Mālavikā and Agnimitra is constructed. The symbolism of women as ever auspicious is implied by this art and hence here *aśokadohada-krīḍā* action is more powerful and inevitable for the monument.

The Saṅghol (S.P. Gupta *fig.* 17, p. 80) and Mathurā (U.N. Roy *figs.* 44, 45) versions show the face of the lady in three-quarter view and the body in complete profile, as she stands leaning against the tree trunk of the flowering *aśoka*. Her left leg is lifted to kick the base of the tree which animates her body. Her hands are pulling at a scarf-like object from one of the branches of the tree. It could also be a garland. A sculpture from Bodha-Gayā represents the lady almost perched on the tree entwining her legs around the tree trunk, while a man seated below supports her. This is a unique version of the *aśoka-dohada* in which both male and female participate. Here the fertility connotation comes a full circle (*fig.* 60).

The most unusual of "the woman and the tree motif" is the lady plucking flowers with her back to the spectator. She stands on a crouching dwarf. The lady could either be in the act of embracing the tree or collecting flowers, *puṣpapracāyikā* (*fig.* 77, 78).

The *keśanistoyakāriṇī*[54] or *sadyasnātā* and *dugdhadhārī* (S.P. Gupta *fig.* 10, p. 71, *fig.* 16, p. 78) are sensually inclined representations, which are symbolizing the inherent fecundity. Woman symbolically is equivalent to water. Bathing motif is connected with erotic attraction and impregnation.[55] The lady is represented wringing her hair when a crane stretches its long neck aspiring to catch the drops of water dripping from her hair.

fig. 75. *Stambha-yoṣita, nṛtyābhinaya*, second century CE, Mathurā, Giridharpur, Mathura Museum.

fig. 76. Lady with a rattle, second century CE, Saṅghol, National Museum, New Delhi.

There is little doubt that a close association with water cosmology, the giver of life and riches, stimulating procreation and growth, is implied (S.P. Gupta *fig.* 3, p. 62, U.N. Roy *figs.* 57, 60). Another representation of *nirjharasnāna* shows a woman bathing under a natural spring. Here again the connotation of pure nature and the natural form of the woman are compared.

Dugdhadhārī (*fig.* 124) are two examples from Saṅghol (S.P. Gupta fig. 10, p. 71, fig. 16, p. 78) and Mathurā (*figs.* 125, 126) (V.S. Agrawala fig. 139a, 139b), in which the lady is shown squeezing or simply touching her breast, while holding a branch of the tree. This act of invoking nourishment and abundance signify the benevolent nature of the *yakṣī*. Some of the sculptures also represent mother and child, *putravallabhā*, an imagery which is supported by *Matsya* and *Vāyu Purāṇa*, with reference to *apsaras* who are called *mātar* and *dugdhavatsā*. In the imagery of *dugdhavatsā*, the nourishment aspect is suggested, which is a role ascribed to *apsaras* in the *Matsya* and *Vāyu Purāṇa*. In that sense both the *yakṣīs* and the *apsaras* seem to share the element of nourishment that vegetation and

fig. 77. *Puṣpabhañjikā* lady seen from the back, second century CE, Mathurā.

fig. 78. Lady holding lotuses, second century CE, Saṅghol, National Museum, New Delhi.

water offer to the human beings. Some Vedic goddesses like Puraṁdhī (plenty and activity). Dhīṣaṇā (abundance), Iḷā (nourishment), Bṛhaddivā (mother), Rākā (rich and bountiful), Sīnīvālī (a broad hipped goddess who is implored to grant offspring)[56] can also be recalled to understand the cultural meaning and antiquity of the motif of *dugdhavatsā*. The *apsaras*es of the Purāṇas and the Vedic goddesses together lend a strong thematic base to the generically called *yakṣī* figures (U.N. Roy figs. 55, 56).

The rest of the sculptures either represent women acrobats balancing a *kalaśa* or a ball on the raised elbow or engaged in drinking (S.P. Gupta 2, 62, V.S. Agrawala fig. 137c), looking into the mirror (S.P. Gupta fig. 8, p. 68) and observing the nail marks (S.P. Gupta 1, 61, U.N. Roy fig. 54). Some women are also shown playing with the pet parrot, who is supposed to tease the lady and reveal the secrets of love play before the elders. Parrot is often used as an erotic inducer.[57] Often referred to as *śukasārikā*, the lady with the parrot is frequently represented at Mathurā where the parrot is perched on her shoulder. At Bhūteśvara the parrot has been released and it is perched on the *nāyikā*'s shoulder. At Mathura the parrot is seated on the girdle of a "dancing" woman nibbling at the knot in order to untie it (*fig.* 70).

The *khaḍgadhārī*, *khaḍgābhinayā* (*fig.* 71), are some of the most bold representations of women weilding weapons, and their frequent occurrence at Mathurā completes the imagery of the *yakṣī–apsaras–nāyikā* full circle, starting with *śṛṅgāra* and ending with *vīra*. The variation in the imagery signifies the various roles ascribed to these figures on a *stūpa* monument which ranges from sensuous to erotic on the one hand (*śukakrīḍā*, *śālabhañjikā* to *nartakī*, *vasanabhraṁśā*) and brave to dangerous on the other (*khaḍgadhārī*). Agrawala calls this as an *abhinaya* of sword dance. The Bhūteśvara pillar from Mathura Museum No. 152, and Lucknow Museum pillar No. J.275, repeat the same *khaḍgadhārī* under a *kadamba* tree. It is difficult to surmise what a *khaḍgadhārī* could be doing under a *kadamba* tree. It certainly evokes questions, such as, is it a *yakṣī* or a *pratihārī*? Many references have been found from classical literature referring to this character (Agrawala *figs.* 137b, c, d). Agrawala observes that in later art this subject was styled as

fig. 79. River goddess, entrance doorway, lintel, *c.* fifth century, cave I, Ajanta.

Urvaśī or Menakā, but the exact references in early art are wanting.[58] The above point will be elaborated in the section on *devāṅganā* sculptures in Chapter 6. But it is heartening to note that Agrawala has pointed out the continuation of this motif in later art, a "connection" on which the main thesis of the present exploration is based. The main objective of introducing a section on Kuṣāṇa period sculptures was to elaborate upon the continuity of some of these very motifs and their re-emergence in medieval temples nearly a 1,000 years later.

fig. 80. Lady with *vita,* Cave 4, Ajantā.

One more conspicuous motif is that of a lady removing the lower garment from Bhūteśvara which Agrawala identifies as *mahānartakī* (*fig.* 167). The implication is that of a dancing girl or a prostitute. But this is not convincing. The lady's stance and gesture are bold and nonchalant, but the element of eroticism has been overridden by fecundity and suggestion of procreation. In later *devāṅganā* sculptures the same action will be performed more artistically by letting the garment slip slightly, which the *devāṅganā* tries to catch by

fig. 81. *Śālabhañjikā-nadīdevatā,* detail of left side of doorframe, upper part, Cave 5, Ajantā.

standing in *baddhācārī*. Another occasion on which the lady startled by the touch of a scorpion advancing under her garment, shrugs it off by opening it. See this at Rānī Vāv (*fig.* 177). The nomenclature, *kharjūravāhaka* often found in the context of Khajurāho sculptures, evolves out of the *vasanabhraṁśā* imagery.

Thus, the *yakṣī* imagery absorbs numerous aspects from various sources so much so that it has encompassed aspects of *śṛṅgāra* and various other *rasa*s as expressed in profane human activities besides the symbolic imagery implying fertility. Thus, the so-called *stambha-yoṣitā* are not mere decorative appendages of the *stūpa* but bear an implicit continuity and logical meaning. Thematically, they belong to the folk and mass culture which does not get

fig. 82. *Śālabhañjikā-nadīdevatā* detail of right side, Cave 5, Ajantā.

entangled with the cultic demands on a religious monument and continue to grow independently of the iconographical injunctions. Stylistically, as sculptures, they stem from a perennial, unbroken tradition of wooden domestic architecture in which the brackets supporting the pillars generally represented female figures. To this day, in states of western India like Gujarat, Rajasthan and parts of Maharashtra, one can see carved timber architectural brackets with representations of winged fairies wearing *ghāgharā-colī* or Marāṭhī-style *sāṛīs* playing musical instruments. They adorn as pillar brackets both religious and domestic architecture.

fig. 84. *Śālabhañjikā-nadīdevatā* with a parrot, doorframe of a side shrine, second half of fifth century Ajantā, Cave 27,

Emergence of the Nāyikā-Viṭa Kuṭilaka Motif

It was a chance meeting with this motif at Ajantā that began my exploration and I keenly observed and found the *kuṭilaka* (the dwarf with a crooked stick) almost everywhere, from *vihāra* doorways to medieval temple doorways, accompanying the *nāyikā* alone, dallying with her or simply watching her or providing a jestful interlude when she is with the *nāyaka*. It seems that this character is a direct quotation from Sanskrit literature. Both Hindu and Buddhist monuments

fig. 83. *Śālabhañjikā* with *viṭa,* doorway, cave 14, Ajantā.

fig. 85. *Nāyaka-nāyikā* with *viṭa*, theatrical scene, Khilchipura pillar, ninth century Mandsaur, Madya Pradesh

fig. 86. *Śālabhañjikā* with *viṭa*, pillar bracket, note the palm tree, sixth century, Jogeśvarī, Mumbai.

represent this character who is always seen as a minor accompanying figure but with a direct reference to the main figure. The sites where this motif of *kuṭilaka* occurs with the *nāyikā* alone or with both *nāyaka* and *nāyikā* are listed below as they help to assess the diffusion of this motif and its popularity shared in contemporary literature. The frequency with which this motif occurs in western India particularly in Madhya Pradesh, Rajasthan, Gujarat and Maharashtra as listed below suggests the artistic norms and guild association of this motif.

(1) Doorways of Ajantā Cave 1, 4, 5, 20, 14 (*figs.* 79, 80, 81, 82, 83, 84).

(2) Pillar capital, Roḍā, Temple No. 6 (*figs.* 97, 212).

(3) Vestibule panel, south, Auraṅgābād Cave 1, 7 (*figs.* 89, 90).

(4) Pillar capital, Ellorā, Cave 21 (*fig.* 92, 93, 94).

(5) Pillar, Khilchipura, Mandsaur (*fig.* 85).

(6) *Maṇḍovara*, along with *putravallabhā*, Jagat, Ambikāmātā Temple.

(7) Mātṛkā, Jhālarāpāṭan (*fig.* 158).

(8) Śāmalājī, Gaṅgā fragment (*fig.* 95).

(9) *Maṇḍovara*, along with *alasā*, Kekind (*fig.* 216).

(10) Vestibule, cave 14, Rāvaṇa kī Khāī, Cave 17, Ellorā.

(11) Doorway, Jogeśvarī Cave (*fig.* 86).

(12) *Garbha-gṛha* doorway, Lakṣmaṇa Temple, Sirpur (*fig.* 96).

This motif occurs frequently on the doorways of the Buddhist and Hindu cave architectures and subsequently on the brackets, capitals and *maṇḍovara*s of the medieval temples. The observation regarding the *kuṭilaka* on rock-cut architecture, may have some connection with theatre on one hand and the evolving concept of the river goddess on the other. The connection between theatre and water cosmology is not apparent, but the presence of this character along with a river goddess on Ajantā Cave 20, and with *nāyaka-–nāyikā* pair on Khilchipura pillar, are evidences that need some explanation.

Here is an architectural-design-oriented explanation. When Buddhist architecture in the Mahāyāna period shifted its focus from outdoor free-standing monuments (e.g. Sāñcī, Mathurā) to rock-cut cave architecture (Ajantā, Ellorā, Auraṅgābād, etc.) a number of sculptural patterns and formats had to be changed and readjusted. A closer scrutiny will show that as the *vedikā* and its ornamented pillars got eliminated in cave architecture, much of the female sculptures got eliminated. The doorway became the focus of attention. The place of *toraṇa śālabhañjikā* from Sāñcī was taken over by the *nadī-devī*, who for some time occupied the T-shaped corner on both sides of the lintel and then slowly occupied the *udumbara*, threshold level. In the evolving stages of the river goddess imagery, the *vṛkṣikā* "Woman and Tree" motif was originally used. Then slowly the *makara* and *kūrma* were differentiated and the nature of Gaṅgā and Yamunā got separated out of the single generic female form of a *nadī-devī*. The Gupta period temple architecture had also contributed to the evolving nature of river goddesses, but the character of the dwarf with *kuṭilaka* is generally not found on Gupta doorways. *Viṭa-kuṭilaka* is peculiar to Ajantā and temple architecture from the western India. Specially noteworthy are the Khilchipura pillars from Mandsaur wherein the dwarf is seen several times.

(facing page)
fig. 87. *Śālabhañjikā* with *viṭa*, Antechamber, Cave 1, Ajantā.

The *vṛkṣikā-nadī-devī* (a generic *nāyikā*, in its evolving phase) usually stands on the left side of the doorway under a mango or *śāla* tree in *svastika* or *daṇḍapādācārī* holding either a lotus (Ajantā, Cave 1, 21, 14, 5) (*figs.* 89, 84) or a parrot, *śukasārikā* (Cave 27). The other hand rests on the head of the dwarf (almost), which gives a *prasārita* movement to the waist of the *nāyikā*, whose posture strikes a perfectly rhythmic *tribhaṅga*. The dwarf rests his forearms and head gleefully on his characteristic curved stick and watches the *nāyikā* (Ajanta, Cave 14, 27, 5; Auraṅgābād Cave 1, 7; Ellorā Cave 21). The dwarf has monkey-like feet, long toes and short legs and in some cases large ears. This gives him a comical appearance; is he a *viṭa*? (*figs.* 89, 90, 91, 92, 93, 94).

(facing page)
fig. 89. Avalokiteśvara, with *yakṣa* Maṇibhadra (*viṭa*)?, Cave 1, Auraṅgābād, Maharashtra.

On the entrance doorway of Cave 20 at Ajantā, the River Goddess Gaṅgā stands on the *makara* in *svastika pāda*, while her dwarf companion holding *kuṭilaka* on the left shoulder, stands in *svastika* on a tortoise. Who is this accompanying figure, a *viṭa*, or a *vidūṣaka*?

Viṭa was a stage character and nothing else, whereas *vidūṣaka*s were jesters, who attended the courts of kings. They were mere comedians, who made their livelihood by their wit and friendly advice. They were real characters in social life in the second century BCE and were not mere dramatic inventions.[59] A proof of this can be provided by citing examples from Amarāvatī and Mathurā reliefs on which male and female dwarfs have been shown in court scenes.

A.B. Keith[60] has pointed out that in the epics there are ample references to court life, yet there is no single reference to professional jesters. The same is true of Kauṭilya's *Arthaśāstra* (first century CE) where the word *vidūṣaka* does not occur either.[61]

But *Daśakumāracarita* of Daṇḍin (*c*. CE 550) refers to *vidūṣaka* as a man who had an access to the harem and who was sitting there near the king, a skilful mind reader, a royal favourite, an adept in song, dance, instrumental music and related arts, a connoisseur of

fig. 88. *Śālabhañjikā* with *viṭa* cave 20, Ajantā.

unconventional women, shrewd, talkative, clever in enigmatic speeches (*bhaṅgī*), critical, a buffoon (*parihāsa-yitra*), a scandalmonger, an adept in calumny, ready to take bribes even from ministers of state, an instructor in all naughtiness, a pilot in the science of love (*kāmatantra*) and the king's servant from the time the former was a prince.[62] *Vidūṣaka* has been again referred to as *kāmatantra-saciva*, councellor in matters of *kāmatantra* or in amorous adventures (*Mālavikāgnimitra* IV.17.10).[63] Even in Bāṇa's *Harṣacarita* (shortly after CE 600) the reference to *vidūṣaka* as a court jester is mentioned along with *kubjā*, *vāmā*, etc. living in and around the court. Somadeva Sūri (about CE 970) in his *Nītivākyāmr̥ta* (14.8), refers to a lot of spies engaged by the king, which includes along with *naṭa, nartaka, gāyaka,* etc. *viṭa*, *vidūṣaka* and *pīṭhamardaka*. For the first time this group occurs in *Kāmasūtra* of Vātsyayāna (around first century CE) in the order of *pīṭhamarda-vīṭa-vidūṣaka* (1.4.44-46). *Agni Purāṇa* refers to the *pīṭhamarda*, *viṭa*, *vidūṣaka* as the companions of the *nāyaka* in his erotic amusements as his attendants (A.G.339.39).[64] As stated by Kuiper and G.K. Bhat, *Kāmasūtra* mentions the *vidūṣaka* as a synonym for the urban *nāgaraka*, who is considered a play-thing (*krīḍanaka*).[65]

According to *Daśakumāracarita*, *pīṭhamarda*, *viṭa*, *vidūṣaka*, *bhikṣukyādi*, were used to advertise a young courtesan in the town by having her beauty, character and sweetness praised in the gathering of the *nāgarka*s.[66]

In dramaturgical texts from *Nāṭyaśāstra* onwards, *viṭa* (35-77) has been taken as a stage character and Bharata describes its use in *prakaraṇa* (20.53) and *bhāna* (20.110). But for *viṭa* there is no reference to prove that he was a social figure.[67] In the *caturbhānī* also *viṭa* has been accepted as a stage character. S.K. De has found later theoreticians mentioning some kinds of plays in which a *viṭa* is acting, such as *Durmallikā*, *Śr̥ṅgāra Prakāśa* (between 1000-50), *Bhāva-Prakāśa* (between 1175–1250), etc.[68] V.S. Agrawala has pointed out palace scenes on Mathurā pillars representing the scene from Aśvaghoṣa's *Saundarānanda*. It is interpreted by Agrawala as representing a scene of palace amusement in which a *vidūṣaka*'s scarf is being pulled by a lady. But the *vidūṣaka* shown here is neither a

(facing page)
fig. 90. *Viṭa* with Tārā and attendant female groups identified as *yakṣa* Maṇibhadra, seventh century, Cave 7, Aurangabad, Maharashtra.

dwarf nor holding a *kuṭilaka*. However dwarfs have been represented in toilet scenes.[69]

But in non-dramatic Sanskrit literature *viṭa* means a paramour (*Mālatīmādhava* 8.8, *Śiśupālavadha* 4-48) and a voluptuary, sensualist (*Bhāgavata Purāṇa* X.1327). The terms used in *Mālatīmādhava* are *kanyāviṭaḥ* or *kanyādūṣakaḥ* (violator of girls), while in *Śiśupālavadha* there is a pure *madhukaraviṭa*, meaning "the bee acting as lover". *Kathā-Sarit-Sāgara* 6.51 mentions the *viṭa* as a rogue who even deceives clever women.[70]

Therefore, *viṭa* is different from *vidūṣaka*. It has a clear mention as a conventional stage character, as a professionally skilled dramatic group and according to *Bṛhad-Kathāśloka Saṁgraha* (10.69) there is an existence of a whole Viṭaśāstra. The character of *viṭa* as a *pīṭhamarda*, *vaihāsika* and an expert in *Kāmasūtra*, interests us at this juncture since in sculptured representation it is this character of *viṭa* that is uppermost. By enumerating all the above data we arrive at a notion of *viṭa*, *vidūṣaka*, as dramatic characters but the visual data before us is still not explained by it. Why *kuṭilaka*? Is the dwarf with a crooked stick representing the *viṭa*?

On the doorway of Ajantā Cave 4 (*fig.* 80) the lady (a courtesan?) is shown necking the male companion with *kuṭilaka* and pouring a cup of wine. Is it a scene of *madhupānā*? While above this group on the same doorway on the left side lintel corner, the lady stands leaning against the tree in an erotic *śṛṅgārika* posture.

From *Padatāḍitakam* of Śyāmīlaka, one of the *Caturbhāṇī*

fig. 91. *Śālabhañjikā* with *viṭa*, cave 17, Ellorā, Aurangabad, Maharashtra.

fig. 92. *Śālabhañjikā* with *viṭa*, pillar bracket, *c.* seventh century, Cave 21, Ellorā, Auraṅgābād, Maharashtra.

plays, it is learnt that the *viṭa* or dwarf is used for the *pādā prahāra* of the *nāyikā* and takes great pleasure in being honoured by her foot. The foot of a damsel (*vilāsinī*) decorated with red lac and anklet, has been compared to the staff of the cupid (*madanasya ketuḥ*) and held worthy of worship, while lying prow with face steadily placed on the ground (verse no. 7).

The *viṭa,* while eulogizing the touch of the foot sole of a charming lady under intoxication, proclaims that her leg adorned with tinkling anklets and raised upwards in dispute of love with the edge of the thighs exposed to the view, because of the transparent lower garment having slipped down, has been victorious (verse no. 8).

At Roḍā, we find a representation of woman and *viṭa*, whose dress appears to be slipping and the *viṭa* is shown watching her gleefully. (*fig.* 97)

From *Padmaprabhṛtakam* of Śūdraka we find the mention of *vaiśikīkalā*, the art of loving a hetaerae. It narrates that a certain Dattaka wrote a handbook on this art, in which a *viṭa* ridicules a hypocritical Buddhist monk, who cultivates this *kalā* and is caught in the act of entering a hetaerae's house. On the Buddhist monument of Ajantā, Cave 4, there is a representation carved right on the doorway, of a woman with a wine cup entwining her arm around a man's neck holding a *kuṭilaka*. It has an air of sarcasm about it and in the light of the story mentioned in *Padmaprabhṛtakam*, the presence of this character on a Buddhist monument might be didactic, but not iconographically prescribed. (*fig.* 80)

There are large-sized representations of dwarfs with *kuṭilaka* in Gaṅgā fragment from Śāmalājī (*fig.* 95), Auraṅgābād Cave 7 (*fig.* 90), and Ellorā Caves 14, 21, (*fig.* 91, 92, 93, 94) standing next to river

goddesses and gazing at their beauty. At one point in his investigative study on Varuṇa as *vidūṣaka*, Kuiper observes that *vidūṣaka* impersonated as Varuṇa who was too inauspicious to act as the protector of a dramatic character (p. 176). Could it be possible to identify the dwarf with *kuṭilaka* standing on a tortoise next to the *nadī-devī*, as an impersonator of Varuṇa? Here water cosmology and dramatic impersonation have combined to produce a unique kind of visual imagery, which has evolved in the transitional phase, only to vanish very soon. In the later river goddesses, only the dwarf with a water pitcher is used and not with the *kuṭilaka* (Ajantā, Tigowā, Besnagar, Nachnā-Kuṭhārā), and they themselves hold a lotus or water pitcher followed by an attendant with a parasol. The tree with flowers and fruits is completely eliminated. Thus, the *vidūṣaka* in the Varuṇa connotation carries forward the evolving iconography of the river goddess via *vr̥kṣikā* and *nāyikā* implying vegetal force and aquatic potency (*figs.* 98, 99, 100, 101, 102, 103, 104).

fig. 93. *Śālabhañjikā* with *viṭa*, pillar bracket, *c.* seventh century, Cave 21, Ellorā, Auraṅgābād, Maharashtra.

fig. 94. *Śālabhañjikā* with *viṭa*, pillar bracket, left, south wall, *c.* seventh century, Cave 21, Ellorā, Auraṅgābād, Maharashtra.

The other interpretation which is solely dramatic and less conjectural as the previous one, is convincing from the Khilchipura pillars. Here the *nāyikā* is pulling the beard of the dwarf and the dwarf makes clear attempts at wooing the *nāyikā* to the annoyance of the *nāyaka* standing beside him. The kneeling *viṭa* is pushed to one side by the *nāyaka*, who pushes forward to woo the shy *nāyikā*. The last scene shows the *nāyikā* accepting the flower and the amorous advances of the *nāyaka*, while the *viṭa* and another attendant gleefully look on (*fig.* 85).

fig. 95. Gaṅgā on *makara*,
viṭa dangling on the creeper
oozing out of *makara* mouth,
fifth century,
Śāmalājī, Baroda Museum.

The occurrence of this motif does not end at the cave sites but continues on temple architecture as well. Foremost among them are Roḍā and Kekind. I came across this motif in conjunction with the *nāyikā* on the capitals of the Roḍā Temple 6 and the *maṇḍovara* niches on the Śiva Temple at Kekind. U.P. Shah[71] in his article does not identify the *viṭa-kuṭilaka* character. At Roḍā the dwarf accompanies the *nāyikā* in *alasā* pose or playing with a ball or blindman's buff. (*figs.* 161, 212).

fig. 96. *Mithuna*, lady in *śālabhañjikā* pose with *viṭa,* Lakṣmaṇa temple doorway, seventh century, Sirpur.

At Kekind, the dwarfish pot-bellied man appears to look at the *nāyikā* in *alasā* pose and another one holding something in her hand (*fig.* 216). Both the sculptures are quite damaged and therefore nothing more can be said but the curved stick and dwarf twining his leg around it are clearly visible. These sculptures of the medieval period could be interpreted in the light of the data from Daṇḍin, Bāṇa and Rājaśekhara. The continuity of this character in the literature from first century of our era, right into the medieval period, helps in connecting the motifs such as the *vṛkṣikā*, *nadī-devī* and *devāṅganā* into a holistic group, parallel and overlapping but heterogeneous in character.

The motif originates in sculpture from Gupta-Vākāṭaka art seen at Ajantā doorways and Mandsaur region, but its absence on Gupta temple doorways should be mentioned. After its life on Buddhist

fig. 97. *Vasanabhraṁśā devāṅganā* with *viṭa*, pillar capital, temple 6, *c.* eighth century, Roḍā, Gujarat.

fig. 98. *Vṛkṣakā* leaning against the tree trunk, doorway, left side, upper portion, cave 4, Ajantā.

and Brāhmanical cave temple doorways, this motif develops in the western Indian temples. Roḍā is the foremost example, but the architectural positioning of this motif changes at Roḍā from doorways to pillar capital. After its spread in Śāmalājī and Roḍā region it is again seen at Kekind where it appears along with the *devāṅganā* sculptures. This progression goes to illustrate the regional development of a larger concept of feminine power of abundance, prosperity and sensuality that share common motifs and imageries, with literary characters.

The Water Cosmology

The *yakṣa*s are vegetation spirits directly controlling and bestowing upon their *bhakta*s, fertility and wealth, in one word-abundance.

Yakṣas have an intimate connection with the waters. For example, Kubera's inexhaustible treasures are a lotus and a conch, innumerable *yakṣīs* have *makara* or other fish-tailed creatures as their vehicle; Kāmadeva, has the *makara* as his cognizance; the greater tutelary *yakṣa*s control the grains essential to prosperity; and in the earliest mythology, that germ which the waters held first and in which all the gods exist, rose like a tree from the navel of the unborn who in the oldest

fig. 99. *Vita-vṛkṣakā* on pillar capital, Cave 1, Auṛṅgabād.

fig. 100. Gaṅgā,
holding mirror,
Kaṅkālīdevī temple,
fifth century, Tigowā, Madya Pradesh

fig. 101.Yamunā,
śālabhañjikā pose, with *gaṇa*,
Kaṅkālīdevī temple,
fifth century, Tigowā, Madya Pradesh

fig. 102. Doorway with river goddesses, Pārvatī temple, fifth century CE, Nachnā, Madya Pradesh

(facing page)
fig. 103. Gaṅgā with a dwarf and lotus flower, Khilchipura pillar, fifth century, Mandsaur.

passages in the *Atharvaveda* is called a *yakṣa*. In decorative arts, vegetation is represented as springing either (1) from the mouth or navel of a *yakṣa*, (2) from the open jaws of a *makara* or other fish-tailed creatures, (3) from a "brimming vessel", and (4) from a conch, but never directly from any symbol representing the earth.[72]

*Yakṣa*s are the "lords of life", closely connected with the waters, though their habitat is terrestrial. The *yakṣa* control not so much the waters as mere waters, but that essence (*rasa*) in the waters which is one with the sap in trees, with the *amṛta* (elixir) of the *deva*s, especially Agni, with the Soma, and with the seed in living beings.

Coomaraswamy places *yakṣa* at an important position in what is called "life cult", to suggest that this life cult, with which is also connected the worship of the Great Mother, may have been the primitive religion of India, and to show that the "plant style" is actually nothing more or less than the iconography of the water cosmology.

Rightly pointed out by him, a belief in the origin of life in the waters was common to many ancient cultures, and must have arisen very naturally in the case of

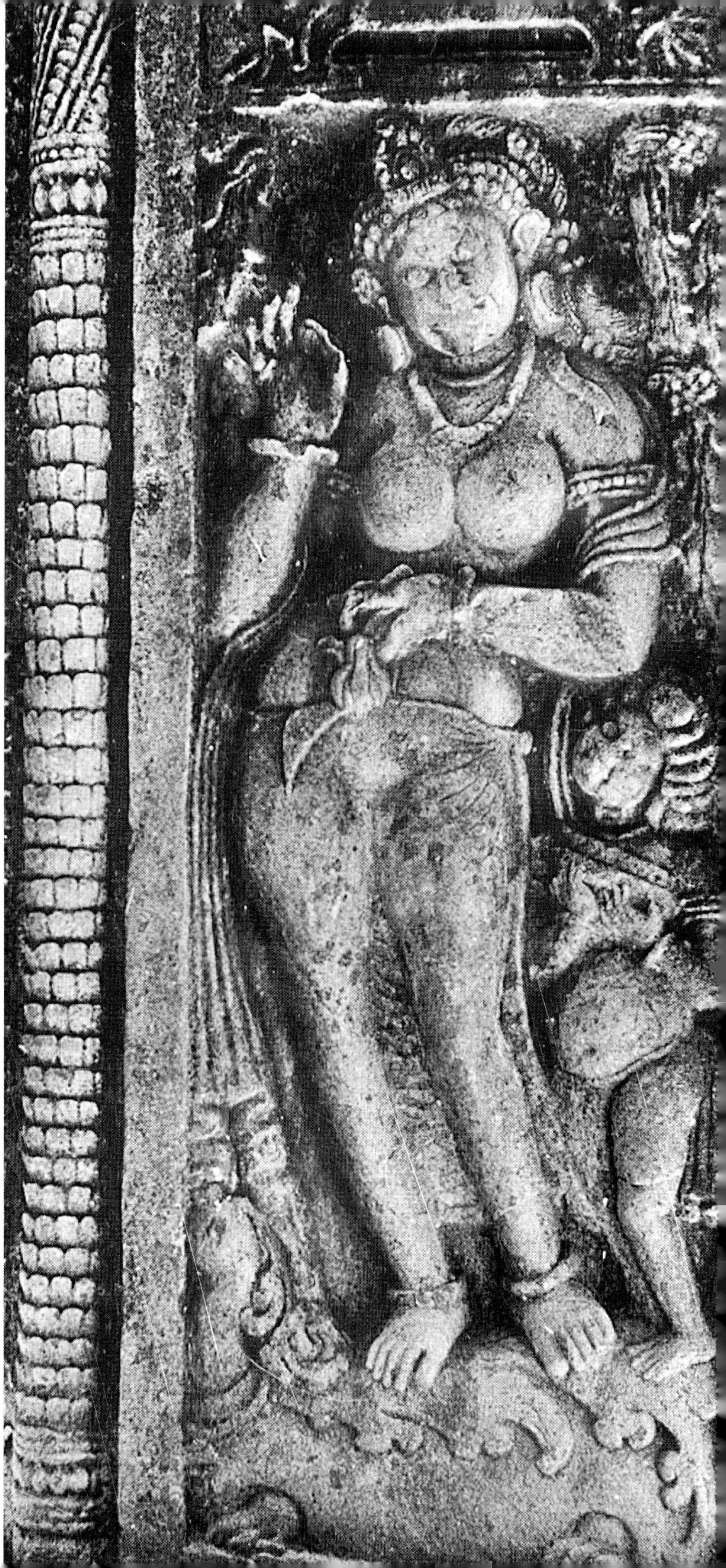

peoples like those of the Nile, the Euphrates, or the Indus Valley, amongst whom water, in the form either of seasonal rains or of ever-flowing rivers was the most obvious prerequisite of vegetative increase, nor can the belief be regarded as in any way unreasonable. Taken in a purely physical sense, it may indeed be called a fair anticipation of modern scientific ideas.[73]

The term "water cosmology" was first employed by Hume in his introduction to *Thirteen Principal Upaniṣads* (pp. 10-14), with reference to such passages as *Bṛhadāraṇyaka* (5.5) "in the beginning this world was just water" and (3.6.1) "all this world is woven warp and woof, on water" and *Kauṣītakī* (1.7), where *Brahman* declares "the waters, verily, indeed are my world".[74]

The reason for incorporating this discussion here is to bridge the connection between *yakṣa–yakṣīs*, *apsaras–gandharvas*, aquatic concepts of *makara*, lotus, *pūrṇa ghaṭa*, Varuṇa, Soma as analogous and complementary. This is intended to create a base for the concept of *nadī-devatā* which comes to the fore on Gupta architecture. The visual connection between the imageries of the *nadī-devatā* and the earlier *vṛkṣikā* are self-explanatory, but the continuation of this motif in medieval temple architecture is seldom explored by scholars as antecedents for *apsaras-devāṅganā* imageries. However, many scholars refer to it, but a focused study is still wanting. Coomaraswamy has observed a number of synchronic fundamentals in mythology and art to support a number of conceptual formulations but did not develop it further.

fig. 104.Gaṅgā, with *chatra* and attendants, site unknown, Madya Pradesh

Water cosmology is closely connected with the feminine powers of fertility and abundance which can be observed in the pre-historic nude goddess, the Great Mother Aditi or Śrī, they are all represented as aspects of women in human form.

Water is the source of all creation and all creation is sustained by water. The *Yajurveda* and

fig. 105. Doorway, Gaṅgā on *makara*
no Yamunā distinction identifiable
Cave 21, late fifth century, Cave 21, Ajantā.

fig. 106. Doorway,
Cave unknown, Ajantā.

Atharvaveda are rich in references on water. "Let flow the divine waters, the honey sweet, for health, for progeny" (*ŚB* VI.4.3); "water, lightning, clouds, rain, let the liberal one favour you. Anoint the earth, O Parjanya, with thy milk, poured out, let abundant rain come" (*AV* IV.5, 6, 9); "The waters divine do then pour full of sweetness to avert diseases from men, from their place, let arise plants with fair leaves" (*YV* IV.1.2); and "From rain originate virility, sap, well-being" (*ŚB*, 1.8, 3.15).[75]

"The essence (*rasa*) of all beings is the earth, the essence of the earth is water, etc." (*Chāndogya Upaniṣad* 1.1.2). "In the waters, O Agni is thy seat, thou enterest the plants" (*YV* IV.2, 3). Besides the nourishing and reproductive power of the water, earth and creation are also implied; the lotus means the water, and this earth is a leaf thereof, even as the lotus leaf here is spread on the waters, so this earth lies spread on the waters (*ŚB* X.5.2.8). *Mithuna*, a productive pair is also connected with water cosmology; *yakṣa–yakṣī* pair is constantly recognized in Śuṅga terracottas. The word *mithuna* is constantly used in connection with ritual coitus, e.g. that of the *mahiṣī* and the sacrificial horse (*ŚB* XIII.5.2.2), and in connection with *Mahāvrata* festival (*AitĀr.* V.1.5), "From Prajāpati, when, dismembered, couples (*mithuna*) went forth, birth originates from a *mithuna* (*ŚB* IX.4.1.2-5).[76] This shows the association of *mithuna* with fecundity and to signify auspiciousness.

According to Coomaraswamy, Varuṇa is another deity connected with water of a settled agrarian culture. He is a chthonic principle connected with seasonal festivals, ritual eroticism and possibly human sacrifice, shared commonly by cultures from Mediterranean to Indus. Varuṇa was originally the root of the tree of life, the source of all creation (*R̥V* 1.24.7) and it is presumably still Varuṇa who is called the unborn in *R̥V* I.24.7. Maybe it is the *aśvattha* or *nyagrodha* with which Varuṇa is identified (*Gobhila-Gr̥hya-Sūtra* IV.7, 24).[77] In *ŚB* XIII.4.3, 7.8 king Varuṇa's people are said to be *gandharva*s and those of king Soma, *apsarase*s. These are closely associated divinities of the waters and of fertility, and originally of more significance than when in the later literature they became little more than the musicians and dancers of Indra's Court. These *gandharva*s and *apsarase*s are tree and fertility spirits (*nyagrodha, udumbara, aśvattha, plakṣa* are

fig. 107. Shrine doorway, Cave unknown, Ajantā.

the homes of the *gandharvas* and *apsarases YV* III.4.8) connected with Varuṇa and Soma, but later on their function was taken over by *yakṣas* and *yakṣīs*.[78] Coomaraswamy points out that both these groups are identical but is not able to delve deeper into the supportive argument.

It is in the context of Varuṇa again, that the mention of river goddess occurs for the first time in *Viṣṇudharmottara* III.52. Here, Varuṇa is described as having a large belly, a pouch (for treasure) holding lotus and fetters, a conch and an umbrella. His wife is Gaurī (or Vāruṇī) holding a blue lotus. Attendants are Gaṅgā on the right, holding a lotus, standing on *makara,* said to represent virility (*vīrya*), and Yamunā on the left, holding a blue lotus, standing on tortoise, said to represent time (*kāla*).[79] It is the various symbolic attributes and chthonic principles which enable the analogous chain of link between the Varuṇa, Soma and Indra groups of semi-divine characters, who float around in supportive unison to create an ambience of auspiciousness. This mythology has a lot of vision and scenic brilliance rather than logical ordering.

Emergence of the Nadī-devatās and its Continuation in Later Devāṅganās

The *yakṣas* and *yakṣīs*, who are connected with *gandharvas* and *apsarases* on the basis of water and vegetation, are represented as standing on aqueous animals like *jalebha*, *jalaturaga*, lion, lotus or *makara*. This attribute connects them as deities of fertility with life-giving waters.

On Gupta and Vākāṭaka period architecture (*figs.* 102, 105, 106, 107, 108, 109, 110) at sites such as Ajantā, we find the first-ever representation of *nadī-devatā*s (in female form) placed on the door jambs, at the ends of lintels, the place where at one time *toraṇa śālabhañjikā*s were placed in the *stūpa* architecture a few centuries ago. They carry *pūrṇa ghaṭa* and their imagery is directly derived from that of the *yakṣī*-dryad, which implies that despite the vegetal and apparently terrestrial habitat they were still primarily a spirit of the waters. Over time, they are differentiated as Gaṅgā and Yamunā attributed with different vehicles, namely crocodile and tortoise respectively. This again recalls the *yakṣī*s' *vāhana*s which consisted of *jalaturaga, jalebha,* etc. They are often made to stand in the *śālabhañjikā* pose holding the branch of a flowering tree while holding a lotus, metamorphosed into a vegetal motif, which is also accompanied by a dwarf genii holding a vessel standing next to the river goddess. Often it is a dwarf with a crooked stick which has already been cited in the earlier section.

Longhurst (*Hampi Ruins*, p. 116) points out that the undifferentiated twin figures are not met with in south of the Gañjam

fig. 108. Shrine doorway with river goddesses, *c.* second half of fifth century, Cave 1, Ajantā.

fig. 109.
River goddesses,
outer doorway,
c. second half of
fifth century,
Cave 26, Ajantā.

fig. 110. River goddesses, Central doorway of *caitya*, second half of fifth century, Cave 26, Ajantā.

district, but it is seen in Orissan architecture, as *dohada* motif. The *śālabhañjikā* has even reached the Draviḍian architecture.[80]

An inscription of Vaidyānātha Temple, Baijnātha, Kāṅgṛā, refers to Gaṅgā and Jamunā as separate names (Vogel, *Gaṅgā et Yamunā*, pp. 387, 388), even from an inscription at Bherāghāṭ (Cunnigham, *A.S.I. Reports* IX, pp. 66-69) and from the description of Varuṇa in *Viṣṇudharmottara* referred earlier. Rivers are called the consorts of Varuṇa at all times.[81]

A combination of *śālabhañjikā-nadī-devī* are seen on Nāgārjunakoṇḍa narrative friezes (see Vogel, *Gaṅgā et Yamunā*, p. 1. Ia) (*fig.* 111) on the outer ends standing in the *svastika pada-kaṭisama* pose, holding the branch of a tree in *uromaṇḍalī hasta* on a composite crocodile, lion or deer *vāhana*. This could be a visual device to separate each frieze or to suggest a symbolic meaning.

From a railing pillar at Amarāvatī, two similar nymphs, each standing on a fish (possibly intended to be a *makara*) and bearing a tray of food at shoulder level, and a water vessel, are found approaching a theriomorphic *nāga* (*fig.* 112). This paired formula also

fig. 111. Buddhist Secne with *vṛkṣikā* standing on *makara*.

fig. 112. Water nymph or river goddesses with food dishes standing on *makara*, first century CE, Coomaraswamy, pl. 19, Amarāvatī.

serves as an example of duplicate river goddesses supported by fish or *makara*. These relate to the *yakṣī* carrying basket and water jug from Faizabad (*fig.* 267) and indirectly hints at the concept of Śrī Lakṣmī as carved on Sāñcī *stūpa* II (*fig.* 113). Thus, the undifferentiated river goddesses connect on one hand with those of *yakṣī*s or dṛyads, on the other hand they exhibit in the vase attribute, what may well have been the immediate source of this motif, as it appears held by the differentiated river goddesses at the close of the Gupta period and subsequently.

According to Coomaraswamy, Varāha cave at Udayagiri (inscribed to CE 402) represents the first-ever Gaṅgā–Yamunā amid *nṛtya-gīta-vādya*, but because of their differentiated form, he does not see it as later in date. But the cap worn by Varuṇa prompts him to call it closer to Kuṣāṇa in style, and therefore, in time as well (*fig.* 114). The association of Varuṇa and the river goddesses with theatre has already been referred to in the earlier section. Reiterating the same point the dwarf carrying vessels along with the *nadī-devī*s in langurous *alasā* or *śālabhañjikā* poses, have to be interpreted from a fresh perspective. The Khilchipura pillars have to be mentioned here once again, since on one of their sides river goddess is represented standing on a *makara* with a lotus in hand and accompanied by a *gaṇa*

(facing page)
fig. 113. River goddess holding lotus standing on lotus pedestal, pillar upright, first century CE.
Sāñcī

fig. 114. Representation of *gīta-vādha-nṛtya*, early fifth century, Cave 19, Udayagiri, Vidiśā, Madya Pradesh

holding a dish or a vessel (*fig.* 103). Here the *nadī-devī*s' attributes are clear, whereas in the above registers some scenes from theatre are depicted, revolving around the *nāyaka-nāyikā-viṭa* group. This is a rare example of its kind and belongs to the same period, but never seen in the light of the above data.

At Ajantā Caves 1, 4, 5, 16, 20, 21, 23 and 26, the doorways represent the river goddesses. There are mostly *vihāra*s with individual shrines and most of them belong to the Mahāyāna phase. The only caves which are a bit different from the rest are those in which the *viṭa* with *kuṭilaka* are represented. Note the Jogeśvarī cave doorway river goddess with *viṭa* holding *kuṭilaka* (*fig.* 86).

Most often, the *makaras* are repeated as *vāhanas*, before the tortoise is introduced. The continuation of foliage and creepers oozing out of *makara* mouths and *yakṣa* navels continue on the doorways, but in a slightly different form. Even the *mithunas* are repeated. In a way, one can say that much of the water cosmology fundamentals have been repeated on the temple doorway by readjusting and reformulating the same old motifs.

At Udayagiri Amr̥ta Cave 19 (*fig.* 115) the *nadī-devīs* are shown standing with *makara*, the influence of which goes to Ajantā, Jogeśvarī and Elephaṇṭā. At Nachnā Kumāramaṭha, the river goddesses are shown at the *udumbara* level, when they are shifted from the lintel to the *udumbara*, their iconography becomes more formal, they are accompanied by attendants holding *chatra* and also

fig. 115. Doorway, river goddesses under rich foliage, early fifth century Cave 19, Udayagiri, Vidiśā, Madya Pradesh

accompanied by *dvārapāla*s (Tumain, Barwāsāgar, etc.) This is a medieval period phenomenon when besides the *nadī-devī*s flanking the *garbha-gṛha* doorway, a number of other female figures have also been introduced on the *maṇḍovara*, e.g. Koṭai, Jagat, Tusā, etc. where they are placed on lotus pedestals, holding lotus, water pitchers or floral garlands. It is these very forms which later on develop into *apsaras* and *devāṅganā* motifs. In action and gestures, the *devāṅganā* figures resemble the *yakṣī*s who are recalled from the architectural memory of decorative motif vocabulary and reused on the temple. From the river goddesses they carry forward the idea of aquatic connection, vegetal fecundity and the concept of abundance and prosperity. They are also considered auspicious and good.

An interesting terracotta Gaṅgā from Mathurā of the fifth century CE (Museum for Indian Art, Berlin) (*fig.* 116) is a voluptuous woman seated on the *makara* head, almost riding it, holding a *kalaśa*, out of which thick foliage is emerging. This is a very direct representation of the river goddess motif with its essential attributes signifying aquatic connection and vegetal growth. The river goddess is represented with bare breasts and wet drapery below the waist indicated with incised lines.

fig. 116. Gaṅgā seated on *makara*, with a waterpot, terracotta, Berlin Museum.

The same motif, during the sixth century CE, is represented at Rājim on a pillar standing on a lotus pedestal above a *makara* (*figs.* 117, 118), holding a floral stick. Both are accompanied by attendants, one of them is holding a container full of pearls. The river goddess has a halo at the back of her head and an umbrella. The artist has also represented birds holding worms in their beaks (*fig.* 118).

The early sixth-century CE temple of Daśāvatāra at Deogaṛh (*fig.* 119) has river goddesses placed on the main *garbha-gṛha* doorway. They are

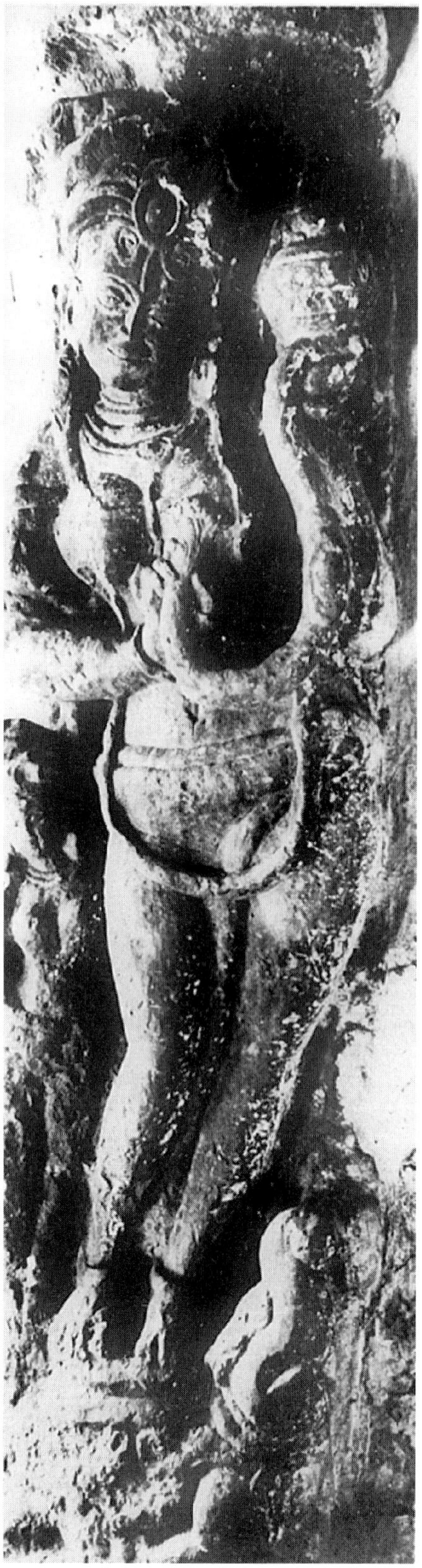

fig. 117. River goddess Gaṅgā, holding a water pot, *c.* CE 600, lower Kosala area, Rājim.

fig. 118. River goddess Gaṅgā on *makara,* holding a pearl stick, *c.* CE 600, Rājim,

fig. 119. Doorway,
Daśāvatāra temple, *c*. fifth-sixth century, Deogaṛh.

at the lintel level with *vāhanas* distinguishing them as Gaṅgā and Yamunā. But at the *udumbara* level there are dwarfs holding *ghaṭapallavas*, out of which a floral *śākhā* emerges. There are auspicious females carrying pearl strings and wearing fluttering sashes. There are *yakṣa* dwarfs also shown, out of whose navels a creeper with rich foliage is emerging on the doorway. All these are aquatic elements which come together on the doorway of the temples in Gupta period, which then get carried forward and repeated on pan-Indian temple doorways..

At Osiā on the Saccīyamātā temple (*fig.* 120) doorway the river goddesses have a richly stylized foliage above their heads turning into a *chatra*. The auspicious female standing in a *svastika pada*, might be holding a *kalaśa* (arms are broken). At Harihara Temple I, the same sculpture has been replaced by *sadyasnātā* squeezing her hair after a bath. Thus, the aquatic connotation continues (*fig.* 121).

It continues in Kaliṅga region in the form of *nāginīs* on the doorways. Sometimes even *śālabhañjikās* are represented instead of river goddesses.

The river goddesses on the Khajurāho temples, like Lakṣmaṇa and Kandarīya Mahādeva, etc. are represented with abundant foliage, which almost covers them like a *parikara*. But what attracted my attention was the representation of the *nāginīs*, with snake hoods flowing down from the *karṇa* conjoints and holding *añjalī-mudrā*. Some of them were represented in the *devāṅganā* imagery engaged in *keśanistoya* or holding a lotus flower, *vasanabhraṁśā*, holding a *darpaṇa* for applying *bindī*, standing in *alasā* pose and so on. This intrigued me because at Lakṣmaṇa Temple this iconographical arrangement is not only unique but also unconventional. The sculptors have freely and creatively filled up the empty spaces on the vast arena of the *maṇḍovara* wall with *devāṅganā* and *nāginīs* depicting similar motifs. The fluvial connection not only connects *nāginīs* and *devāṅganās* but even river goddesses. For this point an illustration of the doorway from Kauśāmbī in Allahabad Museum (*fig.* 257) and a doorway lintel from Ābanerī in the Bharat Kala Bhavan Museum are noteworthy (*figs.* 122). The river goddesses holding ripe lotus buds with a long stalk are placed on their *vāhanas*

fig. 120. *Vṛkṣakā*
near the doorway,
Sacchīyamātā temple,
tenth century, Osiā.

fig. 121. *Sadyasnātā*,
Harihara I,
ninth century, Osiā.

at the *udumbara* level. But on corners of the *lalāṭabimba* of the lintel two *devāṅganā*s are placed, flanked by *vyāla*s, in *vasanabhraṁśā* and *darpaṇa-prasādhikā* poses. They have the foliage at the back which continues the *vṛkṣika* connotation intact. Such examples of medieval doorways shed new light on *devāṅganā* imagery and its complex connections and continuities with water cosmology and *yakṣa* cult of the earlier era. Since the programmatic arrangement of a temple doorway is not the focus of this study, we end this discussion here.

fig. 122. Doorway with *vṛkṣakā* holding a mirror, Ābanerī. Bharat Kala Bhavan Museum, Varanasi.

References

1. Eric Neumann, *The Great Mother: An Analysis of the Archetype*, New York, English tr., 1955.
2. Ibid.
3. Irene Gjjar, 1971, refer figures 36, 52, 144, 246 to 254, 285 and 286.
4. Pupul Jayakar, *The Earthen Drum*, New Delhi, p. 48.
5. Ibid., p. 55.
6. Ibid.
7. Eric Neumann, op. cit., 1955, pp. 102-03.
8. Ibid., pp. 261-62.
9. Vogel, "The Woman and Tree, or Śālabhañjikā in Indian Literature and Art", *Acta Orientalia*, VII, 1928, p. 216; R.N. Misra, *Yakṣa Iconography*, New Delhi, 1981, pp. 140-41.
10. R.N. Misra, op. cit., 1981, pp. 140-41.
11. V.S. Agrawala, *Indian Art*, 1965, Varanasi, p. 224.
12. Vogel, op. cit., p. 216 and ibid., p. 225.
13. V.S. Agrawala, op. cit., 1965, p. 225.
14. R.N. Misra, op. cit., 1981, pp. 140-41.
15. Ibid., pp. 14-15.
16. Ibid., p. 56.
17. Ibid., pp. 56-98.
18. Ibid., p. 99.
19. D.D. Kosambi, *Myth and Reality*, Bombay, 1962, p. 57.
20. R.N. Misra, op. cit., 1981, p. 101.
21. V. Dehejia, *Yoginī Cult and Temples: A Tāntric Tradition*, New Delhi, 1986, p. 36.
22. A.K. Coomaraswamy, *Yakṣas,* Smithsonian Institute, Washington, 1928, Indian edn., 1971, p. 5.
23. Ibid., p. 32 and our Chapter 4, I.I.
24. A.A. Macdonell, *Vedic Mythology*, rpt. 1981, p. 154.
25. Coomarswamy, op. cit., 1971, p. 33.
26. J.Ph. Vogel, *ASIAR 1906-07*, p. 146.
27. *Atharvaveda* VI.8.1 "as the creeper embraces the tree on all sides so do thou embrace me". Coomarswamy, op. cit., 1971, p. 32.
28. A.K. Coomarswamy, op. cit., 1971, p. 33.

29. B.M. Barua, *Bharhut*, Parts I, II, III *Stone as a Story Teller*, Patna, 1979.

30. V.S. Agrawala, op. cit., 1965, pp. 134, 36.

31. K. Rama Pisharoti, in *JISOA*, vol. III, No. 2, p. 28.

32. B.M. Barua, op. cit., 1979, p. 81.

33. Ibid., p. 83.

34. Ibid., refer *Jātaka Tales*, p. 83.

35. Ibid., p. 56.

36. Iravati, "All Female Theatre: As Depicted in Ancient Indian Literature and Art", *Purātana*, vol. 7, 1989, Madhya Pradesh Commissioner, Archaeology and Museums, Bhopal.

37. Agrawala, op. cit., 1965, p. 221.

38. J. Marshall and A. Foucher, *The Monuments of Sāñcī*, 3 vols., London, n.d.

39. J.Ph. Vogel, "La Sculpture de Mathurā", *Arts Asiatica*, XV.

40. C. Sivaramamurti, "Sanskrit Literature and Art-Mirrors of Indian Culture", *Memoirs of the Archaeological Survey of India*, no. 73, Delhi, 1955.

41. K.S. Srinivasan, *The Ethos of Indian Literature: A Study of Its Romantic Tradition*, Delhi, 1985, pp. 86, 205.

42. A.H. Longhurst, "Buddhist Antiquities of Nāgārjunakoṇḍā, Madras Presidency", *Memoirs of the Archaeological Survey of India*, no. 54, Delhi, 1938.

43. S.P. Gupta, ed., *Kuṣāṇa Sculptures from Saṅghol,* New Delhi.

44. V.S. Agrawala, op. cit., 1965, p. 219.

45. A.K. Coomaraswamy, *History of Indian and Indonesian Art*, New York, 1927, p. 64, and M. Rosenfield, *Dynastic Art of the Kuṣāṇas*, 1967, p. 224.

46. R.C. Sharma, *Mathura Museum and Art: A Comprehensive Pictorial Guide Book*, 1971, p. 59.

47. V.S. Agrawala, "Mathura Museum Catelogue", *JUPHS*, pp. 130-32.

48. V.S. Agrawala, op. cit., 1965, p. 221.

49. Ibid., p. 224.

50. Kapila Vatsyayan, *Śālabhañjikās, Puṣpañjali*, Bombay 1980, p. 27, has observed the dance postures and referred to the development of this motif by sculptors of different ages in a very systematic way.

51. S.J. Czuma, *Kuṣāṇa Sculptures*, Cleveland, 1985, see plates 31, 34.

52. Ibid., pp. 98, 99.

53. U.N. Roy, *Śālabhañjikā in Art: Philosophy and Literature,* Allahabad,

1979, see plates 33, 34.

54. V.S. Agrawala, op. cit., 1965, p. 227.

55. Wendy O'Flaherty, *Asceticism and Eroticism in the Mythology of Śiva*, Delhi, 1973, p. 25.

56. A.A. Macdonell, 1981, for the names of Vedic goddesses, pp. 124, 125.

57. K.S. Srinivasan, 1985, p. 205.

58. V.S. Agrawala, op. cit., 1965, p. 228.

59. (i) F.B.J. Kuiper, *Varuṇa and Vidūṣaka: On the Origin of the Sanskrit Drama*, Amsterdam 1979, p. 223; (ii) S.N. Dasgupta and S.K. De, *A History of Sanskrit Literature: Classical Period,* vol. I, Calcutta, 1962, pp. 654 f.

60. A.B. Keith, *Sanskrit Drama*, p. 28.

61. F.B.J. Kuiper, op. cit., 1979, p. 224.

62. Ibid., p. 225 and *Daśakumāracarita*, ed. Agashe, pp. 130, 131 and ed. M.R. Kale, 1966, p. 190.

63. F.B.J. Kuiper, op. cit., 1979, p. 225.

64. Ibid., p. 227.

65. Ibid., p. 228.

66. Ibid., p. 230; *Daśakumāracarita*, ed. Agashe pp. 42, 7.

67. Ibid., p. 234.

68. S.K. De, *Sanskrit Poetics*, II, p. 270, n. 25; F.B.J. Kuiper, op. cit., 1979, p. 233.

69. V.S. Agrawala, *Studies on Indian Art*, pp. 164-66.

70. F.B.J. Kuiper, op. cit., 1979, pp. 234, 235.

71. U.P. Shah, *Rodana Mandirna Nāyikā Svarupo*, Gujarat Dipotsavi Anka, VS 2032.

72. Coomaraswamy, op. cit., 1971, p. 14.

73. Ibid., p. 14.

74. Ibid.

75. Ibid., p. 23.

76. Ibid., p. 27.

77. Ibid., p. 29.

78. Ibid., p. 33.

79. Ibid., p. 37.

80. Ibid., p. 68.

81. Ibid., p. 68.

6

Devāṅganā Sculptural Image Study II

Post-Gupta and Medieval Devāṅganās

How *śālabhañjikā*, *nadī-devatā*, *nāyikā-kuṭilaka* group, *mithunas*, Varuṇa and aquatic motifs came together on Indian architecture has been explored in the previous chapter. Through their representation on religious architecture, they lead us to the study of individual *devāṅganā* imagery. In this chapter we shall focus on their individual representation as well as the varied contexts in which they have been placed on temple architecture. The aquatic connection emerges as a major connecting link between the graceful imageries of celestial women, an aspect from which a lot of details are drawn. What has often been interpreted by scholars as representations of *nāyikā*s in stages of love and exhibiting their charms has much more deeper sensibility inspiring its imagery than just *śṛṅgāra*. Scholars quickly identify them as *apsarases* and dismiss them as quickly as they were identified. One author suggests those infamous alluring "snare"-like characters of the Purāṇas, who when depicted on the temples, perform their graceful charms on spectators. The antithesis between woman and wisdom, the sorrow lurking behind the sensual, are observed by some as the reasons why the so-called *apsarases* are carved in profusion on temple walls.[1] This gross generalization needs further probing and an integrated or holistic approach to interpretation. From the information presented in these chapters highlighting individual *devāṅganā*s, the attempt is to define and demonstrate the nature of the imagery and the psychology which necessitates their occurrence on temple walls, pillars, and ceilings. This typological classification was the most convenient way to show that some of the forms repeat from monument to monument and region to region and across many centuries suggesting their "recall" in artistic imagery and hence their psychological, religious and emotional appeal with patrons, *sthapati*s and public alike.

In the previous chapter, we built a foundation bridging the *śālabhañjikā*, *yakṣiṇī*, *nadī-devatā*s and *apsarases*, to unravel the more chthonic level of meaning which can be traced back to the Vedic sources. The presence of the woman is ever auspicious and protective, her nourishing and sensual aspects fuse together, implying fertility, and these concepts have remained in the Indian psyche perennially. Besides sharing the common auspicious thread, the feminine sculptures bear sensual charm sometimes making Khajurāho

fig. 123. *Vṛkṣākā* in *sva-stana-sparśā* pose, second half of fifth century, cave 19, Ajantā.

fig. 124. *Sva-stana-sparśā*, second century, National Museum, New Delhi

devāṅganās more sensuous than Jagat or Mathurā *yakṣīs*. In the hands of Khajurāho artists they indeed became examples of ideal Indian beauties, whose representation from various angles suggests a keen sense of detailing. Conceptually, *devāṅganā* motif and its essential attributes do not vary dramatically, only their imagery differs now and then at the hands of the master artist. It will be demonstrated in the following sections that even visually, in terms of postures, actions and attributes, there is continuity in imageries of *devāṅganās* which were originally conceptualized in the Vedic literature and visually represented in *yakṣī* figures. The core *devāṅganā* imagery and iconography, some known earlier and some freshly identified by me are cited here: *darpaṇā*, *alasā*, *vasanabhraṁśā*, *markaṭaceṣṭā*, *vīrā*, *naṭī*, *prasādhikā*, *nūpurapādikā*, *nalinī kamaladhāriṇī*, *saṅgītavādinī*, *sva-stana-sparśā*, *keśanistoyakāriṇī*, *śālabhañjikā*, *putravallabhā*, and *kanduka-krīḍā*. We shall now examine each of them inasmuch detail as I could gather at the time of writing this book, but mainly with a view to uncover their meaning, similarity in their representation and their iconological development over several centuries in most of the western and northern India.

Sva-Stana-Sparśā

The motif of the "lady touching her own breast" has been represented in various ways in pre-historic art, Buddhist architecture as well as temple architecture. The term *sva-stana-sparśā* has been specially coined to describe the action of this *devāṅganā*. There are distinct variations in this imagery, such as:

(1) *Sva-stana-sparśā* woman squeezing her breast while holding the branch of the *śāla* tree (Ajantā, Cave 19, *c.* fifth century, Mathura, Saṅghol, second century) (*figs.* 123, 124, 125, 126).

(2) *Putravallabhā* offering the milk from her own breast to the child (Saṅghol pillar upright, *c.* second century) (*fig.* 156).

(3) *Keśanistoyakāriṇī* offering water droplets from her freshly washed hair and squeezing her breast at the same time (Sander, Rānī Vāv, tenth-twelfth centuries) (*fig.* 142).

(4) Admiring one's own sensual charm (Gurgī, Jagat, ninth-eleventh centuries) (*figs.* 127, 128) (Khajurāho, Lakṣmaṇa Temple, tenth century) *fig.* 129.

(5) *Paribhogadarśinī* enjoying the nail marks after love-making left by the lover around the breast (Khajurāho Kandarīya Mahādeva Temple) *fig.* 129.

(6) Touching the breast with one hand and the sole of the foot lifted behind, near the hip, in *pṛṣṭha svastika* pose, which appears more of an acrobatic dance pose, Gurgī wall fragment (*fig.* 130).

From the above range of *sva-stana-sparśā* representations and various connotations implied by their actions, it is clear that there is erotic as well as maternal connotation to this action.

Our visual conditioning of the action of woman touching her own breasts and an understanding of this motif goes back to the pre-historic mother goddesses, who are represented with large procreative organs (*figs.* 131, 132, 133, 134). The same action is repeated on a pillar from Saṅghol of the Kuṣāṇa period. Further, on a Mathurā pillar, the lady holding a flower and squeezing her own breast by slightly bending to one side, has been placed on a water pitcher with creepers sprouting out of it. Here the nourishing and fertility aspects are combined. She has been

fig. 125. *Sva-stana-sparśā*, second century, collection unknown, Mathurā.

fig. 126. *Sva-stana-sparśā* standing on water pot surrounded by foliage, National Museum, Mathurā.

identified as Śrī Lakṣmī by Sivaramamurti, but the identification of Pr̥thvī would be more appropriate. For her roles as the mother, milk-bearing and mother of the mankind, this goddess has been extolled in the *R̥gveda* and *Atharvaveda* as the one who is asked to *duḥ* (*AV* 12.17.45), she holds the world in her womb (*viśva-garbha*) (*AV* 12.2.43), she is the *viśva-dhāya* (nurse) (*AV* 12.1.27).[2] The non-existent (*asat*) came into existence from her (*AV* 4.19.6), is said to have been born in her (*AV* 13.1.54). The Vedic earth goddess is conceived anthropomorphically as possessing a body (*tanu*) (*AV* 12.12.30), head (*mūrdhā*) (*R̥V* 10.88.6), chest (*vakṣa*) (*AV* 12.1.6.26), (*AV* 13.3.25-26) and breast full of milk (12.1.59). The earth goddess is said to have many streams (*AV* 12.1.9) and is asked to suckle *pāyas*. The Pr̥thvī is also conceived as a mother and a youthful maiden and *sajośa* (*R̥V* 8.34.23).[3] The connotation of Pr̥thvī is carried on in later *yakṣī* and *devāṅganā* imageries as their action implies aspects of youthfulness, fertility and nourishment. This is one *devāṅganā* typology which has

(facing page)
fig. 128. *Sva-stana-sparśā*, Ambikā temple, south wall, Jagat.

fig. 127. *Sva-stana-sparśā*, Gurgī fragment, tenth century, Rewa Kotwali, Rewa.

endured for many centuries and carried on the connotation of fertility without alteration.

The Ajantā Cave 19 shows the *śālabhañjikā* standing in *svastika pada* holding the branch of a tree with one hand and her own breast with the other. Here the tree connects her with the vegetal force of nature (*fig.* 123).

The Gurgī *toraṇa* detail of the *kumbhika* of about the tenth century (Rewā Mahārāja's Palace) represents the lady pulling an *āmralumbī* with the outstretched left arm, while touching the breast from the right. She stands bending forward her head with downcast eyes (*fig.* 135).

There are two *devāṅganās* in Ambikā Temple at Jagat, represented standing next to each other. One is in *sama* posture while the other is crossing her feet in *svastika maṇḍala*. There is no symbolic allusion to aquatic or vegetal aspects of nature as no vegetation is represented. The figure in *svastika maṇḍala* actually strikes a stylized posture (*fig.* 128).

The combination of woman wringing out water from her hair and simultaneously squeezing her breast is found at Badoli, Kirāḍu, Rānī Vāv, Sander, etc. O.C. Ganguli observes that the imagery of the earth and her tress of hair saturated with water, can thus be independently derived from the Vedic sources without reference to the Buddhist tradition, which itself may have borrowed the imagery from the original Vedic source.[4] From the Vedic point of view, it may be suggested that the earth goddess will carry in her tresses all the water that descends from the rain clouds, and she could easily wring out any amount of water from her flowing tresses.[5] This imagery connects the earth goddess with

fig. 129. *Paribhogadarśinī*, Kandarīya Mahādeva temple, Khajurāho.

fig. 130. *Sva-stana-sparśā* touching the sole of the foot in *pṛṣṭhasvastika* pose, eleventh century, Gurgī, Rewa Kotwali.

fig. 132. Primordial goddesses, *sva-stana-sparśā*, Cyprus, clay, *c.* 2500 BCE (Neumann pl. 8), British Museum.

fig. 131. Precursor of *sva-stana-sparśā*, fragments of the figure of Goddess Beltis, stone, Susa, seventh century BCE, from Hollander, Aeskulap und Venus, p.206.

fig. 133. Goddess, terracotta, Crete, from a cave near Lapethos (Neumann pl. 13), British Museum.

fig. 134. Isis Hathor, Suckling Horus, bronze, Egypt, seventh-sixth centuries BCE (Neumann, pl. 44), Louvre, Paris.

(facing page)
fig. 135. *Toraṇa* pillar, *sva-stana-sparśā* with *āmralumbī*, tenth century, Rewā Mahārāja's palace, Gurgī.

fig. 136. *Sva-stana-sparśā*,
Saccīyamātā temple, Osiā.

(facing page)
fig. 137. *Sva-stana-sparśā*,
Śiva temple, standing in
baddhācārī, *c.* CE 900,
Kodal, Damoh, Madya Pradesh

rivers of the country and the same imagery can be extended to the *devāṅganā*s holding the breast, wringing hair, holding a water pitcher or a lotus with the later so-called river goddesses. Since the concept of Lakṣmī is Purāṇic, the identification of a certain motif of abundance, prosperity, fertility and vegitation could be more suitably identified as Pṛthvī or Iḷā, Puraṁdhī, Dhīṣaṇā.

On Saccīyamātā Temple at Osiā (*fig.* 136, 137), the *devāṅganā* is shown standing in the *gatāgata* pose while touching her breast. She is attended upon by a *ṛṣi* holding a plate and a dwarf, almost pulling at her *sāṛī*. This seems to imply some ritual and indicates a unique example seen thus far.

The action of squeezing one's own breasts while swaying gracefully has a clear erotic connotation which is greatly explored by the Khajurāho artists. They not only depict women observing the nail marks of love play, but shyly enjoying one's own sensual charm. Some are depicted revealing boldly their charms, while others are shown from profile or back view as if hiding or partially revealing themselves. Stella Kramrisch calls this tendency of revealing-hiding

as *vyakta-avyakta*[6] (Kandarīya Mahādeva Temple, north wall) (*fig.* 170). This group of *devāṅganās* add a completely new dimension to "the woman touching the breast" imagery.

The motif of woman watching the nail marks after love play has fascinated Indian poets from a very early period, and this motif actually bridges the link between poetic and artistic imageries; e.g. lady observing the nail marks around the breast from Lakṣmaṇa and Kandarīya Mahādeva Temple, Khajurāho (*figs.* 129, 138).

A verse from *Subhāṣita Ratnakośa* of Rājaśekhara, a medieval poet of north India (615) refers to this charming act of the lady.

> Now she opens, now she covers, her hard and full grown breasts. She looks, gazing on the nail marks he had made, like a beggar who did find a gem.[7]

Two verses from Kālidāsa's *Ṛtusaṁhāram* 4.12, 5.15,[8] refers to the *nāyikās* watching the fine nail inscriptions on breasts which reveal the passionate enjoyment, relentlessness of women in the first flush of youth. These coveted signs of love's fulfilment are rejoicing, and women decorate themselves again as the sun rises.

But the pearl necklace resting on the breasts of the *nāyikā* delights in what the *nāyaka* wish he could take:

> It is *puṇya* that might help, that man may be born again as rain drop and ride a cloud so as to reach an oyster's mouth. May his virtue then serve to turn him into lovely form, which would play upon your rising breasts (*SR* no. 408), a form which the lover would want to take.[9]

Rājaśekhara voices his poetic admiration of women whose attributes besides round breasts and triple folds, are the crescent moon-shaped nail marks[10] (*SR* no. 623, p. 213).

The intense *kāma* has overtaken the *nāyikā* in another verse of Rājaśekhara, the cut of lover's nail upon her breast shows drops of blood as red as lac, as if of Kāma's fire, grown strong within, the sparks and burst forth through her heart (*SR* no. 612).

What better examples than Khajurāho *apsaras*es be cited to augment the meaning of Rājaśekhara's verses. Thus there are many

fig. 138. *Paribhogadarśinī,*
Lakṣmaṇa Temple, Khajurāho.

shades of interpretations and representations possible to comprehend the act of *sva-stana-sparśā* that evolve from human imagination and experience, ranging between generative fertility and consummate eroticism.

Keśanistoyakāriṇī

The visual representation of the lady bathing under a water stream (*sadyasnātā*) and squeezing her freshly bathed hair, whose droplets are held by the eager swans (*keśanistoyakāriṇī*), were first carved on Mathurā pillars. Any earlier representation has either not survived or was not conceived of. The above term is found in *Matsya Purāṇa,* while the same action is described in *Śṛṅgāra-Mañjarī* of Bhoja as *kabariniścyotana*.[11]

The *devāṅganā keśanistoyakāriṇī* is generally represented frontally with slight or exaggerated bend from the waist. The legs are either placed in *sama*, *svastika* or *baddhācārī* pose. Very often the *gatāgata* position is also favoured. But some interesting postural configurations are also tried by the sculptors at Badoli, Ghaṭeśvara Mahādeva Temple, *maṇḍapa* pillar (*fig.* 242), Gurgī, Rewa Kotwali wall fragment, Śiva Temple, Kodal and Viśvanāth Temple, Khajurāho (*figs.* 145, 146, 147). In these sculptures the legs are in extreme *svastika*, upon which the torso is bent and stretched, twisting around the axis, a reminder of European Mannerist phase sculpture. Yet another unusual representation is from Jabalpur (Rani Durgavati Museum) (*fig.* 148), where the *devāṅganā* is shown in complete profile, bending forward with the weight of her upper body and drenched hair.

Slight variations in the representation of this imagery are observed in the following sculptures:

(1) Woman standing in a gently swaying pose holding her wet hair under a foliate tree bearing fruits is accompanied by an eager swan catching the droplets (Mathurā, Cleveland Museum; Saṅghol, National Museum (*fig.* 139); Roḍā, pillar capital, Temple 6 (*fig.* 140); Sander and Osiā, Harihara group I).

fig. 139. *Keśanistoyakāriṇī*, Saṅghol, National Museum, New Delhi.

fig. 140. *Keśanistoyakāriṇī,*
Temple 6, pillar capital, Roḍā.

fig. 141. *Keśanistoyakāriṇī,*
Ambikā Temple, south wall,
Jagat.

(2) While engaged in this act she is accompanied by a male companion who holds her by the waist (Nāgārjunakoṇḍa, *āyāga* relief) (*fig.* 67).

(3) While squeezing hair the *devāṅganā* also squeezes her breast as if implying nourishment (Jagat, Rānī Vāv) where the foliage, fruits and wet drapery enhance the eroticism and fertility (*figs.* 141, 142).

(4) While engaged in the act of squeezing the hair, the wet garment slips down revealing her vulva and she stands shyly in *baddhācārī* posture overcome by embarrassment (Kekind, Gwalior) (*figs.* 143, 144). An element of surprise and coyness are intermingled in this representation of the erotic motif.

fig. 143. *Keśanistoyakāriṇī* and *vasanabhraṁśā*, Nīlakaṇṭha temple, kekind.

The "bathing" motif is connected with erotic attraction and impregnation at the same time. But here the woman herself is a personification of the waters and the woman/swan pair finds its origin in the *apsaras–gandharva* pair (refer *apsaras* in the chapter on the Vedic Literature). This imagery also represents the idea of the earth drenched with rain water which supplied nourishment to the mankind and the nature. Thus, the male–female, *apsaras–gandharva*, *dyāvā–pṛthvī* pairing is implied. The placement of the Rānī Vāv *devāṅganā* sculptures, in the niches of the buttressing

fig. 142. *Keśanistoyakāriṇī* and *sva-stana-sparśā*, south buttress wall, Rānī Vāv, Pāṭan.

walls of a subterranean architecture, juxtaposing the various forms of Viṣṇu (residing in waters), represents the spirit of the reservoir which sustains human life. Here, the importance of *devāṅganā* figures is raised to another height. Their association with Viṣṇu is firmly established for the first time in association with water. Subterranean architecture is highly specific and regional to western India and underscored by folk traditions as well. These need further study as their antiquity may be further than what we assume.

Impregnation and exposure are alluded to by the exposure of the vulva in some cases, which implies the tertiary connotation of the present motif. This also implies the iconological continuation from sensual charm to implicit procreativity of water and vegetation symbolized by woman.

fig. 144. *Keśanistoyakāriṇī, vasanabhraṁśā* Sās temple, Gwalior.

fig. 145. *Keśanistoyakāriṇī,* Gurgī fragment.

Putravallabhā

The imagery of *putravallabhā* is most auspicious and pleasant where in the concepts of eroticism and fertility culminate into blissful maternity, the representation of which is most natural and reveals a proud mother firmly holding her baby. The conventional mother principle which develops from Aditi into Durgā, the highest goddess of feminine energy, to create, sustain and destroy, is not implied here. Rather it reveals a more chthonic earthy spirit of mother, appealing to

fig. 146.
Keśanistoyakāriṇī,
Śiva temple, Kodal.

fig. 147. *Keśanistoyakāriṇī,*
Viśvanātha temple, Khajurāho.

the masses benevolently. There is a sense of assuring, inviting and nourishing aspect in these images which are informal, amiable and human. See the mothers from Suhāniā and Khajurāho (*figs.* 149, 150, 151).

The iconography of the great goddess is highly complex and refers to all her attributes, while depicting a *putravallabhā* in contrast, requires just the baby held by the woman, who is often shown holding an *āmralumbī* from the tree above her. This juxtaposition makes the fertility-maternity commonly shared by nature and mankind as cognate phenomena. At Saccīyamātā Temple, Osiā, this imagery is found on the northern wall of its eastern *devakulika*. She stands next to Varuṇa (*fig.* 152).

Putravallabhā holding child and *āmralumbī* are also found from Alwar, Nīlakaṇṭha Mahādeva Temple, on the pillars of the *maṇḍapa*s, Gurgī Rewā Mahārājā's Palace (*fig.* 153), Tusā, Sun Temple (*fig.* 154) and Moḍherā, Sun Temple (*fig.* 155) where it is represented next to Indra on the *maṇḍovara*.

The Vedic goddesses, the *apsarase*s, the *yakṣī*s are known mother concepts and hence the Indian psyche from early on was habituated with this imagery and represented it widely. Either in poetic imagery or in visual imagery, the mother as youthful, bountiful and cajoling, has remained unchanged (*fig.* 156).

fig. 148. *Keśanistoyakāriṇī*, c. tenth-eleventh centuries, Rani Durgavati Museum, Doni, Jabalpur.

fig. 149. *Maṇḍovara*, Ambikā temple,
eleventh century, Suhāniā, Madya Pradesh

fig. 150. *Putravallabhā* with waterjug and *āmralumbī,* Suhāniā.

fig. 151. *Putravallabhā* from back view, Kandarīya Mahādeva Temple, Khajurāho.

fig. 152. *Putravallabhā* with Varuṇa, South wall, Sacchīyamātā temple, Osiā.

The Saṅghol mother is represented from her back lifting the child aloft, as if swinging him. The representation of her taught body stretching forward is unique. Another sculpture of mother and child playing with a rattle are depicted at Saṅghol, an imagery which repeats again after a long gap on Auraṅgābād Cave 1 pillar bracket. The *putravallabhā* is standing under a tree with the child and a dwarf *nidhi*. It has been identified as Hārīti by some scholars (*fig.* 157).

At Tusā, Sun Temple, *raṅga-maṇḍapa*, the mother and child are accompanied by attendants holding toys, etc. The *āmralumbī* from the tree behind hangs forward. The *vitāna* is often adorned by the *devāṅganā*s, but the placement of *putravallabhā* here is unusual (*fig.* 154).

The mother from the Jagat Ambikā Temple holds the baby aloft and looks adoringly at the child. There is no *āmralumbī* indicated, but the dwarfish attendants holding *kuṭilaka* draw our attention. Next to

fig. 153. *Putravallabhā,*
Gurgī fragment.

fig. 154. Ceiling *putravallabhā,*
Sūrya Temple, Tusā.

fig. 155. *Putravallabhā*, Sūrya Temple,
south wall, Indra panel,
1st quarter of eleventh century,
Moḍherā, (Mehsānā), Gujarat.

her is Kubera in the *bhadra* niche on the north wall, who also has a similar attendant.

A Mātr̥kā from Jhālarāpāṭan (Jhalarapatan Museum, No. 15) represented on a pillar, is also accompanied by a similar dwarf with a bent stick and resting one leg on it. Since the Mātr̥kā has no *vāhana*, it would be more appropriate to call her *putravallabhā*. The dwarf, with *kuṭilaka*, who has been identified earlier in section 2 of Chapter 4 as a *viṭa* (*fig.* 158) is an interesting inclusion here.

Thus the motif of woman holding a child, touching a fruit, squeezing her own breast, holding a branch of mango fruits, bathing in spring waters — are analogous principles of fertility, which revolve around the aspect of sensual beauty and eroticism. Here the difference lies in the suppression of sexuality and seductiveness, which also emerge out of the same erotic flavour. Thus the erotic principle has the potency to develop into sexual and seductive representation as do the maternal representations. The following five imageries of *kanduka-krīḍā*, *darpaṇā*, *alasā*, *vasanabhraṁśā* and *markaṭaceṣṭā* conform to the sexual tendency.

Kanduka-Krīḍā

The motif of playing with a ball, just like the *śālabhañjikā* motif is an identifiable social construct which finds its way into the realm of religious art. The imagery of *kanduka-krīḍā* is found in Mathurā and Saṅghol (Kota, U.N. Roy *fig.* 46) (*figs.* 159, 160) which implies that perhaps this motif was adapted by the artists of the Kuṣāṇa period into religious art as a profane motif of social pastime. The Saṅghol sculpture shows a *kalaśa* instead of a ball acrobatically balanced on the *nāyikā*'s bent elbow. But this motif is not without its sensuous overtones and could have emerged as a result of an influence of poetic imagery of a woman's beautiful, charming movements. While playing with the ball, the woman's body bends, twists, turns, and this spontaneous gesticulation allures the onlooker. Hence,

fig. 156. *Sva-stana-sparśā, putravallabhā, madhupānā,* Saṅghol.

like the interest generated in the movements of a *naṭī*, the sculptors may have explored to create fascinating representations of the woman in admiration of her graceful actions. *Kanduka-krīḍā* is a mundane activity which has found currency on the temple architecture whose origin most probably is in literary imagination. The alluring element of feminine beauty are cited in Ṛṣiśṛṅga/Apsaras and Śiva/Mohinī stories. In the Āraṇyaka-Parva of the *Mahābhārata*, the prostitute assumes the sensuous postures while playing with the ball. Like a creeper she keeps clinging to Ṛṣiśṛṅga. She also bends the branches of the *śāla*, *aśoka* and *tilā*, and poses to be shy and engrossed, hangs on to the bent branches or plucks flowers from them (3, 111, 15-16). Here the *śālabhañjikā* motif is also implied. In the eighth *skandha* of the *Bhāgavata Purāṇa*, the Mohinī form of Viṣṇu playing with the ball, displaying her grace, bewitched even Śiva, the most steadfast of the *yogī*s.

fig. 157. *Putravallabhā*, Hariti, pillar capital, Cave 3, Auraṅgābād.

The *kanduka-krīḍā* of Mṛgāṅkavatī in *Viddhaśālabhañjikā* has been rendered excellently by Rājaśekhara, creating a delightful picture of the beauty of the woman's body in movement and concentration which steals the heart of the king. It is called *kanduka keli-tāṇḍava*. He observes that the mark of the *tilaka* has got washed off by the drops of perspiration on the forehead. She was exhibiting wonderful agility in course of the repeatedly quick beating of the ball (*varam vareṇa vinatā dṛśaḥ*), in accordance with the manner of the movement of the ball falling down (*paṭa*) and then jumping

fig. 158. *Putravallabhā* with *vita-kuṭilaka*, pillar fragment, tenth century, Jhalawar Museum, Jhālarāpāṭan.

fig. 159. *Kanduka krīḍā*, pillar upright, second century, Mathurā.

fig. 160. *Ghaṭa* balancing, same pose as above, second century, Saṅghol.

up (*utpaṭa*) time and again. At every step, she is gratifying her spectators by her lovely display (*līlā-lālitya*), of striking (*tāḍana*) and throwing the ball in the air (*uttala*) (Act II, 6, 7, 8). Even from *Padmaprabhr̥takam*, one of the Caturbhānī plays, an instance of *kanduka-krīḍā* of *priyaṅgu yaṣṭika* is known, which is staged to show her *nr̥tya kauśalyam*.[12]

In *Daśakumāracarita* of Daṇḍin, princess Kandukavatī of Dāmalipta, propitiated Goddess Vindhyavāsinī by performing before her on the day of the *kr̥ttikā* every month, the *kanduka-nr̥tya*. She adopted the three tempos of *madhya, vilamba* and *druta*. She displayed rapid to and fro movements, plied both her hands, sang and sent the ball in all directions. She executed a number of *karaṇa*s and moved in *maṇḍala*s, wavy lines (*gomūtrikā*) and other movements referred to as *gītamārga* and *pañca-bindu prasr̥ita*. The commentary refers to a text on ball playing as an art, called *kanduka tantra*. Jayappa refers to *kanduka-nr̥tta* as a group dance in which the women, besides beating it on the ground threw and exchanged the ball and ran to catch it.[13]

Roḍā probably is the first site where this imagery is found on the pillar capitals of Temple 6 (*fig.* 161) in the context of temple architecture. It is thc only site where this imagery is found and not repeated on any other temples of the Roḍā complex. Thc *nāyikā* has lifted one leg and placed it in *svastika*, while the body bends diagonally opposite. This gives an effect of abandon while the raised arms in *uromaṇḍalī* clutches the ball. She is accompanied by a dwarf who tries to catch the ball and in unison this composition creates a dynamic effect.

fig. 161. *Kanduka-krīḍā* with *viṭa*, pillar capital, Temple 6, eight century, Roḍā.

fig. 162. *Kanduka-krīḍā*, *pṛṣṭha-svastika*, Ambikā Temple, south wall, Jagat.

At Jagat, Ambikā Temple (*fig.* 162) and Tusā, Sūrya Temple (*fig.* 163) the lady is more articulate, her posture being represented in some kind of *pṛṣṭha svastika* pose. The carving of this image is superb for its firm bends and soft flexions are highly graceful. But the figure appears at rest as she drops down the ball from behind her head. The fluttering garments add dimension and breadth to the figure. The Khajurāho lady holds the ball in such a way that one wonders whether she is playing or just displaying her charm. The *vivṛtta kaṭi* bend is extremely difficult and carved with precision. The *kanduka-krīḍā* from Rānī Vāv and Āhaṛ is too stiff and static compared with that of Jagat, Nāgdā and Tusā representations (*figs.* 164, 165, 166).

The artist's imagination reigns supreme in praising the charm and beauty of the woman. When this praise turns into a visual configuration of the woman either playing with a ball or squeezing the wet hair soon after bath, the artist articulates the postures of the female form by swaying or twisting it.

fig. 163. *Kanduka-krīḍā*, same pose as above, accompanied by *vita*, Sūrya Temple, north wall, Tusā.

Vasanabhraṁśā

The instances of representation of the "woman exposing her vulva" by untying her lower garment or by lowering it suggestively in an act of

fig. 164. *Kanduka-krīḍā*, *ūrdhvajānu* pose, Rānī Vāv, buttress wall, Pāṭan.

fig. 165. *Kanduka-krīḍā*, *ūrdhvajānuvi vivr̥tta karaṇa* Ādinath temple, north wall, Ahāṛ.

fig. 166. *Kanduka-krīḍā, ūrdhvajānuvi vṛtta karaṇa*, Nāgdā, Rajasthan, fourth century, National Museum, New Delhi.

fig. 167. *Vasanabhraṁśā*, Bhūteśvara, pillar upright, second century, Mathura Museum.

fig. 168. *Vasanabhraṁśā* in a niche,Gadarmal temple, south wall, Badoh-Paṭhārī.

self-exhibition, provoking erotic stance, are found from the Kuṣāṇa period onwards. But the veneration of the female generative organ goes back to the pre-historic period, represented by the Mother Goddess figurines with large pudendas, broad hips and heavy bust. The cult of the Aditi Uttānapāda, the faceless or lotus-headed goddess represented in the birth-giving posture, exposing the full vagina for ritual worship. This cult was prevalent from the earliest times right into the medieval period. Anterior to the Aditi Uttānapāda, is the ritual worship of the ring-stones on which the representation of the nude goddess with tree and lizard is found in profusion. This then hints at the primitive female power or energy to reproduce, to enhance productivity and to assure offsprings. This fecundating power shared commonly by animals, humans and nature are supportive and transferable from one to the other. Hence the act of *vasanabhraṁśa* is an exposure of female nudity, which was sensuously but spontaneously depicted in early Indian art.

There is another way of representing this imagery, in which a scorpion is shown perched on the lady's thigh, out of fear and haste, her clothes seem to loosen-up and slip off (*figs.* 170, 174). But the auspiciousness of this concept seems to be very strongly favoured, and so in my observation one of the early representations of *devāṅganā* imagery on temple architecture is found at (1) Paraśurāmeśvara Temple, Bhubaneswar (mid-seventh century CE) on the doorway along with amorous *mithunas*, (2) Temple 6, Roḍā (*c.* eighth century

fig. 169. *Vasanabhraṁśā* and *markaṭaceṣṭā*, Harṣad-Mātā Temple, pillar capital, Ābanerī.

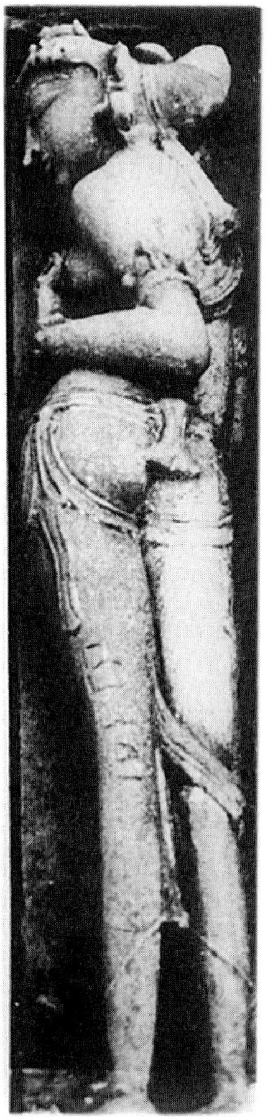

fig. 170. *Vasanabhraṁśā*
with a scorpion, *sva-stana-sparśā*
Kandarīya Mahādeva temple,
Khajurāho.

fig. 171. *Vasanabhraṁśā*,
Ṭoṭeśvara temple,
Kaḍwāhā.

fig. 172. *Vasanabhraṁśā* and *markaṭaceṣṭā*, pillar fragment, *c.* ninth century, Rani Durgavati Museum, Doni, (Damoh), Madya Pradesh

CE) on the pillar capitals, (3) Gadarmal Temple, Badoh–Paṭhārī (*c.* ninth century CE) (*fig.* 168) on the north wall of the *maṇḍovara*.

This points to a possibility that the chthonic principle of female generative power became part of the architectural fabric since very early period, in the form of symbols of auspiciousness. Buddhist and Hindu art both welcomed this imagery and gave it a prominent place on their religious architecture. But in terms of iconography not enough data is found, however, there is no denial that this imagery stems out of folk cults and gets absorbed into higher religious art without losing its identity or much alteration.

The Bhūteśvara *yakṣī* standing in contraposto presses below her weight the dwarf, and opens the lower garment by holding its hem near the waist. This full-bodied voluptuous Kuṣāṇa lady has been identified by V.S. Agrawala as *mahānartakī*, the textual source for which has not been mentioned. Above the *yakṣī* stand two men on a balcony, one of whom holds a stick. Such an image is found for the first time from Mathurā and hence it gives rise to a number of questions. Does it symbolize sexuality, fertility or auspiciousness? Is this a representation of a *yakṣī*, a *nartakī* or a prostitute inducing fertility? (*fig.* 167).

The motif of *vasanabhraṁśā* is not found so far on the cave temples of Ajantā, Ellorā, Auraṅgābād, etc. but suddenly reappears on Roḍā Temple 6 along with other *devāṅganā*s, prominently placed on the pillar capitals. The same motif is also found gracefully standing on the same architectural juncture on Nīlakaṇṭha Temple, Ābanerī (*fig.* 169). The Roḍā *devāṅganā* is accompanied by a *vidūṣaka* or *viṭa*-like character holding a stick, *kuṭīlaka*.

The Gadarmal Temple *devāṅganā* (*fig.* 168) *c.* ninth century CE, placed in one of the niches of the north wall seems to imply sexual implications with her exposed pudendum and the *baddhācārī* posture.

At Kekind, on the Nīlakaṇṭha Temple, ninth century CE (*fig.* 143), one observes that eroticism is the commonly shared component of the *avasthā*s (situations) of most of the *devāṅganā*s. The overlapping shades of imagery of revealing oneself, are gracefully concealed with

inherent eroticism. The wet drapery seems to cling to the limbs revealing nudity, whereas the end of the drapery is held by the *nāyikā* suffused with grace, langour and elegance of a dancer. Their stances too denote the sprightliness and repose of dancers. The partial exposure of the nude figure is also found in *markaṭaceṣṭā* and *keśanistoyakāriṇī* that maintain the *aucitya* of the situation while more virile and animated stance of *ūrdhvajānu* is employed for *markaṭaceṣṭā* (Saccīyamātā Temple, Osiā, *fig.* 188). The *keśanistoyakāriṇī* is shown with slightly lifted heel of her right leg in *gatāgata* posture.

The Kekind lady seems to be freshly bathed and seen arranging her wet drapery. The Jagat *devāṅganā* appears to begin untying and her erotic fervour rising. Its location on the temple wall next to Cāmuṇḍā and Yama also seems to be purposeful, since they preside over the southern side. The friezes of couples above them on the *pratiratha* and *salilāntara* depict the couples in modes of passionate kissing. The other *devāṅganā*s near her are *sva-stana-sparśā* (fertility) and *khaḍgadhārī* (*vīrā*).

The representations of this imagery in the decorative schemes of temple architecture are significant. *Maṇḍovara*, entrance doorway, *maṇḍapa* pillars, interior walls of the *sāndhāra* temple, are generally the favoured placements for these imageries.

The pillars from Doni, Damoh district Madya Pradesh (Rani Durgavati Museum no. 107) (*fig.* 172) and pillar reinstalled at Rewa Kotwali, (*fig.* 251, 252) both represent this imagery. At Doni, the *devāṅganā* has been lifted up on a pedestal supported by the *bhāraputra*. She stands in *baddhācārī* revealing herself, while below her another lady stands in *gatāgata* posture, whose body is turned in *vivṛtta*, with one arm lifted up and caressing a boar-like animal with the other.

At Rewa Kotwali the typical *svastika* posture holding the border of the cloth and shy bent head is noticeable. Each figure is placed in pillared niches all around the pillar base.

fig. 173. *Vasanabhraṁśā* with *kharjūra* and a *mithuna* couple, Devī Jagadambī Temple, Khajurāho.

fig. 174. *Sadyasnātā*, *keśanistoyakāriṇī* and *vasanabhraṁśā*. Note *viṭa* with *kuṭilaka*, Lakṣmaṇa Temple, Khajurāho.

fig. 175. *Vasanabhraṁśā*, Devī Jagdambi temple, Khajurāho.

SHN-55/74

(facing page)
fig. 176.*Vasanabhrṁśā* detail, Ambikā temple, Suhāniā.

fig. 177. *Devāṅganā* alternate with *dikpālas* and consorts. *Vasanabhraṁśā* pose like Bhūteśvara, Scorpion visible, Rānī Vāv, south wall, Pāṭan.

The most unique feature of the Khajurāho *devāṅganās* is the addition of the scorpion, *kharjūravāhaka* symbol, to the imagery of the *devāṅganās*, which intensifies the erotic aspect of the present imagery. The coy lady gracefully holds the hem of her lower garment while a scorpion perched on her thigh heightens the erotic sensation. It appears that this is just a "concealed metaphor" or sexual excitement, or rather a sophisticated version of the Mathurā *yakṣī*, who unselfconsciously exhibits her nudity. They are found prominently on the *jaṅghā* of the *maṇḍovara* and the interior walls of the *sāndhara pradakṣiṇāpatha* on the wall of the *garbha-gṛha*. (*figs.* 173, 175)

The case of the Sās–Bahū Temple at Gwalior (*fig.* 144) brings to notice a different placement programme. The *maṇḍapa* walls from the interior are also carved with single niche images of *devāṅganās*,

especially on the conjoint of the subsidiary directions. It has been found that the imagery of *vasanabhraṁśā* is repeated at three out of four corners, which are concealed from general notice of the spectator. Does this refer to a special ritual offered to them in secrecy or are they placed here for the appreciation by the *rasika*? Their proximity with the small *devī* shrines inside the *maṇḍapa* does not deny the fertility connotation, even though the sexual overtones are more prominent.

The Rānī Vāv architecture is a class by itself, unmatched in size, architectural intricacy and profusion of sculptures on both sides of its buttress walls and in the circular interior of the shaft. It has the maximum number of *devāṅganā*s placed in niches which alternate with the ten incarnations of Viṣṇu, Dikpālas, Durgā, Pārvatī, etc. One can safely call it a Vaiṣṇavaite monument because of the predominance of the Vaiṣṇava iconography. But the association of Viṣṇu with an aquatic subterranean monument is not surprising, because he is the lord of the primeval waters, the *kṣīrasāgara*. But the centrality accorded to the *devāṅganā*s in numbers and placement, suggests the fertility connotation as well as connection with water and vegetation. The symbolism of the Vāv is therefore not very obscure and suggests the continuity of thought from the Vedic *apsaras*es to representations of *yakṣī*s to river goddesses on temples and finally to *devāṅganā*s in Vāv architecture. The continuous chain of analogous representation of cognate principles cited here, is the fundamental source that confirms our approach to the *devāṅganā* study.

The entire galaxy of *vasanabhraṁśā* images found at Rānī Vāv (*figs.* 177, 178) are wide ranging and follow two distinct prototypes. The one placed on the *kuṇḍa* wall of the southern side stands in *baddhācārī*, while the manner in which she holds her garment reminds us of the Bhūteśvara *yakṣī*. It is a singular representation of its kind which has never been repeated. The scorpion is shown very realistically clinging to the hem of the cloth.

The other type of *devāṅganā* is standing in *baddhācārī*, but sensuously enhancing the *tribhaṅga* by lifting her shoulder to bend the torso and the head sidewards. The lifted foot of the leg which crosses in *svastika*, remains slightly raised above the ground. This lends agility to the whole posture. The lady is accompanied by a dwarf. The scorpion now appears on the thigh while the folds of the garment suggest that it is on the cloth. She gently lowers the garment to expose the pudenda.

This posture is not only repeated at Rānī Vāv several times, but even at Sunak (*figs.* 179, 180), Gorad, Sander, etc. in Gujarat. The motif and its postures were profusely used at Khajurāho before they travelled to Gujarat. The association too is unique to these two regions. It is possible to assume that this imagery could have developed at the hands of Khajurāho masters.

As regards the terminology, the term *skhalita vasana* has also been used by scholars for describing the same imagery. There is a subtle difference in the sense of both these words, one denotes the slipping of the garment unawares while the other denotes an intentional exposure.

Markaṭaceṣṭā

The motif of woman harrassed by monkey is very much in use from the medieval period but its associations with literature or earlier sculpture traditions of Kuṣāṇa period, have not come to my notice. Since it is not found along with the typical *yakṣī* sculpture from Mathurā (and now from Saṅghol), there is no mention of this motif in V.S. Agrawala's work.[14]

The motif of woman harrassed by a monkey can be interpreted as an erotic motif of seduction for which the *gandharva*s are considered responsible. From T.A. Gopinath Rao, it is learnt that the *gandharva*s are semi-divine beings. The *Atharvaveda* calls them as hairy like monkeys or dogs, they assume at will handsome appearances to seduce the females of this earth. They are the knowers of the secrets of the divine truths and reveal them to the world. They are included in the class of *parjanya*s. Sāyaṇa links them with the *apsarase*s while the Āgamas do not mention them.[15]

The swiftly moving posture of the lady whose soft curves revealed by the falling garment, suggests a discerning ability of the artist to carve the female figure in complicated postures. The Badoli

fig. 179. *Vasanabhraṁśā* with scorpion, *baddhācārī*, *c.* twelfth century, Nīlakaṇṭha Temple, north wall sunak,

(facing page)
fig. 178. *Vasanabhraṁśā* with a scorpion, *baddhācārī*, Rānī Vāv, north wall, Pāṭan.

fig. 180. *Vasanabhraṁśā, markaṭaceṣṭā,* Nīlakaṇṭha Temple, north wall, Sunak.

fig. 181. *Markaṭaceṣṭā*, *maṇḍapa* pillar, ninth century, Ghaṭeśvara Mahādeva Temple, Badoli.

(facing page)
fig. 182. *Markaṭaceṣṭā*, *nāyikā* represented from the back, Khajurāho area, site unknown, eleventh century National Museum, New Delhi.

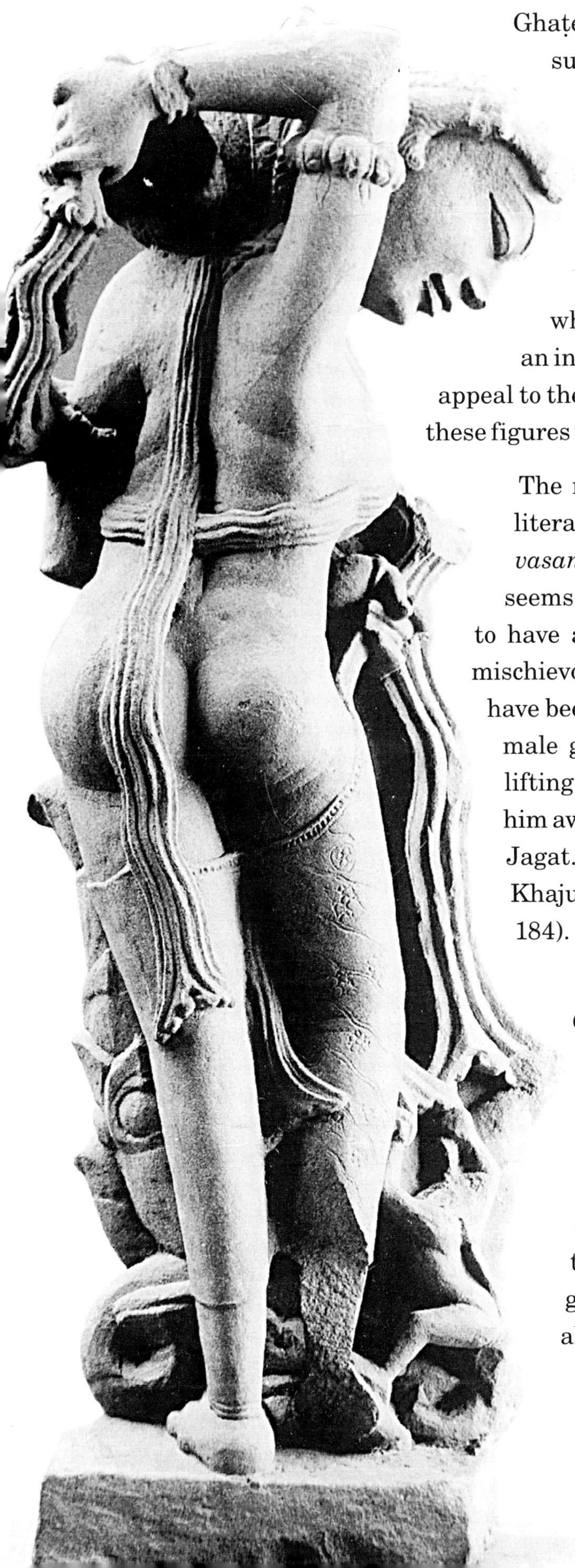

Ghaṭeśvara Mahādeva Temple (*fig.* 181) *maṇḍapa* pillar suggests the mastery and virtuosity of *ālīḍha* while the *kaṭi* is *vivṛtta*. The sculpture in parts is quite mutilated but still appears magnificent. Pillar base, probably, is the original place of *devāṅganā* imagery, whose prototype came from its wooden architecture background. The *devāṅganās* are placed one next to the other in a circular fashion which are not separated by smaller pillars. This allows an interplay between the *devāṅganās*, and their imageries appeal to the viewer in unison. Even in their formal arrangement these figures imply the three-dimensionality.

The monkey is often shown clinging to the lady's leg or literally pulling her garment off. Here many *devāṅganās* of *vasanabhraṁśā* and *markaṭaceṣṭā* seem to look alike. It seems that this imagery is pretty playful and does not seem to have any specific connotations of fertility. The idea of a mischievous animal like monkey harrassing women, seems to have been used as a similie of erotic pleasure obtained by the male gaze. The restrained reaction of the lady by gently lifting her hand above, holding a branch of a tree to drive him away, is invariably pretended and not natural as seen at Jagat. But the anger on the face of the *nāyikā* is distinct. Khajurāho has amply represented this motif (*figs.* 182, 183, 184).

Markaṭaceṣṭā in *baddhācārī* pose are also found at Gurgī (fig. 185), Sohāgpur (fig. 186) and Jagat (fig. 187).

But the sculptures from Osiā, Saccīyamātā Temple (*fig.* 188), and Sander (*fig.* 189) represent the *nāyikā* in *ūrdhvajānu*, whose *ardha-maṇḍalī* posture often makes the vagina visible. The monkey placed in the centre bending towards her, pulling at her lower garment makes a very dynamic pose. The dress has already been lowered while the *devāṅganā* grips the

fig. 183. *Antarāla*, *devāṅganā*s, *markaṭaceṣṭā*, *mithuna*s, Lakṣmaṇa Temple, south wall, Khajurāho.

(facing page)
fig. 186. *Markaṭaceṣṭā*,
west *jaṅghā*,
Virāṭeśvara temple,
twelfth century, Sohāgpur,
Shahdol, Madya Pradesh

fig. 184. *Markaṭaceṣṭā,*
interior pillar bracket,
Devī Jagdambi temple,
Khajurāho.

fig. 185. *Markaṭaceṣṭā*, with *vyālas*,
Gurgī, near *toraṇa*, left jamb,
Rewā Mahārāja's Palace,
tenth century, Rewā, Madya Pradesh

folds of the cloth together. The artist represents the volume of the cloth in a subtle manner.

The Sander Temple repeats this posture on both its temples. The Temple 2 shows a small frieze of seated group of *r̥ṣi* and *kanyā*. Could it indicate some tāntric ritual in progress or just a group of *guru-śiṣya*s?

The dancer-like stance enhances the grace and postural flexibility in the representation of this imagery. Yet another type found from Osiā Saccīyamātā Temple is represented in *ālīḍha* posture (*fig.* 41) while looking backwards at the monkey pulling her garment. The posture is similar to the *ūrdhvajānu* posture of the *vīrā nāyikā*.

Vīrā

It is an exhilarating change from the self-indulgent representations of *śr̥ṅgārika devāṅganā*s for a dynamic, self-asserting, weapon-wielding *vīra nāyikā*s. Under this heading, I will be discussing the *devāṅganā* sculptures represented on temple architecture as personifications of strength, courage, fierce and destructive aspect of the feminine power. The temple thus adorns itself with *devāṅganā*s of all types — bringing the uroboric cycle full circle — erotic, sexual, motherly, ascetic and terrible.

They can be classified thus:

(1) *khaḍgadhārī*, one holding a sword (*khaḍga*), noose (*khaṭvāṅga*), bow and arrow

(2) *sarpadhārī*, holding entwined snakes

fig. 187. *Markaṭaceṣṭā*, south wall, Ambikā temple, Jagat.

fig. 188. *Markaṭaceṣṭā*, frontal view, *nāyikā* in *ūrdhvajānu* pose, Sacchīyamātā Temple, Osiā.

fig. 189. *Markaṭaceṣṭā* in *ūrdhvajānu* pose, twelfth century, Śiva temple, Sander.

fig. 190. *Khaḍgadhārī vīrā* or *pratihārī*, pillar upright, Mathurā.

fig. 191. *Khaḍgadhārī vīrā*, *pratihārī,* pillar upright, Mathurā.

(3) *yoginī* or *tapasvī*, one who practises asceticism and appears austere and ferocious.

About half a dozen images of women holding *khaḍga* or a broad sword, have been conceived first by the Mathurā artists of the Kuṣāṇa period. According to V.S. Agrawala they may be Amazonian guards of the royal palaces. In later art, the lady with sword or bow and arrow, came to be known as Menakā or Urvaśī.[16]

One lady with sword in the right hand, has kept the other hand in *kaṭisama* and stands with her legs apart in *sama*, while the other one standing in *svastika* and holding the sword in the left hand, has kept the other arm above the head in *uromaṇḍalī*. The rich foliage at the back is the recurrent *śālabhañjikā* motif (*figs*. 190, 191). There are no *vīrā nāyikā* at Roḍā and Chittor but at Jagat the same type of *khaḍgadhārī* in *svastika pada* is found (*fig*. 192). One more *nāyikā* holding a curved long knife and a *kapāla*, is shown standing in a *trisra* pose, she is accompanied by a dwarf. But the strength, vigour and animation is absent.

At Osiā (*fig*. 3) there is a bold representation of a *devāṅganā* holding a bow. She holds the *haṁsāsya hasta* and is not actually releasing the arrow. The transparent fluttering garments thrown around the lady and the upper part of the body gently bent backwards, make the figure look charming and graceful. Could she be Rati or Urvaśī?

The most dynamic images of lady aiming an arrow at the crouching animal, is a feature of Maru–Gurjara temples, because this posture began to occur only from this age onwards. Both the *devāṅganās* stand in the *bhujaṅgatrāsita* or *ālīḍha* posture, a posture very appropriate to depict Gajāsura-Saṁhāramūrti in south India. The upper torso stretches and curves in the direction opposite to the bow, which is powerfully aimed at the crouching animal below (*fig*. 193). The expression of tension and force is fully explored here. One more lady with a bow

fig. 192. *Vīrā* with a sword, Ambikā temple, south wall, Jagat.

fig. 195. *Khaṭvāṅgadhārī* with a bowl, *ḍamarū* and *muṇḍamālā* wearing *jaṭābhāra*, accompanied by a dog, Sacchīyamātā Temple, Osiā.

fig. 194. *Khaṭvāṅgadhārī* holding fish-plate, *ūrdhvajānu* pose, accompanied by a drummer, Rānī Vāv, south buttress wall, Pāṭan.

(facing page)
fig. 193. *Vīrā devāṅganā*, Urvaśī or Gaurī aiming a bow, arrow at a lion, twelfth century, Śāraṇeśvara Temple, east wall, Abhapur, Antarsuba, Gujarat.

is found from Kirāḍu, although she is not in action but stands in *atibhaṅga*, the bow fitting into the curve of her waist, she too is accompanied by dwarf figures.

There are two *khaṭvāṅgadhārī devāṅganā*s represented at Osiā on Saccīyamātā and at Rānī Vāv (*figs.* 194, 195). The former holds the *khaṭvāṅga*, *ḍamarū* and a cup in one hand, while the other hand is lifted up in *uromaṇḍalī*. A dog is also seen accompanying her. The *jaṭābhāra* has skulls for decoration. The lady stands slightly swaying herself to one side. But for this action there is no movement in this sculpture. *Vīra nāyikā*s are mentioned in *Kṣīrārṇava* as Urvaśī, Rambhā, Gaurī, etc. who are weapon wielders and fight with human or animal opponents.

The Rānī Vāv (*fig.* 194) image of the *devāṅganā* holding the *khaṭvāṅga* stands in an *ūrdhvajānu* pose bending to the side, the leg is lifted up. She is accompanied by a drummer, which suggests that probably this lady is engaged either in a performance or a ritual.

The imagery of the *sarpadhārī* is most unusual and difficult to explain. This particular *nāyikā* is depicted completely nude with serpents entwining around the legs. She holds a dish with a fish on it to feed the snake. The other hand is lifted up. There are owls and a peacock placed in this composition, probably to suggest a nocturnal ritual of some sacred fluvial rites? The same motif is repeated inside the shaft portion of Rānī Vāv (*figs.* 196, 197).

The category of *vīrā nāyikā* also includes *tāpasī* and *yoginī*, because of their acts of austerity and bravery. The Rānī Vāv and Sander are the only two sites on which *tāpasī* or lady mendicants are

fig. 196. Nude *devāṅganā* with serpent entwining her body, performing a nocturnal ritual? south buttress wall, Rānī Vāv, Pāṭan.

fig. 197. Serpent goddess,
Faience, Crete,
middle Minoan III period,
British Museum.

fig. 198. *Toraṇa* pillar,
yoginī, with knife, *kapāla*,
jaṭābhāra and *muṇḍamālā,*
Mahādeva temple complex,
Ghaṭeśvara, Badoli.

(top left)
fig. 199. *Yoginī* with *kartāra* wearing yogic costume, Śiva Temple, west wall, Sander.

(top right)
fig. 200. North *jaṅghā* upper register shows numerous demonic figures, Mohajamātā Temple, Terahi.

fig. 201. Details of *fig* 200.

fig. 202. Kubera and Kirāti, or *vīra devāṅganā* with bow, arrow, matted hair (left). Vāyu and *devāṅganā* with *āmralumbī* (right), Saccīyamātā Temple, Osiā.

represented holding tongs, wearing simple costumes devoid of jewellery but *rudrākṣa* berries as ornaments. Their ears are elongated and their hair are matted. They are accompanied by dogs (*figs.* 198, 199, 202). At Terāhī, grotesque faced *devāṅganā* welding lethal weapons and skeletal figures, stand flanking images of Durga-Mahisā-suramardini and Vārāhi. (*fig.* 200, 201)

The *vīra* quality of strength and power do not reveal through completely in their postures and gestures, but the very act of indulging in playing with such dangerous objects, qualifies these images as *vīrā*, a category clearly distinct from the erotic objects of enjoyment the other *devāṅganā*s represented.

Darpaṇā

Darpaṇā is the lady with mirror and one of the most vital imageries of feminine beauty found in Indian art and literature. The imagery is often represented by woman putting a *bindī* or adjusting her earring while looking into the mirror. This act could be classified as *prasādhanā,* and therefore, the *nāyikā-prasādhikā*. Thus, within the motif of *darpaṇā*, there are three distinctions: (1) the woman admiring herself by looking into the mirror, (2) engaged in make up, and (3) looking at the nail marks made by the lover and recalling their love play.

The motif of *darpaṇā* goes back to Bharhut (*fig.* 203) and Mathurā *stūpa* railing sculptures, where this motif is represented with clear allusion to the *darpaṇā paribhogadarśinī* and *prasādhikā* (*Darpaṇā* from Maholi, U.N. Roy, fig. 26) (*Bharhut*, Barua, pl. LIX, 68, XXXI, 25) (*Prasādhikā*, Saṅghol, S.P. Gupta, 8, 68) (*Paribhogadarśinī*, Saṅghol, S.P. Gupta 1, 6) (Bhūteśvara, U.N. Roy fig. 54, Govindnagar, *figs.* 203, 204).

fig. 203. *Darpaṇā*, first century BCE, collection: Unknown, Bharhut.

There are other reliefs found from Mathurā wherein the *nāyaka-nāyikā* are engaged in dressing up each other, attended upon by dwarfish attendants holding the mirror in front of them. The popularity of this motif is unquestionable and can be measured by the repetitions to which its imagery has been subjected to. After Bharhut and Mathurā this motif is seen on the doorways of temples of the Gupta period (e.g. Tigowā, Kaṅkālī Devī Mandir, *garbha-gṛha* doorway) where at one time *śālabhañjikā*s were placed, for example on Sāñcī *stūpa* gateways. The motif of *darpaṇā* is not only significant for having an uninterrupted usage throughout, but also because it is one of the first imagery types to be represented on the temple pillars, capitals, ceilings and finally the lintel of the doorway (*figs.* 257, 258).

At Roḍā Temple 6 on the pillar capital the motif of *darpaṇā* occurs (*fig.* 10) so also on the *devakulikā* of the Harihara group I at Osiā, a largish figure of a lady (river goddess or *nāginī*) holding a mirror is to

fig. 204. *Darpaṇā*, Ṭoṭeśvara Temple, south wall, Kaḍwāhā.

be seen (*fig.* 1). Hence in the Pratihāra architecture the presence of *darpaṇā* is probably the earliest, which gradually, towards the tenth century, finds its place on the corners of the temple doorways. Both the *prasādhikā* and the *darpaṇā* are the favourites of the sculptors. On Sander ceiling, as well, this motif is included, Khajurāho, Lakṣmaṇa and Kandarīya Mahādeva temples (*figs.* 205, 206, 207); Kaḍwāhā Ṭoṭeśvara Temple (*fig.* 204), Sohāgpur Virāṭeśvara Temple; Pāṭan Rānī Vāv and Jagat, Ambikā Temple (*figs.* 204, 208) are some of the best examples representing the *darpaṇā* and *prasādhikā*.

In Sanskrit Kāvya literature, the connotation of woman looking into the mirror is not only restricted to admiring one's beauty or being made up, but also to admire the marks of love-making imprinted by the lover. Thus, mirror acts as a stimulant to relive the moments of conjugal bliss by mirroring it to the *nāyikā* after the union is over, Kālidāsa in *R̥tusaṁhāram*, Canto IV, Hemanta *r̥tu*, describes a certain young woman's mental state thus:

> Sharp imprint of love-bites on bruised lips, the lover's fine nail inscriptions on breasts, these clearly reveal the passionate enjoyment, relentless of women in the first flush of youth (IV.12).
>
> A certain young woman, mirror in hand, decorates her radiant face, basking in the gentle warmth of the mild morning sun, and gazes with interest pouting at the love bites her beloved left when he drank his fill of the nectar of her lower lip? (IV.13).[17]

Philosophically *darpaṇā* could be identified as a mirror of the human soul — the conscience, the self, which is metaphorically cleaned by entering the temple and concentrating upon the *Brahman*. This motif is often found on the *garbhagr̥ha* doorways. This interpretation is too idealistic and could be developed to explain the higher quest within an individual. Thus, a *darpaṇā* could on one hand evoke introspection while *paribhogadarśinī* on the other hand definitely implies in expressed and suggested sense a popular erotic connotation.

fig. 205. Same as above *prasādhikā,* Jagat.

fig. 206. *Devāṅganā* applying *āltā* on her foot, eleventh century, Kandarīya Mahādeva Temple, Khajurāho.

fig. 207. *Devāṅganā* painting the foot and forehead, *pṛṣtha-svastika,* south wall, Ambikā temple, Jagat.

fig. 208. *Devāṅgnā* applying *altā* on her her foot, Lakṣmaṇa Temple, tenth century, Khajurāho.

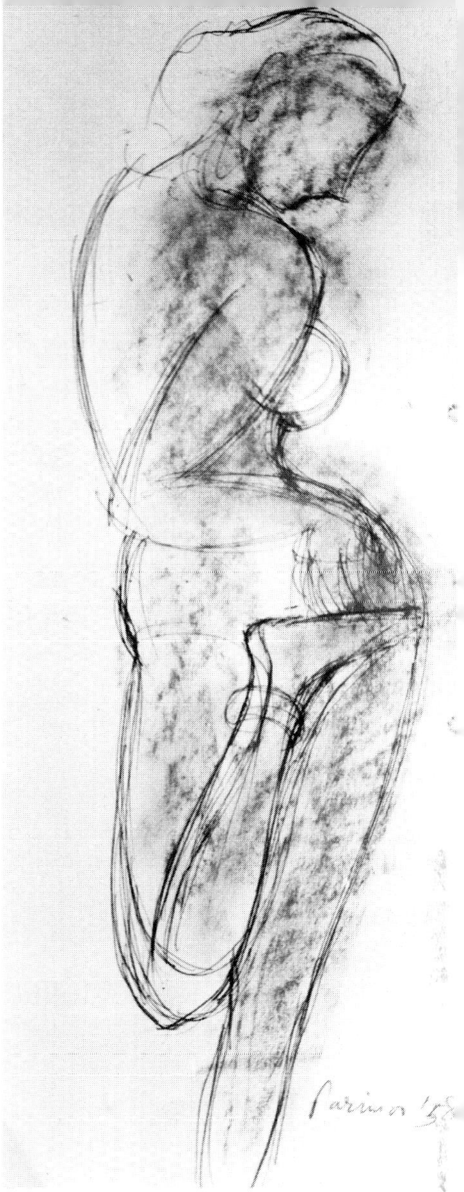

fig. 209. Drawing of the same *devāṅganā* by Ratan Parimoo, 1958.

Prasādhikā

This category hardly refers to an imagery which can have a scope beyond the denotative, and hence the women engaged in toilet, adjusting their earrings, tying the hair, decorating with flowers, painting their lips, feet or applying *bindī* and *kājala*, are highly graceful activities of women, that one generally comes across in everyday life. The connotation of *lakṣaṇā* or *vyañjanā* is absent in these motifs, which do not elevate beyond the mundane. The indirect suggestivity of fertility in *śālabhañjikā* or *vasanabhraṁśā* elevates the female motif beyond its physical form into a metaphorical sphere, whereas in *prasādhikā*, such a transformation does not occur. The *prasādhikā* frankly evokes desire in the hearts of the onlooker.

> Swaying hips, soles tinted deep rose, anklets with tinkling bells, imitating at each step the cry of the wild goose, men's hearts are churned by desire" (I.5 Kālidāsa, *Ṛtusaṁhāram*).[18]

Darpaṇā indicates *śṛṅgāra rasa* and both the types of situations — *saṁbhoga* and *vipralambha* are implied.

fig. 210. *Prasādhikā* painting foot, lifted at the back, *vivṛtta kaṭi*, Saccīyamātā Temple, Osiā.

Alasā

This erotically charged *devāṅganā* is found to illustrate that aspect of feminine charm and grace by which even the greatest seers and ascetics were distracted from their path of meditation and knowledge. The *alasā nāyikā*s stand in *baddhācārī* or *svastika sthāna*, while their arms are lifted above their heads in *uromaṇḍalī hasta*. Their posture itself has an evocative tinge which takes recourse to sensual moves, seductive glances and body flexions. Such a *devāṅganā* has much closer links with (1) *naṭī*, as a dancer, because of its physical disposition

fig. 211. *Alasā*, pillar upright, second century, Saṅghol, National Museum, New Delhi.

(top right)
fig. 212. *Alasā* with *vita*, Temple 6, pillar capital, Roḍā.

on one hand while (2) on the other it continues the fertility eroticism dialogue further. (3) The element of *śṛṅgāra* and *nāyikā bhāva* is also denoted by the *alasā* imagery which convincingly displays one such *nāyikā* in *utkaṇṭhitā* condition, the erotic fervour rising. Both *prasādhikā* and *alasā* can be classified as those *nāyikā*s (distinct from *devāṅganā*s) which represent instances from psychological stages of the *aṣṭanāyikā*s, as described in the *Nāṭyaśāstra* and performed by classical dancers even today. (4) Their postures also denote their expectation in awaiting their lovers. The *Saṅgīta-Ratnākara* calls the posture of *alasā* type *nāyikā* as *uromaṇḍalī*, posture which is employed by women in all the stages of love, and it tallies exactly with the *alasā* in medieval sculptures. (5) The generic term *alasā kanyā* has found currency in Orissan temple architecture and text. This denotes that the entire category of such women are referred to as *alasā kanyā*s while consciously or unconsciously they indicate mortal as well as celestial women. Thus *devāṅganā* as *alasā kanyā* indicates the semi-divine nature of these female divinities, which draw their sources from the earlier *apsaras* concept.

The *alasā* or the indolent type is represented at Saṅghol (*fig.* 211) in the *moṭita hasta* crossing the palms behind the neck in an act of yawning or shedding laziness. The posture is almost the same, save for the slight bend at the knee shifting the weight to the single leg. Such a contraposto is a typical feature of Kuṣāṇa *yakṣī*s.

The Roḍā Temple 6 *alasā* (*fig.* 212) is a dreamy one, who is almost lost in her youthfulness. The exaggerated *tribhaṅga* of the waist and

fig. 213. *Alasā* standing next to Viṣṇu, tenth century, Lakṣmaṇa temple, Khajurāho.

fig. 214. Drawing of the same *devāṅganā* by Ratan Parimoo, 1958.

fig. 215. *Alasā,* south wall, Ambikā temple, Jagat.

fig. 216. *Alasā* in *pratīratha,* south wall, Nīlakaṇṭha temple, Kekind.

fig. 217. *Maṇḍovara, mulaprāsāda*, western *juṅghā*, early tenth century, Sūrya Temple, Tusā, Udaipur, Rajasthan.

fig. 218. *Alasā* and *kanduka-krīḍā* flanking Āditya, denoting time, space and movement, (details of *fig.* 215) Tusā

fig. 219. *Alasā*, Ambikā temple, Suhāniā.

fig. 220. *Alasā*, *vasanabhraṁśā* and *markaṭaceṣṭā*, temple 1, Khirniwālā group 7, Kaḍwāhā.

arms thrown backwards, is accentuated by the profile face and *baddhācārī* posture. She is also accompanied by the *kuṭilaka*, a dwarfish *viṭa* who is a companion of *nāyaka–nāyikā*s in Sanskrit literature. The aquatic vegetation suggests the emergence of this *nāyikā* from acquous source.

fig. 221. *Alasā, prasādhikā,* Śiva Temple, Koḍal.

A slightly stiff but interesting representation of *alasā* is found from Saccīyamātā Temple, Osiā. The *uromaṇḍalī hasta* and *baddhācārī* are neatly struck, but the whole figure is frontally positioned, that leaves the movement static.

A highly mutilated image of a *devāṅganā* in *moṭita* pose is seen at Kekind, Nīlakaṇṭha Temple, whose body bends in a gentle *tribhaṅga* while legs are firmly placed in *svastika* (*fig.* 216). The long single-chained necklace hanging in front leans gently towards one side. Such a swaying *alasā* pose is not seen before. As in Roḍā she too is accompanied by a *kuṭilaka–viṭa* character. At Suhāniā too this iconography is repeated.

The Khajurāho, Lakṣmaṇa Temple and Jagat, Ambikā Temple (*figs.* 213, 214, 215) and Tusā, Sūrya Temple (*figs.* 217, 218) and

(facing page)
fig. 222. *Nartakī* in *karihasta* pose, north wall, Śaraṇeśvara temple, twelfth century, Abhapur, Gujarat.

Suhāniā (*fig.* 219) have representations of *alasā* sculptures, which excel as the best specimens of poise and balance. The *devāṅganā* stands in *baddhācārī* without accentuating the *tribhaṅga* and hence the torso remains straight. But the head and arms lifted above bend gently, implying the *devāṅganā*'s pose to be that of a celestial nymph in an amorous act. At Kaḍwāhā Temple and Koḍal, Śiva Temple, there are many *devāṅganā*s in many moods, some of them striking the *alasā* pose (*fig.* 220).

(facing page)
fig. 223. *Nartakī, ūrdhvajānu*, Udayeśvara Temple, Sukanāsa, CE 1056, Udaipur, Madya Pradesh.

Naṭī–Nartakī

She could be a dancer and an acrobat, but what she could be doing on the *maṇḍovara* of the temple architecture is a question. The legendary Indrasabhā is endowed with such veteran beauteous *apsaras*es, also are ace dancers and bless the major celestial and earthly festivals, the *nitya-sumaṅgalī*s, who are expected to participate in all the major rituals of the temples. They perform dance, in the form of *seva*, beside the *garbha-gṛha*, as well as outside, during the procession of the *utsava-mūrti*. Could the *naṭī* sculptures be inspired from the dance movements of the *devadāsī*s? The sculptor's answer in stone to the virtuosic display of the dancer's movements? Or, are they purely imaginative? The subject of *naṭī–nartakī*, the dancer, has to be dealt with more from the point of view of dance analysis than from the fertility-eroticism-asceticism-*vīra* dialectic point of view. The motif of the woman as a dancer can either be interpreted as the celestial dancer or as *devadāsī* of the temple, beyond which the attention has to concentrate on the postures of the arms, legs, waist, *hasta* and so on. Our tendency is to keenly tally the postures and gestures with *Nāṭyaśāstra* or *Saṅgīta-Ratnākara* and thus essentially technical. While doing this, our attention rests more on the physical than on the metaphorical meaning, emerging out of this imagery. The motif of *naṭī*, therefore, is radically opposite to the motifs of *putravallabhā*, *śālabhañjikā*, *sva-stana-sparśā,* etc. which has *abhidhā*, *lakṣaṇā* and *vyañjanā* levels of interpretation. It leads the attention of the onlooker from its physical charm and titillating presence even in silence, beyond the physical plane of the symbolic,

of which the sculpture is only a pregnant signifier. Very often people have got stuck at the physical element, without being able to transcend it and have interpreted the *apsarases*, *devāṅganās* and *mithuna* sculptures, as though they bear testimony to the degradation of the general moral values of the Indian society. This fallacy has gone too far, especially in the case of *mithuna maithuna* groups at Khajurāho, with which even some of the *devāṅganās* are clubbed.

fig. 224. *Nartakī*, *pṛṣṭha-svastika* pose, twelfth century, Jamsot, Allahabad Museum.

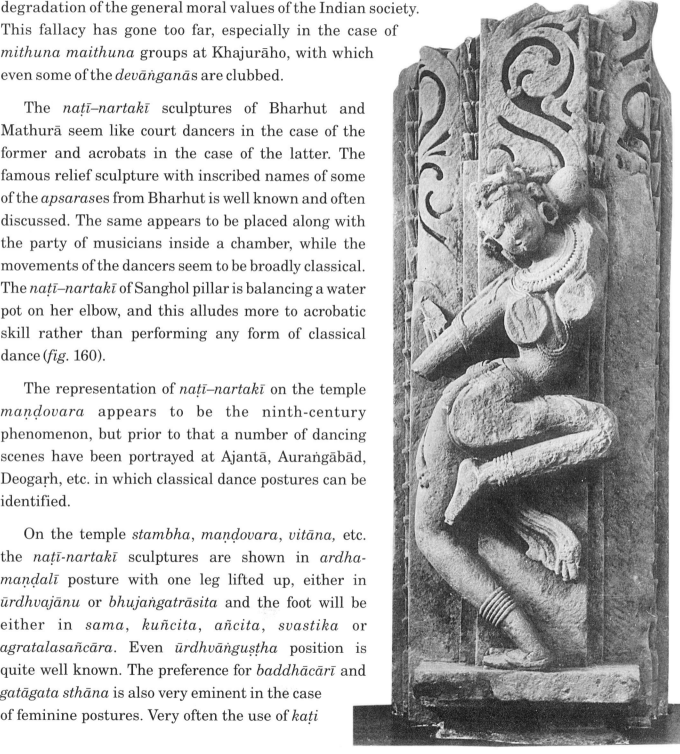

The *naṭī–nartakī* sculptures of Bharhut and Mathurā seem like court dancers in the case of the former and acrobats in the case of the latter. The famous relief sculpture with inscribed names of some of the *apsaras*es from Bharhut is well known and often discussed. The same appears to be placed along with the party of musicians inside a chamber, while the movements of the dancers seem to be broadly classical. The *naṭī–nartakī* of Sanghol pillar is balancing a water pot on her elbow, and this alludes more to acrobatic skill rather than performing any form of classical dance (*fig.* 160).

The representation of *naṭī–nartakī* on the temple *maṇḍovara* appears to be the ninth-century phenomenon, but prior to that a number of dancing scenes have been portrayed at Ajantā, Auraṅgābād, Deogaṛh, etc. in which classical dance postures can be identified.

On the temple *stambha*, *maṇḍovara*, *vitāna,* etc. the *naṭī-nartakī* sculptures are shown in *ardha-maṇḍalī* posture with one leg lifted up, either in *ūrdhvajānu* or *bhujaṅgatrāsita* and the foot will be either in *sama*, *kuñcita*, *añcita*, *svastika* or *agratalasañcāra*. Even *ūrdhvāṅguṣṭha* position is quite well known. The preference for *baddhacārī* and *gatāgata sthāna* is also very eminent in the case of feminine postures. Very often the use of *kaṭi* movements that lead to sensuous bends are found leading to *vivṛtta* position. Of course, the *tribhaṅga* is the hallmark of the kinesthetics of Indian classical dance and sculpture, which gets revealed on every *devāṅganā* sculpture of the medieval period. The more exaggerated the posture, the more strī kingly medieval the character of the sculpture. Kuṣāṇa and Śuṅga images of *yakṣī*s are not images of dancers, but their postures conform to the *Nāṭyaśāstra* tradition. Acrobatic feats are usually displayed by men and women together or by women alone. The *naṭī–nartakī* of Saṅghol is seen balancing a waterpot on her elbow in the same manner in which *kanduka* ball is balanced by the Mathurā *naṭī* (*fig.* 159).

In the post-Gupta era the delineation of *naṭī–nartakī* figures adhering to some basic principles of "balance and the deviation from the centre of gravity", "shift of weight", "faithful representation of *hasta*s and *sthānaka*s", grows, and more and more dancing images of *devāṅganā*s and other divinities come into practice.[19] The Vaḍaval Mātṛkās (*fig.* 231) and Karvan Mātṛkās (*fig.* 232) are cases in point from Gujarat of the seventh and eighth century. The postures are delineated with firmness and classical balance, which controls the accentuation of bends and contortions. By the tenth century CE, the postures employing *ardha-maṇḍalī*, *ūrdhvajānu*, *bhujaṅgatrāsita*, *ālīḍha, daṇḍapādācārī*, *baddhācārī* will become the preferred postures with sculptors who excel in their attempt with each sculpture. The frontality is often dropped for profile views, three quarter views, back views and circularly turned (*vivṛtta*) views in which the figure is turned almost half a circle from the waist. It has been observed that post-tenth-century sculptures of *devāṅganā*s are more dynamically charged with accentuated bends, and covering more planes of space around them. This is a medieval character which will slowly get degenerated towards acrobatic movements, devoid of suppleness and classical restraint.

Note Ābhāpur, Śāraṇeśvara Temple dancer in *uromaṇḍalī-ūrdhvajānu* pose (*figs.* 193, 222); *pṛṣṭha svastika* pose, Udaipur, Udayeśvara Temple; *śukanāsā* figures of dancers in *bhujaṅgatrāsita* (*fig.* 223); two figures of *devāṅganā*s in *vivṛtta kaṭi* posture in *atibhaṅga*, revealing their back and profile from Khajurāho,

fig. 225.
Nūpurapādikā,ūrdhvajānu pose,
Pārśvanātha Temple,
Khajurāho.
(photo Shama Kilanjar)

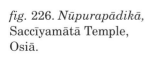

fig. 226. *Nūpurapādikā,*
Saccīyamātā Temple,
Osiā.

fig. 227. *Nūpurapādikā*,
well portion,
Rānī Vāv, Pāṭan.

fig. 228. *Saṅgītavādinī*,
second century, Saṅghol,
National Museum.

Lakṣmaṇa Temple (*fig.* 213), Saccīyamātā Temple, Osiā (*figs.* 210) and Jamsot (*fig.* 224).

Some dynamic postures of *vīrā nāyikās* combating with the opponents in *ālīḍha* and *bhujaṅgatrāsita*, are common in the twelfth-century sculpture of Gujarat, such as the one found at Ābhāpur, Ghumlī and Sejakpur and at Osiā in Rajasthan.

Nūpurapādikā–Saṅgītavādinī

The *naṭī–nartakī* classification also includes the *nūpurapādikā* and *saṅgītavādinī* category, because one is employing a dance-like posture lifting the leg in *ūrdhvajānu* or *daṇḍapakṣa*, (*figs.* 225, 226, 227) while the other represents the woman playing on musical instruments like drums, cymbals, *ekatārā,* and flute. Even women involved in singing are sometimes represented (viz. Jagat) as it appears from their expression. A lady playing a hermonica standing on a crouching *yakṣa* has been found at Saṅghol (*fig.* 228).

There are different references found from texts mentioning the use of drums for accompaniment and for solo dancing. Abhinavagupta refers to it several times and quotes from a composition called *Cūḍāmaṇi Ḍombika* by poet Rāṇaka, and perhaps from another composition also, called *Guṇamālā*. The *ḍombī* is a type like the dance performed by a single *nartakī*, songs are sung by accompanying singers, and the dancer, the *ḍombī*, dances. The difference is in the person of the *ḍombī* and the nature of the theme. *Ḍombī* is a kind of drum and also a class or community of people accomplished in music and dance. The

fig. 229. *Saṅgītavādinī*, tenth century, Harṣanātha Temple, Harṣagiri, Sīkar, Rajasthan.

fig. 230. Flutist, bracket figure, Viśvanātha Temple, Khajurāho.

Rājataraṅgiṇī refers to *ḍombagāyana*s and a *ḍomba-maṇḍala* consisting of one *raṅga* and his two daughters called *ḍomba-gāyikā*s. The *ḍombankuṭṭadi*s were till recently found in the countryside of south India. The *ḍombī* dance also involves *abhinaya* in a crude way, they also strike poses in between dance movements, a *hudukka* drum is played as an accompaniment which Abhinavagupta says is called *cillimārga* in vernacular.[20]

Another mention of dancing with a drum is mentioned by Sayappa, whose correct name is not recovered but seems to be *chatisiri* (*sani*) in which a *cāṇḍāla* woman dancer sings philosophical songs, *caryī gīta*s to the accompaniment of a *hudukka* drum hanging from her shoulder. She is also accompanied by male and female singers and players of flute, *hora*s, cymbals and drums, while the subject of songs is Śiva and Pārvatī in their appearance as the "hunter" and "huntress". As these songs are sung and instruments played, she dances in the delicate style with graceful movements.[21]

Some other examples of *saṅgītavādinī* are the flautist (Khajurāho) and the *ekatārā* player (Harṣagiri (*figs.* 230, 229), who drape the body of the temple as if resounding and revelling in music. They also represent the playing of the *maṅgala vādya*, which constitute the string, wind and percussion instruments.

A significant aspect of the interpretation of the *naṭī–nartakī* sculptures which have evolved in the Nāgara temple architecture from tenth century onwards, has an interesting angle to its study in the light of the then existing *devadāsī* system attached to the temple. It was more rigorously practised in south India, since Āgamas and epigraphical sources mention profusely about it, but the north was no less deprived. It is interesting to note that north Indian temple sculptural programming was so evolved that many interesting forms of *nartakī–saṅgītavādinī* type of *devāṅganā*s found a prominent place on the *pratiratha*s of the *jaṅghā*. Even *devāṅganā*s holding a *cāmara*, *kumbha*, *dīpa*, etc. are also shown attending upon the deities of the *bhadra koṣṭha*. It is quite intriguing to unravel the role of these *devāṅganā–Surasundarī*s on the Nāgara temple architecture, since the Draviḍa architecture does not have this imagery type at all on the *jaṅghā* section (i.e. *bhīta*) of the *garbha-gṛha* or *maṇḍapa* (but on doorways and pillars they occur occasionally). But in the ritual worship of the presiding deity the *rājagaṇikā*s, etc. have quite an important role. Their auspicious intervention has also been noted by Āgamic texts, which confirms the religious sanction. Our question is, are the *naṭī–nartakī* sculptures inspired from the dance of the *rājagaṇikā*s? If they are, then how is it that this tradition got almost wiped out from north India, both in terms of its ritual practice and the practice of the dance tradition? Are the sculptures superficial depiction of the dances, ritualistic and popular, or do they also have a deeper suggestion?

The most characteristic task of the *devadāsī* in the ritual of *nityārcanā* is *dīpārādhanā*. *Devadāsī* should offer the *kumbhadīpa* and either recite or perform *puṣpāñjali*.[22] Due to her role as a *nityasumaṅgalī*, she is not only involved in removing the evil, but also engaged in the task of *liṅgālayam* (reabsorption of the *liṅga*) which connects the *devadāsī* with Tantrism, especially with *kuṇḍalinī yoga*, when the *kuṇḍalinī* which lies asleep in the individual *mūlādhāra* is awakened. It is slowly brought to the *sahasrāra cakra*, where Cosmic Energy, the aggregate of all *kuṇḍalinī*s, resides in inseparable union with Paramaśiva, and by merging with it the *yogī* obtains spiritual release. In this process there is reabsorption of the world into undifferentiated unity. This process is known as *laya*. Thus, the *devadāsī* not only offers the *āratī*, *naivedya*, flowers and *nṛtya*, but cools off the energy produced during the *āratī*. For this purpose she is required and has been proclaimed as *nitya-sumaṅgalī*.[23]

The role of *devadāsī* in the procession of *utsavabhera* is also described by various Āgamic texts such as *Kumāratantra*, *Ajitāgama*, *Kriyākramajyoti* of Aghoraśivācārya, etc. The *Śrīpraśna Saṁhitā* advises that *dāsī*s, instrumentalists and musicians must dance before the deity on earth (ch. XXXIV, 42).[24] According to *Kriyākramajyoti* the idol in the palanquin should be accompanied by *rudragaṇikā*s on both the sides, while Vedic scholars and servants should follow at the back. In front of the palanquin should stand the king, dance master, flutist and other musicians. While still further ahead Śaiva devotees, subsidiary gods, bull and drummer should walk. The *Śrīpraśna Saṁhitā* mentions along with many other details of musical instruments, about *nartakī* the female dancer, who should perform *abhinaya* with an abundance of *rasa*s, like *śṛṅgāra*, while singing, etc. After the procession returns back to the *prākāra* of the temple, the *rudragaṇikā*s should perform the *miśra nṛttam* and Śaiva *gaindharvyam* in the *maṇḍapa*. For *miśra nṛttam* they should wear silver or bronze anklets. In the *prākāra* of the Mahāmārī Temple, *rudradāsī*s should perform *kevala nṛttam*, while *grāmadāsī*s and *rudradāsī*s perform *nāṭakam* (dance-drama) in the temples of the goddesses, Kālī and Durgā, says Sadyojāta Śivācārya commenting on *Kāmikāgama*.

As found from the survey report by Saskia Kersenboom Story, the *devadāsī*s were required to perform at the *sāyarakṣai* (dusk *pūjā*), by doing *kumbhāratī* at the time of *sandhi*s of dawn and dusk. This is an auspicious moment as well as potentially dangerous. They should wear black beads to remove the effect of the evil.[25]

Kāmikāgama distinguishes three types of *devadāsī* — *rudragaṇikā*, *rudrakannikai*, and *rudradāsī*, who should perform *śuddha nṛttam*, employing *karaṇas* belonging to Śivajñāna and *miśram*, to which Purāṇas are added and *kevalam*, which is secular version (*lokavṛttanāma*) of this dance, respectively.[26]

Having brought to light the above data, one begins to look at *devāṅganā* sculptures as possible reflections of *devadāsīs*, who are not only the dancers but an integral part of the temple ritual. The *devāṅganās* holding *kumbha*, *dīpa* and such other imagery could now be seen in new light.

References

1. Kanwar Lal, *Erotic Sculptures of Khajurāho*, Delhi, 1970, pp. 24-30.
2. Vaijayanti Navangule (Shete), Lecturer, Dept. of Art History & Aesthetics, Faculty of Fine Arts, has helped me to formulate the terms and translations of some verses.
3. M.C.P. Srivastava, *Mother Goddess in Indian Art: Archaeology and Literature*, New Delhi, 1979, pp. 51-52.
4. Ibid.; O.C. Ganguli, *IHQ*, vol. XIX, no. 1, March, 1943, p. 10.
5. Ibid.
6. Stella Kramrisch, in *Khajurāho*, Marg Publications.
7. K.S. Srinivasan, op. cit., 1985, p. 20.
8. Chandra Rajan, *Kālidāsa, The Loom of Time: A Selection of His Plays and Poems*, Calcutta, 1989, pp. 124-28.
9. *Subhāṣita Ratnakośa*, K.S. Srinivasan, op. cit., 1985, p. 12.
10. H.H. Ingalls, *Subhāṣita Ratnakośa*, 1965, p. 213.
11. V.S. Agrawala, op. cit., p. 227.
12. U.N. Roy, op. cit., *Śālabhañjikā*, 1979, pp. 22-23.
13. V. Raghavan, *Uparūpakas and Nṛtya Prabandha*, Sangeeta Natak, p. 21.
14. The term *markaṭaceṣṭā* has been formulated after consultation with Vaijayanti Shete.
15. T.A. Gopinath Rao, *Elements of Hindu Iconography*, vol. II, Varanasi, 1971, p. 568.
16. V.S. Agrawala, op. cit., p. 228.
17. *Kālidāsa, Loom of Time*, op. cit.
18. Ibid.
19. Kapila Vatsyayan, *Classical Dance in Literature and the Arts*, New Delhi, 1968, has amply demonstrated this: chapter IV, Sculpture and Dancing.
20. V. Raghavan, "Uparūpaka and Nṛtya Prabandhas", *Sangeet Natak*, no. 76, New Delhi, 1985, pp. 35-55.
21. Ibid.
22. Saskia Kersenboom Story, *Nitya Sumangali: Devadāsī Tradition in South India*, New Delhi, 1987, pp. 119-25.
23. Ibid., p. 120. See also John Woodroffe, *The Serpent Power*, London, 1922.
24. Saskia Kersenboom Story, op. cit., p. 122.
25. Ibid., p. 112.
26. Ibid., p. 118.

7

Medieval Western Indian Sculpture

Modelling the Medieval Form and Style

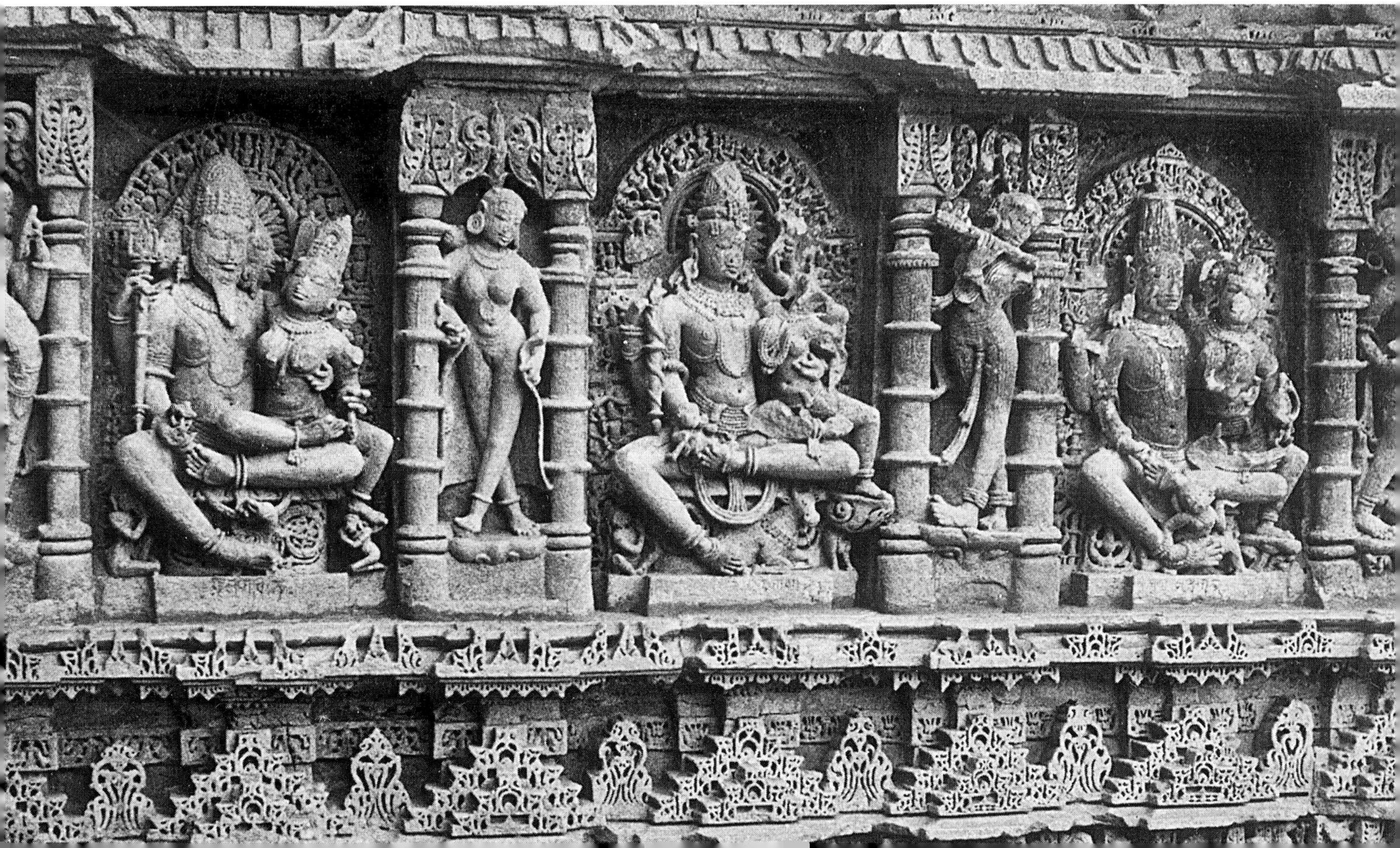

Possible Sources for the Foundation of Sculptural Style in Western India During the Eighth Century CE

SCULPTURAL development in western India has its own independent growth which coincides with the architectural form from time to time, based on its demand from monument to monument. In the following sections, we examine the sculptural form as such and probe sources for possible influences and indigenous elements which matured during the period under examination. When confronted by the eighth-century *devāṅganā*s on the pillar capitals of Roḍā in Gujarat, one gradually begins to dissect and discern the sculptural data of fifth, sixth and seventh centuries to formulate their stylistic lineage. U.P. Shah points out that art under the Kṣatrapas during the first four centuries of the Current Era was parallel to the Kuṣāṇa art of Mathurā and sees its extent in Sindh, Punjab, Rajasthan, Gujarat, Nasik, Khandesh, Bombay and parts of Mālwā.[1]

The sites of Devni Mori and Śāmalājī in Gujarat and Ḍūṅgarpur and Udaipur in Rajasthan, have yielded important examples which call for a stylistic assessment based on a regional variant exclusive to western India. A large number of sculptures of this area portray Mātṛkās or the Mother Goddesses (*figs.* 231, 232). A particular regional style that flourished in this area binds them into a homogeneous tradition of robust naturalism. This robustness can be traced back to Madhyadeśa in the art of Bharhut and Sāñcī and the Śaka–Kuṣāṇa–Sātavāhana schools. P. Pal points out

> . . . the females are clearly descendants of the portly *yakṣī*s of Mathurā and the amazonian donatories at Kārlā and Kānherī of the early centuries of the Current Era, but they are no longer as monumental and earthly as their ancestors.[2]

While assessing the western Indian sculpture of the sixth century CE, the influence of Gupta classicism can neither be overlooked nor over-emphasized. It is obvious that there is a

fig. 231. Vārāhī *Mātṛkā*, sixth century, Vaḍaval, Museology Department M.S.U. Baroda, Gujarat

fig. 232. Indrāṇī in dancing pose, *kṣiptā, kuñcitā, kaṭisamā*, seventh century (*in situ*), Karvan.

link between Deogaṛh, Udayagiri, Mandsaur and Sondhani sculptures with Śāmalājī, Koṭyarka, Aṁjhara, Jagat, Mt. Ābu and other such sites in Ḍūṅgarpur–Udaipur areas. Shah goes further in observing that in the treatment of the heavy and somewhat stunted and sturdy bodies, the Mandsaur and Deogaṛh artists have followed the traditions not of the Sārnāth school but of western India, which again inherited the traditions of the Madhyadeśa art of Bharhut and Sāñcī and of the Śaka–Kuṣāṇa–Sātavāhana schools. The art of Mandsaur and Deogaṛh, though of Gupta age, broadly sixth century CE, is not derived from the Sārnāth school, and now with the evidence of Śāmalājī, Devni Mori, Aṁjhara, etc. discovered in the last few years, we are led to believe that like Sārnāth, a separate school, existed covering a region roughly comprising Deogaṛh, Eraṇ, Śāmalājī, Aṁjhara (whole of old Ḍūṅgarpur state) parts of Ābu region and north Gujarat. Kalyanpur and Mandsaur were already centres of sculpture during the fifth and sixth centuries CE.[3]

Going by the numismatic evidences, Gupta rule in Gujarat was short-lived, it lasted for less than a century, and no Gupta coins after Skandagupta have been found in the area. From Devni Mori only Kṣatrapa and later Vallabhi coins were found, while Gupta coins were totally absent.[4]

Concluding from here, a less sophisticated but earthly and voluptuous form of female figure hailing from Udayagiri, Deogaṛh, Sondhani and Mandsaur in connection with the Ḍūṅgarpur–Udaipur Mātṛkās (the characteristic style which the Roḍā *devāṅganā*s are going to inherit), represents a phenomenon of "simultaneous diffusion" rather than "actual transmission" of style.

The concerted influence of Śuṅga–Sātavāhana style from Kārle, Bharhut and Sāñcī represents the Koṅkaṇ and Madhyadeśa styles fusing at western India in which the role of Mathurā or Sārnāth has already been minimized. This allows us to view the *śālabhañjikā* figures placed on the *stūpa* gateways, etc. as the predecessors of the *devāṅganā*s of the temple *maṇḍovara*. Even their formal conception, ornamentation, dignity and grace amidst a general earthly voluptuousness, shows clear affinity with Roḍā capital figures which were first noticed by U.P. Shah in a small article.[5]

For the stylistic analysis of the post-Gupta sculpture in western India we have chosen the *śālabhañjikā/devāṅganā* motif. This motif is an important stylistic typology to link Ḍūṅgarpur–Udaipur area on one hand with Gupta tradition, and the Koṅkaṇ, i.e. Kārle, Kānherī, Elephaṇṭā, Shivdi style on the other. Since western India is geographically situated at such a receptive juncture, it has absorbed stylistic elements from Koṅkaṇ and Mālwā at the same time. This broad parallelism has been seen in the light of Śāmalājī, Tanesara group of Mātṛkās, for sixth-century sculptural activity by Sara Schastok, U.P. Shah, Karl Khandalawala and S. Gorkshakar. I am trying to extend it to the eighth-century sculptural development, which is analogous to that of architecture as well. It would be worthwhile to suggest the contemporaneity between Shivdi Mātṛkā, which has been identified as Skanda Mātā, with Śāmalājī Mātṛkās, Koṭyarka Mātṛkās, for the similarity between their drapery tying pattern and folds, ornaments, hairstyle; the child pulling at the earring and his robust *gaṇa*-like look wearing *kākapakṣa* hairstyle on the head, are very striking.[6] The similarity is so unmistakable that Gorkshakar writes "but for its findspot and difference in the stone, the image could be easily accepted as from Śāmalājī". Gorkshakar accepts the affinity and contemporaneity between Shivdi and Śāmalājī, and also the influence of Shivdi (the loop type waistband) in the drapery at Śāmalājī, and their independent growth in western

fig. 233. Mātr̥kā Indrāṇī, dancing mode, eighth century, Kanauj.

India, but does not specify the magnitude of high Gupta classicism and its inheritance absorbed by this school. Gorkshakar finds it difficult to lend credence to the theory that disbanded groups of sculptors from Ajantā moved in to provide labour for the new undertakings, which were coming up in the region of Bombay Islands. The Parel Aṣṭamūrti and Gharapurī Maheśamūrti are products of the distinctive local guild and outstanding examples of contemporary sculptural art in this area.[7]

Exploring and assessing the stimulus that Ajantā sent to the surrounding area in terms of style and iconography, I accidentally observed the *viṭa–nāyikā–nāyaka* group on the doorways of Caves 4, 5 and 20 at Ajantā, which represents a portly, dwarfish comical figure carrying a wavy, crooked walking stick, *kuṭilaka*, and dallying with the *nāyikā* or attending upon the couple. It is not easy to assess whether Ajantā sent this stimulus to Mandsaur Khilchipura pillars, Kekind and Roḍā, where this image type is emerging, but the simultaneous representation cannot be overlooked. The elements of *śr̥ṅgāra* and *hāsya* overlap here, along with it theatrical themes enter into artistic illustration. This also throws light on secular life, which became the source of subject matter for the contemporary dramas. The course of transmission of this iconography from Ajantā to Roḍā is a matter of 300 years but its immediate dissemination to Mandsaur region and then to Kekind is not insignificant.

While exploring secular subject matter, even Deccan influence from Amarāvatī and Nāgārjuna-koṇḍa should be explored, since they assign significance to bracket *śālabhañjikā* and couples or *mithuna*s which punctuate the narrative scenes from the life of Buddha. The characteristic *daṇḍapakṣa* or *nūpurapādikā* posture is seen at Nāgarjunkoṇḍa which is noticed at Ajantā and Roḍā.

Roḍā *devāṅganās* are characterized by broad pelvic region and transparent drapery with inner edge of the lower garment hanging from one side. They also wear waist ornament with chains hanging on the thigh which the Koṭyarka Mātr̥kās also adorn themselves with. The links can also be drawn in the *dhammilla* type of hairstyle in which a huge bun is tied over the head encircled with some beaded ornament. In fact, this style continues from Deogaṛh to Ābanerī in western Rajasthan up to the eighth and ninth centuries on sculptures of Gurjara–Pratihāras (*fig.* 233). The sash, so characteristically flying over the head of the *gandharvī* at Sondhani, and hanging from the right arm of the *cāmaradhāriṇī* from Akoṭā of the mid-eighth century CE, is seen at Koṭyarka, Aṁjhara and Roḍā as well. One can recall the flower-holding female figures from Mandsaur, Aṁjhara and Roḍā in the same light. Despite the ornamentation, which is rapidly increasing, the female form has a serene grace and dignified countenance.

fig. 234. *Dvārapāla*, eleventh century, Atru Kota Museum, Rajasthan.

The period between the sixth and eighth centuries witnessed the rule of the great Harṣavardhana of Kannauj in northern India. In the west the Gurjara–Pratihāras under Haricandra and his sons, consolidated their political power and fostered cultural activities, which suffered a temporary setback during the Hūṇa inroads. The seventh century was also the age in which Maitraka power was at its height. Śilāditya I, the Dharmāditya, occupied the throne towards the close of the sixth century (sometime after CE 580). The latter was a man of learning, piety and a great patron of art, with the result cultural activities received a great impetus and continued to flourish during the next century.

In Lāṭa, the period was marked by the rule of the Gurjaras of Bharuch and Nandipuri that began some time in the latter half of the sixth century CE. The boundaries of the Maitrakas of Vallabhi in the north and Mālwā in the north-east, can be very well imagined. If the founder of the Bharuch line was one of the sons of Haricandra of Bhīnmāl and Mandor, as appears likely, then relation with Mārwāṛ too would be certain, so that these parts formed a cultural unit.[8]

Examining the sculptural style from historical perspective lends credence to conclusions drawn on stylistic basis. Let us examine some

fig. 235. Lady holding lotus, fragment, Atru Kota Museum, Rajasthan.

regional styles of the ninth and tenth centuries which emerged from the post-Gupta medieval form.

A Brief Survey of Regional Styles in Western India

After surveying the post-Gupta sculptural style at various sites in western India, let us concentrate on the major ninth- and tenth-century stylistic groups, which when examined microscopically, bear the stamp of individuality and maintain some unique indentities.

Marumaṇḍala shows a continuous stylistic development with Osiā in the eighth century; Auwa, Lamba, Harṣa in the ninth century and Kekind, Phalodī, Pālī in the tenth century. In the Medapāṭa region, Jagat and Chittor have sculptural examples from the eighth and ninth centuries, while a full culmination of their regional style comes in the tenth century. Chittor has a continuous stylistic development which in itself can be studied to illustrate the beginning of medieval idioms and its degeneration in the thirteenth-fourteenth centuries. Medapāṭa curiously has more stylistic affinity with Gurjara than Marū, and therefore, at sites such as Tusā, Jagat, Ekaliṅgajī and Nāgdā the influence of Marū is much less. Medapāṭa in itself, under Guhila dominion, shows a rich efflorescence of sculptural development in conjunction with architecture (*figs.* 234, 236).

Thc Uparamāla region has its own variation of Mahā-Marū style seen at Menal, Amvan, Badoli and Atru, bearing sophistication and superb carving.

The north Gujarat comes into action more spiritedly with the rise of the Solaṅkīs of Anhilpur Pāṭan, while the style of architecture and sculpture that developed in this period (not necessarily under the aegis of the Solaṅkīs) saw the major confluence of two strong stylistic trends, the Marū and the Gurjara. This confluence does not have its political parallel with the glory of the Solaṅkīs, although the later rulers like Siddharāja and Kumārapāla, were not only great patrons of sculpture but also were wielding power over a wide area infiltrating into Mālwā as well as Gopagiri. The major sites of Marū–Gurjara[9] style of architecture and sculpture are Moḍherā, Pāṭan, Siddhapur, Ābu, Kumbhariā, Vaḍnagar, which are within the diameter of the capital itself. The outlaying areas where this influence transmigrated are Kirāḍu, Chittor, Atru, Ghumlī, Sejakpur, Thān and Prabhās Paṭan, etc. In Kutch there is already a presence of Gurjara style of the earlier centuries at Koṭai, Kerākoṭ and Kaṇṭhkoṭ, which gives a clear scope for the development of Marū–Gurjara in the adjoining area of Saurāṣṭra.

fig. 236. Sva-stana-sparśā, Saccīyamātā Temple, Osiā.

Paramāra style in Mālwā and Vāgaḍa is particularly significant for its distinct identity observable at sites such as Mandsaur, Arthuṇā, Jhālarāpāṭan, Indore, and Udaipur in particular. The sites of Kirāḍu, Choṭan in the extreme western part of Rajasthan, represents the Paramāra idiom retained even though the style passes on to Marū–Gurjara phase.

The central Indian style is represented by the Dāhala region temples of Nohṭā, Marai, Damoh, Gurgī, Sohāgpur, which designate Kaḷacuri–Cedi idiom. In the Jejākabhukti region, the major sites are situated at Khajurāho. The sculptures of Candella style evolve out of the Cedi style and so the tradition of sculpture is quite superior in this region. In the entire sculptural contingent from central India, the most unique style is represented by the sculptures of Kaḍwāhā, Terāhī, Gyāraspur, Paḍhāvalī, Suhāniā and Gwalior — the Gopagiri style of Kacchapaghātas. Their sculptural form is heavy despite their plasticity. The proportions are bulbous and contours are rounded. This makes their style distinct and noticeable.

Before plunging into finding stylistic typologies and the development of a generic idiom of a sub-region or a dynastic school, it is imperative to mention that the manner in which the iconography-imagery of the *devāṅganā* has developed, its stylistic development does not correspond to the same development; even for that matter, the architecture. In my view, sculptural form has its own, developmental path, its own manner and its determinism is intrinsic or immanent. It develops irrespective of the architecture that gives it scope and direction, growing in an unhampered way. Thus, sculpture comes into "being" on medieval temple architecture by finding its place on *maṇḍovara*, pillar, *devakoṣṭha*, *vitāna,* etc. thereby the entire temple gets draped and symbolically enriched.

Defining the "Medieval" Form

The sculptures of western and central India should be studied in stylistic and geographic homogeneity and not in isolation. The common heritage of this vast area, must be considered a prime force behind the widespread use of simpler motifs and modes of expression. The kindred patterns are due to the presence of itinerant craftsmen, who travelled from site to site.[10]

The sculptural styles of medieval period between the eighth and twelfth centuries stem out of the combination of local idioms and Gupta heritage which can be identified in the Gurjara–Pratihāra style at Osiā, Roḍā, Kekind, Telīkā Mandir (Gwalior) and finally at Kannauj (*fig.* 233). But the regional styles also branch off from the common heritage received from Gupta and Gurjara–Pratihāra, which eventually lead to a dozen stylistic types or variations from site to site and region to region. Even though the homogeneity can be felt in their general disposition, by carefully observing their proportions and physiognomy, coiffure and ornamentation, posture and gesture, the individual trends could be identified. Classifying the styles based on sites, the following key styles emerge: (a) Harṣagiri, (b) Badoli, (c) Tusā, Jagat, (d) Kirāḍu, Moḍherā, (e) Khajurāho, (f) Kaḍwāhā, (g) Pālī, (h) Ṭoṭeśvara and (i) Chittorgaṛh. The Marū–Gurjara

(facing page)
fig. 237. *Mātṛkā* with broken arms, Nīlakaṇṭha temple, Kekind.

combination offers yet another range of sculptural styles represented by the images on Rānī Vāv, Sunak, Sander, Ābu, Moḍherā *naṭa-maṇḍapa*, Badoli *naṭa-maṇḍapa*; Gwalior, Bahū Temple; and Ghumlī, Navalakhā temple.

Very early on, Stella Kramrisch observed two major trends namely, Gujarātī and Rājpūt in the western Indian schools. The qualities she ascribes to them are:

a. Strained motion, over-stressed curves and a tendency to become angular,

b. The curves of the limbs and body frequently deflect from the convex into the concave, and this the more the later the date of the relief,

c. The slender and rounded limbs are bent in sharp angles and seem to split the linear composition into many fragments. Their joints act the same time as so many centres where nervous energy is bundled up and from where it radiates to its next station,

d. The treatment of accessories, like jewellery, has a tendency to become flat and sharply edged, or else by contrast the volume of such devices is even exaggerated and gives them an undue prominence, heavy, intricate and dissociated from the body and from the plastic context as a whole,

e. The material of the major part of the sculpture (white marble) lent itself to being worked to the utmost possibilities of nervy fragility. Over-wrought gestures and positions not only express an almost unbearable inner tension, more and more stress, but also increasingly rigid as time goes on, and

f. The central Indian trends or sculptural styles are mingled with the tendencies of the east and the west.

The Candella sculpture does not have the nervous elegance of the westernmost branch or the earth-bound futility of the Rājpūt type. An intensity near to violence clasps the modelling with sharply curved outlines. This is flattened out or else it conceals under its tightness.

The modelling is stagnant and renders the softness of the flesh to control it from flattening out.[11]

The above enumeration of Stella Kramrisch's perceptive formulations on "medieval" quality of the life of sculptural form, indicates various stages of development, almost nearing stagnation. Our aim is to discern the qualities of sculptural styles, which are in transition and are about to get heavy, drowsy, flat and angular. This gradual movement towards degeneration threatens our study as we traverse the region looking for that "medieval quality" which flowers today and withers tomorrow. Apparent similarity in figural conception of Udaipur–Ḍūṅgarpur region of the sixth-seventh century with Osiā and Roḍā sculpture of the eighth-ninth century, clearly signify that the short, heavy and fleshy type of figures, having broad pelvic region and full round breasts with a heavy hairdo, was the model in this region. At Osiā though, one comes across a different variation of the broad pelvic type, which is the short torso long-legged variety. On the Harihara I doorway at Osiā such figures are placed in *svastika pada*. They are slender-armed compared with Roḍā Temple 6 *devāṅganā*s, although their coiffure is very heavy and imposing.

The other type which is broad and full but more elongated than the previous one, with a not so broad pelvic region, is found at Jagat, Tusā Ābanerī (*fig.* 238) and Kekind (*fig.* 237). In fact, the Tusā sculptures are comparable with Lakṣmaṇa Temple sculptures of Khajurāho, while Kekind figures are really very slender. They are tall, well composed, dynamically charged and highly plastic. Their sophistication is unique. It hints at a guild, which was masterly but rare. Jagat and Tusā sculptures can be called "sculpture of environment" using Focillon's formulation,[12] since they are not bound by *rathika* frames; they move about, bend and flex their bodies over their axes. They articulate the body movements creating ever-changing profiles. When studied singly or in totality of the other sculptures on the *jaṅghā*, they appear to move in rhythmic undulations. This quality of "medieval efflorescence of sculpture" is celebrated at many sites such as Khajurāho, Udayeśvara and Mt. Ābu, in their distinctive ways.

fig. 238. Capital pillar *in situ*, *devāṅganā* with flower garland, *vita*, note similarity with Roḍā, ninth century, Abaneri, Rajasthan.

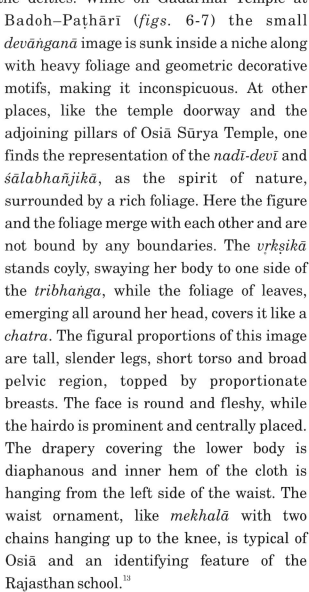

Analysis of Some Major Stylistic Trends

The fascination for the female form in medieval sculpture on the temple begins from the ninth century at sites like Osiā, Harihara group I (*figs.* 1-4) where the figures of the *devāṅganās* are as profuse as the sculptures of the deities. While on Gadarmal Temple at Badoh–Paṭhārī (*figs.* 6-7) the small *devāṅganā* image is sunk inside a niche along with heavy foliage and geometric decorative motifs, making it inconspicuous. At other places, like the temple doorway and the adjoining pillars of Osiā Sūrya Temple, one finds the representation of the *nadī-devī* and *śālabhañjikā*, as the spirit of nature, surrounded by a rich foliage. Here the figure and the foliage merge with each other and are not bound by any boundaries. The *vṛkṣikā* stands coyly, swaying her body to one side of the *tribhaṅga*, while the foliage of leaves, emerging all around her head, covers it like a *chatra*. The figural proportions of this image are tall, slender legs, short torso and broad pelvic region, topped by proportionate breasts. The face is round and fleshy, while the hairdo is prominent and centrally placed. The drapery covering the lower body is diaphanous and inner hem of the cloth is hanging from the left side of the waist. The waist ornament, like *mekhalā* with two chains hanging up to the knee, is typical of Osiā and an identifying feature of the Rajasthan school.[13]

It is noticeable that the eighth- and ninth-century sculptures at Osiā have a monumentality of conception, which vanishes in the tenth century and later. But Osiā is the first site where sculptures occupy the *maṇḍovara*, and begin to pulsate the space of the *ratha*, *pratiratha*, *karṇa* walls with their presence. They begin to absorb light, and create shadows as the sun's rays change their direction, imparting ever-changing fabric design to the architectural edifice. One has only to wait for the tenth-eleventh-century development of the *maṇḍovara*, to fathom the skill of the expert sculptors and architectural planners.

The Ghaṭeśvara Mahādeva Temple at Badoli serves as an intermediary step, between the sculptural interpretations of Osiā and the later, more flamboyant styles of Harṣagiri and Jagat. Post-Gupta overtones still persist but are not so strong, even though the overall handling of the imagery is reminiscent of Osiā.

The imagery of the *devāṅganā* is not represented on the *maṇḍovara*, which is bare save for the central *bhadra* niche, but the pillars have some of the finest examples of "space as an environment" represented in the gestures and postures of the *devāṅganā*s. According to Focillon[14] "the space as an environment" is indicated when there is scattering of volumes, interplay of voids, sudden and unexpected perforations, modelling of multiple, tumbling planes which absorb light and shade. Thus, on the pillars the "space as an environment" experiment begins at Badoli, which by the tenth-century capture the whole *maṇḍovara* and run riot with the sculptural form (*fig.* 242).

The figures represent vibrant youthfulness. The forms of the gently curving bodies flow into each other, and there are no sharp angles to break the movement.[15] The proportions are more streamlined, the solidity of the mass prominently discernible. The smooth finish of the surface creates the finest tactile urge, evoking the feel of real flesh.

The three-dimensional projection of the *devāṅganā* figures from the shaft of the pillar, emerge out of the main stone mass and turn around the axis, in sudden and surprising manner. This kind of flexion and axial movement in the body is for the first time found at Badoli which is probably the first ever attempt made by any sculptor at animating the human form.

The crispness of the figural contour, precision in rendering the details of the face, ornaments and hairdo, and the general treatment of the solid human flesh, seen at Badoli are also observable at Atru. The Atru master sculptors have chosen a very tall image as the model for the *devāṅganā* figures (*figs.* 234, 236). The only difference in Badoli and Atru sculptural proportions is the slender, ethereal almost vapourous "content" of the stone mass of the Atru figures, which is distinct from Badoli. More examples of Badoli idiom are likely and have to be located, but by itself this style leaves a strong imprint.

The Harṣagiri sculptures after renovation, have now been installed on the inner side of the sanctum. The *devāṅganā* figures at Harṣagiri are the epitomes of beauty (*fig.* 28). They are *devāṅganā*s, *vṛkṣikā*s, *saṅgītavādinī*s and devotees, who are lined up in venerating postures. A new facial type was introduced here which was accepted at Gyāraspur and Khajurāho. The flexions and sudden projections of the body movements as found on Badoli, are not to be seen here. They are mostly standing in a relaxed contraposto, striking *trisra*, *dvibhaṅga*, *tribhaṅga* and such other postures. They remain strongly aligned to the wall surface, but breathe a gentle air of relaxed mood. The langour of the "medieval" stylistic idiom, has arrived at Harṣagiri as the *devāṅganā* sculptures exhibit a degree of loosened mass. It is often noticed that even though the contours are sharp and details are minutely worked out, the form is still contained and collected, which restrains the undulations, and does not break the continuity of planes. Thus, at Harṣagiri, there is a lingering of classicism, but also a relaxation of the restraint of the classical form.

In the context of Harṣagiri, Atru and Khajurāho, one observes a "mannered" style emerging.[16] The suppleness of the medieval sculptural form, the attenuation and elegant poise of the tenth-century sculptures, represent the height of medieval idiom, (comparable to "maniera" of Mannerism in the European Art)[17] which is a phenomenon of post-classical stylization (*fig.* 235).

Lanius observes Harṣagiri and Jagat sculptures as direct descendants of the Badoli style, and not an isolated phenomenon on the basis of some similarity of ornaments and rendering of details like beads and jewellery. But I beg to differ here since Lanius has got carried away by the minor details and overlooked the general conception of form, proportions, volume, movement and innervation of the organic quality. Extending the idea of the mannered style of medieval sculpture, two features need to be highlighted:

(1) the axes, profiles, proportions and volumes, sculpture conceived as *figura serpentinata*, and

(2) space as an environment, activation of movement within the form, and the total vibration of the architectural surface.[18]

The Ambikā Temple at Jagat represents the high sophistication of the early tenth century in Medapāṭa region. Jagat is seen at the end of an era, which represents the last stage of individual stylistic innovations, for from this time on, the figures become more and more stereotyped.[19] This may be partially true, because at Khajurāho and other sites of central and western India, etc. the style is still going to keep our attention engaged for its individual idioms represented by Ṭoṭeśvara, Pālī, Gurgī, Kaḍwāhā, Arjula and such other sites.

The Jagat sculptures, like the Badoli and Harṣagiri, are not bound by *rathika* frames (*fig.* 128). They stand on a tiny pedestal, and above each of them are found couples, *gandharva*s, *ṛṣi*s, etc. The figures are bulky and heavy, they are tall but not supple like the Harṣagiri figures. But the flexions of their bodies, especially in *kanduka-krīḍā* and *markaṭaceṣṭā*, are more three-dimensional and bend around the axes. The quality of carving is highly crisp, including the representation of ornaments, hairdo, drapery and body contours.

The sculptures of Tusā Sūrya Temple (*fig.* 163), in my view, are more energetic, charged with movement, and contain a bulky yet dignified form. The terseness of the sculptural volume is more discernible in Tusā *devāṅganā* sculptures than Jagat. Their postures, e.g. of the *kanduka-krīḍā* and *alasā*, are highly charged, the body flexions and movements are exaggerated, and extended much beyond the figure, thereby activating the *maṇḍovara* space. For Jagat, Lanius has rightly observed, that they have begun to show a slight boredom and lethargy, as they preen and pose across the walls like the bird's plumes. The forms have become more architectural, and the vitality and spontaneity of the preceding centuries have begun to disappear, to be replaced by a certain regimentation, stiff angularity and mannered portrayal.[20]

This is especially true of the "Marū–Gurjara" sculptural style, a homogeneous style, which developed out of the amalgamation of Marū and Gurjara, probably by a family of sculptors and *sthapati*s, which was carried on for at least 500 years in western India. This merger has wide implications which not only indicate the high drama of stylistic coalescence in architecture and sculpture, but also give birth to a new style. The Marū–Gurjara sculptural style, can be studied at Rānī Vāv, Moḍherā, Kirāḍu, Chittorgaṛh, Sejakpur, Sunak and then in various stages of deterioration. The Marū–Gurjara *maṇḍapa* and *garbha-gṛha maṇḍovara* are very characteristically designed, with elaborately patterned *rathika*s, *vyāla*s, diamond and foliage motifs, which punctuate the niche figures containing deities, *dikpāla*s and *devāṅganā*s. This overwhelming response of the architecture, at integrating sculpture within its fabric, binds the sculpture within its boundaries. But the sculptors design the forms in such a way that they do not feel limited, and quite often the figures bend, sway and turn with their limbs jutting out of the boundary spaces. This can be observed at Rānī Vāv (*fig.* 26), Chittorgaṛh, Kirāḍu (*fig.* 40) and Sunak (*fig.* 43). The Marū–Gurjara idiom as it is represented at Kirāḍu, can be placed in between Jagat and Moḍherā, which mark a century between mid-tenth and mid-eleventh.

The Kirāḍu style has its unique ponderous mass and stylization, which overshadows the Paramāra idiom. The same situation is observed at Moḍherā. There are many sculptural styles on one and the same site, despite the homogeneity of iconographic programming of the Sun Temple. It is quite probable that one of the *śilpī*s may have come from Kirāḍu and the rest from the adjoining north Gujarat and western Rajasthan besides the local geniuses. The Rānī Vāv sculptures could be called the right specimens of medieval style, as represented by Marū–Gurjara. The proportions are slender, contours are smooth, physiognomy is sharp and angular, represented by two or three guild styles. But the innervation of the form as Stella Kramrisch would observe, makes the motion strained, and the plasticity gives way to a flaccid form, heading towards ossification.

The sculptures of the late eleventh century onwards found on Sander (*fig.* 42), Ghumlī, Sejakpur, Ābhāpur (*fig.* 45) Kumbhariā, and Chittorgaṛh, represent the degenerating stage setting into the medieval style. The sculptures of the *devāṅganā*s are articulated with exaggerated movements, flexing the body around multiple axes, but this does not elevate the nature of the form. The plastic form of the figure and the ornament are both rendered with the same precision and aloofness which recalls the arrival of ossification. Such a representation is peculiar not only to Marū–Gurjara, but is also observable in central India.

While discussing the central Indian sculptural style, besides Khajurāho which is a prominent example, I have also focused on the adjoining regions of Dāhala, Gopagiri, Kacchapaghāta and Dakṣiṇa Kosala, which are also equally significant, and show trends of individual innovations.

The sculptures of Gurgī (*fig.* 127), Kaḍwāhā (*fig.* 220), Suhāniā (*fig.* 219) and Padhavali, represent an understanding of form, which is not tense as suggested by Kramrisch for the western Indian Gujarātī style, but flaccid and unanimated. The figures are bulbous, flesh deposited in such a way that arms and legs do not taper at the ends, while the waist is not capable of much exaggerated movements, although Gurgī and Kaḍwāhā do represent highly complex figural structure, which tend to come to life due to their liveliness. In terms of organic unity, Gurgī sculptures are equally masterly, compared to the sculptures of Lakṣmaṇa or Kandarīya Mahādeva at Khajurāho.

Rightly observed by Parimoo[21] in the light of the "mannerist" concept of *figura serpentinata*, Khajurāho sculptures have contortions and swirling body bends around the axes, and extension of the body movements in all the directions in space. The *maṇḍovara* has been filled up by two or three horizontal bands of sculptures. The principle of *figura serpentinata* can be observed in the light of figures placed along each of the vertical bands of *ratha*, *pratiratha*, *salilāntara*, *karṇa* articulations. Comprehending the whole wall in totality and the individual sculpture in detail, they appear to vibrate and pulsate the surface of the temple wall with movement that generates from the *Brahmasūtra* or the central axis of the individual figures. Thus, *figura serpentinata* at individual level, gives rise to dynamism on the entire *maṇḍovara*. The absorption of light and creation of deep shadows, with ever-changing contours, is also the fundamental programme for the Khajurāho masters.

It is thus clearly evident that at Khajurāho, "the tone has been set for the sculpture to dominate". The stone yielded to the chiselling instruments and the hammering hands of the carver, much as it yielded to the yearning emotions of the lovers, especially the *nāyikā*s. The principle of *sthira* and *gati* in the male and female sculptures suggests the idea of conjugation of two opposite principles.[22]

Depiction of the female torso from its back (*figs.* 208, 210, 213) in complex *tribhaṅga* and body bends, bearing "mannerist" elongation and attenuated proportions, have been observed by Parimoo as a pre-occupation of the Gurjara–Pratihāra masters and its continuation in various figures of the later styles in central India especially at Khajurāho. The Pratihāra ideal of feminine beauty epitomized by the Kannauj Mātr̥kās, can be observed at Vaḍaval, Telikā Mandir, Kannauj, Gwalior and Khajurāho (*figs*. 231, 233, 213).

The individual style, proportions and idiom of a region can be observed on the figural sculptures and proportions of Sohāgpur, Pāli, Kodal, Terāhī, Kaḍwāhā, Jañjagīr and some more centres in central India. Qualitatively, they may not be stylistically superior, but in terms of various guild mannerisms, these temple sculptures are outstanding and lend a new meaning to the whole phenomenon of style and its orthogenetic growth.

R.N. Misra in his study on Dāhala sculptures has brought to light a number of references dealing with *śilpī*s, *vijñānika*s, *rūpakāra*s who assisted the *sūtradhāra*s.[23] He distinguishes the specialization of measurer of proportions, sculptors, carvers and designers. Names of generations of Kokaṣa family *sthapati*s, have been brought to light by him. In the light of the above discussion and data, such an information makes the problem of individual style alive and fathomable.

References

1. U.P. Shah, *Western Indian Sculpture and the so-called Gupta Influence: Aspects of Indian Art*, ed. P. Pal, Leiden, 1972, p. 44.
2. P. Pal, *Bulletin of Allen Memorial Art Museum*, vol. 28, no. 2, 1971, p. 115.
3. U.P. Shah, op. cit., 1972, p. 47.
4. Ibid., p. 48.
5. U.P. Shah, *Roḍā na mandiro nā nārī Svarūpo*, Gujarat Dipotsavi Anka, VS 2032.
6. S. Gorkshakar, "Parel Mahādeva Reassessed", *Lalitkala*, 20, New Delhi, 1982, p. 21.
7. Ibid., p. 23.
8. U.P. Shah, *Akoṭā Bronzes*, Bombay, 1959, pp. 64-65.
9. M.A. Dhaky, op. cit., 1975.
10. M.C. Lanius, *Rajasthani Sculpture of the Ninth and Tenth Centuries: Aspects of Indian Art*, ed. P. Pal, Leiden, 1972, pp. 78-84.
11. Stella Kramrisch, *Indian Sculpture*, London, 1933, Indian repr., Delhi, 1981, pp. 105-10.
12. Focillon, *Life of Forms in Art*, 1933.
13. M.C. Lanius, op. cit., 1972, p. 80.
14. Focillon, op. cit., 1933, p. 23.
15. M.C. Lanius, op. cit., 1972, p. 80.
16. Ibid., p. 82.
17. John Shearman, *Mannerism*, London, 1967, repr., 1973.
18. Focillon, op. cit., 1933, p. 82.
19. M.C. Lenius, op. cit., 1972, p. 83.
20. Ibid., p. 83.
21. Ratan Parimoo, "The Aspects of Form and Style in Indian Sculpture", pp. 108-22, *Aspects of Indian Art and Culture, S.K. Sarasvati Commemoration Volume*, ed. Jayanta Chakrabarty, D.C. Bhattacharya, Calcutta, 1983. Also in Ratan Parimoo, *Essays in New Art History Studies in Indian Sculpture*, Delhi, 2000.
22. Ratan Parimoo, "Khajurāho — The Candella Sculptors' Paradise: Is there a Candella Style of Medieval Indian Sculpture? Its sources and Characteristics", *Indian Archaeological Heritage, Soundara Rajan Felicitation Volume,* ed. Margabandhu. Also in Ratan Parimoo, *Essays in New Art History Studies in Indian Sculpture*, Delhi, 2000.
23. R.N. Misra, *Sculptures of Dāhala and Dakṣiṇa Koṣala and their Background*, New Delhi, 1987, p. 132.

8

Iconological and Semiotic Interpretation of the Devāṅganā Motif

Towards Semiosis

THE semiotic method has universal application that opened up a whole range of interpretative possibilities concerning human sciences, literature, art, theatre, music, mass media and the like. The possibilities of more than one meaning evolving out of the signifier–signified relationship has brought analysis of cultural practices (including making art) to another plane.[1] It is not only the subject matter but attributes, characteristics, gestures and postures depicted in the art form as well as its cultural, psychological, historical and other related contexts and motives that collectively contribute to interpretation. The concluding chapter demonstrates the iconological as well as semiotic analyses of the *devāṅganā* motif.

Morris'[2] views of semiosis have been found most suitable in drawing our conclusion here which has three separate dimensions: (a) syntactical dimension of semiosis, (b) semantical dimension of semiosis, and (c) paradigmatical dimension of semiosis. Morris characterizes semiosis as

> a mediated taking account of . . . the designata are what is taken account of, the sign vehicles are the mediators, the interpretants are the taking-account of, and the interpreters are the agents in the process.

Thus, semiosis is the study of the process, participation and relationship between the components, the designata and the related phenomena. This is closely akin to the *abhidhā*, *lakṣaṇā* and *vyañjanā* process postulated by Ānandavardhana.[3] Both shed light on the process of interpretation, how an art work is perceived and what are the various elements which help us to perceive the layers of meaning in an art work.

The syntactical dimension of semiosis is the interrelationship of signs, of which the sign vehicles are products or parts. The syntactic dimension implicates a primary level of sign relationship. *Devāṅganā*s such as *darpaṇā*, *alasā*, *prasādhikā* could be cited here as examples because their iconography suggests their action and its meaning as a primary sign.

While the semantical dimension is the relationship of signs to their designata and so to the objects which they may or do denote and thus the term "denotes" is a primary lexical item in semantics. Here *vasanabhraṁśā*, *markaṭaceṣṭā*, *putravallabhā* type *devāṅganā*s could be cited to denote an abstract quality or a principle. Both *vasanabhraṁśā* and *markaṭaceṣṭā* denote sexuality and eroticism while *putravallabhā* denotes motherhood and love.

The paradigmatic dimension of semiosis deals with the relationship of signs to their interpreters, or more explicitly "with the biotic aspects of semiosis, that is, with all the psychological, biological and sociological phenomena which occur in the functioning of signs". It is governed by paradigmatic rules which state the conditions in the interpreters under which the sign vehicle is a sign, thus providing information about the interpreter. The dominant thesis of psychoanalysis, paradigm and sociology of knowledge, are all applications of the paradigmatic dimension of semiosis. Paradigmatics deals with the functioning of signs as expressions of their interpreters. A clear formulation of paradigmatics presupposes the development of syntax and semantics, as in these latter two the distinction between a descriptive and a pure level in paradigmatics, is crucial in the avoidance of ambiguity and confusion. Here *naṭī–nartakī* type *devāṅganā*s, with links to *devadāsī*s, could be cited that bring the interpretation and the semiotic process in a more wider arena encompassing sociological and psychological spheres. The various paradigmatic constructs prior to the emergence of *devāṅganā*s on temple architecture such as *yakṣī*, *apsaras*, *nadī-devatā* logically and automatically come together as demonstrated in the previous chapters.

According to Saussure,[4] paradigmatic relationship applies to both the signifier as well as the signified and they are all members of a definite category but each is significantly different from the other. He uses these catagories in a broad sense to include both the form and the meaning. Syntagm is a "chain" of interacting signifiers which forms a meaningful whole within a text. In language, a sentence, for instance, is a syntagm of words: so too are paragraphs and chapters. Saussure[5] also refers to syntagm as sequential and can represent spatial relationships. That is where the meaning of the whole *devāṅganā* imagery could be understood against the backdrop of semiotics where the ancient mother goddesses, *yakṣī*s and *nadī-devatā*s form the paradigmatic relationship while the Buddhist, Hindu and Jaina monuments over the years provide the syntactic relationship.

It is truly significant that the principle of *dhvani* in Indian literary criticism is so closely analogous to the semiotic analysis outlined above. The three potential powers of *dhvani*: *abhidhā* (denotative), *lakṣaṇā* (indicative) and *vyañjanā* (suggestive) have their parallel implications in the tripartite levels enunciated by Morris (supra). The *dhvani* theory has already been referred to in Chapter 1, but reiteration of its application to the analysis of the actual *devāṅganā* motif calls for its recollection together with what one understands by the concept of semiotics. The following analysis of the *devāṅganā* imagery from its paradigmatic dimension calls for the secondary or the deeper interpretation, what the *dhvanikāra* would call *vyañjanā*. Having explored and compared individual motifs elaborately in Chapter 6, I now attempt to view the entire range of iconological connotation of these individual motifs in the context of the whole monument collectively. The following analysis (see circular diagram on page 381) has been formulated on the basis of semiotics and *dhvani*, to formulate a macro view of the *devāṅganā* phenomena, sorting individual motifs in a dynamic formula. This schematic diagram helps to view the cultural patterns inherent within the *devāṅganā* matrix from an aerial perspective, where synchronic and diachronic axes converge.

Semiosis of the Devāṅganā Motif

In the preceding chapters, when analysing the *devāṅganā* imagery on medieval Hindu temples of western and central India, I have looked into their postural analysis for the dancer-like imagery of the *devāṅganā*s including their attributes, gestures and main iconography. After analysing their entire imagery, I have collated frequently occurring and shared *devāṅganā* motifs throughout western India which led me to begin this study. This drew my attention to tracing the antecedents of *devāṅganā* motifs, since they do not show up in architectural design abruptly. The search for roots of *devāṅganā*s led me to the primeval fertility goddesses, erotically inclined *yakṣī*s, *vṛkṣikā*s and *śālabhañjikā*s then to *apsaras*es and *nadī-devatā*s, as visually represented on architectural monuments. The search did not end with documenting the visual forms, but went on to explore the imagery of *apsaras* and *yakṣī* in the Vedas, Purāṇas,

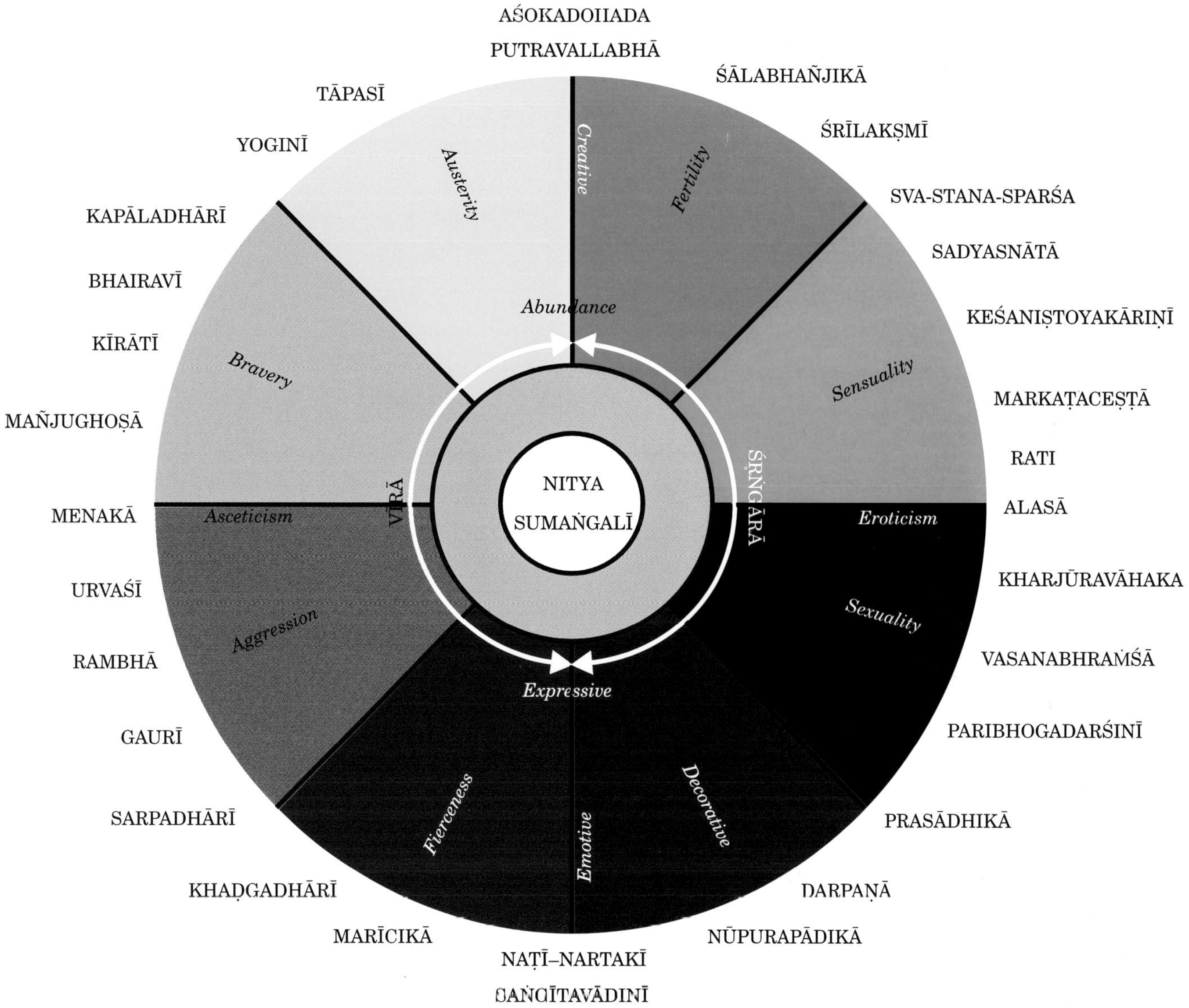

Diagramatic analysis of the *devāṅgaṇā* motif

Epics and the classical Nāṭya and Kāvya. The architectural texts also enriched our understanding of this motif and its integration with architectural structures. Hence, the visual representation on temple architecture refers to the syntagmatic dimension in which similarity of postures, gestures and attributes imply the parallelism in their imagery at a primary level. While the literary data supports the content with cultural and poetic meaning, that designates literary and poetic connotations to their gestures.

In the present section, I try to formulate the paradigmatic analysis, in which, on the basis of visual and literary imageries, the iconological and tertiary level meaning is formulated by branching the imageries into four categories: "ascetic", "erotic", "creative" and "emotive". These are the four overarching values or broad categories which signify dialectical concepts in human nature and society that individuals within it manifest. The "ascetic" and "erotic" are diametrically opposite concepts but not mutually exclusive, since extreme resultant of eroticism can be asceticism (Pārvatī's *pañcāgni sādhanā tapa*) while the "creative" can become "emotive" when overcome by passion (Śiva's *tāṇḍava* dance at Tillai and destruction of Kāma). Thus, fundamental concepts have existed in mythic contexts from ancient times and to stumble upon them in the imagery of *devāṅganā*s is a pleasant coincidence. The imagery of *devāṅganā* thus oscillates between two polarities or extremes which are diametrically opposite, one acting as the cause of the other, but co-existing physically on one and the same monument. I have also attempted to see a dynamic relationship in these images, one that allows homogeneous reordering. This in my view is a new perspective for interpreting these figures.

The inherently and eternally auspicious *devāṅganā*s are divine and coeval with mortal *devadāsī*s. They are considered eternally married and thus *sumaṅgalī*s whose ability to bestow good luck and remove traces of bad luck are considered timeless. The *devāṅganā*s are protective powers personified, embodied by beautiful women, charged either by *śṛṅgārika* or by *vīra* emotions. Looking at their imagery more closely, I found their diametrically opposite characters and plotted them on a vertical, horizontal axis within a circle with the axis intersecting at the centre, and the characters merging or overlapping their imageries like intermediate shades of primary and secondary colours on a "colour circle" (refer *fig.* 381). Thus, at the core of this *devāṅganā* circle is the universal centre, neutral gray in colour represented by *nitya-sumaṅgalī*. On the vertical axis, on the periphery of the circle are the cardinal extremes "creative-emotive" (yellow–orange–red) on opposite ends while on the horizontal axis are "erotic-ascetic" (blue–violet–green). With changing shades and evolving colours, intermediate *devāṅganā*s change their shades accordingly thus coming full circle sharing iconological meaning which changes slightly with each *devāṅganā* type. Hence the imagery not only oscillates between the two polarities but interconnects in a circular manner. The "creative" is the earliest and the most primeval aspect of the *devāṅganā* imagery, whose origin goes as far back as the *yakṣī-śālabhañjikā* and the "woman and tree" motif of the pre-historic times. Thus in this category, I have placed *putravallabhā*, *aśokadohada* and *śālabhañjikā* imagery, which have clear fecundity–fertility connotation. When the "creative" leans towards the "erotic" which is the logical outcome, the intermediate shades of "abundance" implied by the imageries of *nadī-devatā*, *śrīlakṣmī*, *sva-stana-sparśā* and *sadyasnātā* ensue. This category has potent fertility features, but visually shares the erotic representation of *keśanistoyakāriṇī*, *kharjūravāhaka*, *markaṭaceṣṭā* — imageries with blatant erotic intent. This process accelerates, taking sexual turn, when it becomes more expressive of its emotional undercurrents. The demonstration of emotions are observable in *alasā*, *darpaṇā*, *vasanabhraṁśa*, *nūpurapādikā*, *prasādhikā* and *paribhogadarśinī*. They are almost like dancers depicting certain psychological states by striking dance-like postures which have erotic overtones. The "emotive" category carries within its fold the *naṭī–nartakī/saṅgītavādinī* type of *devāṅganā*s, who are performers of ritual dance and music and strike characteristic postures of classical dance. They are inspired by the *devadāsī* tradition, whose emotive role oscillates between realms of human and the divine alike. They "perform" dance and ritual alike. This completes one half of the circle.

The other half is characterized by *vīra rasa*, vibrant and bold, which oscillates between the terrible and the fierce, characterized by

(Facing page)
fig. 239. Śeṣāsāyī Viṣṇu flanked by *devāṅganā*s, well buttress wall, mid-eleventh century, Rānī Vāv, Pāṭan, Gujarat.

demonstrative actions of *sarpadhārī*, *khaḍgadhārī*, *kirātī*, *bhairavī*, Urvaśī and Menakā, holding bow–arrow and slaying the opponent. Their postures are dance-like and charged with passion. The other end of the "ascetic" is the *yoginī*, represented by *tāpasī* and *kapāladhārī* characters, denoting extreme renunciation. They represent austere notions suggesting the ability of the woman to sacrifice, renounce and destroy, an equally powerful aspect of her "will" in comparison with her "will" to create. Thus "asceticism" and "eroticism", "creativity" and "emotionality" contribute to completing the circle of *devāṅganā*s, whom we broadly classified as *śṛṅgāra* and *vīra*. Ingalls has collated two verses which liken the woman in separation (*viyoginī*) to a woman in mystic trance (*yoginī*), thus drawing a parallel between sex and asceticism, that is much indulged into elsewhere by the classical poets,

> Averse from eating, turned from every object of the senses, and this too, that your eye is fixed in trance, again, your mind is single-pointed, and then this silence, and the fact that all the world to you

fig. 240. Śeṣāsāyī Viṣṇu, Rānī Vāv, Pāṭan.

> seems empty: tell me gentle friend, are you a *yoginī* or a *viyoginī*? (No. 703, p. 232)[6]

Another verse makes a pun on the *nāyikā*'s meditative concentration:

> This debility of body and lack of all desire, this fixing of your eye in trance and perfect silence; this state bespeaks a heart fixed on one single object.
>
> What is that one, fair lady, Brahmā or your lover? (No. 715)[7]

The above two verses focus on the close connection between conditions in extreme love-lorn state and asceticism. It is by the *vyañjanā* interpretation that the comparison of the two conditions are paralleled. Thus, the above verses support the circular diagram created to explain the emotional, psychological, sociological and visual forces working in the creation and perpetuation of certain *devāṅganā* imageries.

Devāṅganā on the Temple Maṇḍovara

In the present section, I have attempted to take a closer look at a monument in totality and how the *devāṅganā* images drape them. Is there a logical order of their iconography which dictates the placement of their imagery types in facing a certain direction? Do the *devāṅganā*s have any relation with the *dikpāla*s or the presiding deities of that direction? What light do the texts throw on this issue?

The fact that temples could be Śaiva, Śākta, Saura, Vaiṣṇava or Jaina, provides a new vantage point for studying the role of *devāṅganā*s. While observing the temple site as a symbolic unit or a metaphor in itself, the role of individual

(facing page)
fig. 241 .Wooden door jambs with carved figures of *devāṅganā*s, in continuation of *devāṅganā* imagery in timber architecture, eighteenth century, L.D. Institute Museum, Ahmedabad.

*devāṅganā*s emerges as a micro unit of an *alaṁkāra* or a figure of speech that could be based on suggestion of eroticism, fertility, asceticism and heroism. Coinciding with the presiding cult and functions ascribed to the monument itself by tradition, it would be worthwhile to explore the iconography of *devāṅganā*s from a cultic perspective.

Let us take a look at some monuments such as Jagat, Kekind and Rānī Vāv, to study the pattern of *devāṅganā* placement on the *jaṅghā* of the *maṇḍovara* encircling a temple. Before looking at monuments, one also needs to take note of a textual reference suggesting the manner in which the *jaṅghā* decoration should contain *dikpāla*s and *devāṅganā*s flanking each other and their postures, gestures and attributes. In the *Kṣīrārṇava*, a fifteenth-century text from Gujarat, a chapter is dedicated to the description of a four-faced temple form: *Caturmukha Mahāprāsāda Svarūpādhyāya* which lists 32 *devāṅganā*s, including the order of their appearance, placement on the wall and their actions. They should measure six or eight arms in height, be depicted in dancing postures and looking down, either in *lāsya* or *tāṇḍava* mode, holding *nṛtya hasta*s and representing a festive mood on *jinālaya* along with *dikpāla*s. Yama should be placed in the south, Kubera in the north, Indra in the east and Varuṇa in the west. In the south-west place Kṣetrapāla Nirṛti, in the north-west place Vāyu in dancing posture, his movements should be circular and *tāṇḍava* type, his clothes should be shown fluttering. In the north-east place Īśāna with eight arms while Agni in the south-east. The *devāṅganā* should be placed in *pradakṣiṇā* order starting with Menakā in Īśāna. Rambhā–Indra in *āliṅgana-mudrā* should follow with Rambhā holding an arrow and *vīṇā* in her hands. Even Urvaśī playing flute should be placed here in the *agni-koṇa*. In the south, along with Yama, should be placed Trilocana playing cymbals and Kāmarūpa in dancing pose. In the Nirṛti, place Candrāvalī in *añjalī hasta* while in the west along with Varuṇa place Rambhā holding bow and killing an enemy. On her left place Mañjughoṣā wielding swords. Along with Kubera in the north, place Padminī holding her right hand near the head and dancing (*Kṣīrārṇava*, 82-102). This shows that along with every *dikpāla*, a particular *devāṅganā* is prescribed, but this scheme is not strictly adhered to by sculptors. The above could be treated as a guideline because sculptors seem to have taken liberty in making their favourite choices. Let us observe the arrangement pattern on the Ambikā Temple at Jagat.

Ambikā Temple, Jagat

The elegant temple built during the reign of Guhila ruler Alata or his son Naravāhana of Mewāṛ is datable to CE 960, and stylistically similar to the Śiva Temple, Koṭai; the Lakulīśa Temple, Ekaliṅgajī (CE 971) and the Durgā Temple, Unwas (CE 959).[8] The *devāṅganā* sculptures are placed circumambulating the entire temple at the *jaṅghā* level starting with the *mukhacatuṣkī* and *mukhamaṇḍapa* to the *antarāla-maṇḍapa* and the actual *garbha-gṛha*, barring the transept windows of the *maṇḍapa* projection. The main *devakoṣṭhas* contain images of Durgā Mahiṣāsuramardinī, Sarasvatī, Kṣemaṅkarī and Pārvatī, which are the major manifestations of Goddess Durgā.

The *dviratha* planned temple consists of major *phālanā*s or pilasters which contain *dikpāla*s, *devāṅganā*s, *vyāla*s and smaller *devāṅganā*s standing on elephants projecting out of the wall facets. On the *udgama* level above every *devāṅganā* and *vyāla* sculptures are placed a smaller seated group of figures which represent musicians, dancers, amorous couples and religious rituals. It appears that these groups correspond with the *devāṅganā* imagery and lend meaning to it there by enhance the meaning implicit in the attributes and actions of the *devāṅganā*s.

Fertility and eroticism are guiding principles of the south wall. This *raison d'être* can be discerned in motifs of *nūpurapādikā*, *khaḍgadhārī kapāladhārī*, *vasanabhraṁśā*, *sva-stana-sparśā*, *paribhogadarśinī* and *darpaṇā*, which are inducers of active passion and consummate vigour. Amorous and kissing couples are placed above *devāṅganā*s — *vasanabhraṁśā* and *sva-stana-sparśā*. This is exactly on the *antarāla* which denotes the joining of the *garbhagṛha* with the *maṇḍapa*. This seems to be a case of double entendre and illustrated graphically (*fig.* 14).

The south wall contains *putravallabhā*, *padminī*, *āmralumbī*, *kanduka-krīḍā*, *alasā* and *vasanabhraṁśā* whereas the west wall represents *keśanistoyakāriṇī* and *alasā devāṅganā*s (*figs.* 128, 141). Attempting an interpretation of the entire *devāṅganā* imagery, one can perceive that as the devotee takes the *pradakṣiṇā* direction from the south to the north through the west and back to the east, he first comes across *devāṅganā*s with erotic overtones. This leads him from the realm of the sensual to the inner quest and introspection and finally to cleansing (represented by *darpaṇā*, *keśanistoyakāriṇī*), which then leads to a pure, unconcealed and liberated state (*padminī*, *kanduka-krīḍā* and *vasanabhraṁśā*).

fig. 242. Pillar representing *devāṅganā* imagery all around it, Ghaṭeśvara Temple, Badoli.

Śiva Temple, Kekind

This late tenth-century temple from Rajasthan of Marū–Gurjara style brings to light the first-ever representation of Sapta Mātṛkās on the temple *maṇḍovara* (*fig.* 11) in conjunction with *devāṅganā*s. To my knowledge, this occurrence is not only unique but unmatchable. The *maṇḍovara* design is not repeated, the extraordinary creative ability of the sculptors and architects who worked on this monument is unbeatable. The entire *jaṅghā* is divided into prominently shaped *devakoṣṭha*s. On the *karṇa* position, *dikpāla*s are placed while *devāṅganā*s can be seen on boldly projecting *pratiratha*s. The recesses contain images of four-armed Saptamātṛkās with children who are identified with the help of *āyudha*s and *vāhana*s. The faces are badly mutilated but some *devāṅganā* imagery is identifiable such as, *alasā*, *markaṭaceṣṭā*, *keśanistoyakāriṇī*, *padminī* and *nartakī*. The imagery is difficult to discern due to mutilation but stylistically sculptures of Kekind seem to form a group by themselves which can at the most be compared with the sculptures of Atru for their slim, slender vertically accentuated figures (*fig.* 235).

fig. 243. Large *naṭa-maṇḍapa*, late tenth century, Kirāḍu, Rajasthan.

Rānī Vāv, Pāṭan

This is a magnificent monument and only one of its kind. There are several subterranean architectural monuments all over Gujarat and Rajasthan, but the sculptural decoration and iconographical harmony between its socio-religious purpose and its representation found on this monument are simply unsurpassable. This *vāv* or *vāvaḍī* is the most enormous building of the Solaṅkī period ascribed to the patronage of queen Udayamatī of Bhīmadeva I of late eleventh century CE. This seven-storeyed architecture below ground level has two parts, the well and the tank. On walls of the tank and the well, one observes the placement of sculptures of *devāṅganā*s, *dikpāla*s with their spouses, Daśāvatāra and Śeṣaśāyī forms of Viṣṇu, Pārvatī, Durgā, Mātṛkās, *mithuna*s and Gaṇeśa. The buttress walls facing north and south remind the observer of a typical Solaṅkī temple *maṇḍovara* especially because they alternate with sculptures of *devāṅganā*s (*fig*. 26).

Rānī Vāv has certain features which immediately caught my attention in the light of the representation of *devāṅganā* imagery,[9] namely the presence of the Śeṣaśāyī Viṣṇu, Mātṛkās and *mithuna*s in conjunction with all forms of *devāṅganā*s and *dikpāla*s with their *śakti*s on a monument which is traditionally connected with fertility rites and rituals, and is primarily a source of nourishment for humans and animals alike.

Sculptures placed on walls of terraces and those on walls of the shaft of the well are divided and need to be looked at separately. They are clearly arranged in tiers and rows, alternating with a deity. At the centre of a row, there is Gaṇeśa at the bottom, followed by three Śeṣaśāyī Viṣṇu images one above the other surmounted by Viṣṇu in *yoga-mudrā*. This strong iconographical feature of placement of Śeṣaśāyī form on water reservoirs has been pointed out elsewhere by Ratan Parimoo.[10] Besides Viṣṇu there are sculptures of Mātṛkās and Daśāvatāra, Pārvatī on iguana, *mithuna*s and other gods with their *śakti*s. The reclining Śeṣaśāyī Viṣṇu images are flanked by rows of *devāṅganā*s in different moods.

(facing page)
fig. 244. *Maṇḍapa* with ornately carved pillars, 1043 CE, Pārśvanātha temple, Kumbhāriā,

At the level of the first Śeṣaśāyī image from top, notice *devāṅganā*s such as *darpaṇā-prasādhikā*, *vīrā* holding *khaṭvāṅga* and, *kapāla-ḍamarūdhārī* flanking the image of Viṣṇu in deep slumber. Here, opposing imageries of "erotic" and "terrible" types are placed side by side. Whereas in the middle row all erotic, sensuous and fertility-evoking imageries such as *darpaṇā*, *nūpurapādikā*, *ghaṇṭādhārī*, *cāmaradhārī*, *putravallabhā*, *alasā*, etc. are placed. On the level of the third Śeṣaśāyī image, the overtly erotic *nāyikā*s are placed such as *vasanabhraṁśā*, *sva-stana-sparśā*, and a nude *nāyikā* with snakes entwining around her legs, are noticeable. This imagery is unique to Rānī Vāv which I have observed again only at Mārkaṇḍi (Maharashtra) along with a drummer and at Jalasāṅgī (Karnataka). Further study needs to be carried out to find out rituals associated with serpents and the association of female *yoginī*s with them (*figs.* 196, 239, 240).

For fertility and sexuality associated with a *vāv*, where traditionally young newly-married couples are taken after marriage to invoke the power of fecundity to ensure progeny, the sculptor-designer's intent in placing the above detailed *devāṅganā*s is quite obvious. For example, the *keśanistoyakāriṇī devāṅganā* is not only squeezing the hair but her simultaneous action of squeezing her own breast suggests the implicit metaphor (*fig.* 142), so is the *putravallabhā*, who, while playing with the child, plays with the ripe mango fruits leaning towards her. The motif of *kharjūravāhaka* evoking sexuality, has often been noticed at Khajurāho but its popularity at Rānī Vāv, Sunak, and many other sites in the eleventh century and later, testifies the potential generative power of the woman and its evocation through erotic imagery. This motif seems to have travelled from Madhya Pradesh to Gujarat and Rajasthan within 200 years (*figs.* 170, 173, 174, 175, 177, 178, 179).

Devāṅganā on Pillars of the Naṭa-maṇḍapa

In this section, we focus our attention on pillars and especially the *kumbha*, a portion on the base which bear three-quarter-sized images of *devāṅganā*s and their entire imagery. While exploring pillars, one finds an affinity between *nṛtya maṇḍapa* pillars of Badoli, Moḍherā, Kirāḍu and Gwalior. All these sites have independent, free-standing *maṇḍapa*s in front of temples, known generally as *naṭa-maṇḍapa*.

The *devāṅganā* imagery carved on their bases bear notice to the survival of its tradition first on the *maṇḍapa* pillar. It appears quite likely that it was later on adapted for *maṇḍovara* decoration, a case in point is Badoli. I am almost eager to suggest that it is quite likely that the *devāṅganā* imagery was always delincated in timber architectural tradition. Hence, in stone it may have stopped somewhere after the Kuṣāṇa period, but the wood carving tradition on architectural pillars the purpose and the *devāṅganā* imagery continued. Two wooden door jambs from L.D. Institute Museum, Ahmedabad (*fig.* 241) represent similar *devāṅganā* imagery on its pillars as can be found on the developed *maṇḍovara* of the Nāgara temple architecture. The Badoli, Ghaṭeśvara Temple (*fig.* 242) has a small *mukhamaṇḍapa* and its pillars contain the most elegant, sensuous and almost three-dimensional images of *devāṅganā*s on the octagonal shafts of the pillar bases. They are neither framed nor limiting in their action. This provides a great sense of freedom in their movements and body flexions. Even pillars of the adjoining *toraṇa* on the same site contain *devāṅganā*s and *dvārapāla*s on pillar bases. Curiously enough, the *maṇḍovara* of Ghaṭeśvara Temple is still bare and no *devāṅganā* embellishment seems to have caught the fancy of the artists. Therefore, the early ninth-century period (as has been demonstrated in the chapter on architecture) shows a hesitant beginning of *devāṅganā* imagery on *maṇḍovara*, but on pillars it survives and thrives, carrying forward the tradition of railing uprights from the ancient period.

The large *naṭa-maṇḍapa* of Kirāḍu (*fig.* 243) also bears notice to the similar tradition. In the *naṭa-maṇḍapa* of Badoli facing the Ghaṭeśvara Temple, pillars are placed very close to each other and their octagonal shafts are profusely carved with *devāṅganā*s, many of whom are in dancing mode. Thus, even a peep into the *naṭa-maṇḍapa* today can evoke the grandeur of the bygone age when all these *maṇḍapa*s would be resounding with dance, music and religious recitation.

As the eleventh-century approaches, pillars become more and more embellished with the result that no portion is left bare. Even the *devāṅganā* imagery multiplies and more and more images are fitted

on the available space. On the Bahū Temple of the Sās–Bahu group at Gwalior, pillars of the *naṭa-maṇḍapa* bear figures almost intertwining their limbs and striking dance-like postures. Some are musicians while others are male drummers, and *devāṅganā*s. Sculpture, remain embedded on the main stone, just like the *naṭa-maṇḍapa* sculptures on the Moḍherā Temple. They are actually framed and so they merge with the main block of the pillar and thus lack the spirit of individual articulation, organic plasticity and movement. At Moḍherā, both *gūḍha-maṇḍapa* as well as *naṭa-maṇḍapa* pillars bear the *devāṅganā* imagery, although the imagery of *naṭa-maṇḍapa* relates more with the Rānī Vāv sculptures, especially of the *khaḍgadhārī* type.

The pillar sculptures of Śāntināth Temple at Kumbhariā (*fig.* 244) have a special niche on four sides within which are placed *naṭī–nartakī* figures. They are four-armed and confuse us at first glance. But closer observation suggests that in order to show the continuous movement, the sculptor has given the figures additional arms so as to suggest a dynamic movement. The figures are elegant, poised and terse. They strike *ūrdhvajānu*, *svastika* or *pṛṣṭha svastika*-like postures and the arms are either in *uromaṇḍalī* or *ūrdhvamaṇḍalī*.

fig. 245. *Raṅgamaṇḍapa* ceiling, *apsaras*, *devāṅganā*s and Kāmadeva placed on hastimuṇḍī, mid-tenth century, Sūrya Temple, Tusā, Udaipur, Rajasthan.

Samarāṅgaṇa Sūtradhāra, chapter 57, explains quite in considerable detail the placement of *apsaras*es on the various facets of pillar bases and *toraṇa*s along with *makara*, elephants, *vidyādhara*, leaves, flowers and other auspicious symbols. Even on the *vitāna* and the *toraṇa*, the placement of *apsaras*es is prescribed. The imagery is not mentioned but the types of *prāsāda*s on which their placement is essential are: *śrīdhara*, *puṣpaka*, *mahāvraja*, *ratideha* and *vimānam*, besides *meru*.

Devāṅganā on the Temple Vitāna

In the light of the above data, one finds ample examples of *devāṅganā* sculptures on *vitāna*s of temples at Sunak, Tusā, Sander, Devī Jagdambī temple at Khajurāho; Sās Temple at Gwalior, and Udaipur which are still *in situ*, while some have been displayed in museums which were actually fixed on the *vitāna*. The terms mentioned in *Samarāṅgaṇa Sūtradhāra*, chapter 57, refers to *apsarāgaṇa bhūṣitā*, *vidyādhara vadhuvṛnda*, *surānām sundarībhiśca*, *nāgakanyā kadambaiśca* while *Aparājitapṛcchā*, chapter 77, mentions *yakṣī* and *śālabhañjya* to be carved in the *vitāna*. The significance of this verse is to be interpreted symbolically as well as metaphorically as creating the placement of these figures essential to support the structure and not to superficially decorate it.

On the *vitāna* of the Sun Temple of Tusā, mid-tenth century *(fig.* 245) are carved eight figures of *devāṅganā*s along with Kāmadeva in full conformation with the text, standing on *hastimuṇḍī* (*fig.* 246). One can also see the rich foliage of the vegetation under which these *apsaras–devāṅganā*s stand. One of them is *putravallabhā*, *darpaṇā*, *kumbhadhārī* and *āmralumbīdhārī*. Three sculptures are missing. Their garments are fluttering and they are attended upon by small dwarfs. Kāmadeva is shown with *ikṣudaṇḍa* and *puṣpa-bāṇa* while

fig. 246. Ceiling (detail), Kāmadeva, Sūrya Temple, Tusā.

fig. 247. *Gūḍha-maṇḍapa* ceiling, *devāṅganās* placed on the ceiling supported by Vidyādhara, 1059-80 inscribed, Udayeśvara Temple, Udaipur, Vidiśā, Madya Pradesh

fig. 248. Pillar brackets, interior of the *maṇḍapa*, *vyāla*, *devāṅganā* alternate, Devī Jagdambi Temple, Khajurāho.

(facing page)
fig. 249. West *mandāraka* ceiling, dance and music, procession, VS 1288-96, CE 1232-40, Lūṇa Vasahī, Paṭṭaśālā, Sirohī, Mt. Ābu, Rajasthan.

on his youthful body, beard and moustache are represented. The waning away of youth is indicated. A beautifully carved ceiling from the Udayeśvara Temple also represents a similar design and iconography (*fig.* 247).

Some *devāṅganā*s as bracket figures supporting the lintel and the pillar are indicated in both the texts and its representation can be seen especially inside the *maṇḍapa*. This has fascinated me. Observing them on the Devī Jagdambī Temple at Khajurāho (*fig.* 248) and at Sās Temple, Gwalior on interior pillars of the square platform (a sort of *yajña-kuṇḍa* platform) tempted me to connect them with each other and the *Aparājita-pṛcchā*. Six to eight such *śālabhañjikā*s standing under a foliate tree are represented either as *vasanabhraṁśā*, *markaṭaceṣṭā*, *putravallabhā*, *patra-lekhana*, *alasā* and so on. They preside over the place of ritual worship and act as supports of its pillars. This convention of placing dancing images, musicians and *śālabhañjikā* along with *vyāla*s continues till today on timber architecture in Gujarat, Maharashtra and Rajasthan on the *havelī*s, palaces and other residential buildings.

The *vitāna* decoration of the Ābu temple of Vimala Vasahī (*fig.* 249) and later temples such as Lūṇa Vasahī expand the

fig. 250. Entrance gate pillar, decorated with *devāṅganā* imageries in *rathika* frames, Gurgī, Rewā Mahārāja's palace.

(facing page)
fig. 251. Entrance gate pillar, detail showing *alasā devāṅganā*, *bhāravāhakā*, *vyāla*, etc., Gurgī, Rewā Mahārāja's palace.

scope and intricacy of carving. The *vitāna* images of *devāṅganās* multiply to almost twenty-four and sometimes thirty-two. This includes majority of dance postures and the usual *devāṅganā* imagery gets obliterated for more dynamic representations of bodies in kinetic movement. The ceilings take on a gem-like faceted intricacy and opulence.

On Gurgī pillars of the Rewa Kotwali collection (*figs.* 250, 251, 252) one observes rows of *ṛṣi-kanyā* figures indulging in erotic/sexual activity, *devāṅganā-vyālas* alternating and such other motifs placed in rows one above the other. The *vyālas* are frontally placed unlike their profile representations which one comes across on temple *maṇḍovara*. The *devāṅganās* strike postures like *alasā*, *vasanabhraṁśā*, *markaṭaceṣṭā*, to name a few. Such an ornate representation of *toraṇa* pillars is unique and has few repetitions. *Toraṇas* are also found at the Limbojīmātā Temple Delmal, Vaḍnagar and Moḍherā in Gujarat, Vidiśā and Badoli in Madhya Pradesh and Rajasthan, on which *śālabhañjikās* are represented as brackets, as was the tradition at Sāñcī and Amarāvatī in the first century CE, or on the *kumbha* of the pillar base, whose antecedents can be traced to the Buddhist *stūpa* pillar uprights.

fig. 252. Details of *fig.* 250, tāntric sexual rites, group orgy.

Devāṅganā on the Temple Doorway

The observation concerning the placement of *devāṅganā* sculptures on the body of the temple seems to have evolved from the earliest times. The Buddhist and Hindu monuments of Ajantā, Ellorā, Auraṅgābād, Jogeśvarī, Udayagiri and Gupta–Pratihāra period temple architecture, have all incorporated the image of the woman on doorways of their sanctuaries. Whether they be temples, *vihāras* or *caitya*, their doorways have contained first the images of *śālabhañjikā–yakṣī–vṛkṣikā*, transitional motifs of *śālabhañjikā*–river goddess (*nadī-devatā*), to fully developed iconographically evolved Gaṅgā and Yamunā figures. This has been much discussed in the chapter on

fig. 253. Doorway,
eleventh century, Śiva temple,
Nohtā, Madya Pradesh

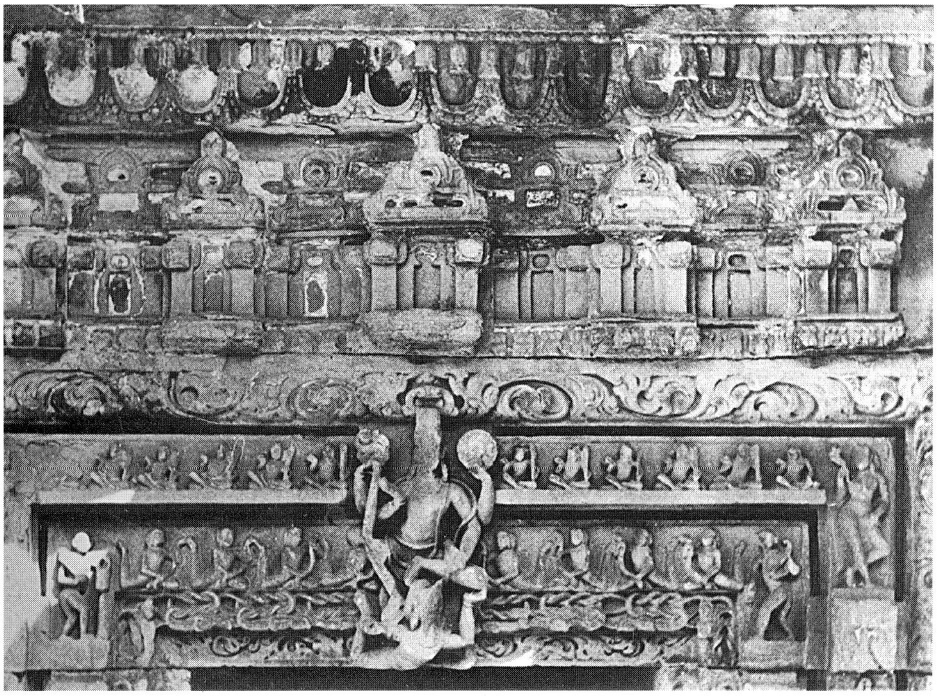

sculpture. It is quite interesting to note how even in the tenth century and later temples (randomly selected here) the *devāṅganā* imagery persists even though the *nadī-devatā* concept has evolved and branched out of it. On the doorway of the Śiva Temple, Nohṭā (*fig.* 253) the *lalāṭabimba* depicts the Naṭarāja, lintel represents *navagrahas*, *dikpālas*, Brahmā, Viṣṇu, Maheśa and door jambs represent dwarfs dancing and couples amorously sporting. The lintel conjoints with pillars represent *devāṅganās* in *svastika pada* and *uromaṇḍalī hasta* without any other attributes.

The same features can be observed on the Śivā Temple at Terāhī doorway lintel, which has Garuḍārūḍha Viṣṇu on the *lalāṭabimba* and *vidyādharas*. The *devāṅganā* holds a lotus with long stalk and another one stands with a child and an attendant (*fig.* 254).

On the doorway of the triple shrine at Menal, the *devāṅganās* are shown in *kaṭisama hasta* and *svastika pada* holding a bunch of flowers under a foliated tree. There are a number of dwarfs dancing, and seated couples indulging in amorous activities. The *nadī-devatās* are as usual at the *udumbara* level holding a waterpot and wearing fluttering garments surrounded by rich foliage.

fig. 254. *Garbhagṛha* doorway *vṛkṣakā-nalinī* on lintel, early ninth century, Śiva Temple, Terahi, Śivapurī, Madya Pradesh

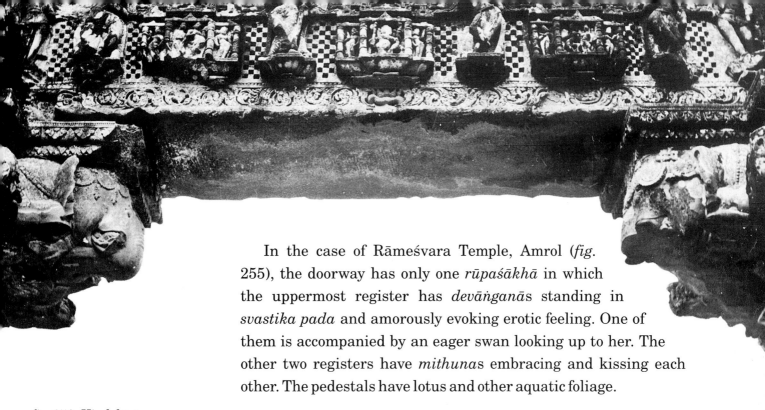

In the case of Rāmeśvara Temple, Amrol (*fig.* 255), the doorway has only one *rūpaśākhā* in which the uppermost register has *devāṅganā*s standing in *svastika pada* and amorously evoking erotic feeling. One of them is accompanied by an eager swan looking up to her. The other two registers have *mithuna*s embracing and kissing each other. The pedestals have lotus and other aquatic foliage.

fig. 256. *Hiṇḍolā, toraṇa, maṇḍapa*, northern architrave, south face, *vr̥kṣikā*, *vasanabhraṁśā*, CE 1011, Gyāraspur, Vidiśā, Madya Pradesh

On the *hiṇḍolā toraṇa*, Gyāraspur (*fig.* 256) which are the lintels of a *toraṇa*, the framed images with *udgama* and attendants of gods, *mithuna*s, etc. are interspersed with *devāṅganā*s striking the most elegant *svastika*, *baddhācārī* or *ālīḍha*. There are *alasā*, *vasanabhraṁśā*, *śālabhañjikā*, *padminī, markaṭaceṣṭā*, and *cāmara,* to note a few. Such a representation is not only rare but testifies to the fact that the idea of *devāṅganā* auspiciousness pervades all the parts of the temple (*figs.* 257, 258, 259).

Thus, doorways, of the *garbha-gr̥ha* either have the "creative", the "erotic" or the "emotive" type of *devāṅganā*s, while the pillar brackets and *vitāna* too have the same class of sensuality, fertility and emotive motifs. The pillar bases do bear the *vīra* imagery which represents the *kapāla*, *khaḍga* and *sarpadhārī devāṅganā*s. Some even hold the *āmralumbī* and parrot, which signify the coalescence of fertility and eroticism. Attempting a semiotic analysis of the *devāṅganā* placement and its ever-auspicious *nitya-sumaṅgalī* character which combines a coalescence of "ascetic", "erotic", "creative" and "emotive" nature, they actually determine the character of the monument in totality by multiplying their imagery, repeating and renewing their potency and the potency of the monuments. The most favoured tendency is the "creative" followed by the "erotic", since the majority of monuments rely upon the presence of the maternal or feminine images. This is followed by the dance and music imagery in which

(facing page)
fig. 255. Sanctum doorway, *devāṅganā* on doorway, *c.* eighth century, Rāmeśvara Temple, Amrol, Gwalior, Madya Pradesh

fig. 257. Doorway,
darpaṇā, *vasanabhraṁśā* and *mithuna*
Sūrya Temple Kauśāmbī,
Allahabad Museum.

fig. 258. Doorway, *devāṅganā darpaṇā* on the lintel, *c.* tenth century, Chandwasa, Mandsor, Madya Pradesh, Indore Central Museum.

fig. 259. Doorway,
apsaras flanking Ādityas,
c. tenth century, Gyāraspur,
Bajramath cntral Sūrya shrine Vidiśā,
Madya Pradesh.

images of *devadāsīs* and their ritualistic performances seem to be captured. The influence of performing tradition can certainly not be overlooked. The ascetic and *vīra* seem to relate to the tāntric rituals and imageries which are difficult to explain on the "denotative" level, but can be explained in the light of the literary or technical data enlightening it.

The presence of *devāṅganās* on pillars, brackets and pilasters not only suggests that they are the *āvaraṇa devatās* but also that they are the support of the whole universe. The concern for fertility in their imagery and its widespread popularity indicates that, in every age motherhood was the ultimate form in which womanhood or femininity was realized. Thus women were not seen as "gates of hell", or what has been so far popularized as the "snare"-like characters, who distracted men from pursuing righteousness (*fig.* 262).

Text and Culture Correlation

In the Vedic–Purāṇic literature we came across several references to the erotic character of the *gandharva* who is identified as the violator of women, who takes form of an ape or a dog or a hairy child and approaches women. The imagery of *markaṭaceṣṭā* has clear allusion to this imagery, where the monkey is shown pulling the garment of the

fig. 260. Āditya flanked by *devāṅganā* Padminī, south wall, Sūrya temple, Tusā.

fig. 261. *Garbha-gṛha*, Āditya flanked by *devāṅganās*, *kanduka* and *alasā*. south wall, Sūrya Temple, Tusā.

fig. 262. *Maithuna* couple flanked by *devāṅganās*, *antarāla* wall, mid-eleventh century, Kandarīya Mahādeva Temple, Khajurāho, Madya Pradesh

nāyikā who strikes him with the branch of a tree. Such comical but sexual interludes make the *devāṅganā* imagery colourful. The *gaṅdharva* is also identified with Soma, and there are number of representations especially of the Kuṣāṇa period, in which they are represented drinking alone or with a partner or swooning under the effect of liquor. On Ajantā Cave 4 the *devāṅganā* is seen embracing a monkey-faced dwarfish male holding a wine cup tempting her to drink. Could this be interpreted as a satirical representation on a Buddhist monument of promiscuous life of *gandharva*s and *apsaras*es? The indulgence in irrational pursuits should be abstained by the monks, thus this illustration might be a subtle way of didactic ethical teaching.

We have already made a note of the correlation between *devāṅganā* and Śeṣaśāyī form of Viṣṇu on a fluvial monument, such as the Rānī Vāv, Pāṭan (*fig.* 240). The element of fertility and powers of the water to lend fertility have been suitably echoed by the figures of the *devāṅganā* imagery on the entire monument. Likewise on the Sūrya Temple of Tusā (Rajasthan) (*figs.* 260, 261), *devāṅganā*s are elegantly juxtaposed along with Ādityas and the *devakoṣṭha* images of Sūrya seated on seven horses. We observe the *alasā* and *kanduka-krīḍā devāṅganā*s topped by *gandharva* couples holding garlands. The *alasā* pose represents *aṅgaḍāī* or an *avasthā* denoting "time", so does the movement of the ball signify the movement of time in the *saṁsāra-cakra*. One evokes stages of love while the other evokes the reality principle or meaning of human existence. More significant suggestion or the *vyañjanā* is of "time", which Sūrya stands for. *Fig* 217 shows the *padminī devāṅganā*s flanking the Sun seated in his car, at Tusā, Sūrya Temple along with a *kanduka-krīḍā* it has been described in the *Viṣnu Purāṇa* that (see page 68) that Sūrya's car every month carries along with an Āditya, two *apsaras*es, *gandharva*s, *ṛṣi*s, *nāga*s and *rākṣasa*s. On the central Sūrya shrine at Bajramaṭha, Gyāraspur (*fig.* 259) one can notice all the Ādityas on the doorway, while the major three on the lintel have the two *apsaras*es each flanking them. Often with Sūrya, Uṣā and Pratyūṣā, represented by figures standing in *ālīḍha sthāna* holding bow and arrow are associated. But medieval period temple doorways represent *apsaras*es as well along with Uṣā–Pratyūṣā.

(facing page)
fig. 263. Bahū Temple *maṇḍapa*, pillars represent dancing figures at the base eleventh century, Gwalior, Madya Pradesh

fig. 264. Bahū Temple, interior view, eleventh century, Gwalior, Madya Pradesh

On the *devakoṣṭha*s of Moḍherā Sūrya Temple as well, one comes across the images of *devāṅganā*s and *apsaras*es flanking the Ādityas, Dvādaśa Gaurīs and the *dikpālas* (*fig.* 36). They are placed on the lower two registers depicting different activities of typical *devāṅganā* imagery. But they do not tally exactly with any śilpa texts, and the sculptors at Moḍherā seem to have applied their own logic and criterion for *jaṅghā* decoration while incorporating *apsaras* images. The association of *apsaras* with Sūrya is definitely strengthened here.

Since we have opened the discussion on the relationship between *apsaras* and Sūrya from written texts, and found it generally tallying with the sculptural representation, I thought of exploring the imagery of the "Uṣas", the Dawn, which is conceived in the feminine form. Macdonell[11] suggest that Uṣas is the most graceful creation of

the Vedic poetry, and there is no more charming figure in the descriptive religious lyrics of any other literature. She is celebrated in about twenty hymns of the *R̥gveda*. Let us study the imagery of Uṣas which implicitly shares many attributes, characteristics and functions with the Vedic *apsaras* and the imagery of the *devāṅganā* as it is represented on temple architecture. Here are some verses which enlighten the imagery of Uṣas. She arrays herself in gay attire like a dancer, she displays her bosom (1.92.4, 6.64.2), she is clothed in light and appears in the east and unveils her charm (1.124.3-4). Does this not remind one of *vasanabhraṁśā*? Rising resplendent as from a bath, showing her charms she comes with light, driving away the darkness (5.80.5-6). This imagery relates well with the *sadyasnātā* imagery. Like a wheel she revolves ever anew (3.61.3) and reveals the paths of men, manifests all beings and bestows new life (7.80.1-2). She dispels the darkness (6.64.3, 65.4) and wards off evil spirits and the hated darkness (7.75.1). She is often called the mother of kine (4.52.2-3, 7.77.2). This signifies the nature of nourishment, sustenance, moral values and general upliftment of human life.

fig. 265. *Vr̥kṣikā*, with drummer, Harṣanātha temple, Harṣagiri, Sikar.

Uṣas' connection with Sūrya is extremely intimate. Sūrya follows her as a young man would follow a maiden (1.115). She shines with the light of the Sun (1.113.9) her lover (1.92.11). Savitr̥ shines after the path of Uṣas (5.81.2). She meets the god who desires her (1.123.10). The dawns are the wives of the Sun (4.5.13). But as preceding the Sun in time, she is occasionally thought of as his mother. The physical phenomenon of dawn followed by the Sun has been transformed poetically into the lover/beloved chase and presented in the form of a metaphor. A verse from *Dhvanyāloka* highlights:

> Twilight is full of love, And the day chases her face to face; But oh, look at the decree of Fate, The twine do never meet! — p. 23, *adhyāya* I.13

This is an example of *rūpaka* (metaphor) and *dhvani* (suggestion) in which the expressed sense refers to something which is not literally expressed.

Uṣas is the sister of the Āditya, Bhaga (1.123.5) and the kinswoman (*jami*) of Varuṇa (1.123.3). Here the connection with Varuṇa, the water god, is implied which in the sculpture section has

fig. 266. *Alasā* on pillar, *raṅga-maṇḍapa*, Viṣṇu Temple, late tenth century, Kirāḍu, Rajasthan.

already been discussed. Just as *apsaras* are connected with Varuṇa and Indra, Uṣas also has much to do with the waters. As the elder sister of night (1.124.8) she is also associated as Naktoṣasa. She has been produced for the production of Savitṛ, and arrives with a bright child (1.113.12). Here the maternal aspect of Uṣas is suggested hinting at the imagery of *putravallabhā*. Uṣas is born in the sky (7.75) and the place of her birth suggests the relationship with it, as most frequently mentioned in the *Ṛgveda*, she is the daughter of the heaven (1.30.22).

(facing page)
fig. 267. *Stambha-yoṣitā* with food basket and a jug, second century, Bharat Kala Bhavan, Varanasi.

The goddess is often implored to look upon the worshipper, bring to him wealth and children, to bestow protection and long life (1.30.22, 48.1, etc.). She is resplendent, shining, divine, immortal and bountiful. She is akin to the Aurora of Greek mythology. But more characteristically the imagery of Uṣas is more cognate with the Vedic *apsaras* and demonstrably with the *devāṅganā*s of the medieval Nāgara temples, which are rich in fertility, eroticism and sensuous expressions of these manifestations by means of dance.

The unresolvable yet unignorable issue is of the imageries of *vīrā* types from Moḍherā and Pāṭan, which are peculiar only to these sites, where one observes the representation of *khaḍga*, *sarpadhārī*, *muṇḍa* and *kapāladhārī*, with serpents entwining around their naked bodies. It is quite possible that the artist sculptors at both the sites, would have belonged to the same guild, and therefore, possibly shared similar imagery. Another type of *vīra* imagery which depicts the *devāṅganā* combating with a lion, a fallen foe or simply brandishing swords and other weapons, is also a favourite with the Gujarat sculptor seen on Kumbhariā, Śiva Temple; Śāraṇeśvara Temple, Ābhāpur, Navalakhā Temple, Ghumlī and Sejakpur temples. Thus, in eleventh and twelfth centuries the combating *vīrā devāṅganā*s caught the fancy of the artists and hence this motif perpetuated on many sites.

I have explored the possible inspiration for the source of *vīrā* imagery from *deśī* dance forms performed at popular level by acrobats, such as dancing with serpents, garlands, balls, knives, swords, pots, cloth, *śaṅkha, cāmara*, stick, *vīṇā*, etc. which are not only auspicious symbols by themselves, but exhibit virtuosity of

dancers. This clearly distinguishes two types of dance forms that have inspired sculptors of medieval temples, one is the *deśī* style while the other is the *mārgī* one. The *deśī* style dances have been brought to light by V. Raghavan[12] from *Nṛttaratnāvalī* and *Nṛtyasarvasva* which refer to pure dance numbers holding the above-mentioned articles. It is known that till recently *nattuvanār*s filled *adavu*s and *jāti*s to sword dances, and trained their dancers doing *varṇa*s to execute the same with swords. In the course of their movements, they would cut vegetables with the sword which were tied to the body of the girl with precision but without hurting her.

The other type of dance movements which I identify as the *mārgī* style depicts classical postures which denote either a *nṛtta* or a *nṛtya* gesture. Thus, within the range of *naṭī/nartakī* sculptures, one observes the references to *deśī* and *mārgī* mode of dance representations.

Imagery–Terminology Correlation

Before concluding, what I would like to emphasize is the basic understanding of idea–image correlation and how spontaneously it was evolved. As has been rightly observed by Coomaraswamy, there is no motif more fundamentally characteristic of Indian art from the first to the last, than that of the "woman and tree".[13] The *yakṣa* and *yakṣī* are the vegetation spirits while the *apsaras* are water-borne and air-borne. They do reside in the trees just like the *yakṣī*s. It was the basic need for fertility and fecundating potential that the two got identified together with the "tree and woman" motif, to coalesce into the concept of the *devāṅganā*, which multiplied its imagery and forms to become tangible and palpable in the most sensuous forms of women. Abstract features like smells are associated with them, their limbs are beautiful, their form is ever-auspicious, thus they generically began to signify the positive and desirable aspects of a woman. The potential of the same imagery also contained elements of heroism and asceticism which can be evoked in particular. Thus, when texts were formulated, for example the *Śilpa Prakāśa*[14] of

Orissa, it clearly mentions a *yantra* or a compositional device which contains *dvibhaṅgī* (or diagonal-shaped lines) that signify *gati*, dynamism and kinetic plasticity, which distinguish the nature of the woman from the man. As has been observed by Parimoo with reference to the *mithuna* sculptures, where the woman stands entwining herself round the male, there the principle of *sthira gati* is implied.[15] Thus, the creation of the whole range of *apsaras*, *yakṣī*, *devāṅganā*, *mithuna*, *dikpāla* images, are a creation of abstract elements of nature, human behaviour and personality transformed and given a physical form, attributes, gestures and postures. This coexistence of worlds of nature and humans suggests the concern of the medieval mind to conceive and symbolize the cosmic order, in giving a structure to the smaller units of that order, namely the individual imageries, decorative motifs and architectural parts.

A study of architectural texts suggests that by the medieval period the term *śālabhañjikā* had fossilized into a technical term, denoting a generic architectural feature, which was totally divorced from its original dynamic metaphor of fecundity, pregnant with meaning. The occurrence of terms such as *yakṣī*s, *surāṅganā*, *apsaras*, *nāyikā*, *devāṅganā*, *alasā kanyā*s became popular and part of the parlance of architectural language. They contributed nothing much to the imagery and the source of the imagery which actually came from the creative literature of the *nāṭya*s, *kāvya*s and the Vedic–Purāṇic narrative sources. This finally led to the evolution of the socio-cultural motif of the auspicious "woman and vegetation" interrelationship which has even inspired socio-religious rituals and folk cults.

Therefore, at the level of codification of architectural texts, the motif only remained a denotative term and lost its meaning. But, for the sculptors the tradition had not died, even if the texts had not made any reference to their placement on temple architecture. It is learnt that from the reference notes of the traditional architect families of Gujarat, some names and imageries of *devāṅganā*s had been found, which support my view, that in the local stone and timber traditions, the practice of *devāṅganā* imagery had never ebbed. It was very much alive and thriving.

My last question, while summing up the whole discussion, is whether *yakṣī* and *apsaras* can be interchanged as a nomenclature for analogous principles of vegetation, water, earth, fecundity, abundance and rejuvenation. What kind of mass psychology may have operated in transferring a spring festival as a motif to identify with the imagery of the *yakṣī*? Further, how could a secular motif denoting a chthonic principle get absorbed into the visual imagery of a higher religion and get incorporated to denote an air-borne principle of *apsaras*? The preceding research on the motif, its possible lineage, its perpetuation at several sites of medieval western India, clearly reiterates that fundamentally there is no dichotomy between *apsaras* and *yakṣī*. Needless to say, their origins are different but undoubtedly they perform the same functions — auspicious, fecundating, pleasing, morally uplifting. Dichotomy, if any, is in the character of the imagery itself which has been conceived and experienced by masses. This positive–negative polarity is discussed at length in the beginning of the chapter on "Semiosis of the Devāṅganā Motif", which finally brings to light the implicit dialectic in the nature of the feminine. Thus, a verse from the *Mahābhārata* which voices the ambiguity in the nature of the woman sums up:

> Who are thou that clasping the branch of the *kadamba* tree shinest radiantly in the lonely hermitage, sparkling like a blaze of fire in the night, shaken by the breeze, O! thou of fair brows? Exceedingly pleasing art thou, yet fearest, naught here in the forest. Art thou a *devī*, a *yakṣī*, a *dānavī*, a choicest *apsaras*, or fair *daitya* girl, or the maiden-incarnate of a Nāga king, or a foresteress (*vanecarī*) or consort of a night wanderer in the wood or spouse of Varuṇa, Soma, Yama or Kubera? — Vana-Parva 265.1-3[16]

The above verse in essence conveys more or less the same import that my research has demonstrated in an analytical way. The form of the *devāṅganā* embodies features of all that the above-stated form of the auspicious woman signifies. Her nature as amorphous yet definitive, alluring yet enduring, consistent yet staggering, "śāstric" (standardized) yet "deśic" (variety), physically charming yet metaphorically didactic - is an inherent ambivalence which simply continues.

References

1. (1) Roland Barthes, tr., *Elements of Semiology*, 1967, 9th edn., 1984, 1st published (French) 1964; (2) Ratan Parimoo, "Adaptation of Folk Tales for Buddhist Jātaka Stories and their Depiction in Indian art: A Study in Narrative and Semiotic Transformation", *Journal of M.S. University of Baroda*, Humanities Number 1991/92; also by the same author Vidhura Pandita, "Jātaka, from Bharhut to Ajantā: A Study of Narrative, Semiology and Stylistic Aspects", in *Dr. Debala Mitra Felicitation Volume*, New Delhi, 1991 and *Art of Ajantā: New Perspectives*, New Delhi: Books and Books, 1991.
2. C.W. Morris, *Signs, Languages and Behaviour*, New York, 1946.
3. K. Kunjuni Raja, *Indian Theories of Meaning*, Madras, 1963; *Dhvanyāloka* of Ānandavardhana, critically edited with Intro., tr. and notes by K. Krishnamurthy, New Delhi, 1974, 2nd edn., 1982.
4. Saussure, 1983, pp. 127-28, from "Semiotics for Beginners by Daniel Chandler", *Paradigms and Syntagms*, http://www.aber.ac.uk/media/Documents/S4B/sem03.html.
5. Ibid., 126-28.
6. D.H.H. Ingalls, *An Anthology of Sanskrit Court Poetry, Vidyākara's Śubhāṣita Ratnakośa*, Harward University Press, 1965.
7. Ibid.
8. R.C. Agrawala, "Khajurāho of Rajasthan, The temple of Ambikā at Jagat", *Arts Asiatiques*, 1964, vol. X.

9 See Author's article "Devāṅganā Sculptures in the Rānī Vāv", *India Magazine*, vol. 9, 1989, p. 76.

10 Ratan Parimoo, *Sculptures of Śeṣaśāyī Viṣṇu*, Baroda, 1983.

11. A.A. Macdonell, *Vedic Mythology*, pp. 47-48.
12. V. Raghavan, "Uparūpakas and Nṛtya Prabandha", *Sangeeta Natak*, no. 76, 1985, pp. 36-55.
13. A.K. Coomaraswamy, *Yakṣa*, 1971, p. 32.
14. *Śilpa Prakāśa*, p. 47, fig. 11, *Alasā Yantra* (*SP* 1, pp. 407-09).
15. Ratan Parimoo, "Khajurāho, the Candella Sculptors, Paradise: Is there Candella Style of Medieval Indian Sculpture? Its Sources and Characteristics", in *Essays on New Art History,* vol. I, *Studies in Indian Sculpture*, New Delhi: Books and Books, 2000.
16. *Mahābhārata,* 1-3 from U.N. Roy, p. 265.

Appendix

1. ब्रह्माण्डपुराण

1. शैब्या धन्यानि देवीनां सहस्राणि च षोडशे ।
चतुर्दश तु ये प्रोक्ता गणास्त्वप्सरसां दिवि ॥ (P. III. 71.243)

2. विचार्य देवैः शक्रेण विशिष्टास्त्विह प्रेषिताः ।
पत्नर्थ्यं वासुदेवस्य उत्पन्ना राजवेश्मसु ॥ (P. III. 71.244)

3. चतुर्विंशाश्चावरजास्तेषामप्सरसः शुभाः ।
अरूणा चानपाया च विमनुष्या वरांबरा ॥ (P. III. 7.5)

4. मिश्रकेशी तथाचासिपर्णिनी चाव्यलुंबुषा ।
मारीचिः शुचिभा चैव विद्युत्पर्णा तिलोत्तमा ॥ (P. III. 7.6)

5. अद्रिका लक्ष्मणा क्षेमा दिव्या रंभा मनोभवा ।
असिता च सुबाहूश्च सुप्रिया सुभुजा तथा ॥ (P. III. 7.7)

6. पुंडरिका जगन्धा च सुदती सुरसा तथा ।
तथैवासा सुबाहूश्च विख्यातौ हहाहूहू ॥ (P. III. 7.8)

2. भागवतपुराण

7. ततश्चाप्सरसो जाता निष्कण्ठयः सुवाससः ।
रमण्यः स्वर्गिणां वन्मुगतिलीलावलोकनैः ॥ (VIII. 8.7)

8. गन्धार्वाप्सिसरसः काम वसन्तमलयानिलैः ।
मुनयेर्प्रेषयामास रजस्तोकमदौ तथा ॥ (XII. 8.16)

9. इति प्रगृणतां तेषां स्त्रियोऽत्यद्भुत दर्शनाः ।
दर्शयामास शुश्रूषां स्वर्चिता कुर्वतीर्विभुः ॥ (XI. 4.12)

10. ते देवानुचरा दृष्ट्वा स्त्रियः श्रीरिव रूपिणीः ।
गन्धेन मुमुदुस्तासां रूपोदार्यहतश्रियः ॥ (XI. 4.13)

11. तानाह देवदेवेशः प्रणंतान् प्रहसन्निव ।
आसानेकतमां वृङध्वं सवर्णां स्वर्गभूषणाम् ॥ (XI. 4.14)

12. ओमित्यादेशमादाय नत्वा तं सुखन्दिनः ।
उर्वशीमप्सरः श्रेष्ठां पुरस्कृत्य दिवं ययुः ॥ (XI. 4.15)

3. मत्स्यपुराण

13. मुनिर्मुनीनोन्वगणंगणमत्सरसां तथा ।
तथाकिन्नरगन्धर्वामरिष्टाजनयद्बहून् ॥ (6.45)

14. गन्धर्वैश्वपुरादुग्धावत्सधासाप्सरोगणैः ।
वत्सं चैत्ररथंकृत्वा गंधान्पद्मदले यथा ॥ (10.24)

4. वायुपुराण (आनन्दाश्रम संस्करण, सं० 2049, 1983)

15. तत सृजति भूतानि स्थावराणि चराणि च ।
यक्षान्पिशाचान्गन्धर्वास्तथैवाप्सरसां गणान् ॥ (9.55)

16. अप्सरोगणसंघाश्च समाजग्मुरनेकशः ।
ववौ शिव सुखो वायुर्नानागन्धर्वाः शुचिः ॥ (30.87)

17. गणा अप्सरसां ख्याताः पुण्यास्तै वै चतुर्दश ।
आहूताः शोभयन्तश्च गणा हत्यते चतुर्दश ॥ (69.53)

18. ब्रह्मणो मानसाः मन्याः शोभन्त्यो मनोः सुताः ।
वेगवन्तस्त्वरिष्टाया उर्जायाश्चाग्निसंभवा ॥ (69.54)

19. आयुष्मत्यश्च सूर्यस्व रश्मिजाता सुभास्वराः ।
गभतिश्च सोमस्य ज्ञेयास्ते कुरवः शुभाः ॥ (69.55)

20. यज्ञोत्पन्नाः शुभा नाम ऋक्सामान्यास्तु वहन्य ।
वारिणा हयमृतोत्पन्ना अमृता नामतः स्मृताः ॥ (69.56)

21. वायुत्पन्ना सुदा नाम भूमिजात्रा भवास्तु वै ।
विद्युतश्च रूचो नाम मृत्यो कन्याश्च भैरवाः ॥ (69.57)

22. शोभयन्त्यश्च कामस्य गणाः प्रोक्ताश्चतुर्दश ।
सेन्द्रोपेन्द्रैः सुरगणैः रूपातिशय निर्मिताः ॥ (69.58)

23. धनुरूपा महाभागा दिव्यानारी तिलोत्तमा ।
ब्रह्मणश्चाग्नि कुण्डाच्च देवनारी प्रभावली ॥ (69.59)

24. रूपयौवनसम्पन्ना उत्पन्ना लोका विश्रुता ।

25. वेदीतलसमुत्पन्ना चतुर्वक्त्रस्य धीमतः ।
नाम्ना वेदवती नाम सुरनारी महाप्रभा ॥ (69.60)

26. तथा यमस्य दुहिता रूपयौवनशालिनि ।
वरहेमनिभा हेमा देवनारी सुलोचना ॥ (69.61)

27. इत्येते बहुसाहस्त्रं भास्वराः हयप्सरोगणाः ।
देवतानामृषीणां च पत्न्यस्ता मातरश्च ह ॥ (69.62)

28. सुगन्धाश्चम्पवर्णश्च सर्वाश्चाप्सरसः सभाः ।
संप्रयोगे तु कान्तेन माधन्ति मदिरा विना ॥
तासामाप्यायते स्पर्शादानन्दश्च विवर्धते । (69.63)

29. चतुस्त्रिंशधवीयस्यस्तेषामप्सरसः शुभाः ।
अन्तरा दाखत्या च प्रियमुख्यां सुरोत्तमा ॥ (69.64)

30. मिश्रकेशी तथा चाशी वर्णिनी वाऽप्यलम्बुषा ।

मारीचि पुत्रिका चैव विधुद्वर्णा तिलोत्तमा ॥ (69.65)

31. अद्रिका लक्षणा चैव देवी रम्भा मनोरमा ।
सुवरा च सुबाहुश्च पूर्णिता सुप्रतिष्ठिता ॥ (69.66)

32. पुण्डरिका सुगन्धा च सुदन्ता सुरसां तथा ।
हेमा सारद्वती चैव सुवृत्रा कमल च या ॥ (69.67)

33. सुभुजा हंसपादा च लौकिक्योऽप्सरसस्तथा ।
गन्धर्वाप्सरसो ह्येता मौनयाः परिकिर्तिताः ॥ (69.68)

34. एवमादिनी देवीनां सहस्राणि च षोडश ।
चतुर्दश तु ये प्रोक्ता गणाश्चाप्सरसां दिवि ॥ (96.325)

5. विष्णुपुराण द्वितीयंश, दशमोध्याय

35. धाता कृतस्थली चैव पुलस्त्यो वासुकिस्तथा ।
रथभृद् ग्रामणीर्हेतिस्तुम्बुरूश्चैवसप्तमः ॥ (10.3)

36. एते वसन्ति वै चैत्रे मधुमासे सदैव हि ।
मैत्रेय स्यन्दने भानोः सप्तमासाधिकारिणः ॥ (10.4)

37. अर्यमा पुलहश्चैव रथौजाः पुञ्जिकस्थला ।
प्रहेतिः कच्छवीरश्च नारदश्च रथे रवेः ।
माधवे निवसन्त्येते शुचिसंज्ञे निबोध मे ॥ (10.5)

38. मित्रोऽत्रिस्तक्षको रक्षः पौरूषेयोऽथ मेनका ।
हाहा रथस्वनश्चैव मैत्रेयेतेवसन्ति वै ॥ (10.7)

39. वसिष्ठो वरूणो रम्भा सहजन्याः हुहूर्बुधः ।
रथचित्रस्तथा शुक्रे वसन्त्याषाढ़संज्ञिते ॥ (10.8)

40. इन्द्रो विश्वासुः स्त्रोता एलापुत्रस्तथाङिराः ।
प्रम्लोचा च नमस्येते भसप्तिश्चार्के वसान्ति वै ॥ (10.9)

41. विवस्यानुग्रसेनश्च भृगुरापुरणस्तथा ।
अनुम्लोचा शङ्खपालो व्याघ्रो भाद्रपदे तथा ॥ (10.10)

42. पूषा वसुरूचिर्वातो गौतमोऽथ धनञ्जयः ।
सुषेणोऽन्यो धृताची च वसन्त्याश्वयुजे रवौ ॥ (10.11)

43. विश्वावसु भरद्वाजः पर्जन्यैरावतौ तथा ।
विश्वाची सेनजिच्चाप कार्तिकै वसन्ति वै ॥ (10.12)

44. अंशकाश्यपताक्ष्र्यसहसु महापद्म तथोर्वशी ।
चित्रसेनस्तथा विधुन्मार्गशीर्षेऽधिकारिणीः ॥ (10.13)

45. क्रतुर्भगस्तथोर्णायुः स्फूर्जः कर्कोकटस्तथा ।
अरिष्टनेमिश्चैवान्या पूर्वचित्तिर्वराप्सराः ॥ (10.14)

46. पौषमासे वसन्त्येते सप्तभास्करमण्डले ।
लोकप्रकाशनार्थाय विप्रवर्याधिकारिण ॥ (10.15)

47. त्वष्टाथ जमदग्निश्च कम्बलोऽथ तिलोत्तमा ।
बघ्नपेतोऽथ ऋतजिद् धृतराष्ट्रोऽथ सप्तमाः ॥ (10.16)

48. माघमासे वसन्त्येते सप्त मैत्रेय भास्करे ।
श्रूयतां चापरे सूर्ये फाल्गुने निवसन्ति ये ॥ (10.17)

49. विष्णुरस्वतरो रम्भा सूर्यवर्चाश्च सत्यजित् ।
विश्वामित्रस्त्था रक्षो यज्ञोपेतो महागुनेः ॥ (10.18)

6. समराङ्गणसूत्रधारः (अध्याय 57) मेर्वादिविंशिका नाम सप्तञ्चाशोऽध्यायः ।
GOS, No. 25, 1966

50. तस्योपरि स्यात कलशो वर्तुलस्त्रिपदोच्छ्रितः ।
तोरणैर्मकरैः पत्रैः साग्रैश्च सव(म) रालकैः ॥46 ॥

हस्तिमुण्डैः समाकीर्णमध(प्स) रोगणभूषितम् ।
इदृशं श्रीधरं कुर्यात् सर्वालंकारभूषितम् ॥47 ॥

51. विचित्रभूमिके (सप्तदशम्मिल्लिख्यराक्षणप्यपि?) ।
स्तम्भैर्विविध विन्यासैर्बहुभङ्गविनिर्मितैः ॥

भूषितैः कर्मभिश्चित्रैः सर्वत्र शुभलक्षणैः ।
चन्द्रशालादिसंयुक्तैस्तोरणैश्चारूचामरैः ॥ (P. 404)

52. मदान्धातिककुळाकीर्णगजवक्त्रविभूषितैः ।
विद्याधरवधूवृन्दैः क्रीडारम्भतिभूषितैः ॥ (P. 404)

53. सुराणां सुन्दरीमिश्च वीणाहस्तैश्च किन्नरैः ।
सिद्धगन्धर्वयक्षणां वृन्दैश्च परितः स्थितैः ॥ (P. 404)

54. अप्सरोभिश्च दिव्याभिर्विमानावलिभिस्तथा ।
चारूचाभिकरान्दोलाक्रीडासक्तैश्च (निःसराम?) ॥ (P. 404)

55. नागकन्याकन्दम्बैश्च सर्वतः समलङ्कृतम् ।
एवंविताभिः सर्वत्र भूमिकाभिर्निरन्तरम् ॥ (P. 404)

7. अपराजितपृच्छा (अध्याय 190, वितानवर्णन)

56. अष्ट द्वादश द्विरष्ट चतुर्विंशतिर्द्वात्रिंशत् ।
चतुःषष्टिर्विद्याधरास्तदूर्ध्वे च वराङ्गनाः ॥14 ॥

57. ततानद्धनाद्येश्च वादित्रैः सुस्वरैस्तथा ।
नाटकैनृत्यरङ्गनद्यैर्गीतनादैरकधा ॥15 ॥

(गृहग्रामनगरशोभा, 85-26)

58. धटीस्थानोत्तरे कार्या विचित्रा नृत्यशालिकाः ।
वितानैः शालभञ्जिभिर्घण्टाछाद्यै विभूषिताः ॥26 ॥

(नागरप्रासादविभक्तिप्रस्तरप्रमाण, अध्याय 127-21, 24)

59. कार्या तदूर्ध्वे जङ्घण च पञ्चत्रिंशत्समुच्छिता ।
भ्रमनिर्माणतः स्तम्भैर्नासिकोपाङ्गफालना ॥21 ॥

60. मूलनासासु सर्वासु स्तम्भैः स्युश्चतुरश्रिकाः ।
गजश्च सिंहव्यालैश्च मकरैः समलङ्कृताः ॥22 ॥

61. कर्णेष्वष्टौ च दिक्पालाः प्राच्यादिषु प्रदक्षिणम् ।
नटेशः पश्चिमे भद्रे हयन्धकैः सह दक्षिणे ॥23 ॥

62. चण्डस्य चोत्तरे देवी दंष्ट्रानन सुशोभिताः ।
वीतरागे च शासनदेव्यश्चैव दिशाः प्रति ॥24 ॥

(भूधरादिब्रह्मनगरं, अध्याय 70, 21)

63. कर्णे कर्णे तु कर्त्तव्या वृत्ताहालकशोभना ।
(त्रि) सहस्रान्ते पुनः कुर्याद्योधविधरी तथा ॥21 ॥

(सभाष्टकवेदीनिर्णयो, अध्याय 77-7)

64. निष्कान्ता च चतुर्भद्रैर्यक्षी कार्या सुशोभना ।
भद्रे-भद्रे द्विशालीनि सा गता रत्नसंभवा ॥7 ॥

65. तरस्याश्च प्रत्येकशालं प्रतिभद्रविभूषितम् ।
उत्पला च समाख्याता महाराजेन्द्रवल्लभा ॥8 ॥

66. अम्बिन्याख्यावितानानि विचित्राणि च मध्यतः ।
अनेककाररूपाश्च राजक्रीडोचिताः स्थिताः ॥9 ॥

67. शालभञ्ज्यादि प्रतिमा स्तम्भविमानसम्भवाः ।
मुक्तलूमच्छाद्योपरि घण्टाकूटैरलंकृताः ॥10 ॥

68. दिव्यसौवर्णकलशैर्मतवारणसम्युताः ।
सुरसद्नोपमाश्चैव नृपसद्माग्रमण्डपाः ॥11 ॥

8. लक्षणसमुच्चय **(अध्याय 26-9, 11)**

69. रविभाषा न कुऽयानि भ्रमणत् नखांशकैः ।
अष्टाविंशतिभिर्भित्तिः शासनस्तम्भ कुमारिके ॥9 ॥

70. हृदासारेश्वतुर्दिक्षु मंडपस्त्रिंशदशकैः ।
चतुस्तम्भाश्च तन्मध्ये द्वादशास्यकुमारिके ॥10 ॥

71. तिस्रस्तिस्रस्तु कोणेषु स्तम्भाग्रे कुमारिके ।
पाश्र्वयोरग्रमो वापि कुर्यादिसार संयुते ॥11 ॥

9. काश्यपशिल्पपटल **(अधयाय 48-49,51)**

72. अतिकान्तियुता रक्ताः कोशाभारालकान्विताः ।
नानाबन्धनसंयुक्ता नानापुष्पैरलंकृताः ॥49 ॥

73. दुकूलवसनां सर्वाः पीनोरूणघनास्तनाः ।
मध्यसूक्ष्माश्च सौम्याश्च किंचितप्रहसिताननः ॥50 ॥

74. नानागन्धानुलिप्ताङ्ग भद्रपीठोपरि स्थिताः ।
समभङ्गयुताः सप्तसङ्ख्या अप्सरसागणः ॥51 ॥

Glossary

agratala sañcāra pose: feet position, heels are raised up, the toe is thrust forward as if striking the ground

alaṁkāra: decoration, figure of speech

ālīḍha pose: warrior pose, one leg bent forward or sideways, the other leg stretched

amātya: minister

antarāla: space in front of the sanctum door, vestibule, conjoint space between the sanctum and the hall

añcita pose: one foot rests on the ground and the other foot's forepart is raised

apsaras: divine nymph, *surasundarī*

aśrama: forest dwelling

aśvattha: *pīpal* tree, *Ficus religiosa*, a type of fig tree

aśoka: *Saraca asoca*, "sorrow less" tree

atibhaṅga pose: many extreme bends in the body, many twists and turns in the posture

āyudha: weapon

baddhācārī pose: both shanks of the legs are crossed over and thighs move sideways

bhadra: central offset of the temple wall

bhadrapīṭha: auspicious seat

bhakti: devotional approach to religion

bhāravāhaka yakṣa: dwarf atlantid figures supporting super structure

bhitti: wall

bhūmi: storeys or levels of the superstructure

bhujaṅgatrāsita pose: After throwing up a foot, there is a three-cornered twist in the leg starting from the hip and the knee

bhūmija: a type of temple superstructure popular in western India, northern Karnataka and Malwa region of central India

cāmaradhāriṇī: female attendant who holds a fly whisk

daṇḍapādā cārī pose: leg lifted up as if tying an anklet, stretched and turned quickly

devadāsī: female servant of the gods, dancer who also conduct ritual worship

devakoṣṭha: niche

dhvani: implied meaning

dikpāla: directional deities of the eight cardinal directions

dvārapāla: door guardians

dvāraśākhās: door jambs

Gaṅgā: river Ganges personified as a goddess, placed on the sanctum doorway

gandharva: male celestial beings

gaṇikā: prostitute

garbha-gṛha: womb house or the sanctum of a temple

gavākṣa: cow's eye, horse shoe-shaped niche with figures placed in it

gatāgata pose: a movement of walking and halting suddenly

gati: movement

haṁsāsya gesture: hand gesture where thumb and index finger join and the other fingers are stretched out

hasta: hand gestures

hastimuṇḍī: elephant-faced capital

hāsya: laughter

ikṣudaṇḍa: sugar-cane bow of Kāma, the god of love

jaṅghā: wall frieze between plinth and superstructure

kakṣāsana: seatback or backrest

kalpavṛkṣa: wish-fulfilling tree

kapota: overhanging cornice

karṇa: corner or angle

kaṭisama pose: hands resting on the waist

khaḍgadhāriṇī / khaḍgavāhinī: women holding spears

*kumārikā*s: virgins

kumbha: pot-shaped base of a pillar

kumbhāṇḍaka: dwarf potbellied figures

kuñcita pāda: toe pressed to the ground and heel raised up, foot position

kuṇḍala: earplugs

lalāṭabimba: central portion of the door lintel

luma: pendentive in the centre of the ceiling

makara: composite crocodile-like sea creature, mythical vehicle of Gaṅgā

maṇḍapikā: canopied hall

mekhalā: waistband

mithuna: auspicious couple

mithunaśākhā: column of erotic couples on temple doorframe

mukha-maṇḍapa / mukha catuṣkī: front or entry hall

mṛdaṅga: two-sided drum

Nāgara: north Indian temple *śikhara* also known as *latinā* or *anekāṇḍika śikhara*

nāgakanyā / nāga nāyikā: female serpent

nārībandha: a band of female figures on the temple plinth

naṭī: female acrobat

nadī-devatā: river goddesses

padmadala: lotus stalk

phalanā: pilaster

piśāca: nocturnal, ghostly beings

pradakṣiṇā: circumambulation

pratiratha: wall-offset flanking *bhadra*, main niche

pratimā: image or visualization

praśasti: eulogy

pṛṣṭha svastika pose: feet crossed at the ankle, waist turned round and arms raised in *pārśvamaṇḍalī*, kept to the sides of the body

pratihārī: female attendant

pūrṇaghaṭa / kumbha: vase of plenty, a decorative motif in the shape of a brimming pot with foliage

puṣpabāṇa: flower arrow

rākṣasa: demons

ṛsi: sage

rūpaśākhā: doorjamb with human figures

śakti: energy or female consort of a male god

śālabhañjikā: woman and tree motif, bracket or pillar support

salilāntara: recess between wall bays

samudra-manthana: churning of the ocean

samabhaṅga: standing in equipoise, balanced posture

sandhivigrahika: officer who settles disputes

sthānaka: standing postures

sthapati: master architect, chief planner of the temple

sthira: stationary

śilpī: sculptor

śr̥ṅgāra: love

śubha: auspicious

surasundarī: heavenly dancers, *apsaras*

svastika(maṇḍala) pada: feet crossed over posture

tāpasī: female practitioner of *yoga* and meditation

toraṇa: gateway

tribhaṅga: standing posture in which the body bends at three places in an S curve

udgama: pediment of interconnected *gavākṣa* patterns

udumbara: threshold

udyāna-krīḍā: garden sport

uromaṇḍalī pose: after circling movement, one hand is to be raised up, the other is hanging down and certain movement takes place near the breast

ūrdhvajānu pose: one leg is lifted up to the knee level where the lifted knee comes to the chest level while the other rests on the ground holding the balance of the body

uttaraṅga: lintel

Uṣas: Dawn, consort of the sun-god, Sūrya

vāhana: mount, vehicle of the deity

varṇasaṅkara: hybridization, mixed population

vārimārga: water outlets, pilasters

vāv / *vāvḍī*: step well

vedikā: balustrade or railing

vīṇā: string instrument

vidyādhara: mythical beings having magical knowledge

vidyādevī: goddesses bearing knowledge, one of the sixteen Jain goddesses

vitāna: ceiling

vivr̥tta kaṭi: the waist turns round around the sacrum

vyāla: composite mythical animal

yajña: fire sacrifice

yoddhā: warrior

yogī: a male practitioner of *yoga* and meditation, usually a Śaiva monk

yoginī: female counterpart of *yogī*

yoga-mudrā: yogic pose

yakṣa: male nature spirit, benevolent as well as malevolent, worshipped in Jain and Buddhist religion and iconography

yakṣī: female nature spirit, benevolent as well as malevolent, worshipped in Jain and Buddhist religion and iconography

Yamunā: river Jamunā personified as a goddess, placed on the sanctum doorway

yāyāvarīya: one who travels from place to place

Bibliography

Agrawala, R.C., "Khajurāho of Rajasthan: The Temple of Ambikā at Jagat", *Arts Asiatiques*, X, 1964.

Agrawala, V.S., *Bṛhat Kathāśloka Saṁgraha: A Study*, Varanasi: Prithvi Prakashan, 1975.

———, *Studies in Indian Art*, Varanasi: Vishva Vidyalaya Prakashan, 1965.

———, *Harṣacarita: Ek Sānskṛtika Adhyayana* (Hindi), Patna: Bihar Rashtra Bhasha Parishad, 1964.

———, *Matsya Purāṇa: A Study*, Varanasi: All India Kashiraj Trust, 1963.

———, "Mathura Museum Catalogue", *Journal of Uttar Pradesh Historical Society*, 1951.

———, The *Handbook of the Curzon Museum of Archaeology, Mathura,* Allahabad: Government Printing Press, 1938.

Anand, Mulk Raj, ed., "Khajurāho", *Marg*, 3rd Edition, Bombay, 1968.

———, "Rajasthani Sculpture", *Marg*, vol. XII no. 2, Bombay, 1959.

Aparājitapṛcchā of Bhuvanadevācārya, ed. P.A. Mankad, Gaekwad Oriental Series, CXV, M.S. Baroda: University of Baroda, 1950.

Banerjea, J.N., *Development of Hindu Iconography*, New Delhi: Munshiram Manoharlal, 3rd edn., 1974.

Banerjee, Projesh, *Apsaras in Indian Dance*, New Delhi: Cosmo Publications, 1982.

Barthes, Roland, *Elements of Semiology*, tr. Annette Lavers and Colin Smith, London: Jonathan Cape, 1967.

Barua, B.M., *Bharhut: Stone as a Story Teller*, Indian Research Institute Series, Calcutta, 2nd edn., Patna, 1934.

———, *Bharhut*, Part I, *Stone as a Story Teller*; Part II, *Jataka Scenes*; Part III *Aspects of Life and Art*, Patna: Indological Book Corporation, 1979.

Bhāgavata Purāṇa, ed. J.L. Shastri, Delhi: Motilal Banarsidass, 1973.

Bharata, *Nāṭyaśāstra*, tr. Manmohan Ghosh, Calcutta: Asiatic Society of Bengal, 1950.

Bombay Gazetteer, vol. I, part I, *History of Gujarat*, Bombay, 1896.

Boner, Alice and S.R. Sharma, *Śilpa Prakāśa: Medieval Orissan Sanskrit Text on Temple Architecture*, by Ramachandra Kaulacharya, Leiden: E.J. Brill, 1966.

Brahmāṇḍa Purāṇa, ed. J.L. Shastri, New Delhi: Motilal Banarsidass, 1973.

Bruhn, Klans, *The Jain Images of Deogaṛh*, Leiden: E.J. Brill, 1969.

Buddhasvami, *Bṛhat Kathā Śloka Saṁgraha*, ed. V.S. Agrawala, Indian Civilization Series IV, Varanasi: Prithvi Prakashan, 1974.

Burgess, Jas and Henry Cousens, *The Architectural Antiquities of Northern Gujarat, Districts Included in Baroda state*, Archaeological Survey of India Western India, vol. IX, 1902, 1st Indian edn., Varanasi, 1975.

Chattopadhyaya, B.D., *The Making of Early Medieval India*, New Delhi: Oxford University Press, 1994.

———, *Historiography, History and Religious Centres, Early Medieval North India, circa AD 700-1200*, New Delhi: Oxford University Press, 1994.

Coomaraswamy, A.K., *History of Indian and Indonesian Art*, New York: Dover Publications, 1927.

———, *Yakṣas,* Washington: Smithsonian Institute, 1928, Indian edn., 1971.

Czuma, S.J., *Kuṣāṇa Sculptures*, Cleveland Museum of Art in cooperation with the Indiana University Press, 1985.

Daśakumāracarita, ed. M.R. Kale, New Delhi: Motilal Banarsidass, 1966.

Das, S.K. and M.C.P. Srivastava, *Mother Goddess in Indian Art, Archaeology and Literature*, New Delhi: Agam Kala Prakshan, 1979.

Das, S.K., *Śakti or Divine Power*, Calcutta: Central Press, 1934.

Dasgupta, S.N. and S.K. De, *A History of Sanskrit Literature*: *Classical Period,* vol. I, Calcutta: University of Calcutta Press, 1962.

De, S.K. and Edwin Gerow, *Sanskrit Poetics as a Study of Aesthetic*, Berkeley: University of California Press, 1962

Dehejia, V., *Yoginī Cult and Temples*: *A Tāntric Tradition*, New Delhi: National Museum, 1986.

Dehejia, Vidya, ed., *Representing the Body: Gender Issues in Indian Art*, New Delhi: Kali for Women in association with The Book Review Literary Trust, 1997.

Desai, Devangana, *Erotic Sculpture of India*: *A Socio-Cultural Study*, New Delhi: Tata-MacGraw Hill Pub Co, 1975.

———, "Sculptural Representation on the Lakṣmaṇa Temple on Khajurāho in the Light of Prabodhacandrodaya", *National Centre for the Performing Arts*, *Quarterly Journal*, Special Issue, vol. XI no. 324, 1982.

Desai, Vishakha and Darielle Mason, eds., *Gods, Guardians and Lovers: Temple Sculptures from North India AD 700-1200*, New York: The

Asia Society Galleries and Ahmedabad: Mapin Publishing Pvt. Ltd., 1993.

Deva, Krishna, *Kachchapaghata Temples*, The Researcher, 1969.

Deva, Krishna, *Seminar on Indian Art History*, Delhi, 1962.

———, *Temples of North India*, National Book Trust, New Delhi, 1969.

Dhaky, M.A., "The Chronology of the Solanki Temple of Gujarat", *journal of the Madhya Pradesh Itihas Parishad,* Bhopal, no. 3, 1961, p. 53.

———, "The Nīlakaṇṭheśvara Temple at Kekind", vol. XXIII, no. 3, March 1973.

Dhaky, M.A., "Genesis and Development of Maru–Gurjara Architecture", in *Studies in India Temple Architecture,* ed. Pramod Chandra, Bombay: American Institute of Indian Studies, 1975.

———, "Kirādu and the Maru–Gurjara Style of Temple Architecture", *Bulletin of American Academy of Benaras*, vol. I, Varanasi, 1967.

———, "The Chronology of the Solanki Temples of Gujarat", *Journal of the Madhya Pradesh Itihas Parishad*, no. 3, 1961.

———, "The Date of the Dancing Hall of the Sun Temple, Moḍherā", *Journal of the Asiatic Society of Bombay* (New Series), Bhaudaji Volume, ed. P.V. Kane, vol. 38, Bombay 1964.

———, "The Old Temple at Lamba and Kāmeśvara Temple at Auwa", *Journal of the Asiatic Society*, Calcutta, vol. VIII no. 3, 1966, p. 147.

———, "The Problems on Pramāṇamañjarī", *Bharatiya Vidya*, vol. XIX nos. 1-2.

———, *The Vāstuśāstras of Western India*, Reprint from Author's Introduction, *Prasādamañjarī* of Sūtradhara Nātha, ed. P.O. Sompura, 1965.

———, *The Vyālas on the Medieval Temples of India*, Indian Civilisation Series II, Varanasi, 1965.

Dikshitar, V.R. Ramachandra, *The Purāṇa Index,* vol. III (Ya to Ha), University of Madras, 1955.

Dimmitt, Cornelia and J.A.B. Buitenen, *Classical Hindu Mythlogy*, 1st published 1978, Indian edn., New Delhi: Rupa & Co., 1983.

Donaldson, Thomas, *The Hindu Temple Art of Orissa*, vols. I, II, III, Leiden: E.J. Brill, 1987.

Dubey, Lalmani, "Aparājitapṛcchā: A Critical Study", *Encyclopaedia of Art and Architecture*, Allahabad, 1987.

Dvyāśraya Kāvya, sarga IX and *Vikramāṅkacarita*, sarga X.3, v. 97, *Indian*

Antiquary, 1975.

Dwivedi, R.C., ed. & tr., *Mammaṭa's Kāvya Prakāśa*, vols. I & II, New Delhi: Motilal Banarsidass, 1966-70.

Epigraphia Indica, XI (1911-12), ed. Sten Konow (reprint 1981).

Epigraphia Indica, XV (1919-20), ed. F.W. Thomas (reprint 1982).

Focillon, *Life of Forms in Art*, 1933, English tr. C.B. Hogan and George Kubler, New York: Wittenborn, 1957.

Fordham, Frieda, *An Introduction to Jung's Psychology*, Harmondsworth, Middlesex: Penguin Books, 1953.

Foucault, Michael, *The Archaeology of Knowledge*, tr. A.M. Sheridan Smith, 1st published in Editions Gallimard, New York: Pantheon, 1972.

Frankl, Paul, "Principles of Architectural History", *The Four Phases of Architectural Style, 1420-1900*, 1st German edn., 1914, 1st English tr., MIT Press, 1968.

Ganguli, K.K., *Cultural History of Rajasthan*, New Delhi: Sundeep Prakashan, 1983.

Ganguli, O.C., *Indian History Quarterly*, vol. XIX no. 1. March, 1943.

Garimella, Annapurna, "Engendering Indian Art", in Vidya Dehejia (ed.), *Representing the Body: Gender Issues in Indian Art*, New Delhi: Kali for Women, 1997.

Ghosh, M., *Nandīkeśvara's Abhinayadarpaṇam, A Manual of Gesture and Posture Used in Hindu Dance and Drama: English Translation and Notes with Introduction and Illustrations*, Calcutta: Manisha Granthalaya Private Ltd., 1975.

Gidion, Seigfried, *The Eternal Present*, Parts I, II, New York: Pantheon Books, 1964.

Gjjar, Irene, *Ancient Indian Art and the West: A Study of Parallels, Continuity, and Symbolism from Proto-Historic to early Buddhist Times*, Bombay: D.B. Taraporewala & Sons, 1971.

Gopinath Rao, T.A., *Elements of Hindu Iconography*, 4 vols., Madras: Law Printing House, 1914-16.

Gorkshakar, S., "Parel Mahādeva Reassessed", *Lalitkala*, 20, New Delhi, 1982.

Gupta, S.P., ed., *Kuṣāṇa Sculptures from Saṅghol,* New Delhi: National Museum, 1985.

Handa, Devendra, *Osia: History, Archaeology, Art and Architecture*, New Delhi: Sundeep Prakashan, 1984.

Handique, K.K., *Apsarases in Indian Literature*, New Delhi: D.K. Printworld, 2001.

Harsha, M., "Sikar: An Early Chauhan Monument", *The Researcher,* Journal of Rajasthan Department of Archaeology, vols. V & VI.

Ingalls, D.H.H., *An Anthology of Sanskrit Court Poetry, Vidyākara's Subhāṣita Ratnakośa*, Harvard Oriental Series, vol. 44, Harvard University Press, 1965.

Iravati, "All Female Theatre: As Depicted in Ancient Indian Literature and Art", *Purātana*, vol. 7, Madhya Pradesh Commissioner, Archaeology and Museums, Bhopal, 1989.

Jayakar, Pupul, *The Earthen Drum*, New Delhi: National Museum, 1980.

Kāśyapa Śilpaśāstram, ed. S.H. Ganapati Sastri, Anandashram Sanskrit Series, 1986.

Kālidāsa, *Meghadūtam*, tr. Chandra Rajan, *Kālidāsa*: *The Loom of Time, A Selection of His Plays and Poems*, New Delhi: Penguin Classics, 1989.

Keith, A.B., *Sanskrit Drama,* 1st Indian edn., New Delhi: Motilal Banarsidass, 1992.

———, *The Religion and Philosophy of the Veda and Upaniṣads*, Harvard Oriental Series, vol. 31, 1st edn., Harvard University Press, 1925.

Kleinbauer, W. Eugene, *Modern Perspectives in Western Art History*: *An Anthology of Twentieth Century Writings on the Visual Arts*, New York: Holt, Rinehart and Winston, 1971.

Kosambi, D.D., *Myth and Reality*, Bombay: Popular Prakashan, 1962.

Kramrisch, Stella, *Hindu Temple*, Calcutta: Motilal Banarsidass, 1946.

———, *Indian Sculpture*, Calcutta: Y.M.C.A. Publishing House, London: Oxford University Press, 1933; Indian reprint, New Delhi: Motilal Banarsidass, 1981.

———, *Khajurāho*, Bombay: Marg Publication, 1962.

———, *Pāla–Sena Sculptures*, Calcutta: Indian Society of Oriental Art (Reprinted from Rupam), 1929.

Krishnamurthy, K., *Dhvanyāloka of Ānandavardhana*, Critically edited with Intro., trans. and notes, New Delhi: Motilal Banarsidass, 1974, 2nd edn., 1982.

Kṣīrārṇava, ed. P.O. Sompura, Palitana, 1966.

Kṣemendra, *Samayamātṛkā*, tr. E. Powys Mathers, London, 1927, VIII, 83.

Kuiper, F.B.J., *Varuṇa and Vidūṣaka*: *On the Origin of the Sanskrit Drama*, Amsterdam, 1979.

Kumārapāla Carita, VI.32, I, 1966-67.

Lal, Kanwar, *Erotic Sculptures of Khajurāho*, New Delhi: Asia Press, 1970.

Lanius, M.C., *Rajasthani Sculpture of the Ninth and Tenth Centuries: Aspects of Indian Art*, ed. P. Pal, Leiden: E.J. Brill, 1972.

Lobo, Wibke, *The Sun Temple at Moḍherā*, Forschungen zur allgemeinen und vergleichenden Archeologie, Munchen, 1982.

Longhurst, A.H., "Buddhist Antiquities of Nāgārjunakoṇḍā, Madras Presidency", *Memoirs of the Archaeological Survey of India*, no. 54, Delhi, 1938.

Macdonell, A.A., *Vedic Mythology*, Strassburg: K.J. Trubner, 1898, Indian reprint, New Delhi: Motilal Banarsidass, 1981.

Majmudar, M.R., *Gujarat: Its Art Heritage*, Bombay: Popular Prakashan, 1968.

———, *Historical and Cultural Chronology of Gujarat from Earliest Times to 942 AD*, Baroda: M.S. University of Baroda, 1960.

Majumdar, A.K., *Cāḷukyas of Gujarat: A Survey of the History and Culture of Gujarat, from the Middle of the 10th Century to the end of 13th Century*, Bombay: Bharatiya Vidya Bhavan, 1956.

Mani, Vettam, *Purāṇic Encyclopaedia: A Comprehensive Dictionary with Special Reference to the Epic and Purāṇic Literature*, 1st edn. 1964 (Malayalam), New Delhi: Motilal Banarsidass, 1975 (English).

Mankodi, Kirit, *The Queen's Step-well at Pāṭan*, Bombay: Franco Indian Research, 1990.

Marglin, Frederique Apffel, *Wives of the God King: The Rituals of the Devadāsīs of Puri*, New Delhi: Oxford University Press, 1985.

Marshall, J., and A. Foucher, *The Monuments of Sāñcī*, 3 vols., London: Probsthein, 1940, New Delhi: Swati Publications, 1983.

Matsya Purāṇa, Anandashram Series, no. 54, Poona, 1907.

Mehta, Mohanlal and K. Rishabha Chandra, *Āgamic Index*, vol. I, General Editor Dalsukh Malvania, Lalbhai Dalpatbhai Series, no. 37, Ahmedabad: L.D. Institute of Indology, 1970.

Meister, M., M.A. Dhaky and Krishna Deva, *Encyclopaedia of Indian Architecture*, vol. II, Part I, *North India*, American Institute of Indian Studies, Princeton University Press, 1989.

Merutunga, *Prabandha Cintāmaṇi*, ed. Jinavijayaji, Guj. trans. Khanda, G.O.S., no. CIII, Baroda: M.S. University of Baroda, 1958.

Misra, R.N., *Sculptures of Dāhala and Dakṣiṇa Kośala and their*

Background, New Delhi: Agam Kala Prakashan, 1987.

———, *Yakṣa Iconography*, New Delhi: Munshiram Manoharlal, 1981.

Mitra, Shishirkumar, *Early Rulers of Khajurāho*, Calcutta: Motilal Banarsidass, 1st edn. 1958.

Morris, C.W., *Signs, Languages and Behaviour*, New York: Prentice-Hall, 1946.

Motichandra, *The World of Courtesans,* New Delhi: Vikas Publishing House, 1973.

Munro, Thomas, *Evolution in the Arts, and other Theories of Culture / History*, Cleveland: Cleveland Museum of Art, 1963.

———, *Form and Style in the Arts*, Ohio: Press of Case Western University, 1970.

Nanavati, J.H. and M.A. Dhaky, "The Ceilings in the Temples of Gujarat", *Bulletin of Baroda Museum*, vols. XVI, XVII, Baroda, 1963.

Nath, R., *Khajurāho,* New Delhi: Abhinav Publication, 1980.

Neumann, Eric, *The Great Mother*: *An Analysis of the Archetype*, English tr. 1955, Princeton University Press, 1991.

O'Flaherty, Wendy, *Asceticism and Eroticism in the Mythology of Śiva*, New Delhi: Oxford University Press, 1973.

Śṛṅgāramañjarī, ed. Kalpana Munshi, Bombay, 1959.

Pal, P., *Bulletin of Allen Memorial Art Museum*, vol. 28, no. 2, 1971.

Panofsky, Erwin, *Meaning in Visual Arts*, Chicago: University of Chicago Press, 1955.

———, *Studies in Iconology*, Oxford: Westview Press, 1939.

Parikh, Rasiklal & Hariprasad Shastri, eds., *Solaṅkī Kāla*: *Gujarat no Rajakiya ane Sanskrutik Itihas* (Gujarati), vol. 4, Ahmedabad, 1976.

Parimoo, Gauri, *A Study of Nṛttahastas in Indian Dance* — A dissertation submitted to the Department of Dance, Faculty of Performing Arts, M.S. University of Baroda, 1985-86 (unpublished).

Parimoo, Ratan, *Art of Ajantā*: *New Perspectives*, New Delhi: Books and Books, 1991.

———, *Essays in New Art History Studies in Indian Sculpture*, New Delhi: Books and Books, 2000.

———, *Essays in New Art History*, vol. I, *Studies in Indian Sculpture: Regional Genres and Interpretations*, New Delhi: Books & Books, 2000.

———, *Sculptures of Śeṣasāyī Viṣṇu*, Baroda: M.S. University of Baroda Press, 1983.

———, "Adaptation of Folk Tales for Buddhist Jātaka Stories and their depiction in Indian Art: A Study in Narrative and Semiotic Transformation", *Journal of M.S. University of Baroda*, Humanities Number, 1991-92.

———, "Khajurāho — The Candella Sculptors' Paradise: Is there a Candella Style of Medieval Indian Sculpture? Its sources and Characteristics", *Indian Archaeological Heritage, Soundara Rajan Felicitation Volume,* ed. Margabandhu, New Delhi, 1991.

———, "Some Aspects of Decorative Repertoire of Gujarat Temple Architecture", *Decorative Arts of India*, Salarjung Museum Seminar Papers, ed. M.L. Nigam, Hyderabad, 1987.

———, "The Aspects of Form and Style in Indian Sculpture", *Aspects of Indian Art and Culture, S.K. Sarasvati Commemoration Volume*, ed. Jayanta Chakrabarty, D.C. Bhattacharya, Calcutta, 1983.

———, "The Myth of Gupta Classicism and the Concept of Regional Genres: Historical and Cultural Overview I & II", *New Quest*, November–December, 1990, January–February, 1991.

———, "Uncovering the Meaning of the Picture Puzzles of Bihari Satsai painted by Jagannath: A Semiotic Study", *East & West,* Rome, vol. 45 nos. 1-4, 1995.

Parimoo, Ratan and Vidhura Pandita, "Jātaka, from Bharhut to Ajantā: A Study of Narrative, Semiology and Stylistic Aspects", in *Dr. Debala Mitra Felicitation Volume*, ed. Gaurishwar Bhattacharya, New Delhi, 1991

Parimoo-Krishnan, Gauri, "Devāṅganā Sculptures in the Rānī Vāv", *India Magazine*, vol. 9, 1989.

Pisharoti, K. Rama, "Dohada or the Woman and Tree Motif", in *JISOA*, vol. III no. 2, Albany: SUNY Press, 1935.

Pollock, Griselda, "Feminist Interventions in the Histories of Art: An Introduction", *Vision and Difference*: *Femininity, Feminism and Histories of Art*, London: Routledge, 1988.

Raghavan, V., *Śṛṅgāra Prakāśa*, Hindi tr. P.D. Agnihotri, Bhopal, 1981, 1st publ., Ministry of Education and Social Welfare, Government of India, Madras, 1963.

———, "Uparūpaka and Nṛtya Prabandhas", *Sangeet Natak*, no. 76, New Delhi, 1985.

———, *Studies on Some Concepts of the Alaṁkāraśāstra*, Adyar Library Series, vol. 33, Madras, 1942.

———, ed., *Aestheticians: Cultural Leaders of India*, New Delhi: Publications Division, 1983.

Raja, K. Kunjuni, *Indian Theories of Meaning*, Madras: Adyar Library and Research Centre, 1963;

Raja, K. Kunjunni and Radha Burnier, *Saṅgīta Ratnākara of Śāraṅgadeva*, vol. IV, Adyar Library Series, vol. 108, Madras: Adyar Library and Research Centre, 1976.

Rajan, Chandra, *Kālidāsa, The Loom of Time: A Selection of His Plays and Poems*, Calcutta, 1989.

Rājataraṅgiṇī, VII, VIII, Westminster: Archibald Constable and Company Ltd., 1900.

Ray, H.C., *Dynastic History of North India,* New Delhi: Munshiram Manoharlal, 1973.

Rosenfield, M., *Dynastic Art of the Kuṣāṇas*, University of California Press, 1967.

Rowland, Benjamin, *The Art and Architecture of India*, Middlesex: Penguin, 1953.

Roy, U.N., *Śālabhañjikā in Art: Philosophy and Literature,* Allahabad: Lokbharati Publications, 1979.

Samarāṅgaṇa Sūtradhāra, ed. Ganapati Sastri, Gaekwad Oriental Series, no. 25, Baroda: M.S. University of Baroda, 1966.

Sankalia, H.D., *Prehistoric and Historic Archaeology of Gujarat,* New Delhi: Munsihram Manoharlal, 1987.

Saussure, 1983, pp. 127-28, from "Semiotics for Beginners by Daniel Chandler", *Paradigms and Syntagms*, http://www.aber.ac.uk/media/ Documents /S4B /sem03.html.

Sewell, Robert, *Prabandha Cintāmaṇi, The Journal of the Royal Asiatic Society of Great Britain and Ireland*, no. 3 (July 1920), pp. 333-41, Cambridge University Press, 1920.

Shah, U.P., *Akoṭā Bronzes*, Bombay, Department of Archaeology, Government of Bombay, 1959.

———, *Roḍā na mandiro nā nārī Svarūpo*, Gujarat Dipotsavi Anka, VS 2032.

———, *Sculptures of Shāmalāji and Roḍā*, Baroda, 1961,

———, "Some Medieval Sculptures from Gujarat and Rajasthan", *Journal of the Indian Society of Oriental Art, Western India, 1966*, ed. U.P. Shah & K.K. Ganguli.

———, *Western Indian Sculpture and the so-called Gupta Influence*: *Aspects of Indian Art*, ed. P. Pal, Leiden: E.J. Brill, 1972.

Sharma, Dasarath, *Early Cauhān Dynasties* (*AD 800-1316*), New Delhi: S. Chand & Co., 1959.

Sharma, Gopinath, *Rājasthan ke Itihās ke Srota*, Jaipur: Panchsheel Prakashan, 1973, p. 66 (Hindi).

Sharma, R.C., *Mathurā Museum and Art*: *A Comprehensive Pictorial Guide Book*, Mathura: Government Museum, 1971.

Sharma, R.P. Pandey, *Rājaśekhara aur unakā Yuga*, Patna, 1977.

Shearman, John, *Mannerism*, London: Penguin Books, 1967, reprint, 1973.

Singh, Mahesh, *Bhoja Paramāra and His Times*, New Delhi: Bharatiya Vidya Prakashan, 1984.

Sivaramamurti, C., *Citrasūtra of Viṣṇudharmottara*, New Delhi: Kanak Publications, 1978.

———, *Śrī-Lakṣmī in Indian Art,* New Delhi: Kanak Publications, 1982.

———, "Amarāvatī Sculptures in the Madras Government Museum", *Bulletin of the Madras Government Museum*, New Series, vol. IV, Madras, 1942 & 1977.

———, "Sanskrit Literature and Art: Mirrors of Indian Culture", *Memoirs of the Archaeological Survey of India*, no. 73, New Delhi, 1955.

Sri Aurobindo and the Mother, *On Women*, Aurobindo Ashram, Pondicherry, 1st edn., 1978.

Srinivasan, K.S., *The Ethos of Indian Literature*: *A Study of Its Romantic Tradition*, New Delhi: Chanakya Publications, 1985.

Srivastava, M.C.P., *Mother Goddess in Indian Art*: *Archaeology and Literature*,New Delhi: Agam Kala Prakashan, 1979.

"Moḍherā, Modha-Vaṁsa, Modha-Gaccha and Modha-Caityas", *Journal of the Asiatic Society of Bombay*, Bhagavanlal Indraji Memorial Volume, ed. Devangana Desai, vols. 56-59, 1981-84, Bombay.

Stein, Burton, *Peasant State and Society in Medieval South India,* New Delhi: Oxford University Press, 1980.

Storr, Anthony, *Jung*, London: Fontana Press, 1973.

Story, Saskia Kersenboom, *Nitya Sumaṅgali*: *Devadāsī Tradition in South India*, New Delhi: Motilal Banarsidass, 1987.

Stutley, Margaret, *Ancient Indian Magic and Folklore*, New Delhi:

Munshiram Manoharlal Publishers, 1980.

Srinivasan, K.S., *Subhāṣita Ratnakośa*, New Delhi, 1985.

Tewari, S.P., *Royal Attendants in Ancient Indian Literature, Epigraphy & Art*, New Delhi: Agam Kala Prakashan, 1987.

Tripathi, L.K., *Temples of Badoli*, Varanasi, 1975.

Upadhye, A.N., ed., *Udyotanasuri Kuvalayamālā*, Singhi Jain Series, Bombay: Bharatiya Vidya Bhavan, 1957.

Upadhyay, Baldev, *Sanskrit Sāhitya ka Itihāsa*, vol. I, *Kāvya Khaṇḍa*, Varanasi, 1947, 10th edn., 1978.

Vāstusūtra Upaniṣad: The Essance of Form in Sacred Art, text, tr., ed. Alice Boner, S.R. Sharma, B. Baumer, New Delhi: Motilal Banarsidass, 1982.

Vatsyayan, Kapila, *Classical Dance in Literature and the Arts*, New Delhi: Ministry of Information and Broadcasting, 1968.

———, *Traditional Indian Theatre, Multiple Streams,* New Delhi: National Book Trust, 1980.

Vāyu Purāṇa, Anandashram Series, no. 49, Poona, 1983.

Viennot, Odette, *Les Divinites Fluviales, Gaṅgā et Yamunā, aux portes des Sanctuaries de L'inde*, Paris, 1964.

Viṣṇu Purāṇa, Bombay: Oriental Press, 1889.

Vogel, J.Ph., "The Mathurā School of Sculpture", *Archaeological Survey of India Annual Report, 1906-07.*

———, "La Sculpture de Mathurā", *Arts Asiatica*, XV.

———, "The Woman and Tree, or Śālabhañjikā in Indian Literature and Art", *Acta Orientalia*, VII, Leiden, 1929.

Wilson, H.H., *Viṣṇu Purāṇa*, A System of Hindu Mythology and Tradition, translated from the Original Sanskrit, Published by John Murray, Oxford: Oxford University, 1840.

Willis, Michael D., "Religion and Royal Patronage in North India", *Gods, Guardians and Lovers*, ed. Vishakha Desai, Darielle Mason, Nelson Atkins Museum, Asia Society Galleries in association with Mapin Publishing, Ahmedabad, 1993.

Woodroffe, John, *The Serpent Power*, London: Luzac & Co., 1922.

Zannas, Eliky, *Khajurāho,* The Hague: Mouton & Co., 1960.

Zimmer, Heinrich, *The Art of Indian Asia: Its Mythology and Transformations*, 1st published Princeton University Press, 1st Indian edn., New Delhi: Oxford University Press, 1984, vol. I.

Index

A.S.I. Reports IX, 256
Ābaneri, 264, 305, 362
Ābhāpur, 178, 347, 350, 373, 416
abhayagarika, 88
abhaya-hasta, 98
abhidhā, 15, 76, 344, 378, 380
abhidheya-sambandha, 16
Abhimanyu, 39
Abhinavabhāratī, 49
Abhinavagupta, 49, 350-51
abhinaya, 78, 351
abhyudāgama, 82
Ābu (Mt.), 4, 37, 40, 42, 145, 165, 168, 171, 359, 364, 367-68
Achalgaṛh, 178
adavus, 417
adholoka, 74
Aditi, 4, 20, 55, 58-59, 248, 289
  Uttānapāda, 303
Āditya(s), 67, 166-67, 410, 414
  twelve, 67
Āgama(s), 94, 311, 351
Āgamic
  indexes, 74
  sources, 9
  tradition, 75
  texts, 352-53
Aghoraśivācārya, 353
Agni, 56, 61-62, 65, 70, 210, 247, 251, 387
Agni Purāṇa, 236
agni-koṇa, 97, 387
agnikuṇḍa, 33
Agnimitra, 223
agrāmya, 47
agratālasañcāra, 346
Agrawala, V.S., vii, 3, 6, 88, 208, 211, 220, 225, 227-28, 236, 305, 311, 323
Āhaṛ, 44-45, 140, 146, 148, 150, 156, 300
  temple, 145
Ahila, 43
Ahmedabad, 36, 394
Ajantā, 4, 87, 210, 214-15, 230-32, 234, 238-40, 242, 253, 259-60, 273, 278, 305, 361, 401, 409
Ajayapāla, 43
Ajitāgama, 353
Ajitnātha, 42
Akālavarṣa, 36
Akoṭā, 362
  sculptures, 47
akṣapāṭalikā, 44
Alakāpurī, 79
alaktaka, 81
alaṁkāra(s), 13, 44, 47, 49-50, 387
  school, 49
  theories of, 47
Alaṁkāra Śāstra, 44, 48-49
Alaṁkāra Sarvasva, 49
alaṁkārikā(s), 59, 78
  terminology, 209
alasā(s), 4, 17, 91, 93, 97, 138, 148, 150, 156, 162-63, 171, 173, 219, 232, 242, 257, 264, 273, 337, 342, 372, 378, 383, 389-90, 392, 399, 401, 410
  *devāṅganā*s, 389
  imagery, 336
  *nāyikā*s, 144, 336
  pose, 145
  sculptures, 342
  imageries of, 296
alasākanyā(s), vii, 2-3, 6, 9, 11, 92, 337, 418; see also *apsaras*(es)
  sculptures of, 2
Alberuni, 85
Alhaṇa, 83
ālīḍha, 315, 320, 323, 347, 405
āliṅgana-mudrā, 387
Allahabad Museum, 264
Allaṇadeva, 42
Allaṭa, 44
allegorical imageries, 14
alluring movements, 78
Alwar, 171, 292
*āmalaka*s, 137
amānuṣī, 70
Amarakośa, 88
Amarāvatī, 33, 58, 87, 201, 214, 234, 256, 361, 401
  sculptures, 7
  Nāgārjunakoṇḍa, 208, 214
Amaruśataka, 217
amātya, 44
Amazonian
  guards, 323
  origin, 86
American Institute of Indian Studies, 4
Aṁjhara, 145, 359, 362
Amoghavarṣa, 36
āmralumbī, 278, 292, 294, 405
āmralumbīdhārī, 389, 396
Amrol, 120, 403
amṛta, 65, 247
Amwan, 166
Ānadavardhana, 15
Anahilawāḍa, 37-38, 45
Anahilawāḍa Pāṭan, 43
ānanda, 66
Ānandavardhana, viii, 17, 48-49, 378
Ānartta, 34, 118, 130, 142, 168
  temples, 140
ancient Indian psyche, 74
añcita, 78, 346
Andhaka, 93
Andhakāsuravadha Śiva, 161, 168
Āndhra, 77
  art, 215
anekāṇḍikā śikhara, 120, 142, 146, 163
aṅga, 80, 168
aṅgaḍāī, 410
aṅgadāyī, 146
āṅgikābhinaya, 48
Aṅgkor Vat, 94
Anhilpur Pāṭan, 363
añjalī hasta, 97-98, 387
añjalī-mudrā, 264
Añjār, 140
antaḥpurika, 87
antarāla, 150-51, 162, 164, 167, 388
antarāla maṇḍapa, 388
antarapatra, 142-43
Antarsuba, 178

anti-caityāvāsa, 84
Apabhraṁśa, 42, 44, 48, 84
apāna, 71
apāna bhūmi, 80
Aparājitapṛcchā, 10-11, 46, 85, 90, 93, 96, 146, 396, 399
Aphrodite, 196
Apsarā-Diśākumārī Interrelationship, 74
apsarāgaṇa bhūṣita, 396
apsaras(es), vii, 2-9, 11-12, 26, 55, 57, 59-67, 69-77, 86, 89-91, 94-95, 97, 106, 109, 138, 142, 150, 166, 171, 187, 191, 198-99, 201, 208, 211, 225, 251-52, 272, 288, 292, 297, 311, 337, 344, 346, 379-80, 396, 409-10, 413, 416-19
- imagery, 66
- imagery of, 380
- images, 413
- lover of, 62
- motif, 59
- sculptures of, 2
- thirty-four, 66
- tradition, 13
- with Sūrya, 413

apsaras(es), names of
- Adrikā, 66
- Alakanandā, 210
- Alambuṣā, 7, 64, 66, 72-75, 210
- Alasā, 91, 336
- Ānandā, 75
- Aniṁdiā, 74
- Anurāginī, 200
- Aparājitā, 75, 93
- Ariṣṭā, 64-65
- Arjunī, 64
- Aruṇā, 66
- Asitā, 66
- Avantīsundarī, 48
- Bakulādevī, 40
- Bhaddā, 75
- Bhāvacandrā, 97-98
- Bhogalakṣmī, 59
- Bhogamālinī, 74
- Bhogaṁkarā, 74
- Bhogavatī, 74
- Bhūdevī, 58
- brackets, 163
- Bṛhaddivā, 54-55, 227
- Cāmuṇḍā, 20, 37, 138, 306
- Caṇḍikā, 93
- Candrāpīḍā, 88
- Candrarekhā, 97-98
- Candravaktrā, 99
- Candravaletrā, 97
- Candrāvalī, 97-98, 387
- Carcarī, 85
- Chasī, 66
- Citriṇī, 97-98
- Cittā, 75
- Cittaguttā, 75
- Cittakanāgā, 75
- Ḍālamālikā, 91
- Dedadarā, 130, 136
- Devadattā, 64
- Devasakhā, 97-98
- Devasenā, 64
- Dhanalakṣmī, 59
- Dhanapāla, 48
- Dhanurūpā, 65
- Dhānyalakṣmī, 59
- Dhīṣaṇā, 54, 227, 283
- Dhṛti, 64
- Divyā, 66
- Egaṇasā, 75
- Gajalakṣmī, 210
- Ghṛtāci, 69, 73
- Gūḍhaśabdā-Padmanetrā, 97
- Guhavāsinī, 200
- Guṇā, 154
- Guṇāḍhya, 87
- Hāhā, 64
- Haṁsapādā, 66
- Haṁsāvalī, 97-98
- Hasā, 75
- Hemā, 66
- Hirī, 75
- Hūhū, 64
- Iḷā, 54-55, 59, 283
- Iḷādevī, 75
- Indumatī, 89
- Irāvatī, 211
- Jagandhā, 66
- Jalasāṅgī, 392
- Jayā, 97, 99
- Jayantī, 75
- Kalabhā, 64
- Kalāvatī, 72
- Kalyāṇī, 37-38
- Kāmeśvarī, 199
- Kanakamatī, 199
- Kandukavatī, 299
- Kapiśā, 220
- Keśinī, 64
- Ketakībharaṇā, 91-92
- Kṣemā, 66
- Kṣemaṅkarī, 388
- Kuhu, 54
- Kulavardhanā, 89
- Lakṣmīmatī, 210
- Lāvaṇya Sundarī, 86
- Mahābhāgā, 65
- Mālavikā, 223
- Mānahaṁsā, 97-98
- Mañci, 73
- Māninī, 91, 97-98
- Mañjughoṣā, 97, 99, 387
- Mañjukeśī, 64
- Manobhavā, 66
- Manohāriṇī, 199

apsaras(es) Cont.
- Manoramā, 64, 66
- Mardalā, 92-93
- Maricī, 66
- Maricikā, 97-98
- Markandi, 392
- Māyādevī, 5, 77
- Mehaṁkarā, 74
- Mehamālinī, 74
- Mehavatī, 74
- Menakā, 64, 73, 97, 228, 323, 385, 387
- Miśkosī, 210
- Miśrakeśī, 64, 66, 72, 74-75
- Mohinī, 99, 297
- Mṛgākṣī, 97-98
- Mṛgāṅkavatī, 297

Mṛgāvatī, 72
Mṛṇālakhādika, 82
Mugdhā, 91
Nalinī, 210
Nandā, 64, 75
Nandīvadhanā, 75
Nanduttarā, 75
Naṭī, 200
Nūpurapādikā, 92
Nūpurapādikā-Saṅgītavādinī, 350
Padmagandhā, 91
Padmanetrā, 98
Padminī, 97-98, 200, 387
Parṇinī, 66
Paruṣṇī, 57
Pradhā, 72-73
Pramadvārā, 73
Prasādhikā, 330, 332
Puṇḍarikā, 66, 75
Puraṁdhī, 54-55, 59, 227, 283
Pūrṇitā, 66
Pūrvacittī, 73
Putravallabhā, 97-98
Putrikā, 66
Rakṣitā, 64
Rambhā, 64, 66, 71-72, 97, 99, 326, 387
Rati, 323
Ratipriyā, 200
Revatī, 134
Sahajanyā, 73
Śaivyā, 66
Samahārā, 75
Santatī, 64
Śaradvatī, 66
Saralā, 64
Sarvakalā, 97-98
Saudāminī, 64
Sīnīvālī, 4, 54, 56, 59, 227
Śubhagāminī, 97-98
Subhogā, 74
Subhujā, 66
Śuci, 71
Sucibhā, 66
Sudalī, 66
Sudantā, 66
Sudarśanā, 210
Sudatī, 64
Sugandhā, 66, 97-98
Sukasārikā, 92
Sumālā, 64
Sumehā, 74
Sumukhī, 64
Sunandā, 64, 89
Sundarī, 64, 97-98
Supabudhā, 75
Supainnā, 75
Supratiṣṭhitā, 66
Supriyā, 64, 66
Supuṣkalā, 64
Suradevī, 75
Surajā, 64
Surasā, 66
Surottamā, 66
Susvabhāvā, 97-98
Sutarā, 75
Sūtrapāḍā, 114
Suvacchā, 74
Suvarā, 66
Suvratā, 66
Suyaśā, 198
Tamasundarī, 200
Tilottamā, 64-66, 72-73, 99
Toyadharā, 74
Tusā, 140, 145, 155, 261, 292, 294, 300, 342, 363, 365, 372, 396, 410
Ūrjā, 71
Urvaśī, 54, 64, 69-73, 97, 99, 323, 326, 385, 387
Vaccamittā, 74
Vārāhī, 330
Varisenā, 74
Varṇinī, 66
Vāruṇī, 75, 252
Vedavatī, 65
Vejayantī, 75
Vicittā, 74
Vidagdhā, 64
Viddhaśālabhañjikā, 26, 47-48, 80, 297
Vidhicitrā, 97-98
Vidyutparṇā, 64, 66, 72
Vijayā, 74-75, 97
Vilāsavatī, 89
Vindhyavāsinī, 83, 299
Vinyāsā, 91-92
Vīrā, 320
Vīralakṣmī, 59
Viśvāci, 73
Vṛkṣikā, 201
Yakṣarātri, 83
Yakṣiṇī, 210
Yaśaprāptā, 210
apsaras–śālā, 58
apsaras-devāṅganā imagery(ies), 56, 99, 199, 248
*apsaras-devāṅganā*s, 396
apsaras–gandharva(s), 58, 248, 288
pair, 288
apsaras–moon, 58
apsaras–soma, 58
ap-sāriṇī, 60
āpya, 57, 70
apyā yoṣā, 60
aquatic bird, 60
aqueous nymph, 60-61
Arabs, 39
āratī, 352
Arbudā, 34, 46, 111, 118
Maṇḍala, 37
Medapāṭa, 120
archaeological excavation, 21
archaeology, 21
archetypal
feminine, 19
figure, 19
image, formation of, 20
archetype, 19
symbolism of, 19
universality of, 20
architectural
contexts, 7
development of Nāgara temples, 106
fabric, 305
motif, 5
parts, development of, 109

planning, 106
programmes, 46
programming, 8
schema, vii
sites, 2
structure(s), 11, 382
style(s), 4, 11, 34, 46
texts, 27, 89, 95, 111, 146
texts of Gujarat, 11

architecture,
and literature, 34
development of, 145
Maru–Gurjara style of, 364
morphology of, vii
religious, 272
stylistic development of, 14

ardha-maṇḍalī, 315, 346-47
Arikesarī, Thānā plates of, 38
Arjula, 372
Arjuna, 35, 39, 73
Arjunavarman, 37
Arṇorāja, 41, 45
art,
and literature, 5
consumption of, 24
forms, 46
historical problems, writing on, 10
of Kuṣāṇa period, 56
production, 27
production of, 24

art history, 24, 25
discipline of, viii

artha, 17, 49
Arthaśāstra, 88, 234
arthāntara saṁkramita vācya, 17
Arthuṇā, 364
praśasti, 37

artistic
imagery, 272
material, 22
tradition, 14

artists' guilds, 34
Āryāvarta, Mahārājādhirāja of, 35
Āṣāḍha, 72
asaṁlakṣyakrama vyaṅgya, 17
āsana paṭṭaka, 117
Asarāja, Bali inscription of, 41
asat, 276
asceticism, 5
Asia Society, New York, 12
asiggāhaka, 86
aśoka, 221, 223, 297
flowers, 81
tree, 81, 200, 203

aśoka dohada, 6, 16, 79, 81, 192, 197, 224
imagery, 383
krīḍā, 218, 223
motif(s), 6, 192, 203, 221

Aśoka Vihāra, 81
aśokottamsika, 81
āśrama, 69
Aṣṭamīcandra, 81
aṣṭanāyikās, 337
Astarte, 20-21, 195
Aṣṭāvakra, 72
asura(s), 72
Asurāja, 41
Aśvaghoṣa, 6, 78, 236
aśvattha, 60, 190, 251
Aśvins, 56
Atantīya Sutta, 76, 210
atayaḥ, 60
Atharvaveda, 54, 56-57, 59-63, 95, 199, 201, 247-48, 276, 311
Atibāhu, 64
atibhaṅga, 323, 347
Atru, 144, 165-66, 363-64, 371, 390
master sculptors, 371
sculptural proportions, 371

attitudes, 10
atyanta tiraskṛta vācya, 17
aucitya, 49, 306
Aucitya Vicāracarcā, 49
aukṣagandhī, 199
Auraṅgābād, 231-32, 234, 239, 294, 305, 346, 401
Aurora of Greek mythology, 416
Auwa, 106, 112, 116, 136, 146, 165, 363
avahita, 156
Avantī, 41, 43
temples of, 86

Avantinātha, 41
āvaraṇa devatās, 9, 49, 91, 409
avaspanditā, 156
avasthā(s), 305, 410
avivakṣita vācya, 17
āyāga
cornice, 217
relief, 286
paṭṭas, 201

āyata, 156
maṇḍala, 161

āyudha(s), 96, 390

Babylonia, 192
Babylonian tradition, 201
bad goddess, 20
Badarī grove, 71
baddhacārī, 152, 156, 229, 288, 305-06, 310, 336-37, 342, 344, 346-47, 405
pose, 286, 315

Badoh, 112, 120
Śiva Temple, 112
Paṭhārī, 129-30, 137, 161, 305, 369

Badoli, 4, 112, 136, 138, 171, 278, 286, 363, 365, 370-72, 392, 394, 401
Ghaṭeśvara Mahādeva Temple, 311
naṭa-maṇḍapa, 367
pillar *devāṅganās*, 171
sculptural proportions, 371

Bāḍmer, 167
Baijnātha, 256
Bajramaṭha, 154, 410
temple, 158

Bajranātha, 158, 161
Bālabhārata, 35, 47-48
Balahavā, 74
Bālakavi, 47
bālakhilyas, 67
bālapañjaras, 117
Balarāma, 134
Bālarāmāyaṇa, 48

balikrīḍā, 82
Bāṇa, 6, 80, 84, 86, 88-89, 236, 242
Banerjea, J.N., 7
Banerjee, Projesh, 8
Bāṅswāṛā, 37
Bappaka, 44
Barthes, Roland, 3, 17-18
Barua, B.M., 5, 76, 208, 210, 330
Barwāsāgar, 112, 118, 120, 261
Baṭesar, 120, 129
bathing motif, 224, 288
Besnagar, 240
bhadra, 118, 130, 132, 134, 137-38, 142-44, 148, 150, 161, 163-64, 168, 171, 173, 294, 370
  devakoṣṭha(s), 106, 109, 144-45
  koṣṭha, 352
  kṣobhanas, 164, 168
  pratiratha, 148
  udgama, 134
bhadraka, 117
bhadrapīṭha, 94
Bhaga, 191, 414
Bhāgavata Purāṇa, 67, 238, 297
Bhāgyalakṣmī, 59
Bhairava, 65
bhairavī, 385
bhaktas, 244
bhakti, 198
  ideology, 33
Bhāmaha, 49
bhāna, 48, 236
bhaṅgī, 236
Bhānu, 46
bharaṇī, 143, 150
bhāraputra(s), 158, 306
Bharat Kala Bhavan, 55
Bharat Kala Bhavan Museum, 264
Bharata, 64, 88, 198, 236
Bharatanāṭyam, 146
  disciplines of, 2
Bhāratas, 64
bhāravāhaka yakṣa, 210
Bharhut, 6-7, 25-26, 58, 201, 208-11, 215, 330-31, 346, 358-60
  apsaras Misakosi, 7
  imagery, 211
  sculptures, 6, 208
  stūpa, 76, 221
  yakṣīs, 26
Bhartravaddha, 35
Bhartṛpaṭṭa, 44
Bharuch, 43, 362
Bhat, G.K., 236
Bhaṭṭa, Kumārila, 16
Bhavana Vai, 74
bhāvanodyāna, 80
Bhāva-Prakāśa, 80, 236
bhikṣukyādi, 236
Bhīma, 42
Bhīma I, 38, 40, 42-43
Bhīma II, 40
Bhīmadeva I, 165, 173, 391
Bhīmdeva II, 173
Bhīmnātha, 114
Bhīnmāl, 40, 84, 362
bhiṣagādhirāja, 44
bhīta, 352
bhitti, 94
Bhoja, 6, 34, 36-40, 46, 48-49, 80-82, 85, 90, 286
Bhoja I, 34-35
Bhoja Paramāra, 85
Bhojadeva, 39
Bhojarāja, 38
Bhṛgukaccha, 44
bhṛkuṭi, 79
Bhṛṅgī, dance of, 78
bhrū-vilāsa, 79
bhruvañcitaiḥ, 78
Bhubaneswar, 303
  temples, 26
bhujaṅgatrāsita, 323, 346-47
Bhumarā, 120
bhūmija, 46
  style, 129
Bhūmija temples, 178
Bhūtaḍāmaratantra, 199
Bhūteśvara, 227-28, 330
  yakṣī, 305, 310
Bhuvanadeva, 90
Bhuvanadevācārya, 93
Bhuvanapāla, 46
Bilāspur, 154
bindī, 98, 264, 330, 336
Bodādit, 116, 140, 144
  Sun Temple, 118
Bodha-Gayā, 58, 201, 224
bodhisattva, 78
Bombay, 358
  Islands, 361
Boner, Alice, 8-10
boon-bestowing, 65
  protective spirits, 164
bracket figures, vii
Brahmā, 64-65, 67, 72-73, 97, 386, 403
  wife of, 56
Brahma-Kṣetra, 95
Brahman, 248, 332
  power of, 9
Brāhmanical cave temple doorways, 244
Brāhmaṇa(s), 33, 54, 56-57, 62
  priests, 85
  texts, 63
Brahmāṇḍa Purāṇa, 66
Brahmasūtra, 374
Bṛhad-Kathāśloka Saṁgraha, 238
Bṛhadāraṇyaka, 248
Bṛhatkathā, 79, 87
Bṛhatkathā Mañjarī, 79
Bṛhat-Kathā-Śloka-Saṁgraha, 87
British Museum, 214
Buchkala, 112, 114, 116, 130
Buddha, 78, 214
  life of, 361
  Nativity, 203
Buddhacarita, 5, 78, 81, 214
Buddhaswāmi, 87
Buddhism, 198
Buddhist, 4-5
  architecture, 76, 186, 232, 273

art, 55, 89, 199, 305
cave architectures, 232
cave temple doorways, 242
iconography, 76, 201
lore, 215
monk, 239
monument(s), 201, 223, 230, 239, 379, 401, 409
remains, 189
sources, 76
stūpa, 25, 76
*stūpa*s of, 219
stūpa pillar, 401
text(s), 62-63
tradition, 278
buffalo woman, 192
building activity, tradition of, 45
Bulandshahr, 35
Bundānā, 116, 130
Bundelkhaṇḍ, 153

Cāhamāna(s), 35, 37, 39, 40-46, 109, 120, 151
monuments, 145
temples, 145
Caitra, 81
Caitra Śīta Caturdaśī, 81
caitya, 84, 89, 401
*gavākṣa*s, 215
cakita netra, 79
Cāḷukya(s), 37-39, 43, 45
kingdom, 41
Cāḷukyan domain, 37
cāmara(s), 92, 134, 151, 352, 416
cāmaradhārī, 392
cāmara-dhāriṇī(s), 91, 132, 148, 156, 362
Cambay, 35
Cambodia, 94
Cāmuṇḍarāja, 37
Cānda Bardāī, 42
cāṇḍāla woman dancer, 351
candanānulepana, 80
Candella(s), 34-36, 39-41, 43, 46, 83, 109, 138, 143, 153-54
art, 163
idiom, 162
monarchs, 121
sculpture, 367
style, 163, 364
Candella Yaśovarman, 39, 163
caṇḍita, 92
Candra *yakṣī*, 208
candraśālā, 91
Candraulī, 97
Candra-vaṁśa, 72
candrikātalana, 82
cannibal *yakṣī*, 198
Cāpotkata princess, 39
cārī(s), 2, 7, 82
Carcarī, 85
dance, 80
*caryī gīta*s, 351
Cassirer, Ernst, 3, 23
caturaṅga, 168
*caturasra nṛtya hasta*s, 211
caturbhaṅgī, 98
Caturbhāṇī, 48, 236, 238
plays, 299
Caturmukha, 120
caturmukha mahāprāsāda, 96, 178
Caturmukha Mahāprāsāda Svarūpādhyāya, 387
Cauhān(s), 42
houses, 43
kings, 43
Cauḷa Devī, 40, 85
caurī(s), 75
bearers, 118, 168
Cedi, 34, 37
style, 121, 364
Cedideśa, 111, 120
celestial
gandharva, 70
maidens, 65
nymphs, 64, 67
water nymph, 60
celestial women, 12
imageries of, 272
celukkhepa, 88
central India, 111-12, 120, 130, 137-38, 146, 153, 213, 364-65, 372, 374-75, 380
central Indian
Jejākabhukti, 120
sculptural style, 374
sites, 120
style, 364
temples, 152
Ceras, 21, 194-95
*chanda*s, 43
Chāndogya Upaniṣad, 57, 251
Chandra, Pramod, 3
charming women, beauty of, 77
chatisiri, 351
chatra, 161, 264, 369
Chattopadhyaya, B.D., 33
China, 195
Chittor, 37, 42, 44-45, 95, 114, 116, 173, 323, 363-64
Chittorgaṛh, 45, 112, 130, 132, 365, 373
Chorepura, 154
Choṭan, 364
cillimārga, 351
cintana-mudrā, 98
Circe, 20
Citragupta, 163
Citragupta temple, 121, 163
Citraratha, 64
Classical Dance in Literature and the Arts, 7
classical
*karaṇa*s, 11
literature, 66
period, 32-33
Cleveland Museum, 286
cloud
spirit, 61, 63
messenger, 79
Coḷa, 38
collective unconscious, 19
colloquial language, 48
connotation(s) of
divine courtesans, 3

lakṣaṇā, 336
prostitutes, 3
vyañjanā, 336
fertility, 315
conographic function, 109
consecration ceremony, 74
constancy and change, 21
contemporary phenomena, 46
Coomaraswamy, A.K., vii, 3, 5-6, 59, 200-01, 247-48, 251-52, 257, 417
Cosmic
Energy, 352
event, 64
Cosmos in stone, 165
Courtly Pastime, 79
cow–bull, 58
creation, mothers of, 71
Cretan goddess, images of, 194
Crete, 192
cula, 208
Culakoka Devatā, 208
cūḍāmaha, 211
cūḍāmaṇi dombika, 350
cult objects, 194
cultural
affinity, 2
connotations, 2
history, 32
overview, 45
process, 13
cultural symptoms, history of, 18
cūraṇapada, 82
cūtabhañjikā, 82
cūtalatikā, 82
cūtamādhavī, 82
Czuma, S.S., 221

Dadhīca, sage, 72
Dahala, 34, 39, 111, 139, 153, 364, 374
region, temples of, 121
sculptures, 375
daitya, 419
Daiva Kṣetra, 95
Dakṣiṇa Kosala, 111, 374
Dāmalipta, 299
ḍamarū, 326
Dammara, 38
Damoh, 154, 156, 306, 364
dānavī, 419
dance
forms, 77
postures, identification of, 7
references, 89
text, tripartite comparative analysis of, 2
dancing girls, 6
daṇḍapada, 215
daṇḍapadacārī, 214-15, 234, 347
daṇḍapakṣa, 350, 361
Daṇḍin, 48, 234, 242, 299
darpaṇa, 217, 264, 330, 332, 336
darpaṇā, 4, 91, 150, 162-63, 211, 273, 330-31, 378, 383, 388-89, 392, 396
devāṅganā, 134
imageries of, 296
darpaṇa paribhogadarśinī, 330
darpaṇadhāriṇī, 218
darpaṇa-prasādhikā, 266, 392
Dasārṇa-Cedi, 136
Dasārṇa Cedideśa, 50
Dasārṇa-Cedi-Mālava, 117
Dasārṇa-Mālava, 111
Daśakumāracarita, 82, 234, 236, 299
Daśarūpaka, 48
Daśāvatāra, 391
dāsī(s), 87, 353
Dattaka, 239
dauvārika, 87
de Saussure, 17-18, 379
De, S.K., 236
Dehejia, Vidya, 3, 25-26, 200
deity–devotee relationship, 33
Delmal, 173, 176, 401
Temple, 173
Demeter, 194-96
demon-faced figures, 161
Deogaṛh, 120, 261, 346, 362
sculpture, 359
Desai, Devangana, vii, 47
Desai, Vishakha, 3, 12
deśī, 48, 417
dance, 416
krīḍās, 79-80
literature, 79, 90
Nāmamālā, 48
Śabdakośa, 48
style, 417
deva(s), 56, 66, 91, 247
devadāsī(s), 8, 12, 18, 54, 76, 83, 85-86, 89, 344, 352-53, 379, 382, 405
system, 351
tradition, 13, 18, 383
types of, 353
Devadatta, 16
devakoṣṭha(s), 143-44, 152, 155, 157-58, 162, 166, 365, 388, 390, 410
devakulika(s), 109, 116, 132, 134, 173, 292, 331
devakumārī(s), 76, 209-10
devāṅganā(s), 2, 4-5, 8-9, 11, 16-17, 20, 22, 26-27, 44, 49, 54-55, 57, 59, 74-75, 77, 89, 95-97, 99, 106, 109, 118, 129, 132, 134, 137-39, 142-46, 148, 150-52, 155-58, 161-64, 166-68, 171, 173, 176-78, 186-87, 210, 228, 242, 264, 266, 272-73, 278, 283, 286, 288, 294, 305-06, 309-10, 315, 320, 323, 326, 330, 336-37, 342, 346-47, 352, 358, 360, 365, 368-71, 373-74, 378-80, 383, 385-88, 390-92, 394-96, 399, 401, 403, 405, 409-10, 414, 416-19; see also *apsaras*(es)
circle, 383
concept, 60
figures, 13-14, 27, 120, 134, 155, 171, 261, 288, 371
figures, three-dimensional projection of, 370
forms, 137
grips, 315
iconography, 137
image(s), 22, 150, 369
images of, 309
matrix, 380
phenomena, 380
prototypes, 156

study, 310
types, 17, 106
typology, 276
devāṅganā imagery(ies), 11, 15-18, 20-24, 26-27, 34, 47, 49, 54, 58, 75, 106, 134, 136-39, 150, 164-65, 186-87, 218, 264, 266, 272-73, 276, 303, 315, 379-80, 382-83, 388-91, 394-95, 401, 409, 413, 419
efflorescence of, 2
devāṅganā keśanistoyakāriṇī, 286
devāṅganā motif(s), viii, 13, 87, 109, 136, 186-87, 261, 273, 360, 378, 380
diagramatic analysis of, 381
dragametic analysis of, viii
semiosis of, 419
devāṅganā placement, pattern of, 387
devāṅganā sculpture(s), vii, 3, 17-18, 21, 27, 114, 121, 129, 132, 139, 148, 153, 164, 171, 173, 177-78, 186, 228, 244, 320, 346-47, 353, 371-72, 388, 396, 401
devāṅganā-nāginī, 164
*devāṅganā-surasundarī*s, 352
devāṅganā-vyālas, 401
devatā(s), 76, 208-10
imageries, 208
devī(s), 66, 90, 161, 166, 419
concepts of, 188
shrines, 310
Devni Mori, 358-59
Dhaṅga, 34, 39, 163
Dhaky, M.A., viii, 3-4, 10, 96, 111-12, 114, 118, 129-30, 136, 139, 146, 150, 152, 167-68, 176-78
methodologies of, 11
dhammilla, 362
Dhanañjaya, 48
Dhāra, 38, 41, 48, 129
praśasti, 37
Dharmāditya, 362
dhatūrā arkakṣīra, 199
Dhṛtarāṣtra, 76
dhvani, viii, 13, 15, 47, 49-50, 58, 380, 414
concept of, 15
principle of, viii, 380
theories of, 47
theory, 380
dhvanikāra, 78, 380
Dhvanyāloka, 49, 414
Dhvanyāloka Locana, 49
Dhyānākarṣitā, 91-92
Dīdāragañja, 55, 77
*dik nāyikā*s, 9
dikpāla(s), 9, 11, 75, 91, 96, 106, 118, 129-30, 132, 134, 137, 142-44, 146, 150, 152, 155, 157-58, 161, 166-68, 173, 310, 373, 386-88, 390-91, 403, 413, 418
Dilwāṛā, 33
group, 171
temple(s), 139, 168
Dionysus, 194
dīpa, 352, 354
dīpārādhanā, 352
Dīpārṇava, 46, 96
Dīpāvalī, 83
directional deities, 74
diśākumārī(s), 21, 74-76; see also *apsaras*(es)
genre, 75
mahāttariyas, 74
Div, 42
divine beings, 65
dohada, 197, 209, 214, 256
dohada śālabhañjikā, 209
ḍolovilāsa, 82
ḍombagāyanas, 350
*ḍomba-gāyikā*s, 350
ḍomba-maṇḍala, 350
ḍombī, 350
dance, 351
Doni, 306
Doṣa Prakaraṇa, 49
Draviḍa architecture, 352
Draviḍadeśa, 178
Draviḍian architecture, 256
druta, tempos of, 299
Dūbakuṇḍa, 39
stone inscription, 35
dugdhadhārī, 221, 224
dugdhadhāriṇī, 218
dugdhavatsā, 64, 225
duh, 276
Duladeo, 154, 163
Temple, 121
Ḍūṅgarpur, 37, 358-59
Ḍūṅgarpur–Udaipur, 359-60
Ḍūṅgarpur–Udaipur Mātṛkās, 360
Durgā, 20, 26, 55, 59, 289, 310, 353, 391
Durgā Mahiṣāsuramardinī, 143, 330, 388
Durlabhadevī, 37
Durlabharāja, 37
Durmallikā, 236
Durvāsā, 73
dūtī(s), 9, 77
Dvādaśagaurī, iconography of, 11
*dvāraśākhā*s, 217
dvārapālas, 261, 394
dviaṅga, 116, 173
dvibhaṅga, 371
dvibhaṅgī, 418
dviratha, 388
*dviśālā*s, 93
Dvyāśraya Kāvya, 38, 42
dwarf-like form, 69
dyāvā-pṛthvī, 288

earlier writings, critique of, 5
earth, odour of, 62
eastern
India, 90, 111
Ruyagga, 74
Egypt, 192, 194-95
Egyptian
art, 194
tree goddess Nut, 21
eight *devakumārī*s, 76
Ekaliṅgajī, 45, 118, 150, 363, 388
Ekaśālmali, 81
ekatārā, 350
player, 351

ekāvalī, 77
Elephaṇṭā, 260, 360
Ellorā, 4, 210, 231-32, 234, 239, 305, 401
Encyclopedia of Temple Architecture, 4
Engendering Indian Art, 27
enunciative
  analysis, 21
  derivation, tree of, 21
Epic(s), 66
  literature, 64
  periods, 61
epigraphical sources, 351
Eraṇ, 120, 359
erotic
  gestures, 11
  motif of seduction, 311
eroticism, 5
esoteric cults, 33
eternal presence, 19
Euphrates, 248

factual imageries, 14
fairies, 19
Faizabad, 220, 257
Fata Morgana, 62
fecundity–fertility connotation, 383
female
  archetype, 19
  demons, 19
  energy, significance of, 76
  figures, 9
  imagery, 25-26
  motifs, range of, 209
  power of, 3
  powers, sevenfold, 71
  principles, 27
  representation, 27
  sculptures, 6
  sexuality, 27
feminine, 20-21
  concept, 21, 187
  concept of, 20, 22-23
  figure on temple walls, 55
  form, 21
  masculine energies, 190
  power, 9
  principle(s), 21, 54
feminine beauty,
  concept of, 77
  glory of, 78
  Pratihāra ideal of, 375
femininity of Śakti, 9
feminist analysis of gendered representation in Indian art, 24
feminist intervention, 24-27
  perspective of, 13
Ferguson, vii
fertility
  connotation, 75
  lines of, 22
  symbols of, 21, 194
feudal, 33
  culture, 33
  society, 33
feudalism, 33
figura serpentinata, 372, 374
figural or visual images, 13
figural sculpture, 136
fly whisks, 75, 86
Focillon, 368, 370
Foucauldian, 22
  approach, 187
  sense, 21
Freud, Sigmund, 3, 18

Gadarmal Temple, 112, 120, 129-30, 137-38, 305, 369
  devāṅganā, 305
Gahasattasai, 80
Gajāsura-Saṁhāramūrti, 323
gajathara, 138, 168, 171
Gala inscription, 41
gaṇa(s), 10, 96, 257, 360
  figures, 134
Ganda, 39
gandha, 62
gandhabba, 62
Gandhāra, 220
Gāndhārī, 97-98
gandharva(s), 55-57, 60-65, 67, 69, 73, 91, 94-95, 106, 118, 142, 155, 201, 251-52, 311, 372, 409-10
  Ūrṇāyu, 62
  couples, 410
  kanyā, 198
  Viśvāvasu, 60-61, 63
gandharvī(s), 6, 201, 362
Gaṇeśa, 391
  six-armed, 134
Gaṅgā, 7, 57, 109, 232, 234, 239, 252-53, 256, 261, 264, 401
  makaravāhinī, 210
Gaṅgā et Yamunā, 256
Gaṅgā–Yamunā, 117-18, 136, 257
  imagery of, 7
  Valley, 111
Ganges, 35, 60
Gāṅgeya, 38
Ganguli, K.K., 37
Ganguli, O.C., 278
gaṇikā, 40, 86
Gañjam, 253
garbha-gṛha, 9, 130, 143, 150, 155, 164-67, 177, 261, 309, 331-32, 344, 352, 388, 405
  doorways, 332
  maṇḍovara, 146, 373
Garimalla, Annapurna, 27
Garuḍārūḍha Viṣṇu, 134, 403
gatāgata, 152, 156, 286, 306
  pose, 283
  sthāna, 346
gatamārga, 82
Gāthā Saptaśatī, 217
gati, 418
  principle of, 375
gauḍī, 47
gauṇī vṛtti, 16-17
Gaurīs, 97-98, 166, 252, 326
gavākṣa, 91, 93
gāyaka, 236
gaze and spectatorship, 25, 27
gender issues in Indian art, 25

generic female divinities, 56
geometrical configurations, 95
ghāgharā-colī, 230
ghana dundubhi, 78
Ghānerāo, 140
ghaṇṭā, 93
ghaṇṭādhārī, 392
Gharapurī Maheśamūrti, 361
ghaṭapallava(s), 117-18, 132, 134, 137, 264
ghaṭisthāna, 93
Ghorī, Muhammad, 37
ghṛta, 70-71
Ghumlī, 173, 178, 350, 364, 367, 373
  Temple, 416
Gidion, Seigfried, 19-20
Giridharapur Ṭīlā, 220
Girnār, 41-42
  inscription, 40
gītamārga, 299
Gobhila-Gṛhya-Sūtra, 251
Godāvarī, 37
Goddess
  Āśāpurī, 44
  Durgā, manifestations of, 388
  Lakṣmī, 69
  Vāruṇī, 69
Golden
  Flower, 195
  maṇḍapikā, 38
Golmaṭh, 157
gomūtrikā, 82, 299
Gopagiri, 34, 111, 129, 154, 364, 374
  style, 364
Gorad, 173, 176, 311
Gorgon, 20
Gorkshakar, S., 360-61
Govaka I, 35
Govinda IV, 35
Govindnagar, 220, 330
Grahapati, 114
grāmadāsīs, 353
Great Goddess, 19, 194
Great Mother, 19, 22, 196, 247-48
  concept of, 187-88
greater whole, individual parts of, 12
Greek, 21, 194
  art, 196
  mythology, Aurora of, 416
grīṣma, 82
gūḍha-maṇḍapa, 150, 155, 164, 177, 395
guggula, 199
Guhila(s), 44-45, 109
  dominion, 363
  family, 44
  monuments, 145
  rule, 44
  ruler Alata, 388
  temples, 145
  territory, 45
Guhilots, 35, 44
guhyakas, 69
Guhya-Samāja-Tantra, 199
Gujarat, 2, 4-5, 12, 34-41, 45-46, 48, 85, 91, 95, 99, 106, 112, 114, 129-30, 136, 139, 146, 148, 150, 153, 168, 173, 176, 178, 230-31, 311, 347, 350, 358-59, 387, 391-92, 401, 416, 418
  temples, 10, 177
  western, 140
Gujarātī style, western Indian, 374
guṇas, 47
guṇamālā, 350
Gunthanā, 92
Gupta
  age, 129
  architecture, 210, 248
  art, extension of, 111
  coins, 359
  heritage, 365
  period, 8, 77, 87, 112, 117, 120, 232, 257, 264, 331
  rule, 359
  tradition, 120, 360
Gupta, S.P., 223-24, 227, 330
Gupta-Vākāṭaka, 242
  temple, 136
Gupta–Pratihāra period, 401
Gurgī, 139, 171, 274, 286, 292, 315, 364, 372, 374
  pillars, 401
  sculptures, 374
  toraṇa, 278
Gurjara(s), 41, 111, 114, 139, 165, 362-64, 373
  style(s), 168, 364
Gurjaradeśa, 46
Gurjara-Pratihāra(s), 362, 365
  elements, 155
  phase, 152
  masters, 375
  period, 161
  style, 365
guru-śiṣyas, group of, 320
Guvaka I, 43
Gwalior, 39, 112, 120, 161-62, 171, 288, 309, 364-65, 367, 375, 392, 395-96, 399
  Fort, 120, 129-30, 139, 154
  Museum, 77
Gyāraspur, 112, 129, 154, 158, 364, 371, 405, 410
  vṛkṣikā, 77

Hāla, 78, 80
Hampi Ruins, 253
haṁsalīlāvalokana, 82
haṁsasya hasta, 323
Handa, D., 11
Handique, K.K., 13
Hansot, 35
Haṛappā, 188-90
Haṛappan forms, 189
Haras, 43
Hari, 69
Haribhadra Sūri, 84
Haricandra, 362
Harihara, 286, 331, 368, 369
  group, 109, 112, 130, 134
Harīpāla, 40
Hārīti, 20, 294
Harṣa, 32, 84, 88, 363
  stone inscription, 43
Harṣacarita, 80, 236
Harṣagiri, 351, 365, 370-72

Hill, 151
sculptures, 371
Temple, 151
Harṣanātha, 44
Temple, 44, 83, 114, 116, 140
Temple Inscription, 83
Harṣapur, 45
Harṣavardhana, 362
Harsola, 36
hastas, 45, 347
hastimuṇḍī, 396
hāsya, elements of, 361
havelīs, 399
headless trunks, dance of, 79
heaven, vault of, 62
heavenly
court dance, 211
nymphs, 67
singers, 67
Hecate, 20
Heeramanik Collection, 214
Hemacandra, 16, 42, 48
Hemacandrācārya, 49
Hemanta *ṛtu*, 332
Himalayan kingdoms, 111
hiṇḍolā toraṇa, 405
Hindu
architecture, 186
art, 89, 305
cave architectures, 232
gods, 26
iconography, development of, 7
monument(s), 230, 379, 401
pantheon, 67
rule, 36
Hindu temple(s), vii, 8, 12, 23, 75
architecture, 7
Hiraṇyakaśipu, 72
historical information, 18
horas, 351
Horus, 192
hudukka drum, 351
human
culture, 3
form, 78
mood, 78
sciences, 18
humanity, 43
Hume, 248
Hūṇa(s), 32, 362
Huviṣka, 220

iconic deities, 106
iconographers, writings of, 7
iconographic construct, 4
parallelism, phenomenon of, 34
programming, 106
vocabulary, 106
iconographical
analysis, 14
compilation, 11
programming, 8
representations, 4
iconography styles, 34
iconological
interpretation, viii, 14
method, 14
iconology, 3, 13, 18-19
theory of, 14
Idar, 42
idea–image correlation, 417
ikṣudaṇḍa, 396
image
making, process of, 26
of Sūrya, 145, 157
typology, 3
imagery(ies) of
alasā, 296
apsaras, 380
celestial women, 272
darpaṇā, 296
devāṅganās, 11, 15, 273, 382
Gaṅgā–Yamunā, 7
kanduka-krīḍā, 296
markaṭaceṣṭā, 296, 409
nadī-devatā, 383
nāyikās, 6
religious, vii
vasanabhraṁśā, 296
yakṣī, 7, 380, 419
images of
Cretan goddess, 194
devāṅganās, 309
Ishtar goddess, 194
India, 32
south, 83, 323, 351
western, 90, 129, 139, 145, 230-32, 273, 289, 358-60, 363, 372-73, 380
Indian
aesthetic(s), 13, 47
architecture, 14, 272
civilization, 32
classical dance, 346
culture, 5
epigraphy, 83
feminine beauty, 77
literary criticism, 380
literature, 21, 209, 330
monuments, 2
Museum, 214
poets, 284
psyche, 54, 77, 272, 292
scholars, 3
sculpture(s), viii, 14, 81, 209, 346
society, 89, 346
thought, 21
tradition(s), 4, 191
tradition of poetic expression, 15
woman, 77
Indian art, vii, 6, 21, 24-25, 58, 303, 330, 417
gender issues in, 25
historian, 24
indologists, writings of, 7
Indore, 112, 120, 364
Indra, 67, 69, 72-74, 81, 96-97, 211, 251, 387, 416
sabhā of, 74
Indra III, 35, 40
Indra-Agni, 56
Indradhvaja festival, 81
Indrarāja, Mahāsāmanta, 35
Indra's court, dancers of, 3

Indrasabhā, 61, 65, 211, 344
Indrotsava, 81
Indu, 58
Indus Valley, 22, 189, 191, 248
Indus–Sarasvatī, 187, 189
  cultures, 186
Irene Gajjar, 189
Īśāna, 97, 387
Ishtar, 194
  goddess, images of, 194
Isis, 20, 194

Jabalpur, 286
Jagat, 4, 22, 45, 55, 118, 120-21, 139-40, 142-45, 148, 152, 155, 165, 231, 261, 274, 278, 288, 300, 315, 323, 342, 350, 359, 363, 365, 368, 370, 372-73, 387-88
  devāṅganā, 306
  sculptors, 142
  sculptures, 371-72
  temple, 142, 150, 332
  Temple sculptures, 142
  yakṣīs, 273
Jagat Ambikā Temple, 145, 294
Jagat Swāmin, 84
Jaggeyapeṭa, 201
Jaina(s), 4, 44, 76, 171, 386
  affiliation, 163
  architecture, 76, 186
  āyāga-paṭṭa, 223
  iconography, 76, 150
  monks, 84
  monuments, 223, 379
  philosophy, 42
  stūpas, 220
  stūpas of, 219
  temple(s), 12, 23, 75, 120, 139, 150, 171
  temples at Deogaṛh, 112
  work, 84
Jaipur, 43
jala-krīḍās, 6
jalantara, 99
jalaturaga, 252
jalebha, 252
Jālor, 37, 42-43
Jamālpur, 220
jami, 414
Jamsoṭ, 347
Jamunā, 256
jaṅghā, 90, 93, 97, 99, 118, 142-46, 148, 152, 155, 171, 173, 177, 309, 352, 368, 387-88, 390
  decoration, 413
  design, 176
  sculptures, 143, 158, 165, 171, 173, 176
Jañjagīr, 121, 375
janmotsava, 73
Jarai Mātā, 120
jaṭābhāra, 173, 326
Jātaka(s), 199, 214
  stories, 86
jāti(s), 16, 417
Jāvālipura, 37
Jayadeva, 78
Jayakar, Pupul, 191-92
Jayākhyā Saṁhitā, 199
Jayamaṅgala, 44, 81-82
Jayamaṅgalā, 80
Jayappa, 299
Jayasiṁha II, 38
Jayasiṁha Siddharāja, 40-41
Jejākabhukti, 34-35, 39, 121, 139, 154, 364
Jhālarāpāṭan, 129, 178, 231, 296, 364
Jhalarapatan Museum, 296
Jina, 97
Jina Maṇḍana, 41
Jinadatta Sūri, 84
jinālaya, 387
Jinavallabha, 84
Jodhpur, 36, 37
Jogeśvarī, 232, 259-60, 401
Jojaladeva, Rājā, 83
Jośaharā, 75
Jung, C.J., 3, 18, 22, 192

kabariniścyotana, 286
Kacchapaghāta(s), 35, 39, 109, 129, 154, 364, 374
  architecture, 162
  Mahipāla, 162
  structure, 158
  style, 129
  temples, 161
Kacchapaghāta Vikramasiṁha, inscription of, 39
kadamba, 91, 419
  blossoms, 82
  tree, 227
  yuddha, 82
kādambaka, 88
Kādambarī, 84, 86, 88-89
Kaḍwāhā, 154, 161-62, 365, 372, 374-75
  sculptures of, 364
Kaḍwāhā Ṭoṭeśvara Temple, 129, 332, 344
kājala, 336
Kakanmaṛh, 161
  Temple, 154
kākapakṣa, 360
kakṣāsana(s), 151, 164, 177-78
kāla, 239, 252
Kalacuri(s), 39, 41
  court, 48
  Gāṅgeya, 38
  Gāṅgeyadeva, 39
  Karṇa, 40
  Yuvarājadeva, 48
  temples, 158
Kaḷacuri–Cedi
  idiom, 364
  style, 153
Kālañjar, 83
  Fort, 41
kalaśa, 142, 227, 261, 264, 296
Kāla-Svarūpa-Kulaka, 85
Kalhaṇa, 85
Kālī, 20, 353
Kālibaṅgan, 189-91
Kālidāsa, 6, 78-79, 81-82, 88, 223, 284, 332, 336
Kaliṅga, 178, 264
kalpavṛkṣa, 67

Kalyanpur, 359
Kalyāṇa plate, 38
Kalyāṇasundaramūrti, 109, 136
kāma, 69, 74, 284, 382
Kāmaśāstra, 80, 236
Kāmadeva, 81, 87, 244, 396
Kāmadhenu, 69
Kāmarūpa, 97, 387
Kāma's fire, 284
Kāmasūtra, 80, 236
kāmatantra, 236
  saciva, 236
Kāmikāgama, 353
Kaṁsa, 41
kañcuka, 88
kañcukī, 87-88
kañcukin(s), 83, 87
kañcukoṣṇiṣṭa, 88
Kandarīya, 163
Kandarīya Mahādeva, 164, 264
  sculptures of, 374
Kandarpa Cūḍāmaṇi, 80
kanduka, 347
  keli-tāṇḍava, 297
  nṛtta, 299
  nṛtya, 83, 299
  tantra, 83, 299
kanduka-krīḍā, 4, 6, 17, 79, 82, 145, 150, 162, 219, 273, 296-97, 300, 372, 389, 410
  imageries of, 296
  devāṅganās, 410
Kāṅgṛā, 256
Kānherī, 358, 360
Kaṅkālī Devī Mandir, 331
Kaṅkālī Ṭīlā, 201, 220, 223
Kannauj, 32, 34-36, 39, 112, 130, 362, 365, 375
  Mātṛkās, 375
Kaṇṭhkoṭ, 364
Kanwarlal, K., 11
kanyā(s), 10, 106, 320
kanyābandha, 91
kanyādūṣakaḥ, 238
Kanyakumari, 13
kanyāviṭaḥ, 238
kapāla, 173, 323, 405
kapāladhārī, 385, 388, 416
kapāla-ḍamarūdhārī, 392
kapilī, 138, 142, 144, 155, 173
kapotālī, 142-43, 150
karaṇas, 299, 353
karihasta, 215
Kārle, 358, 360
Karṇa, 38, 40
karṇa(s), 93, 109, 118, 130, 132, 134, 137, 142-44, 146, 152, 161, 164, 167-68, 173, 264, 369, 374
  devakoṣṭha, 106
  kṣobhana, 164
  position, 136
Karṇadeva II, 40
Karṇadeva Phase, 173
Karṇāṭa, 37, 178
Karnāṭa-Maharashtra style, 129
Karpūramañjarī, 48, 97-98
Kārttika festival, 199
Kārttikeya, 79
Karvan Mātṛkās, 347
Kashmir, 13, 15
  temples of, 85
Kaśyapa Prajāpati, 72-73
Kaśyapa, Ṛṣi, 64
Kaśyapa-Śilpa-Paṭala, 94
kaṭākṣa, 79
Kathā-Sarit-Sāgara, 79, 198, 238
kaṭi movements, 346
kaṭisama, 221, 323
  hasta, 403
kaṭyāvalambita, 109
Kaula texts, 200
kaumudī jāgaraṇa, 83
Kaumudīmahotsava, 80
Kauśāmbī, 264
Kauṣītakī, 248
kaustubha, 69
Kauṭilya, 85-87, 234
kavipratibhā, 48
kāvya(s), 42, 80, 382, 418
Kāvya Kalpalatā Vṛtti, 84
Kāvya literature, 18, 54, 76, 79
Kāvyālaṁkāra, 49
Kāvyamīmāṁsā, 47-48
Kāvyānuśāsana, 48-49
Kāvyaprakāśa, 49
Kāyāvarohaṇa, 99
Keith, A.B., 7, 62-63, 234
Kekind, 116, 118, 121, 139-40, 151-52, 156, 162, 165, 168, 173, 232, 242, 244, 288, 305-06, 342, 361, 363, 365, 368, 387, 390
  Mātṛkās, 168
Kerakoṭ, 121, 140, 364
keśa saṁskāra, 80
keśanistoya, 215, 264
keśanistoyakāriṇī, 4, 6, 58, 150, 156, 162-64, 171, 217-18, 224, 273-74, 286, 306, 383, 389-90, 392
kevala nṛttam, 353
kevalam, 353
Keyūravarṣa, 48
khaḍga, 99, 320, 405
khaḍgābhinaya, 227
khaḍgadhārī, 87, 218, 227, 306, 320, 323, 385, 388, 395, 416
khaḍga-vāhinī(s), 86-87
Khajurāho, vii, 4, 11, 40, 106, 120-21, 138-39, 152-53, 158, 165, 176-77, 210, 218, 274, 284, 286, 289, 300, 311, 315, 332, 342, 346-47, 351, 364-65, 368, 371-72, 374-75, 392, 396, 399
  apsaras(es), 138, 284
  artists, 163, 273, 283
  devāṅganās, 272, 309
  Kandarīya Mahādeva Temple, 274
  masters, 311, 375
  sculptures, 152, 229, 374
  temple(s), 12, 26, 138, 162, 164-65, 177, 264
Khalji, Ala-ud-din, 36, 40
Khambhaṭ, 42
Khandalawala, Karl, 360
Khandesh, 37, 358
Kharatara-gaccha, 84

Kharataras, 84
kharjūravāhaka, 229, 309, 383, 392
khaṭvāṅga, 168, 320, 326
khaṭvāṅgadhārī devāṅganās, 326
khaṭvāṅgam, 392
Kherat, 129
khilapañjara, 95
Khilchipura, 231
pillar(s), 151, 232, 240, 257
Khirnīwālā, 129
group, 154, 161
King Ruru, 73
kinnaras, 64, 91
Kirāḍu, 37, 42, 140, 165, 167-68, 171, 173, 278, 323, 364-65, 373, 394
style, 373
kirātas, 41
Kirātakūpa, 37
kirātī, 173, 385
Kīrtikaumudī, 38, 41
kīrtimukha(s), 121, 134, 138
Kīrtirāja, 38-39
knowledge, excavation of, 22
Kodal, 154-55, 162, 286, 344, 375
koka(s), 208, 210
Kokasa family *sthapati*s, generations of, 375
Kolkata, 214
Koṅkaṇ, 37-38, 360
Kore, 196
koṣṭha(s), 118
frames, 145
Kota, 296
Koṭāh, 144
Koṭai, 45, 120, 139, 142-44, 155, 165, 176, 261, 364, 388
temple, 150
Koṭyarka, 145, 359, 362
Mātṛkās, 360, 362
Kramrisch, Stella, vii, 3-4, 8-9, 47, 56, 283, 367-68, 373-74
krīḍā(s), 6, 80, 82, 219, 220
pastime, 79
krīḍanaka, 236
Krishna Deva, 111-12, 120-21, 138
Kṛṣṇa, 41, 67
Kṛṣṇa III, 35
Kriyākalpa, 49
Kriyākramajyoti, 353
Kṛtavarmā, 72
kṛttikā, 83, 299
Kṣatrapa(s), 358
coins, 359
Kṣemaṅkarī, 388
image, 132
temple, 116, 130, 132
Kṣemarāja, 40
Kṣemendra, 48-49, 86
kṣetra, 95
kṣetrapāla, 96-97
Kṣetrapāla Nirṛti, 387
kṣipta, 151
position, 211
Kṣīrārṇava, 5, 11, 46, 90, 93, 95-97, 326, 387
kṣīrasāgara, 73, 310
Kṣitipāla, 40
kṣobhana(s), 164, 166
Kṣudrakoka Devatā, 208
Kubera, 73-74, 76, 97, 208, 294, 387, 419
daughters of, 198
Kuiper, 236, 240
Kulārṇava Tantra, 200
kulavṛkṣas, 200
Kullu Valley, 39
kumāra vihāra(s), 42, 85, 178
Kumārapāla Cāḷukya, 34, 38, 42, 45, 84-85, 93, 364
Kumārapāla-Carita, 42
Kumārasambhava, 78
Kumāratantra, 353
kumārikās, 94
kumbha, 134, 142, 352, 354, 392, 401
kumbhadīpa, 352
kumbhadhārī, 396
kumbhaka, 142
kumbhāṇḍakas, 213
kumbhāratī, 353
Kumbhariā, 171, 173, 176, 364, 373, 395, 416
group, 139
kumbhika, 278
kumkum, 199
Kumrahāra, 220
kuñcita, 161, 209, 218, 346
kuṇḍa, 165, 310
kuṇḍalas, 203
kuṇḍalinī(s), 352
yoga, 352
kuḍya, 94
Kuntaka, 49
kūrma, 232
vāhana, 109
Kuṣāṇa, vii, 22, 77, 220, 228, 257, 274, 305
śālabhañjikā, 7
art, 358
images, 346
yakṣīs, 337
Kuṣāṇa period, 8, 138, 186, 219, 296, 303, 323, 394, 409
art of, 56
sculpture traditions of, 311
Kutch, 45, 121, 364
kuṭilaka, 145, 230-32, 234, 238-40, 259, 294, 305, 337, 361
viṭa character, 342
Kuṭṭanīmattam, 86
Kuvalayamālā, 86

L.D. Institute Museum, 394
Lacchimai, 75
lady of
animals, 196
plants, 196, 200
lakṣaṇā, 15-17, 49, 66, 344, 378, 380
Lakṣaṇā Samuccaya, 90, 94
lakṣarasa, 199
Lakṣmaṇa, 66, 154, 163, 264
sculptures of, 374
Lakṣmaṇagaṛh Ṭīlā, 220
Lakṣmī, 20, 55, 59, 66, 77, 195
concept of, 278

Lakṣmī-like form, 69
lalāṭabimba, 266, 403
lalita, 78
bhāva, 78
Lalita Vigraharāja, 44
Lalitavistara, 210
Lamba, 106, 112, 116, 363
*lambhaka*s, 87
Lanius, 371-72
lāsya, 387
latā(s), 116, 203
Lāṭa, 35, 37-38
Latavya, 88
latinā
śikhara, 116, 130, 158
type, 156
Laurīya–Nandanagaṛh, 189
law of transmigration, 62
laya, 352
legend of Soma, 56
life
cult, 247
lords of, 247
principle, 70
līlā-lālitya, 297
Līlāvatī, 97
Lilith, 20
liṅga, 352
liṅgālayam, 352
literary
arts, 7, 46
criticism, notion of, 50
imagery, 59
sources, 76
sources, knowledge of, 18
thoughts, 48
tradition, 50
world-view, 49
Lobo, Wibke, 11
local idioms, 112
lokapāla(s), 76, 96
lokavṛttanāma, 353
lolahasta, 215
*lolahasta nṛtya hasta*s, 211
Longhurst, A.H., 218, 253
lotus
motifs, 211
nymph, 210
inhabiting lady, 59
lower
Ānartta, 120
deities, 61
Medapāṭa, 118, 120, 140
Lucknow Museum, 58, 227
*lūma*s, 93
Lūṇa Vasahī, 42, 171, 399

Macdonell, A.A., 7, 60, 413
Mackay, 221
Mada, 69
madanasya ketuḥ, 239
madanikā, vii, 2
Madanotsava, 81, 197
madhukaraviṭa, 238
madhupānā, 58, 219, 238
mādhurya, 47
Madhya Pradesh, 2, 4, 12, 34, 91, 106, 129-30, 139, 173, 176, 231, 392, 401
madhya
sūtra, 176
tempos of, 299
Madhyadeśa, 111, 117, 358, 360
art, 359
temples of, 153
Madhyamakoka Devatā, 208
madhyapatra, 155, 157
Māgadhī, 64
mahā, 208
Mahāban, 220
Mahābhārata, 7, 48, 72, 81, 198, 297, 419
Mahābhāṣya, 7
Mahādeva, 43
Temple, 116, 120
Mahā-Gurjara, 114, 120, 145
design, 177
feature, 155
site, 136
style(s), 118, 120, 139, 142, 146, 150
traits, 120
*mahākāvya*s, 80
Mahālakṣmī, 44
Mahāmāṇḍalika Cūḍāmaṇi, 36
mahāmaṇḍapa, 162
Mahā-Maru, 114, 171
phenomenon, 120
sites, 120
style(s), 139, 144, 150, 363
temple(s), 114, 116, 118
traits, 120
mahānartakī, 305
mahārājādhirāja, 36
Maharashtra, 4, 46, 114, 191, 230-31, 392, 399
Mahāśakti, 9
mahāttarī, 89
mahāttarika, 89
Mahāvaṁśa, 5
Mahāvastu, 210
*mahāvidyā*s, 91
mahāvraja, 396
Mahāvrata festival, 251
Mahāyāna, 232, 259
Mahendrapāla, 34
Mahendrapāla II, 35
Mahendrarāja, 37
Maheśa, 403
Mahimbhaṭṭa, 49
Mahipāla, 34, 47
Mahipāla I, 35
Mahmūd (of Ghazni), 35, 38, 40, 43
Mahobā, 36, 39, 41
Mahodaya, 34-35
Maholi, 330
Maihar, 157
Maitraka, 112, 362
Maitreya, 67
makara(s), 90, 93, 203, 215, 232, 234, 244, 247-48, 252, 256-57, 260-61, 396
vāhana, 109
Malabar Coast, 38
mālādhara couple, 145
mālāśākhā, 117

Mālatīmādhava, 238
Mālava, 111, 168
Mālavikāgnimitra, 81, 197, 223, 236
Malayānīla, 69
male–female
concept, 58
principle, 58
Malla, 46
Mālwā, 34, 36-37, 39-42, 45-46, 48, 50, 90, 114, 129, 136, 139, 154, 358, 360, 362, 364
Mammaṭa, 16, 48-49
Manabhaṅga, 114
*mānasa kanyā*s, 65, 67
mañcika, 142, 157, 168
maṇḍalabhramaṇa, 82
*maṇḍala*s, 299
Maṇḍana, Sūtradhāra, 95
maṇḍapa(s), 94-95, 99, 116, 121, 129-30, 137-38, 142-43, 146, 151, 157-58, 161-62, 164, 166-68, 177, 292, 309, 310, 352-53, 373, 388, 399
free-standing, 392
open-pillared, 171
pillar(s), 138, 286, 306, 315, 394
projection, 388
maṇḍapikā, 120
mandirodyāna, 80
Mandor, 36
maṇḍovara(s), 16, 75, 96-97, 99, 106, 109, 112, 114, 118, 120, 129-30, 132, 134, 136-39, 142-43, 145, 148, 150, 156-58, 161-63, 166, 171, 176, 178, 231-32, 242, 261, 264, 292, 305-06, 309, 344, 346, 360, 365, 369, 370, 372, 374, 387, 390-91, 394, 401
decoration, 394
design concept, 134
figure sculpture, 136
planning, 144
sculptures, 151, 165
Mandsaur, 145, 231-32, 242, 360, 362, 364
Khilchipura pillars, 361
sculpture, 359
Maṅgaḷa, 59
maṅgala vādya, 351
Maṅgrol, 42
Maṇibhadra, 76
maniera, 371
manifestations, 46
of Goddess Durgā, 388
Maṇimekhalai, 81
mañjīrā, 99
Mañjuśrī Mūlakalpa, 199
Mānkheṛā, 112, 120
Mankodi, Kirit, 11
*mantra*s, 199
Mānyakheta, 35-36, 38-39
Marai, 121, 154, 156-57, 364
mārgasaritā, 198
mārgī, 48, 417
literature, 79
style, 417
Mārkaṇḍeya, 69
markaṭaceṣṭā, 5, 17, 139, 148, 150, 158, 171, 173, 217, 273, 306, 311, 315, 372, 378-79, 383, 390, 399, 401, 405
devāṅganā, 63
motif, 218
imagery(ies) of, 296, 409
Marshall, J., 211
Maru, 111, 114, 139, 144, 150, 165, 363, 373
styles, 168
Maru–Gurjara, 111, 114, 139, 143, 145, 165, 364-65, 374
architecture, 144
features, 171
idiom, 173, 373
phase, 134, 171
sculptural style, 373
style, 165, 178, 390
style of architecture, 364
style of sculpture, 364
temples, 165, 178, 323
Marumaṇḍala, 34, 112, 363
Maru-Medapāṭa-Śākambharī, 111
Maru-Sapādalakṣa, 46, 116, 130, 132, 134, 136, 140
Marusthalī, 34
Marut, 74
Mārwāṛ, 36, 40, 42, 362
Marxist, 24
Mary, 20
Mason, Darielle, 3, 12
mātar, 225
mathematical configurations, 95
Mathurā, vii, 6, 35, 55, 58, 87, 201, 208, 213, 215, 218-19, 223, 225, 227, 232, 234, 236, 261, 273, 286, 296, 305, 311, 330, 346, 358, 360
artists, 323
Museum, 77, 223, 227
naṭī, 347
pillar(s), 6, 151, 274, 286
railing pillars, 221
sculptures, 6
stūpa railing sculptures, 330
yakṣī(s), 273, 309
Mātṛkā(s), 145, 152, 161, 166, 231, 296, 347, 358, 391
Vārāhī, 161
Tanesara group of, 360
Mātṛmūrti, 92
Matsya Purāṇa, 64, 71, 225, 286
mattavāraṇa, 117
Mattavilāsa, 48
Mauryan, 77
forms, 189
period, 188, 209
ring-stones, 209
Māyā, 20, 71, 213
Māyādhara, 72
Medapāṭa, 34, 44, 46, 140, 142, 168, 363, 372
Medapāṭa-Uparamāla, 116, 118, 132
medieval
chivalry, 43
Hindu temples, 380
Nāgara temples, 416
period, 32, 34, 303, 365
quality, 368
sculpture, 369
western India, 419
medievalism, elements of, 33

Medinīpati, 44
Meghadūtam, 78-79
Mehraulī, 220
Mehsānā, 165
Meister, Michael, 4, 111
mekhalā(s), 77, 203, 213, 369
Menal, 363, 403
mental
  derangement, 61
  sphere, 65
meru, 396
Meru, mount, 37
Meru-prāsāda, 75, 90
Merutuṅga, 38, 40-41, 85
methodologies, viii, 3, 13
  of Dhaky, 11
  of Parimoo, 11
metres
  mālinī, 44
  mandakrāntā, 44
  sārdūlavikrīḍita, 44
  sragdharā, 44
Mewāṛ, 44-45, 388
  artists, 145
Miani, 42
Mihira Bhoja, 47, 120
Mīnaladevī (Mayanallā), 40
miśra nṛttam, 353
Misra, R.N., 5, 11, 198-99, 375
miśram, 353
Mitaoli, 154
mithuna(s), 58, 63, 118, 151, 157, 163, 251, 260, 272, 303, 361, 391, 405, 418
  couple(s), 215, 217
  maithuna, 346
  sculptures, 346, 418
mithunaśākhā, 117
Mitra, 56
Mitra-Varuṇa, 56
Moḍherā, 4, 33, 40, 139, 144, 148, 165-66, 171, 176-77, 292, 364-65, 373, 392, 395, 401, 413, 416
  maṇḍovara design, 166
  maṇḍovara devakoṣṭhas, 11
  naṭa-maṇḍapa, 367
  Sūrya, 410
  temples of, 45
Moharājaparājaya, 42, 84
Mohenjo-Dāṛo, 189-91
Mohinī, 99, 297
  form of Viṣṇu, 297
monographs on temple sites, authors of, 11
monument, iconography of, 27
Moon, 62
Morena, 154
morphological features, 47
Morris, C.W., viii, 378, 380
Mother Goddess Durgā, 77
Mother Goddess figurines, 22, 303
mothers of creation, 71
Moti Chandra, 3, 8, 86
moṭita, 342
  hasta, 337
  sthānakas, 156
Mṛcchakaṭika, 81
mṛdaṅga(s), 78, 86
mṛgamada, 199
mudrā, 9
Muhammad of Ghore, 32, 40, 43
mukhacatuṣkī, 116, 130, 136, 142, 155, 388
mukhamaṇḍapa, 138, 144, 157, 164-65, 388, 394
mukhaśālā, 91
mūlādhāra(s), 118, 352
mūlanāsā, 93
mūlaprāsāda, 132, 150, 168
Mūlarāja, 39-40, 43
Multani, Ein-ul-Mulk, 36
muṇḍadhārī, 416
muṇḍamālā, 168, 173
muni(s), 63, 66, 99
Muñja, 48
muraja, 79
Murayat, 161
mūrdha, 276
Murtaẓāgañj, 189
Muse, 20
Museum for Indian Art, Berlin, 261
Museum of Fine Arts, Boston, 214
musical instruments, 78, 201, 350

nābhicchanda, 117
Nachnā, 120
Nachnā Kumāramaṭha, 260
Nachnā-Kuṭhāra, 112, 120, 240
Naḍḍula, 41, 43
nadī-devatā(s), 4, 7-8, 21, 57, 77, 248, 253, 272, 379-80, 401, 403
nadī-devatā, imageries of, 383
nadī-devī(s), 232, 240, 242, 257, 260-61, 369
nadī-devīs' attributes, 259
Nadol, 37, 83
nāga(s), 91, 94, 118, 121, 256, 410
Nāga king, 419
Nāgabhaṭṭa I, 35
Nāgabhaṭṭa II, 34-35, 112, 114
Nāgahrada, 44
nāgakanyā, 91
  kadambaiśca, 396
Nāgānanda, 88
nāga-nāyikā, 91
Nāgara, 10, 90, 111, 153, 210
  architecture, 394
  style, 4
  temple(s), 67, 120, 129
  temple architecture, 129, 158, 217, 351
nāgaraka, 236
Nāgārjunakoṇḍa, 63, 214-15, 217, 256, 286, 361
  sculptures, 217
nāgasakhā(s), 117-18
Nāgāvaloka, 35
Nāgdā, 44-45, 106, 136, 140, 150, 300, 363
  temple(s), 145, 150
nāginīs, 106, 163-64, 264
naivedya, 352
Naktosasa, 416
Nakula, 46

naladi, 199
Nalakubera, 72
nalinī, 138, 148, 163-64
  kamaladhāriṇī, 273
namaskāra, 87
nandikā, 138, 168
Nandipuri, 362
Nara, 71
Nāradapṛcchā, 96
narathara, 138, 168, 171
Naravāhana, 44, 388
Naravīra, 200
Nārāyaṇa, 71
Naresar, 112, 120, 129
nārībandha, 91, 93, 97
Narolī, 220
nartaka, 236
nartakī, 3, 17, 92, 156, 162, 227, 305, 350, 353, 390
nartakī-saṅgītavādinī, 352
Nasik, 358
Nasik-Bulsar, 37
naṭa, 236
nāṭaka(s), 80-81
nāṭakā, 9
nāṭakam, 353
naṭa-maṇḍapa, 139, 146, 162, 392, 394-95
Naṭarāja, 138, 403
Naṭeśa, 93
Nath, R., 11
naṭī(s), 3, 54, 218, 273, 336, 344
naṭī-nartakī, 5, 344, 346, 350, 379, 383, 395
  sculptures, 351-52, 417
National Museum, 286
nāṭya(s), 156, 198, 223, 418
nattuvanārs, 417
nature, beauty of, 77
Nāṭya, 382
  literature, 18, 54, 76, 79
Nāṭyaśāstra, 5, 7, 47, 64, 78, 88, 214, 236, 337, 344, 347
Nāṭyālaṁkāra, 64
navagrahas, 403
navalatikā, 82
navambuda, 82
Navamiyā, 75
navāmrakhādikā, 82
navapatrikā, 82
Navasāhasāṅka Carita, 36
navasamāgama, 82
nāyaka, 215, 217, 230-31, 236, 240, 284
nāyaka-nāyikā(s), 232, 330, 342
nāyaka-nāyikā-viṭa group, 259
nāyikā(s), 3-4, 11, 92, 146, 164, 176, 215, 217, 227, 230-31, 234, 239-40, 272, 284, 299, 306, 315, 323, 332, 337, 361, 375, 392, 409, 418
  bhāva, 336
  imageries of, 6
  kuṭilaka, 272
  prasādhikā, 330
nāyikā's meditative concentration, 386
nāyikā-viṭa kuṭilaka motif, 230
Nefertem, 195
Neumann, Eric, 20, 187, 192, 194-95, 200
nidhi, 294
Nīlakaṇṭha Mahādeva, 177
  Temple, 42, 173, 178, 292
Nile, 248
nirjharasnāna, 225
Nirṛti, 387
Nirukta, 60
Nītivākyāmṛta, 236
nityārcanā, 352
nitya-sumaṅgalī(s), 344, 352, 383, 405
Nohṭā, 121, 129, 154, 156, 162, 364, 403
non-Āryan
  origin, 201
  sources, 201
north
  Gujarat, 171, 363
  India, 273, 284, 352
  Indian temple sculptural programming, 352
northern
  India, 129, 362
  Ruyagga, 75
nṛtta gesture, 417
nṛttahastas, 2
Nṛttaratnāvalī, 417
nṛtya, 80, 352
  gesture, 417
  hastas, 387
  kauśalyam, 299
nṛtyācāryas, 87
nṛtya-gīta-vādya, 257
nṛtya-maṇḍapa, 392
nṛtyaśālā, 93
Nṛtyasarvasva, 417
nūpurapādikā, 150, 156, 158, 173, 273, 350, 361, 383, 388, 392
Nut, 195
nyagrodha, 60, 251
nymphs, 19, 61, 67

Occidental cultures, 21
O'Flaherty, Wendy Doniger, 3
oral tradition, 3
Orissa, 2, 97, 418
Orissan
  architecture, 256
  temple architectural text, 91, 337
Osiā, 109, 112, 114, 116, 120, 130, 134, 137, 144-45, 165, 171, 173, 264, 283, 286, 292, 306, 315, 320, 323, 326, 331, 342, 347, 350, 363, 365, 368-70
  sculpture, 368
Osian, 11, 33

Padatāḍitakam, 238
Padhavali, 154, 364, 374
padmacchara, 211
padma-dala, 64
  gandha, 64
Padmagupta, 36
Padmaprabhṛtakam, 239, 299
padmavara vedikā, 211, 220
Padmāvatī, 83, 150
padminī, 6, 156, 389-90, 405
  devāṅganā(s), 97, 210, 410
  nāyikās, 144

padumaccara, 210
Padumavatī, 210
Pal, P., 358
Pāla-Sena sculpture, 47
Pāli, 42, 88, 154, 158, 363, 365, 372, 375
pānagoṣṭhī, 80
pañca-bindu prasṛta, 82, 299
pañcāgni sādhanā tapa, 382
pañcaratha, 129, 136, 142, 146, 155
  ground plan, 157
pañcaśākhā, 117
pañcāyatana, 163
Pāṇini, 82
pañjara, 117
paññagas, 91
Panofsky, Erwin, viii, 2-3, 14, 18, 186
Paramāra(s), 33-34, 36-37, 39, 42-43, 45-46, 154
  architecture, 129
  Bhoja, 38, 43, 45
  Dhandhuka, 40
  idiom, 364, 373
  kingdom, 41
  Naravarman, 41
  style, 364
  temples, 91
  Cāḷukya relationships, 34
Paramaśiva, 352
Parāśara, 67
Parel Aṣṭamūrti, 361
paribhogadarśinī, 218, 274, 330, 332, 383, 388
paricārīkās, 9
parihāsayitra, 236
pārijāta, 69
parikara, 143, 264
Parimoo, Ratan, 3, 10, 47, 153, 374-75, 391, 418
  methodologies of, 11
Parjanya(s), 251, 311
Pārvatī, 55, 78, 310, 351, 382, 388, 391
Pāśupata devotee, 198
paṭa, 200, 297
patākā caturasra hasta, 211
Pāṭan, 40, 42, 46, 165, 171, 364, 373, 391, 409, 416
Patna Museums, 77
patralekhana, 399
patraśākhā, 117
Paṭṭana, 85
Paumarai, 75
Paurāṇic themes, 95
pāyala, 98
pāyas, 276
peacocks, dance of, 78
*phālanā*s, 93, 163-64, 171, 176-77, 388
Phālguna, 72
Phalodī, 363
pīḍā prahāra, 239
pila, 199
pillars, 272
Pippalāda, 95
Piprahwā, 189
*piśāca*s, 63, 65, 69
Pisharoti, K. Rama, 209
pīṭha, 118, 142, 155, 157, 168
pīṭhamarda, 236
pīṭhamarda-vīṭa-vidūṣaka, order of, 236
pīṭhamardaka, 236
plakṣa, 61, 251
poetic
  expression, Indian tradition of, 15
  feeling, 18
  imagery, 77, 219, 292
  language, 15
poets, writings of, 46
political
  events, pattern of, 32
  history, 32
  skirmishes, 46
Pollock, Griselda, 24
post-Gupta, 32, 109
  medieval form, 363
  overtones, 370
  period, 49
  sculptural style, 363
  sculpture, 47, 360
  Vākāṭaka era, 32
post-Harṣa period, 32
post-Vedic
  literature, 60, 62-63
  mythology, 56
  texts, 61
Prabandha Cintāmaṇi, 38, 40-42, 85
Prabhās Pāṭan, 114, 364
Prabodhacandrodaya, 48
Pracaṇḍa Pāṇḍava, 48
Pracetas, 198
pradakṣiṇā, 87, 93, 97, 387, 389
prahasana, 48
Prajāpati, 251
prākāra, 353
prakaraṇa, 236
Prākṛt literature, 44, 48, 54, 74, 77, 79
prakṛti, 56
pralīna, 93
pramadā-kūla, 84
Pramāṇamañjarī, 46
pramardinī, 199
prāṇa, 70-71
prāṇāgni, 70
praṇāla, 10
prapāṭhakas, 95
prāsāda(s), 9, 93, 396
Prāsāda Maṇḍana, 95
prasādhana, 217-18, 330
prasādhikā, 5, 58, 138, 150, 156, 162, 218, 273, 330, 332, 336-37, 378, 383
prasaṁśā, 16
prasārita, 234
  movement, 221
Prasenajit Pillar, 210
Praśna Upaniṣad, 95
Pratāpgaṛh, 35
pratīka nāṭaka, 48
pratibhadra, 93
Pratihāra(s), 34-36, 39-40, 43-44, 46, 109, 111-12, 114, 120
  age, 112, 117, 120, 136
  architecture, 130, 331
  ideal of feminine beauty, 375
  Mahendrapāla, 47

Mahipāla, 39
period, 129
sculptors, 132
style, 112
temple(s), 112, 129-30, 136
type plan, 144
Pratihāra-Candella, 34
Pratihāra-Paramāra, 34
pratihārī(s), 54, 83, 86-87, 89, 227
pratikarṇa, 168
pratimā, 94
Pratimā Lakṣaṇa, 90
pratiratha(s), 106, 118, 130, 132, 134, 137-38, 142-45, 148, 152, 155, 158, 161, 164, 168, 173, 178, 306, 352, 369, 374, 390
*rathikā*s, 148
sculptures, 118
pratīyamāna, 15
prayoga, 200
pre-historic period, 303
pre-iconographical description, 14
pre-Islamic India, 54
pre-Khajurāho phase, 156
pre-kuṣāṇa development, 187
pre-Maru–Gurjara phase, 137
pre-Mughal times, 32
pre-Solaṅkī period, 112
prekṣaka kula, 87
primordial archetype, 19-20, 22
Priyadarśikā, 84
priyaṅgu yaṣṭika, 299
pṛṣṭha-svastika, 274, 347, 395
pose, 300
Pṛthvī, 276, 283
identification of, 276
Pṛthvīrāja III, 43
Pṛthvīrāja Rāso, 42
Pṛthvīrāja Vijaya, 41
Pṛthvīvallabha, 36
psycho-historical order, 187
Puhai, 75
Punjab, 43, 358
puṇya, 284
Pupphamatā, 74
Purāṇas, 65, 80
Purāṇic, 7-8, 13
apsaras, 54
concept, 211
Hinduism, 33
literature, 18, 54, 64, 72, 74
periods, 61
pūrṇa
ghaṭa, 248, 253
kalaśa, 134
*Pūrṇakumbhanārī*s, installation of, 56
Pūrṇapāla, 37
Pūrvaraṅga, 81
Pururavas, 70-71
puruṣa, 56
Puruṣottama, 45
Puṣkara, 44
puṣpāñjali, 352
puṣpa-bāṇa, 99, 396
puṣpaka, 396
puṣpa-krīḍā, 80
puṣpapracāyikā, 221, 224
puṣpavācayikā, 82
putravallabhā, 4, 6, 17, 55, 150, 162, 173, 218, 225, 231, 273, 289, 292, 294, 344, 378-79, 389, 392, 396, 399, 416
imagery, 383

Queen's Stepwell at Pāṭan, The, 11

Raghu, lineage of, 35
Raghavan, V., 81-82, 417
Raghuvaṁśa, 7, 81
Raja, Kunjunni, 17
Rājaśekhara, 6, 35, 47-48, 50, 78, 80, 242, 284, 297
*rājagaṇikā*s, 352
rajas, 70
Rajasthan, 2, 4, 12, 34-35, 37, 40-41, 43, 45, 85, 91, 94, 106, 112, 120, 129-30, 138-39, 146, 151, 173, 230-31, 350, 358, 364, 390-92, 399, 401, 410
lower, 150
school, 369
sculptures, 121
southern, 140, 144, 171
upper, 150
western, 362
Rājasthānī element, 121
Rājataraṅgiṇī, 350
Rajendra Coḷa I, 38
Rājim, 261
Rājpūt, 367
Rājyalakṣmī, 59
Rājyapāla, 35-36, 39
Rākā, 4, 54, 59, 227
Rakes, ways of, 87
Rākhengāra, 40
rākṣasa(s), 67, 91, 411
Rāmagiri hill, 78
Rāmāyaṇa, 7, 48, 81
Rambhā-Indra, 387
Rāṇā Kumbhā, 95
Rāṇaka, 350
Raṇathambhor, 43
raṅga, 350
raṅgāṅganam, 87
raṅga-maṇḍapa, 117, 168, 173, 294
Rani Durgavati Museum, 286, 306
Rānī kī Vāv, 4, 22, 40, 148, 171, 229, 274, 278, 288, 300, 310, 326, 332, 367, 373, 387, 391-92, 409
architecture, 310
devāṅganā sculptures, 288
sculptures, 373
sculpture of, 148
temples, 55
Rao, T.A. Gopinath, 7, 311
rasa(s), 49-50, 229, 247, 251
rasika, 310
Rasshamra, 194
Rāṣṭrabhrat, 64
Rāṣṭrakūṭa(s), 35-36, 38, 44
Rāṣṭrakūṭa Indra III, 39
Rāṣṭrakūṭa style, 118
ratha(s), 106, 151, 173, 176-77, 369, 374
ratha-pratiratha, 96, 161
ratha-pratiratha-salilāntara facets, 163

rathika(s), 142, 168, 171, 368, 372-73
ratideha, 396
rativilāsa, 80
Ratnāvalī, 81
raudra, 158
Rāvaṇa, 72, 88
Rāvaṇa kī Khāī, 232
Ray, H.C., 39
Rāyapasenīya Sutta, 211, 220
Ṛcā, 65
Reigl, Alois, 10
religious
  imagery, vii
  imagination, development of, 55
retodha, 57
Revanta, 132
Rewa Kotwali, 286, 306, 401
Rewā Mahārājā's Palace, 139, 278, 292
Ṛgveda, 54, 56-57, 59-60, 62-63, 70, 201, 276, 414, 416
rhythmic facets, 132
rīti(s), 47
  theory of, 47
ritual
  traditions, 18
  tradition of, 45
  worship, 352
river goddess motif, 186
Ṛk, 65
rock-cut architecture, 232
Roḍā, 4, 114, 136, 239, 242, 244, 286, 299, 323, 331, 337, 358, 360-62, 365
  complex, 299
  devāṅganā(s), 305, 362
  sculpture, 368
  Temple, 130, 137, 231, 242, 305, 368
Roman, 21
Rome, 194
Roy, U.N., 8, 225, 227, 296, 330
ṛṣi-kanyā figures, 401
ṛṣi(s), 64, 66-67, 71, 92, 106, 166, 171, 173, 283, 320, 372, 410
Ṛṣiśṛṅga, 297
Ṛtusaṁhāram, 79, 284, 332, 336
Ruā, 75
Ruagavai, 75
Ruasiā, 75
rūcaka, 117, 130, 132
Rudra, 56
rudradāsī(s), 353
rudragaṇikā(s), 353
rudrakannikai, 353
Rudramahālaya, 42, 178
Rudraṭa, 49
rūpaka, 49, 414
rūpakāras, 375
rūpapaṭṭikā, 168
rūpasakhā, 403
rūpastambha, 117
Ruyagga, 74
  southern, 75
  western, 75
Ruyyaka, 49

Sābarmatī river, 37
śabda, 17, 49
sabhā, 72
  of Indra, 74
Sabhadā, 210
Saccīyamātā, 326
  group, 171
  Temple, 134, 171, 264, 283, 292, 306, 315, 320, 342, 347
sādhāraṇīkaraṇa, 49
Sādhu Gayapāla, 171
sādhyas, 69
sadyasnātā, 164, 218, 224, 264, 286, 383
  imagery, 414
Sadyojāta Śivācārya, 353
sahakāra bhañjikā, 82
Sahasraliṅga Lake, 42
Sahasrānīka, 72
sahasrāra cakra, 352
sāhitya, 49
Sāhitya Mīmāṁsā, 80
Saindhava, 112
Śaiva, 83, 90, 386
  devotees, 353
  gaindharvyam, 353
  philosophy, 42
  temple(s), 167, 171
  ṛṣis, 155
Sajjana, 40
sajośa, 276
Śākambharī, 35, 39, 41-44
Śaka–Kuṣāṇa–Sātavāhana schools, 358-59
Śakrārca, 81
Śākta, 83, 90, 386
Śakti, 9, 55
  concepts of, 188
  femininity of, 9
śaktis, 391
Śaktikumāra, Atpur inscription of, 44-45
Śakuntalā, 64, 73, 82
Śākuntalam, 88
śāla, 234, 273, 297
śālā, 93, 221
śālabhañjikā(s), vii, 3-5, 8, 11, 17-18, 21, 58, 77, 81-82, 89, 94-95, 151, 192, 197-98, 208, 214-15, 220-21, 223, 227, 253, 256-57, 264, 272-73, 278, 331, 336, 344, 360-61, 369, 380, 399, 401, 405, 418
  imagery, 383
  motif(s), 6, 89, 186, 192, 199, 214, 296-97, 323, 360
  parivādi, 221
  pose(s), 197, 213, 223
  sculptures, 214
śālabhañjikā-aśoka dohada, 221
śālabhañjikā–nadī-devī, combination of, 256
śālabhañjikā–rivergoddess, 401
śālabhañjikā–yakṣī–vṛkṣikā, 401
śālabhañjya, 396
salila-krīḍā, 80, 82
salilāntara(s), 99, 130, 132, 137, 142-44, 146, 148, 152, 155-56, 158, 161-64, 171, 173, 176-78, 306, 374
Śālmalimūla Khelana, 81
Sāma, 65
  pose, 286

position, 211
sama, 278, 323, 346
samabhaṅga, 94, 208
samadala pratiratha, 120, 142
Śāmalājī, 47, 145, 232, 239, 244, 358-60
Mātṛkās, 360
Samarāṅgaṇa Sūtradhāra, 10, 45-46, 81, 90, 93, 146, 396
samatala, 117
samavaraṇa, 138, 168
maṇḍapa, 176
roof, 162
Samayamātṛkā, 86
saṁbhoga, 209, 336
sambhūya krīḍās, 80, 82
saṁlakṣyakrama vyaṅgya, 17
saṁsāra-cakra, 410
samudra-manthana, 64, 69
Saṁyutta Nikāya, 63
Sāñcī, vii, 6, 26, 33, 58, 77, 120, 201, 208, 211, 215, 217, 232, 358-60, 401
pillars, 211
śālabhañjikā, 214
stūpa, 257
stūpa gateways, 331
toraṇa śālabhañjikā, 223
*yakṣī*s, 213
Sander, 173, 176, 274, 278, 286, 311, 315, 326, 332, 367, 373, 396
Temple, 320
sandhāra, 93, 164
pradakṣiṇāpatha, 309
temple, 306
*sandhi*s, 353
sandhivigrahika, 44
Saṅgha Paṭṭaka, 84
Saṅghol, 55, 215, 218, 220, 223, 225, 273-74, 286, 292, 296, 311, 330, 337, 347, 350
pillar, 346
sculpture, 296
saṅgīta, 80
Saṅgīta-Ratnākara, 48, 337, 344
saṅgītavādinī(s), 273, 350-51, 371, 383
Saṅgrāma Singh, Mahāpratihāra, 83
sani, 351
Sankalia, H.D., 178
śaṅkha, 416
Sanskrit
drama(s), 86
kāvya literature, 332
literature, 77, 83, 230, 238, 342
origin of, 81
terminology, 111
Sanudasa, 87
Sapādalakṣa, 34, 39, 41, 43, 118
*sapta kannigai*s, 191
Sapta-Mātṛkās, 152, 390
Sara Schastok, 360
śarada, 82
Śāradātanaya, 80-82
Śāraṅgadeva, 48
Sārasvata, 72
Sarasvatī, 20, 54-57, 195, 210, 388
Sarasvatī-kaṇṭhābharaṇa, 80
Sarayū, 57
śārdūla, 9
sarga, 87
sāṛī(s), 283
Marāṭhī-style, 230
śarīrin, 49
saritpulinakeli, 82
Sārnāth, 33, 359-60
school, 359
sarpadhārī, 17, 320, 326, 385, 416
*devāṅganā*s, 405
sārūpya, 16
Sārvabhauma, 37
Sās-Bahū, temples of, 162
*śāsanadevī*s, 93
Śāstras, 79, 91
sāta
apsaras, 191
saheliāṅ, 191
śataka, 48
Śatapatha Brāhmaṇa, 60, 64
Satnā, 154, 156-57
Śatrumardinī, 97-98
Śatruñjaya, 42
saṭṭaka, 48, 211
saukumārya, 47
Saundarānanda, 236
Saura, 386
Saurāṣṭra, 40-41, 140, 178, 364
style, 112
sauvida, 89
sauvidala, 89
Savitṛ, 414, 416
Savvapabhā, 75
Sāyaṇa, 311
Sayappa, 351
sāyarakṣai, 353
schools, western Indian, 367
sculptural
decoration, 158
development, 358
efflorescence, 14
evidence, 18
figures, 151
form, life of, 368
forms, 139
imagery, 42, 186
interpretations of Osiā, 370
programming, 8
style, Maru–Gurjara, 373
styles, 47, 365
typologies, 10
sculpture for architecture, 145
sculptures of
alasākanyā, 2
apsaras, 2
Dahala and Dakṣiṇa Kosala, 11
devāṅganā(s), 21, 347
environment, 368
Gaurī, 151
Kandarīya Mahādeva, 374
Kaḍwāhā, 364
Lakṣmaṇa, 374
Lakṣmaṇa Temple, 368
Maru–Gurjara style of, 364
medieval efflorescence of, 368
placement of, 145
Rānī kī Vāv, 148

Śeṣasāyī Viṣṇu, 10
styles of, 46
stylistic development of, 14
traditions of Kuṣāṇa period, 311
western Indian, 358
seated figures, group of, 143
seduction, erotic motif of, 311
seductresses, 12
Sejakpur, 173, 177, 350, 364, 373
Temple, 178, 416
Śekhāwatī, 43
semi-divine
characters, groups of, 252
figures, 90
powers, 60
semiological analysis, 17, 21
semiology, 13, 17, 19
semiosis,
dimension of, 379
of Devāṅganā motif, 419
semiotic(s), 3, 25
interpretation, viii
Śeṣaśāyī, 391, 409
image, 392
Śeṣasāyī Viṣṇu,
sculptures of, 10
images, 391
Sesavai, 75
seven constellations, 76
Shah, U.P., viii, 47, 242, 358-60
Shah, Vimala, 171
Shahdol, 154
Sharma, Sadasivarath, 9-10
sheaves, Madonna of, 194
Shivdi, 360
Mātṛkā, 360
Siddhapur, 364
Siddharāja, Jayasiṁha, 34, 41-42, 364
Phase, 173
siddhas, 91
siddhi, 200
Sīkar, 44, 83, 114, 116, 140, 151
śikhā, 99
śikhaṇḍilasya, 82
śikhara, 90-91, 93, 129, 136, 138, 142, 146, 155-57, 161, 168, 177
śākhās, 132
śikhariṇī metres, 44
Śilāditya I, 362
Śilāhāras, 37-38
Śilappadikāram, 81
Śilpa, 3
text, 413
Śilpa Prakāśa, 9, 11, 90-92, 418
Śilparatna, 26
Śilpasūtra, 95
śilpīs, 373, 375
Siṁharāja, 44
Siṁhāsanabattīsī, 5
siṁho devadattaḥ, 16
similes on
dance in literature, 78
nature's beauty, 79
Sindh, 358
Sindhū, 57
Sindhurāja, 36-37
Sirimā Devatā, 208, 210
Sirpur, 232
Sisodiās, 44
Śiśupālavadha, 238
Sītā, 75, 88
sites, western Indian, 139
Śiva, 3, 42, 73, 78, 90, 97, 297, 351, 382
Temple, 13, 112, 114, 116, 120-21, 129-30, 137, 140, 143, 151-52, 154-55, 158, 161, 163, 173, 242, 286, 344, 388, 390, 403, 416
twin temple of, 112
Śivajñāna, 353
Śivaliṅgam, 143
Śiva–Pārvatī images, 148
Śivapurī, 154
Sivaramamurti, C., 3, 7, 214, 274
sixty-four *yoginīs*, 200
Siyaka, 36
Skanda Mātā, 360
Skandagupta, 359
skandha, 297
skhalita vasana, 311
Smith, Vincent, vii
Soddhala, 48
Sohāgpur, 121, 154, 158, 315, 364, 375
Virāṭeśvara Temple, 332
Sohāniā, 364
Solaṅkī(s), 34, 39-40, 42-43, 46, 109, 114, 153, 168, 363
dynasty, 171
period, 391
style, 171
temple *maṇḍovara*, 391
temples, 91, 168
territory, 45
glory of, 364
Soma, 57-58, 60-62, 247-48, 251-52, 419
juice, 60, 62-63, 78
legend of, 56
Somadeva, 43
Somadeva Sūri, 236
Somanātha, 13, 40, 99
Paṭṭana, 85
Phase II shrine of, 42
Someśvara, 38, 41-42
Someśvara I, 85
Sompura, P.O., 99
Sondhani, 145, 360, 362
sculpture, 359
Soṅkh, 220, 223
Sophia, 20, 195
Soyamaṇi, 75
spandita, 92
Spes, 194
sphoṭa, 17
theories of, 15
Śrāvaṇa, 82
sṛgakrīḍā, 82
Śrī, 7, 58-59, 210, 248
Śrī Lakṣmī, 59, 257, 274
Śrī Muñja, 46
Śrīdevī, 75
śrīdhara, 396
śrīlakṣmī, 383
Śrīmā, 58

Śrīmatī, 58, 210
Śrīpraśna Saṁhitā, 353
Śrīsūkta, 58, 69
Śrīvallabha, 36
śṛṅgāra, 227, 229, 272, 353, 385
  bhāva, 336
  elements of, 361
  nāyikās, 20
  rasa, 209, 336
  type, 20
Śṛṅgāra Mañjarī, 86, 286
Śṛṅgāra Prakāśa, 80, 82, 236
śṛṅgārika, 158, 238, 382
  devāṅganās, 320
  events, 151
  love sports, 215
śṛṅgas, 177
stambha(s), 90, 93-94, 346
stambhas gaja siṁhavyāla, 93
stambha-yoṣita, 229
stambhikā(s), 144, 155, 166
stambhika(s), 148, 150, 171
stambhikā-bound frames, 156
stana-sparśā, 138
sthānaka(s), 2, 7, 45, 347
sthapati(s), 3, 26, 32, 109, 272, 373
  families, 5
sthāpatya, 89
sthira, principle of, 375
sthira gati, principle of, 418
Sthūlakeśa, sage, 73
stimulated aestheticians, 49
stone inscriptions, 41
Story, Saskia Kersenboom, 353
strī, 346
structural features, 47
studies in iconology, 14
stūpa(s), 86, 89, 211, 214, 217, 220, 223, 229
  architecture, 6, 253
  gateways, 360
  monument, 211, 227
  of Buddhists, 219
  of Jainas, 219
  sites, 76
styles and iconography, 45
Subāhu, 64, 66
śubha, 65
Subhāṣita Ratnakośa, 284
Śuddha, 65
śuddhā nṛttam, 353
Sudi inscription, 85
Śūdraka, 86, 239
Suhāniā, 129, 154, 161, 289, 342, 374
śuka, 215
śukakrīḍā, 227
śukanāsā, 136, 138, 155, 347
śukasārikā, 6, 218, 227, 234
śukasaritā, 217
Sukeśī, 64
Sukumāra dance, 78
Sulocanā, 64, 66
Sultan Mahmūd, 35
sumaṅgalīs, 382
Sumer, 194
Sumero–Draviḍian connections, 201
Sun, 62
  Temple, 84, 112, 114, 116, 120, 139-40, 144-45, 165-66, 178, 292, 294, 373, 396
Sunak, 173, 178, 311, 367, 373, 392, 396
  Temple, 177
  temples of, 45
Śuṇḍa, 73
Sunda hill inscription, 43
Sunda inscription, 44
Śuṅga, 251
  image, 346
  Kuṣāṇa, 219
  Sātavāhana style, 360
surānam sundarībhiśca, 396
surāṅganā, 89, 418
Surāṣṭra, 34
surasundarī(s), vii, 2-3, 8-9, 11, 26, 56, 59, 76-77, 109, 199; see also *apsaras*(es)
  sculptures of, 2, 6
Surat, 37-38
Surata, 64
Sūravāyā, 161
Surāyana, 65
Surwaya, 154
Sūrya, 67, 72, 74, 76, 97, 145, 410, 413
  shrine, 410
  Temple, 40, 116, 140, 300, 342, 372, 410
  image of, 145, 157
sūtradhāras, 375
Śutudrī, 57
Suvasantaka, 81
sva-stana-sparśā, 5, 16, 58, 148, 156, 162, 173, 273-74, 284, 306, 344, 383, 388, 392
  devāṅganās, 22
svastika, 152, 156, 215, 234, 299, 306, 310, 323, 342, 346, 395, 405
  cārī, 109, 215, 217
  maṇḍala, 278
  pada, 151, 209, 214, 221, 234, 264, 278, 323, 368, 403
  pada-kaṭisama, 256
  pose, 286
  position, 211
  sthāna, 336
svayaṁvara, 37
Śyāmīlaka, 238
symbolic, 23
  expression, 19
  forms, 23
  imageries, 14
  images, 22

tāḍana, 297
Tailapa, 39
tamāla patras, 148
Tamil Nadu, 191
tāṇḍava, 382, 387
  tāṇḍava nṛtya, 97
Tantra, 198
Tantrasāra, 26
Tāntric, 198
  cults, 33
  literary sources, 199
  practices, 198

ritual(s), 200, 409
ritualism, 161
work, 199
Tantrism, 352
tanu, 276
tapas, 73, 99, 106
tapasvī, 323, 326, 385
Tārakāsura, 79
Tāraṅga, 42
tarjanī-mudrā, 210
tatsiddhi, 16
Tauṅgadhanva, 82
technical texts, 54
Tejpāla, 42
Telaṅgānā, 39
Telikā Mandir, 112, 120, 130, 365, 375
temple architects, 74
temple architecture, 2, 6, 9-10, 13, 49, 56, 59, 75, 92, 94, 114, 139-40, 146, 186, 211, 218, 232, 272-73, 297, 303, 306, 344, 365, 379, 382, 414, 418
history of, 13
Temple
Ādinātha, 148, 150, 163
Ambikā, 20, 118, 140, 142, 148, 278, 300, 332, 342, 372, 388
Ambikāmātā, 45, 231
Amvan Śiva, 144, 363
Badoh Śiva, 112
Bahū, 367, 395
Bajramaṭha, 158
Bhaillasvāmi, 86
Bhubaneswar, 26
Bodādit Sun, 118
Brāhmaṇasvāmi, 136
Cāhamāna, 145
Cāṇḍāleśvara, 83
Caturmukha Mahādeva, 112
Chandalmaḍh, 161
Citragupta, 121, 163
Dahala, 162
Daśāvatāra, 261
Devī Jagdambā, 163
Devī Jagdambī, 121, 164, 396, 399
Durgā, 13, 388
Durgā Kṣemaṅkarī, 118
Ghaṭeśvara Mahādeva, 112, 136, 138, 286, 370, 394
Harihara, 2, 106, 109, 116, 264
Harṣanātha, 44, 83, 114, 116, 140
Jagat Ambikā, 145, 294
Jarai Mātā, 112
Kālikā Mātā, 112, 114, 116
Kāmeśvara, 112, 116, 136, 146
Kandarīya Mahādeva, 106, 121, 162, 283-84, 332
Kaḍwāhā Ṭoṭeśvara, 129, 332, 344
Kṣemaṅkarī, 116, 130, 132
Kumbhaśyāma, 112, 114
Temples (Cont.)
Lakheśvara, 140
Lakṣmaṇa, 47, 106, 120-21, 152, 162-65, 210, 232, 264, 274, 284, 342, 347
Lakulīśa, 118, 150, 388
Limbojīmātā, 173, 401
Mahādeva, 116, 120
Mahāmārī, 353
Mahāvīra, 140, 173
Mahāvīra I, 114
Mālādevī, 112, 120
Maniyāra Mahādeva, 130, 136
Mīrā, 140, 146, 148, 150
Mohajamātā, 154, 161
Muni Bāvā, 140, 144
Navalakhā, 173, 177-78, 367, 416
Nīlakaṇṭha, 83, 305, 342
Nīlakaṇṭha Mahādeva, 42, 173, 177-78, 292
Nīlakaṇṭheśvara, 116, 118, 140, 151-52
Harihara, 106
Sūrya, 369
Padhavali Jain, 129
Parśurāmeśvara, 303
Pārśvanātha, 121, 163, 173
Rāmeśvara, 403
Rāṇak Devī, 130, 136
Saccīyamātā, 134, 171, 264, 283, 292, 306, 315, 320, 342, 347
Śāntināth, 173, 395
Saptaratha, 163
Śaraṇeśvara, 44, 178, 347, 416
Sās, 396, 399
Sās-Bahū, 129, 136, 139-40, 150, 154, 161, 309
Śiva, 13, 44, 112, 114, 116, 120-21, 129-30, 137, 140, 143, 151-52, 154-55, 157-58, 161, 163, 173, 242, 286, 344, 388, 390, 403, 416
Sohāgpur Virāṭeśvara, 332
Somanātha, 42
Someśvara, 168, 173
Sun, 84, 112, 114, 116, 120, 139-40, 144-45, 165-66, 178, 292, 294, 373, 396
Sūrya, 40, 116, 140, 300, 342, 372, 410
Śyāma Sundara, 166
Terāhī Śiva, 137
Ṭoṭeśvara, 129, 162
Tusā Sūrya, 146
Udayeśvara, 129, 154, 347, 399
Vaidyānātha, 256
Vāmana, 121, 163
Virāṭeśvara, 154, 158
Viṣṇu, 13, 45, 114, 129-30, 140, 150, 167-68, 171
Viśvanātha, 121, 163-64, 286
temple,
dancers, 77
facade of, 63
maṇḍovara, 386, 390
ritual, 8
sculptors, 74
sculpture(s), 13, 21
sculpture, history of, 13
Sejakpur, 178, 416
sides of, 63
structures, 178
temple(s) of
Ānartta, 140
Bhadreśvara, 140
central Indian, 152
Delmal, 173
Duladeo, 121
Gadarmal, 112, 120, 129-30, 137-38, 305, 369
Ghanerao, 118
Ghantai, 121
Ghumlī, 416
Guhila, 145

Gujarat, 10, 177
Gupta-Vākāṭaka, 136
Hindu, vii, 8, 12, 23, 75
Harṣagiri, 151
iconography, 106
Jagat, 142, 150, 332
Jawarī, 121
Kacchapaghāta, 161
Kakanmaṛh, 154
Kaḷacuri, 158
Koṭai, 150
Kumbhariā, 94
Moḍherā, 11, 165, 395
Roḍā, 130, 137, 231, 242, 305, 368
Śaiva, 167, 171
Sander, 320
Sunak, 177
Suravāyā, 161
Thān, 144
Tusā, 145-46, 150
vitāna, 396
wall(s), 3-4, 10, 94, 109, 272
western India, 244
Terāhī, 112, 129-30, 137, 154, 161, 330, 364, 375, 403
texts, Āgamic, 352-53
textual references, 2
Thān, 140, 142, 364
Thānesara, 40
Tharad, 42
tharas, 138
theoretical writings, 4
Thirteen Principal Upaniṣads, 248
Tigowā, 120, 240, 331
tilā, 297
tilaka, 297
Tillai, 382
timber architectural tradition, 394
timber architecture in Gujarat, 399
tīrthaṁkara(s), 74, 150
Tiwari, S.P., 86, 89
toraṇa(s), 10, 90-91, 396, 401, 405
śālabhañjikā(s), 213-15, 232, 253
gateway, 214
pillars, 401
Ṭoṭeśvara, 365, 372
Mahādeva, 154
Temple, 129, 162
tradition,
Āgamic, 75
age-old, 99
history of, 14
traditional
art history, 24
theatre, 18
transmigration, law of, 62
tree and nature worship, vii
tree spirit, 190, 201
triaṅga, 116
tribhaṅga, 92, 134, 215, 221, 234, 310, 337, 342, 346, 369, 371, 375
Trilocana, 97, 387
triratha, 129, 136-38, 144, 155, 176
plan, 156
triśākhā, 117
trisra, 323, 371
Triṣaṣṭiśalākāpuruṣa-Carita, 42
tryasra, 156
Tumain, 261
Tumburū, 64, 72
Turkish invader, 40
Tusā, 140, 145, 155, 261, 292, 294, 300, 342, 363, 365, 372, 396, 410
Ābanerī, 368
Sūrya Temple, 146
sculpture, 368
temple, 145-46, 150

Udaipur, 145, 358, 364
Udaipur–Ḍūṅgarpur, 368
udakasvedikā, 82
Udayāditya Paramāra, 34, 46, 129, 154
Udayagiri, 58, 257, 260, 359, 401
sculpture, 359
Udayamatī, 40, 391
Udayana, 73
Udayapur, 42, 129, 146, 347, 396
praśasti, 37-38
Udayeśvara, 33, 178, 368
Temple, 129, 154, 347, 399
uddīpana vibhāva(s), 80, 209
Uddyotana Sūri, 84, 86
udgama(s), 118, 132, 137-38, 144-45, 155, 157, 161, 166, 168, 171, 388, 405
udumbara, 61, 117, 232, 251, 260, 264, 266, 403
udyāna krīḍā(s), 6, 80, 211, 221
udyānayātrā, 82
Ugrajīt, 64
Ugrampasya, 64
Ujjain, 41, 129
Ujjayinī, 36
Umā, concepts of, 55
Umā-Pārvatī, 59
union, rites of, 191
Unwas, 118, 388
upabhadra, 176
upacāras, 81
Upadeśarasāyana, 85
upamā, 49
Upamitibhāvaprapañcakathā, 84
Uparamāla, 34, 46, 363
Upendrarāja, 36
ūrdhvajānu, 306, 315, 320, 326, 346-47, 350, 395
ūrdhvaloka, 74
ūrdhvamaṇḍalī, 395
hastas, 211
nṛtya hastas, 211
ūrdhvāṅguṣṭha, 346
uromaṇḍalī, 208, 214, 299, 323, 326, 337, 342, 395
hasta, 152, 215, 256, 336, 403
nṛtya hastas, 211
ūrdhvajānu, 347
Uṣā–Pratyūṣā, 411
Uṣas, 413-14
uṣṇīśa, 88
Utbi, 35
utkaṇṭhita, 337
utpaṭa, 297
utsava mūrti, 344
utsavabhera, 353

uttala, 297
uttama, 73
uttarīya, 88

vāc, 56
Vāc, 56, 62
Vācaspati, 57
vācya, 15
Vaḍanagara *praśasti*, 38, 41
Vaḍaval, 347, 375
Vaḍnagar, 364, 401
Vagada, 364
vāhana(s), 136, 203, 221, 256, 260, 264, 296, 390
vaidarbhī, 47
Vaijayantī Kośa, 89
Vaikhānasa Kāśyapa Janakhaṇḍa, 94
Vaikhānasīya Atri Saṁhitā, 90, 94
vaiparītya, 16
Vaiśampāyana, 88
vaisikikala, 239
Vaiṣṇava, 83, 386
  iconography, 47, 310
  sculptures, 163
  temples, 162, 167
Vaiṣṇavite, 150
  temple, 163
Vājapeya Saṁhitā, 64
Vākāṭaka, 253
Vākpatirāja, 36, 44
Vākpatirāja II, 43
vakrokti, 49
Vakrokti-Jivīta, 49
vakṣa, 276
Vakulavihāra, 81
valita, 156
Vallabhi, 362
  coins, 359
Vāmana, 48-49, 69
  Temple, 121, 163
Vāmana Sāromāhātmya, 69
*vana-devatā*s, 220
vanaspati, 57
vandīpati, 44
vanecarī, 419
varada-mudrā, 98
varāha, 157, 257
varāṅganā(s), 89, 93
vārimārga munīndra, 93
Varman, 136
*varṇa*s, 417
varṇasaṅkara, 33
varṣa, 82
*varṣavara*s, 87
Varuṇa, 56, 60, 74, 76, 96-97, 198, 240, 248, 251-52, 256-57, 292, 387, 414, 419
  court of, 61
vāsanā, 49
vasanabhraṁśā, 4, 17, 138-39, 156, 162-63, 168, 218, 227, 264, 266, 273, 300, 303, 305, 310, 315, 336, 378-79, 383, 388-89, 392, 399, 401, 405, 414
  imagery, 229
  images, 310
  imageries of, 296
Vasanta, 69, 81-82
Vasantgaṛh inscription, 37
Vasantotsava, 81
vaśīkaraṇa, 199
Vasiṣṭha, 70
Vassalage, 46
vastrābharaṇa maṇḍana, 80
Vastūpāla, 42
Vastūpāla-Tejapāla, 171
  praśasti, 38, 41
Vāstuśāstra, 18, 45
Vastusūtra, 95
Vastusūtra Upaniṣad, 90, 95
Vāstuvidyā, 96
Vāsudeva, 67
Vasundharā, 75
vasus, 158
Vatsarāja, 114
Vatsyayan, Kapila, vii, 3, 7
Vātsyāyana, 80, 82, 236
vāv, 391-92
  architecture, 310
vāvaḍī, 391
Vāyu, 96-97, 387
Vāyu Purāṇa, 65, 198, 225
Vedas, 54
vedībandha, 142, 168
Vedic, 7-8
  apsaras(es), 310, 414, 416
  concept, 58
  fertility goddesses, 55
  goddesses, 54, 227, 292
  literature, 18, 54-55, 59-61, 64, 74, 273, 288
  mythology, 7
  passages, 16
  poetry, 413
  point of view, 278
  religion, 63
  religious life, 197
  scholars, 353
  servants, 353
  sources, 272, 278
  texts, 4, 54, 59
Vedic–Purāṇic, 76
  narrative sources, 418
  literature, 409
vedikā, 117, 220, 232
vegetal–aquatic personifications, 176
venerable animal, symbols of, 21
veṇīprasādhanā, 6
veṇukośa, 117
vernacular language, 48
veśa, 87
vetragrahiṇī, 87
vetra-yaṣṭi, 88
vidambi, 88
Vidhūma, 72
Vidiśā, 86, 154, 401
vidūṣaka(s), 234, 236, 238, 240, 305
Vidyādevī(s), 146, 171
Vidyādhara(s), 35-36, 39, 91, 93, 118, 142, 396, 403
  Deva, 35
  thara, 95
  vaduvṛnda, 396

vidyādharī, 93
Vigraharāja, 39, 43
Vigraharāja II, 43-44, 83
Vigraharāja IV, 43-44
vihāra(s), 89, 230, 259, 401
Vijjukumāra, 75
Vijjukumārī *mahāttarīya*, 75
*vijñānika*s, 375
Vikramasiṁha, 35
Vikramorvaśīyam, 88
vilamba, tempos of, 299
vilāsinī(s), 86, 239
*vilāsinī-devadāsī*s, 86
Vimala Vasahī, 40, 171, 399
vimānam, 396
vimānāvalī, 91
Vimānavatthu, 210
vīṇā(s), 86, 91, 97, 151, 387, 416
vīṇādhāriṇī, 150
vīṇāvādinī, 148, 163
*vinoda*s, 82
vipralambha, 336
vipralambha śṛṅgāra, 78
vīrā, 5, 273, 306
vīra, 330, 385, 392, 409, 416
  imagery, 405, 416
  nāyikā(s), 20, 168, 320, 323, 326, 347
  rasa, 383
  type, 20
Vīrabhadra, 80
virahā nāyikā, 146
Virudhaka, 76
Virūpākṣa, 76
vīrya, 252
Viṣṇu(s), 3, 41, 58, 67, 69, 90, 97, 288, 310, 391-92, 403, 409
  *daśāvatāra*s, 11
  Mohinī form of, 297
  Temple, 13, 45, 114, 129-30, 140, 150, 167-68, 171
  ten incarnations of, 310
  wife of, 54
Viṣṇu Purāṇa, 67, 69, 72
Viṣṇudharmottara, 71, 252, 256
Viṣṇu–Lakṣmī images, 148
visual arts, 7, 14, 18, 46
  meaning in, 14
visual imagery, 55, 292
viśva-dhāya, 276
viśva-garbha, 276
Viśvāmitra, 73
Viśvanātha, 16, 163-64
  Temple, 121, 163-64, 286
Viśvāvasu, 69, 73
Viśvedevas, 69
viṭa, 88, 234, 236, 238-40, 259, 296, 305, 342
vitāna(s), 10, 90-91, 93, 95, 97, 99, 112, 117, 146, 151, 173, 294, 346, 365, 396, 405
  śālabhañjikā, 93
  decoration, 399
  images, 399
Viṭaśāstra, 87
viṭa-kuṭilaka, 232, 242
viṭa-nāyikā-nāyaka group, 361
vivṛtta, 306, 315, 346-47
  kaṭi, 300, 347
  movement, 221
viyoginī, 385-86
Vogel, J.Ph., 3, 5, 213-14, 256
vṛkṣikā(s), 4, 17-18, 21, 77, 201, 208, 219-20, 232, 240, 242, 248, 369, 371, 380
  connotation, 266
  sculptures, 219
vṛkṣikā-śālabhañjikā
  motif, 218, 220
  sculptures, 220
vṛkṣikā-nadī-devī, 234
Vṛtra slayer, 57
vṛttasaṁsthāna, 178
*vṛtti*s, 47
vyakta-avyakta, 283
Vyakti-Viveka, 49
vyāla(s), 9-10, 56, 99, 106, 130, 132, 142-44, 146, 148, 150, 157, 161, 163-64, 166, 171, 173, 214, 266, 373, 388, 399, 401
  sculpture, 388
vyāla-makara brackets, 171
vyaṅgya, 17
vyañjanā, 15, 17, 49, 344, 378, 380, 386

Wadhwān, 130, 136
water cosmology, 244, 248
  iconography of, 247
water nymph(s), 61, 191
water pitchers, 109
wedding procession, 61
West, 195
West Asia, 188
West Asian, 22
  cultures, 21
  material, 187
Western, 32
  art, 24
  Cāḷukya dynasty, 38
  scholars, 3
  traditions, 4
wind spirit(s), 61, 63
woman and tree, 186, 201, 221, 232, 383, 417
  motif, vii, 5, 200, 208, 224
woman and vegetation, 418
womanhood, 409
women artists, 26
word and meaning, interrelationship of, 17
World of Courtesans, The, 8
writings of poets, 46

Yādavaprakāśa, 89
yajña, 65
yajña-kuṇḍa, 399
Yajurveda, 57-58, 248
Yakkha Cittarāja, 199
yakṣa(s), 65, 67, 69, 78, 91, 94-96, 197-98, 201, 203, 211, 218, 244, 247, 252, 260, 264, 350, 417
  Cittarāja, 199
  cult, 6, 58, 197
  worship, 198, 200
yakṣarātri, 82

yakṣārohī, 218

yakṣa-yakṣīs, 248

  cult, 223

  pair, 251

yakṣī(s), 4, 6, 8-9, 17-18, 21, 26, 55, 58-59, 76-77, 93, 150, 187, 197-200, 203, 208, 210-11, 213-15, 217, 220-21, 223, 225, 227, 244, 252, 257, 261, 292, 305, 310, 346, 358, 379-80, 396, 417-19; see also *apsaras*(es)

  figures, 22, 214, 227, 273

  imageries, 208, 276

  imagery, 223

  imagery of, 7, 380, 419

  images, 215

  Kumārikā, 200

  sculpture, 311

  spirit of, 191

  worship, 199, 200

yakṣī–apsaras, 7

yakṣī–apsaras-nāyikā, 227

yakṣī–devāṅganās, 215

yakṣī–śālabhañjikā, 383

  connotation, 187

  imagery, 6

  motif, 186-87, 200

  vṛkṣikā motif, 6

yakṣiṇ, 210

yakṣiṇī(s), 9, 198-201, 209, 211, 272

yakṣiṇī sādhanam, 199

yakṣiṇī–śālabhañjikā, 211

yakṣīs' vāhanas, 253

Yama, 61, 66, 74, 76, 96-97, 306, 387, 419

  court of, 61

Yamī, 61

Yamunā, 7, 57, 109, 232, 252-53, 264, 401

yantra, 10, 92, 418

  of Śrī, 9

Yaśapāla, 42

Yāska, 60

Yaśodharā, 210

Yaśovarman, 34, 41

Yavanīs, 86

yāyāvarīya, 47

yoddhā, 93

yoga-mudrā, 98, 391

yogī, 352

yogic powers, 69

yoginī(s), 9, 11, 41, 173, 200, 323, 326, 385-86, 392

  Padmāvatī, 200

yosidvarṣavarapriyā, 87